MW00560288

THE POLI'
ELECTORAL REFORM
Changing the Rules of Democracy

Elections lie at the heart of democracy, and this book seeks to understand how the rules governing those elections are chosen. Drawing on both broad comparisons and detailed case studies, it focuses upon the electoral rules that govern what sorts of preferences voters can express and how votes translate into seats in a legislature. Through detailed examination of electoral reform politics in four countries (France, Italy, Japan, and New Zealand), Alan Renwick shows how major electoral system changes in established democracies occur through two contrasting types of reform process. Renwick rejects the simple view that electoral systems always straightforwardly reflect the interests of the politicians in power. Politicians' motivations are complex; politicians are sometimes unable to pursue reforms they want; occasionally, they are forced to accept reforms they oppose. *The Politics of Electoral Reform* shows how voters and reform activists can have real power over electoral reform.

ALAN RENWICK is a lecturer in Comparative Politics at the University of Reading.

THE POLITICS OF ELECTORAL REFORM

Changing the Rules of Democracy

ALAN RENWICK

School of Politics and International Relations
University of Reading

CAMBRIDGE
UNIVERSITY PRESS

CAMBRIDGE UNIVERSITY PRESS
Cambridge, New York, Melbourne, Madrid, Cape Town,
Singapore, São Paulo, Delhi, Tokyo, Mexico City

Cambridge University Press
The Edinburgh Building, Cambridge CB2 8RU, UK

Published in the United States of America by Cambridge University Press, New York

www.cambridge.org
Information on this title: www.cambridge.org/9781107403253

First published 2010
Reprinted 2010
First paperback edition 2011

A catalogue record for this publication is available from the British Library

Library of Congress Cataloguing in Publication Data
Renwick, Alan, 1975–
The politics of electoral reform : changing the rules of democracy / Alan Renwick.
p. cm.
ISBN 978-0-521-76530-5 (hardback)
1. Elections. 2. Voting. 3. Representative government and representation.
I. Title.
JF1001.R394 2010
324.6–dc22
2009048078

ISBN 978-0-521-76530-5 Hardback
ISBN 978-1-107-40325-3 Paperback

In memory of my grandmother,
Sheila Struthers

CONTENTS

13   Conclusions and implications   239

     Appendix: glossary of electoral system terminology   256
     Bibliography   261
     Index   302

TABLES

FIGURES

ABBREVIATIONS

ACT   Association of Consumers and Taxpayers *or* the ACT Party
ADN   *Alleanza Democratica Nazionale* (National Democratic Alliance)
AN   *Alleanza Nazionale* (National Alliance)
ANC   African National Congress
AV   alternative vote
BA   bonus-adjusted system
BC   Borda count
BV   block vote
CDU   *Christlich Demokratische Union* (Christian Democratic Union)
CGP   *Kōmeitō* (Clean Government Party)
CSU   *Christlich-Soziale Union* (Christian Social Union)
CV   cumulative vote
DC   *Democrazia Cristiana* (Christian Democracy, generally known as the Christian Democrats)
DPJ   Democratic Party of Japan
DSP   Democratic Socialist Party
ENP   effective number of parties, in terms of either votes (ENPV) or seats (ENPS)
ERC   Electoral Reform Coalition
FDP   *Freie Demokratische Partei* (Free Democratic Party)
FPTP   first past the post
GHQ   General Headquarters of the Allied Occupation Forces
JCP   Japanese Communist Party
JNP   *Nihon Shintō* (Japan New Party)
JSP   Japan Socialist Party
JT   *Japan Times*
LDP   Liberal Democratic Party (of Japan)
list PR list proportional representation
LV   limited vote
MMM   mixed-member majoritarian
MMP   mixed-member proportional
MRP   *Mouvement Républicain Populaire* (Popular Republican Movement)
MSI   *Movimento Sociale Italiano* (Italian Social Movement)
NFP   *Shinshintō* (New Frontier Party)

xii LIST OF ABBREVIATIONS

NZH   *New Zealand Herald*
PBV   party block vote
PCF   *Parti Communiste Français* (French Communist Party)
PCI   *Partito Comunista Italiano* (Italian Communist Party)
PDS   *Partito Democratico della Sinistra* (Democratic Party of the Left);
        Partei des Demokratischen Sozialismus (Party of Democratic Socialism)
PLI   *Partito Liberale Italiano* (Italian Liberal Party)
PR   proportional representation
PRI   *Partito Repubblicano Italiano* (Italian Republican Party)
PS   *Parti Socialiste* (French Socialist Party)
PSDI   *Partito Socialista Democratico Italiano* (Italian Social Democratic Party)
PSI   *Partito Socialista Italiano* (Italian Socialist Party)
RC   *Rifondazione Comunista* (Communist Refoundation)
RPF   *Rassemblement du Peuple Français* (Rally of the French People)
SADC   Southern African Development Community
SFIO   *Section Française de l'Internationale Ouvrière* (French Section of the
        Workers' International, predecessor to the PS)
SMD   single-member district
SMP   single-member plurality
SNTV   single non-transferable vote
SPD   *Sozialdemokratische Partei Deutschlands* (Social Democratic Party of
        Germany)
STV   single transferable vote
TRS   two-round system
UDC   *Unione dei Democratici Cristiani e dei Democratici di Centro* (Union of
        Christian Democrats and Democrats of the Centre)
UDF   *Union pour la Démocratie Française* (Union for French Democracy)
UMP   *Union pour un Mouvement Populaire* (Union for a Popular Movement)

ACKNOWLEDGEMENTS

I have incurred many debts while researching and writing this book. At the very beginning, Alan Ware encouraged me to turn what I had envisaged as an article into a larger project; he has continued to offered invaluable guidance ever since. Numerous colleagues and friends have offered support, kindness, and probing questions, including Nancy Bermeo, Nigel Bowles, Martin Ceadel, David Erdos, Elizabeth Frazer, David Goldey, Desmond King, Iain McLean, Marina Popescu, Gábor Tóka, Stephen Whitefield, and Laurence Whitehead.

As a comparativist, I have often leant upon the greater expertise of others in each of the countries I study. On France, I am particularly indebted to David Goldey and Andy Knapp; Ben Clift also gave valuable help. On Italy, Martin Bull, Chris Hanretty, and David Hine answered my questions with knowledge and patience. Ian Neary gave me invaluable initial orientation in Japanese politics, and Sarah Hyde and Arthur Stockwin have provided great advice and encouragement throughout. While in Japan, I spoke with Kentaro Fukumoto, Hiroshi Hirano, Takashi Inoguchi, Ikuo Kabashima, and Steven Reed, and from each conversation I gained new insights. The people of New Zealand deserve a collective medal for their openness and hospitality. During a wonderful month based at the Political Science and International Relations Programme of Victoria University of Wellington, I gained immeasurably from the kindness and insightfulness of numerous colleagues, especially John Leslie, Stephen Levine, Elizabeth McLeay, and Kate McMillan. I also met Peter Aimer and Jack Vowles in Auckland, both of whom have been immensely helpful and encouraging as my work has proceeded. I interviewed many politicians and other public figures while in New Zealand or by telephone afterwards. Many of these interviews are listed in the bibliography; even those not listed contributed to my understanding of New Zealand politics. I am particularly grateful to Murry McCully, who granted me access to his papers in Archives New Zealand,

and Phil Saxby, who has continued to show great interest in the project since we met. Beyond these four core countries, I am grateful to Sarah Birch, André Blais, Ken Carty, Patrick Dunleavy, David Farrell, Richard Katz, Shaheen Mozaffar, Jean-Benoit Pilet, Gideon Rahat, and Ben Reilly for sharing their ideas and enthusiasm for the subject.

I have presented papers on matters relating to this book at various seminars and conferences. Many who attended these events asked questions that forced me to clarify or alter my ideas, and I am especially grateful in this regard to Nancy Bermeo, Philip Giddings, Jonathan Golub, Xiaoming Huang, Des King, Tim Power, Thomas Saalfeld, Michael Steed, Oisín Tansey, Jack Vowles, and Laurence Whitehead.

I am particularly indebted to those who read and commented on previous drafts of the manuscript in whole or in part: Peter Aimer, Sarah Birch, Nigel Bowles, Martin Ceadel, David Erdos, David Farrell, David Goldey, Chris Hanretty, Richard Katz, Maria Pretzler, Gideon Rahat, Ben Reilly, Arthur Stockwin, Alan Ware, and Stephen Whitefield. All made suggestions that greatly improved the book.

I could not have completed this research without the kindness and hospitality of numerous friends and colleagues who supported me in Oxford and on my research trips around the world. I thank Willie Booth, who sadly passed away while this book was in production, as well as Pam and Steve Edwards, Kate Heard, Kerensa Heffron, Cameron and Silvie Hepburn, Sam Kessler, Duncan McGillivray, Jim and Mary McGillivray, John Meade, Catherine Muller, Adrienne Nolan, Sarah Ogilvie, Maria Pretzler, Yasuko Goto, Mark Schaan, Jane Shaw, and Richard Taunt. I finished most of the work for this book while a Junior Research Fellow at New College, Oxford. New College is an extraordinary community of scholars and friends, and my work and life have been immeasurably enriched by my time there. I moved in the final stages of the project to the University of Reading, where colleagues have been warm, supportive, and intellectually challenging.

Finally, I should like to thank John Haslam, Christina Sarigiannidou, Carrie Parkinson, and Fiona Sewell at Cambridge University Press. They have been remarkably supportive, efficient, and helpful throughout our dealings.

To all these people I am truly grateful. I remain wholly responsible, of course, for all errors and deficiencies that remain.

1

Introduction

Elections lie at the very heart of modern democracy. They are typically the occasions when citizens become most directly engaged in the political process; they determine the identity of those who will govern, often for four or five years; and they significantly influence how that governing power can be exercised.

The rules that govern elections therefore matter too, for they can have a major impact upon outcomes. Had different electoral rules been in place, George W. Bush might not have been elected to the American presidency in 2000 and Tony Blair might never have secured a majority of the seats in the British House of Commons. Had less proportional rules been used, Italy might not have been quite so plagued by 'revolving door' governments for the last sixty years. Conversely, had proportional representation not been chosen as part of the interim constitution of 1993, South Africa might not have achieved such remarkable democratic stability after its hard-fought transition from white-only rule.

Given the importance of electoral rules, it matters that we understand where those rules come from. Three questions in particular demand our attention. First, who has the power to choose the electoral system? To what extent do politicians control the decision process? To what extent are they constrained or can they be entirely displaced by others, including citizens, judges, and foreign powers? Second, what interests or values do these choices serve? If politicians are in control, do they simply pursue their own narrow self-interest or can they be motivated by broader values? If citizens are involved, are they also captured by narrow partisan interests or can they focus on the wider good of the polity? In so far as values matter, which are these values and what determines their role? Third, what electoral system changes are likely to take place? How often is reform likely to occur in general, and can we predict its incidence in particular countries? Is it correct, as Colomer (2004a: 62–6) argues, that electoral system choices are largely determined by the prevailing party system – specifically, by the number of parties it contains? Is it true, as

Colomer (2004a: 55–62) again contends, that there is a general drift in the direction of more proportional systems?

These are all big questions. They can be approached using multiple methods, and no single method is likely to yield answers that entirely exhaust our curiosity. Three approaches in particular can be distinguished. One uses formal theory to derive precise hypotheses that can subsequently be tested against reality. This approach has been fruitfully exploited by Benoit (2004), Boix (1999), Colomer (2004a, 2005), and Iversen and Soskice (2006). The second employs evidence, whether statistical or qualitative, from a large number of cases. Boix (1999) and Colomer (2004a, 2005) test their theoretical hypotheses against such data. Gallagher (2005) and Katz (2005) employ inference from broad surveys of cases to ground a variety of propositions. The third uses intensive analysis of a smaller range of cases in order to tease out mechanisms that are harder to discern at higher generality. Notable examples include Birch *et al.* (2002) on post-communist countries, Reilly (2006) on the Asia-Pacific, Mozaffar (1998) on Africa, and Rahat (2008) on Israel in comparative perspective.

Except in single case studies, the last of these three methods has not been used extensively to study reforms in established democracies. But it should be, and this is the method and the empirical focus that I adopt in this book. As I shall argue, the answers we can develop to the questions stated above are enriched greatly if we engage with the complexity and contingency of diverse electoral reform processes. Specifically, the conventional answers to these questions are that politicians dominate the choice of electoral system, that in doing so they pursue their own power interests, and that this implies both a strong connection from the number of parties to the choice of electoral system and a general trend towards the adoption of more proportional systems. I argue that these answers are either wrong or too simple. In fact, ordinary citizens have considerable influence too, conceptions of the public interest can matter, the link from the party system to the electoral system is complex, and there is no clear trend – at least in established democracies – towards greater proportionality.

I focus on *major changes in electoral systems*. Electoral law comprises enormously many elements, including who has the right to vote or run for office, how voters are registered, who conducts elections following what administrative procedures, how campaigns are financed, how people vote, what preferences voters can express, and how votes are translated into seats (on many of these aspects, see Massicotte, Blais, and

Yoshinaka 2004). I cannot cover all of these here, and, in common with most electoral system scholars, I limit the inquiry to the last two elements, concerning the nature of the vote and its translation into seats. It is to these elements that the label of *electoral system* is typically given.

At the most general level, two types of electoral system can be distinguished. First, there are *plurality or majority systems*: those in which the candidate or candidates who gain the greatest number of votes in a voting district win the seat or seats available, while all others win nothing. Second, there are *proportional systems*: those in which the seats available are divided up between candidates or parties in proportion to the number of votes they win. Within each of these categories, however, further distinctions can be made, and some systems do not neatly fit either category. In this book, I employ a classification of fourteen different types of electoral system. This is based on a twelve-way classification developed by Reynolds, Reilly, and Ellis (2005: 35–118), to which I add two further categories – bonus-adjusted systems and cumulative vote – into which some of the cases I discuss fall. These fourteen types are listed in Table 1.1 and explained in the Appendix. I define major electoral system change as a shift from one of these categories to another.

In analysing major electoral system changes, I focus primarily on reforms to the systems used to elect national legislative lower houses. I do not consider changes at sub- or supra-national levels, such as the adoption of mixed-member proportional (MMP) systems for elections to the Scottish Parliament and Welsh Assembly and list proportional representation (list PR) for British elections to the European Parliament. Nor do I analyse upper house reforms – such as Japan's House of Councillors reform in 1982 – or changes in the method of choosing the head of government – notably, the direct election of the French president in 1962 and of the Israeli prime minister in 1992.

I also focus primarily upon reforms in established democracies. That electoral systems often change in the course of democratization is hardly surprising: some authoritarian states allow no legislative elections at all; in others, the electoral system inherited from authoritarian times may not be serviceable for the democratic future. Reforms in new or fragile democracies are also to be expected: these are countries where the institutional framework has not bedded down or is endangered by systemic instability. The association of electoral reform with democratization is illustrated by Figure 1.1, which charts in broad terms the number of cases of major electoral reform in non-authoritarian contexts since World War II. The chart has two peaks. The first, around the 1940s

Table 1.1. *Types of electoral system*

Plurality/majority systems
  Single-member plurality (SMP)
  Block vote (BV)
  Party block vote (PBV)
  Alternative vote (AV)
  Two-round system (TRS)
Proportional systems
  List proportional representation (list PR)
  Single transferable vote (STV)
Mixed systems
  Mixed-member proportional systems (MMP)
  Mixed-member majoritarian systems (MMM)
  Bonus-adjusted systems (BA)
Other systems
  Single non-transferable vote (SNTV)
  Limited vote (LV)
  Cumulative vote (CV)
  Borda count (BC)

Notes: Based on classification in Reynolds, Reilly, and Ellis (2005: 35–118). To their twelve categories two have been added: bonus-adjusted systems and cumulative vote. In accordance with widespread usage, two categories are relabelled: Reynolds, Reilly, and Ellis call single-member plurality 'first past the post (FPTP)' and mixed-member majoritarian systems 'parallel systems'.

and 1950s, encompasses the second wave of democratization that occurred immediately after World War II and through the following period of decolonization. The second, during the 1990s, is associated principally with the quickening of the third wave of democratization following the collapse of communism in East-Central Europe in 1989.

What is analytically most curious, however, is electoral reform in the context of stable democracy. Katz argued in 1980 that such reform was 'unlikely': major change 'seems likely only when, as in France after the Second World War or during the Algerian crisis, the nation seems on the verge of collapse' (Katz 1980: 123). Similarly, Nohlen argued a little later

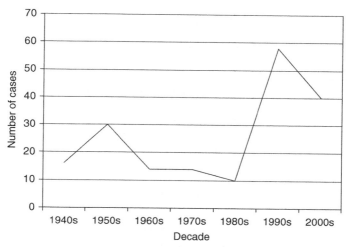

Figure 1.1. Incidence of major electoral reform since World War II.
Principal sources: Colomer (2004a: 74–6); EISA (2009); EJPR (1992–2007); Electoral Studies (2000–2009); IFES (2009); IPU (2009).

that 'Fundamental changes [to electoral systems] are rare and arise only in extraordinary historical situations' (Nohlen 1984: 217). He had in mind fundamental ruptures such as democratization in Spain and Portugal in the 1970s or the transition from the Fourth to the Fifth Republic in France in 1958. In the decades since Katz and Nohlen wrote, however, six episodes of major electoral reform have occurred in established democracies – defined stringently as those countries that were independent democratic states by the end of the second wave of democratization in 1962 (Huntington 1991: 16) and that have remained consolidated democracies ever since – without such ruptures. These cases are summarized in Table 1.2.

The two French cases in the mid-1980s may be thought relatively minor in historical perspective, involving as they did only a very short-lived deviation from the two-round system established at the birth of the Fifth Republic in 1958. At the time, however, they were highly contentious and had major implications for the structure of political competition. There is no doubting the significance of the remaining cases. Italians began to consider ways of reforming their unstable, corruption-ridden political system through electoral reform in the 1980s, leading to the abandonment of full list PR in 1993. The new system was a compromise that left few people happy, but repeated efforts to complete the reform effort

Table 1.2. *Major electoral reforms in established democracies since 1980*

Country	Year enacted	Previous electoral system	New electoral system
France	1985	Two-round qualified plurality	List proportional representation
France	1986	List proportional representation	Two-round qualified plurality
Italy	1993	List proportional representation	Mixed-member majoritarian with partial compensation
New Zealand	1993	Single-member plurality	Mixed-member proportional
Japan	1994	Single non-transferable vote	Mixed-member majoritarian
Italy	2005	Mixed-member majoritarian with partial compensation	Bonus-adjusted proportional representation

throughout the remainder of the 1990s all failed. A significant reform was pushed through in 2005; but it was universally regarded as botched, and pressure for another change has remained high since. In Japan too, the need to tackle rampant corruption was one of the central goals of reform advocates. The unusual system of single non-transferable vote (SNTV) in multi-member districts that had been in place almost continuously since 1925 was widely seen as partly responsible for that corruption; it was hoped that its abolition would bring alternation of parties in power and more programmatic political debate. New Zealand's reform was perhaps the most momentous of all. Aside from brief use of a two-round system in 1908 and 1911, New Zealand had never deviated from plurality rule, and single-member plurality became universal there before even in the UK. In 1993, however, New Zealand broke all Westminster tradition. Not only did it adopt proportional representation: it also opted for a form of PR – MMP – never before used in the Westminster world. A country that previously had shown exceptional electoral system conservatism stepped decisively into the unknown.

In the chapters that follow, I conduct detailed analysis of electoral reform in these four countries – France, Italy, Japan, and New Zealand. In order to increase the size and diversity of the sample, I include not just the six cases of reform since 1980, but all cases of major reform and of attempted but failed reform in these countries since 1945 – a sample that encompasses nineteen episodes in total. My primary method is comparative process tracing, through which mechanisms operating in these cases can be explored and patterns across them identified. My purpose is not just to illuminate these cases – though that is a worthy goal in itself – but also to develop comparative generalizations regarding the nature of reform processes, allowing answers to be developed to the questions about power, interests, values, and outcomes that were stated above.

Before I turn to the empirical study, however, an analytical framework is required. I pursue four main tasks in the remainder of this chapter. First, I consider existing analytical frameworks, arguing that, though they take us far, they do not give us all the tools needed to understand electoral reform. I propose that a revised framework must recognize two key points: that different electoral reform episodes come in quite different types that cannot readily be placed within a single model; and that various aspects of the complexity of each type must be grappled with if we are to derive all the understanding we can of processes and outcomes. Second, I address the first of these two points, considering what different types of electoral reform exist and which are particularly likely to be found among cases of major electoral reform in established democracies. Third, I lay out the terrain for the analysis of each reform type that will take up the bulk of the book. Each type comprises a variety of 'building blocks', concerning who is involved, what motivates them, how their motivations translate into preferences, and how those preferences translate into outcomes. I consider these in detail in Chapters 2 to 4, but I provide a brief outline here. Finally, I round off the chapter by pointing towards the conclusions I will reach on the three fundamental questions regarding electoral reform with which I began.

Existing approaches to analysing electoral reform

Recent analysis of electoral system change has yielded two main theoretical perspectives regarding the reforms of recent decades. One – the power-maximization perspective – is specified most precisely by Benoit (2004), but also underlies the work of Boix (1999) and Colomer (2004a, 2005), among others. It assumes that politicians control the choice of electoral system and that they are motivated to maximize their power. The other, developed by Shugart (2001) and Shugart and Wattenberg (2001c), allows for a wider range of actors – in particular, including

Table 1.3. *Performance of the power-maximization and inherent/ contingent factors approaches in relation to major electoral reforms in established democracies*

Approach	France 1985	France 1986	Italy 1993	New Zealand 1993	Japan 1994	Italy 2005
Power-maximization	Y	Y	N	N	N	Y
Inherent and contingent factors	Y	N	Y	Y	Y	N

Y: approach can interpret reform. N: approach cannot interpret reform.

ordinary citizens as well as politicians – and sees electoral reform as the product of a mix of inherent and contingent factors: the electoral system is vulnerable to reform where it occupies an inherently extreme position on either an inter- or an intra-party dimension; reform can then occur in response to specific instances of systemic failure.

Table 1.3 gives an initial assessment of the empirical performance of these two perspectives in relation to the six major electoral reforms since 1980 that were identified above. As is apparent, both approaches can explain some of the reforms, but not all. The power-maximization perspective can account for President François Mitterrand's decision in 1985 to replace France's two-round system with list PR: it was evident that his Socialist Party was going to lose the election due the following year, and the reform would limit the size of that loss. It can also explain the reversal of that decision by the victorious centre-right coalition led by Jacques Chirac in 1986: PR had diminished the size of the centre-right's majority; Chirac expected that restoration of the two-round system would make it easier to secure comfortable majorities in the future. And, with more effort, it can explain the Italian case of 2005 too: the reform enacted by the government of Silvio Berlusconi enhanced the coalition's expected seat share, but (as I shall argue in Chapter 6) did not maximize it; nevertheless, once a range of other considerations is taken into account, it in various ways advanced the power interests of all the parties that supported it. But the power-maximization account does not explain the three remaining reforms. In New Zealand, two large parties had long dominated politics and could expect their dominance to continue under the status quo; MMP, by contrast, would force them to compete with smaller rivals who would be likely to eat into their seat shares. In Italy in 1993, a shift away from proportional representation was enacted when the party system was going through enormous flux, with old parties vulnerable to collapse and new parties seeking to establish themselves – precisely the context where seat-maximizing parties would be most expected to want proportional rules. In Japan too, the system adopted in 1994 was slightly less proportional than the old (Gallagher 1998: 217), even though the party system had lately fragmented and several parties that contributed to the reform expected their capacity to win seats to be harmed.

The perspective developed by Shugart and Wattenberg, meanwhile, is well able to deal with the reforms in Italy, New Zealand, and Japan in 1993–1994: in each country, the electoral system prior to reform was 'extreme' in terms of Shugart's criteria (Shugart 2001: 43); and all three political systems were subject to severe systemic failures in the run-up to reform. Shugart also categorizes the French two-round system as extreme, and so the approach is compatible with its abandonment in 1985. But the approach cannot account for the return to the extremities in France in 1986, nor for the reform in Italy in 2005: in neither of these cases was the prevailing electoral system extreme.

Thus, each approach captures a significant part of the real-world story, but each leaves much to be explained. The value of the two approaches is not determined solely by their performance in this test. Nevertheless, there is clearly scope for further exploration.

A second reason for probing further is not revealed in Table 1.3: many aspects of the process of reform envisaged by each approach remain underexplored. In the case of the power-maximization approach, for example, the most clearly specified version is Benoit's model, which operationalizes *power*-maximization solely in terms of *seat*-maximization:

> Electoral systems result from the collective choice of political parties linking institutional alternatives to electoral self-interest in the form of maximizing seat shares ... A change in electoral institutions will occur when a political party or coalition of political parties supports an alternative which will bring it more seats than the status quo electoral system, and also has the power to effect through fiat that institutional alternative.
>
> (Benoit 2004: 373–4)

Yet, as Benoit (2004: 367–8; 2007: 378–80) and others (e.g., Blau 2008: 63–5; Katz 2005: 61–2) have pointed out, even if politicians simply pursue power, power may mean multiple things and may be influenced by electoral system choices in many ways. Seats matter, but so, for example, do intra-party relations and possibilities for inter-party coalition-building. In order to develop a full understanding of how power-maximizers approach electoral reform, we need a more nuanced conception of their motivations. In relation to the approach developed by Shugart and Wattenberg, meanwhile, much remains to be learnt about the precise mechanisms through which underlying problems translate into electoral reform. If voters as well as politicians are involved, the motivational complexity increases considerably, and the dynamics of how these different actors relate to one another become important.

In the light of these two issues, I seek to develop a more refined understanding of electoral reform processes through two steps. First, we should acknowledge that there are different types of electoral reform process. The evidence in Table 1.3 already points in this direction: in five of the six cases, one of the two approaches successfully predicts reform while the other does not, suggesting that they may be capturing essential features of different types. Second, with regard to each of the key types, I seek to develop more nuanced understanding by analysing various aspects of the reform process in considerable detail. I turn now to the first of these tasks.

Types of electoral reform

As I have suggested, the traditional idea that major electoral reform will occur only in response to systemic rupture must be rejected in the light of the fact that six major reforms have occurred in unbroken democratic contexts since 1980. Nevertheless, that only six cases of major reform in such contexts exist in thirty (indeed, fifty) years indicates that the traditional view was not far wrong: major electoral reform in established democracies is a very rare event. That is so, in essence, because politicians usually control the electoral system and those politicians with the power to change the system are typically precisely those who benefit from it and therefore want to keep it unchanged. This implies two potential routes to electoral reform: either the politicians in power do decide that they want reform; or those politicians lose control over the decision process (cf. Banting and Simeon 1985: 12). We thus have two broad types of electoral reform. It is useful, however, to subdivide these further, as summarized in Figure 1.2.

Politicians retain control

Among cases in which politicians retain control, the key further question concerns how those politicians approach the electoral system. Following

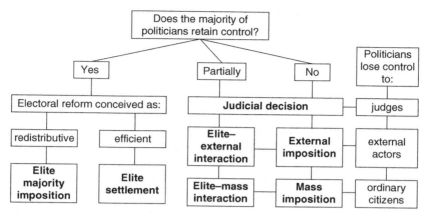

Figure 1.2. Types of electoral reform.

Tsebelis (1990: 104), politicians may conceive of the electoral system as either 'redistributive' or 'efficient'. Efficient institutions 'improve (with respect to the status quo) the condition of all (or almost all) individuals or groups in a society', whereas redistributive institutions 'improve the conditions of one group in society at the expense of another'. As Tsebelis (1990: 104) suggests, electoral systems are in many ways archetypical redistributive institutions: that one party wins more seats under an alternative to the status quo entails that another party wins fewer. Where a particular group or set of groups sees such gains for itself from changing the electoral system over the opposition of consequent losers, we have what I term reform by *elite majority imposition*.

Nevertheless, there are circumstances in which efficient aspects of the electoral system come to the fore. First, where the political system as a whole is threatened by inter-group violence or secession, politicians may place system stability above immediate partisan gain and adopt electoral reform in order to ameliorate tensions – as was the case, for example, in South Africa in 1993 and Fiji in 1997. Second, while it is generally reasonable to assume that most politicians are heavily concerned with their own power (as an end in itself or a means to further ends), they may sometimes be more idealistic, particularly if they have non-standard political backgrounds. In Hungary and Czechoslovakia in 1989 and 1990, for example, former dissidents who participated in negotiations to design new democratic institutions did not give up the ideals for which they had struggled, often at considerable personal sacrifice, for years, and in some cases introduced rules that would not obviously maximize their power (Birch *et al.* 2002: 69; Renwick 2005). Third, where actors face extreme uncertainty regarding their future prospects, they may be unable to calculate the redistributive consequences of alternative systems. They are like actors behind the Rawlsian veil of ignorance: even if entirely self-interested, they act *as if* the electoral system is an efficient institution (Rawls 1971: 136–42). Such uncertainty contributed, for example, to electoral system choice during post-communist transition (Andrews and Jackman 2005; Przeworski 1991: 87–8). All these circumstances can support electoral reform based on wide consensus, which I call reform by *elite settlement*.

Though the distinction between redistributive and efficient institutions is dichotomous, that between elite majority imposition and elite settlement is better viewed as a continuum. Individual actors may have mixed motivations. Across the range of actors, some may treat the electoral system essentially as redistributive, others more as efficient. Furthermore, in some cases a broad coalition may build comprising actors all of whom expect private gain from some aspect of a complex reform; in such cases, there may be wide consensus on the reform even though the various members of that consensus each subscribe to it for differing redistributive reasons.

Nevertheless, major electoral reforms in stable democratic contexts are likely to tend towards the elite majority imposition end of this continuum. The three conditions that can generate elite settlement can, it is true, to some extent be fulfilled in established democracies. In the case of the first condition – systemic threat – Cairns famously argues that the single-member plurality system harms Canada's national integration (Cairns 1968), and Weaver (2001: 567–8) suggests that this may in the future generate electoral system instability. As I discuss further in the final chapter, it is also conceivable that the current growth of popular alienation from politics and politicians might prompt some in the political class to consider serious electoral reform as a means towards restoring their legitimacy. But in general in established democracies, the background stability required for efficient pursuit of power can be assumed to be in place. Regarding the second condition – idealism – Bonney (2003: 459) suggests that the process leading to the founding of the Scottish Parliament in 1999 generated the kind of idealism more typically associated with fresh democratization: it 'was enthused with a vision entailing the transformation of the political process in Scotland to make it more open, transparent, inclusive, consultative, and participatory'. In general, however, established democracies are characterized by 'normal politics' in which a focus on power dominates. As for the third condition – uncertainty – this is always a feature of politics. But in established democracies, uncertainty regarding future electoral prospects is likely to be lower than the uncertainty that would be triggered by electoral reforms that change the contours of political competition.

Thus, it is reasonable to expect that, where politicians retain control, major electoral reform will occur in established democracies primarily by way of elite majority imposition. This is one of the reform types that I examine in detail in the following chapters.

Politicians lose control

Politicians do not, however, always retain control. As we move to the right-hand side of Figure 1.2 – to those cases in which politicians lose control of the reform process – the key question concerns whom politi-cians lose control to. I consider four possibilities here: judges, experts (not shown in Figure 1.2 for reasons given below), external actors, and ordinary citizens. The first three can be discussed relatively briefly.

Judges

Judicial decisions have had a prominent role in crafting many aspects of electoral law in the United States, most notably in relation to reapportionment (Cox and Katz 2002: 66–86). As such, judges have received much attention in the literature on American electoral reform (e.g., Bowler and Donovan 2008: 104; Cain 2007; Engstrom 2004: 168–72; Grofman 1982: 108–12; Richie and Hill 2004: 216). They have been active elsewhere too: in Germany, for example, the Constitutional Court has twice limited the use of electoral thresholds (Williams 2005: 192–5). An active role for judges in deciding electoral law could have major implications for who decides the electoral system: at least in theory, it could give considerable power even to small minorities if judges are persuaded that the prevailing system or a planned alternative violates constitutional provisions. Several minority groups have indeed sought precisely to use this route to change. In the 1970s, the British Liberal Party launched a case before the European Court of Human Rights, alleging that the single-member plurality system violated voter equality (ECHR 1980). A similar and ongoing case has been launched by the Canadian Green Party (Beatty 2005; Test Case Centre 2006).

At the level of major reform of national electoral institutions, however, judges have so far had no wide impact. In the Czech Republic in 2001, the

Constitutional Court blocked changes passed by parliament the previous year that would have substantially reduced the proportionality of the system (Crawford 2001; Kopecký 2004: 351–2). But this has been the exception rather than the rule: more generally, courts have been reluctant to intervene (Williams 2007: 956). The British case was thrown out by the European Court of Human Rights in 1980. At least one scholar has cast doubt on whether such cases are ever likely to get far: given the multiple contingencies involved in generating electoral system effects, it is diffi-cult to present a clear case that any particular system in fact breaches minority rights (Katz 2004). Thus, while reform by judicial decision may be important in the wider sphere of electoral law, it is less relevant to the major national electoral reforms analysed here. Judges may require further attention in the future, but they are not among the primary actors analysed in this book.

Experts

Electoral system experts can also matter. Farrell and McAllister (2006: 25–9) highlight the role of three individuals with expert knowledge – Catherine Helen Spence, Inglis Clark, and Edward Nanson – in the adoption of alternative vote in Australia in 1918. The Fiji Constitution Reform Commission of 1996 was strongly influenced by the political scientist Donald Horowitz in its decision to recommend alternative vote as a means to overcome the country's severe ethnic tensions (Fiji Constitution Review Commission 1996: 62; Fraenkel 2001: 8–9). Experts played important roles also in the cases discussed in later chapters of this book, most notably in New Zealand.

But experts have an advisory role rather than a decision-making one. There is thus no 'expert imposed' category of electoral reform in Figure 1.2. Nor do I include a separate 'elite–expert interaction' category: in fact, in almost all cases, experts play a role, more or less behind the scenes, in defining options or honing specific proposals. In any case of electoral reform, it is important that we understand what options the experts on the ground put forward and what effects they expect these to have.

External actors

Where the electoral system is decided not by domestic democratic actors but by forces external to the normal democratic process, we have reform by *external imposition*. The most archetypical external actors are foreign governments. But other actors who do not ordinarily participate directly in democratic politics – such as bureaucrats or monarchs – can usefully be categorized in the same way (Ishiyama 1997: 104).

Cases of pure external imposition appear to be rare. Even in countries under foreign occupation, such as Japan and West Germany in the 1940s (Friedrich 1949: 465–6; Merkl 1963: 86–7; Ward 1966: 551) and Afghanistan and Iraq in the 2000s (Dawisha and Diamond 2006; Reynolds 2006), domestic forces have had considerable leeway. More common are instances of *elite–external interaction*, where domestic politicians and external forces interact in the generation of the electoral system. A clear recent case is that of Lesotho, where the Southern African Development Community (SADC) intervened amidst violence following the elections of 1998 and in 2002 eventually pressured the domestic actors to agree a system of MMP (Southall 2003). As with judges, so foreign forces may subvert entrenched domestic power structures, with far-reaching implications for the direction of reform outcomes.

In established democracies, however, anything beyond an advisory role for external actors is extremely unlikely. An analogous case may occur where one tier of government has power to determine the electoral system used in another tier. But in focusing upon reforms at the national level I have deliberately excluded such cases precisely because they introduce a further dimension of heterogeneity that would render the analytical tasks in hand intractable. I therefore do not consider this reform type further here.

Citizens

For current purposes, the most relevant actors to whom politicians can lose control are ordinary citizens. Complete loss of control – leading to reform by *mass imposition* – is possible where provisions for citizen-initiated referendums exist. It was through this procedure that Switzerland adopted proportional representation in 1918 (Lutz 2004). Initiatives have been used in many American states too to address various aspects of electoral law: indeed, the very first state-level citizen-initiated referendum, held in Oregon in 1904, introduced direct primaries (Initiative and Referendum Institute 2008; Thacher 1907: 199–200). Of these many initiatives, one has led to major reform of the state-wide electoral system: in 1980, a citizen-initiated referendum reduced the size of the lower house of Illinois's General Assembly by a third and replaced the cumulative vote electoral system that had been in place for over a hundred years with single-member plurality (Everson 1981; Grofman 1982: 121).

⌐ For two reasons, however, complete loss of control by politicians to the
⌐public is unlikely. First, binding citizen-initiated referendums that can
propose new laws (rather than merely abrogate existing laws) are rarely
possible at the national level. Switzerland was for many years the only
country allowing them. The third wave of democratization has created
other cases – including Hungary, Latvia, Lithuania, and Slovenia
(Kaufmann and Waters 2004) – but attempts to use this provision to
change the electoral system have been rare and unsuccessful. Second,
irrespective of the formal decision rules, electoral reform rarely gets off
the ground as an issue without backing from prominent politicians. No
matter how fascinating it may seem to political scientists, the cause of
electoral reform is not one that readily ignites fervour among ordinary
voters, and in order to gain credibility as a serious issue it must gain
support from serious political figures (cf. Hermann 1995: 288). The
citizen-initiated referendum that brought proportional representation
to Switzerland in 1918 was in fact sponsored by two opposition political
parties (Lutz 2004: 285–6). In all three post-war cases of reform at
national level where I shall argue politicians lost significant control –
Italy, New Zealand, and Japan in 1993–1994 – prominent politicians
were central to the initial development of reform momentum. Even in
Illinois in 1980, which comes closest among all electoral reforms in
established democracies to a pure case of reform by mass imposition,
the reform movement was led by Pat Quinn, then a maverick member of
the state lower house (Stepanek 1980). Thus, the phenomenon of primary interest is not mass imposition, but rather reform by *elite–mass
interaction*, where both politicians and voters are essential components
of the reform story.

   This analysis suggests that electoral reforms in established democracies are likely to fall into two types: elite majority imposition and elite–
mass interaction. The six cases included in Table 1.3 split evenly between
these categories: reform by elite majority imposition occurred in France
in 1985 and 1986 and in Italy in 2005; elite–mass interaction characterized the changes in Italy, New Zealand, and Japan in 1993–1994. These
are therefore the two types of electoral reform that I subject to detailed
analysis in this book.

   The identification of these types is already a useful step along the road
to answering the questions with which I began the chapter. Indeed, the
labels that I have given the types already say much about the first
question – who has power over the outcomes in each scenario – and
may seem therefore to have implications for the second question – what

interests or values are served. But much more needs still to be said: in order to answer both these questions and the third question – what trends can be expected in electoral system change – we need to understand the mechanisms at work in each type in much greater depth. That will take the rest of the book. In the following section, I provide an outline.

The road ahead: building blocks and processes

Each type of electoral reform is an aggregate process composed of numerous building blocks. I begin the analysis from the bottom up by investigating these building blocks, before putting the components together to understand the dynamics of the processes as a whole. The building blocks are the subject of Part I of the book, while the processes belong to Parts II and III. My purpose in Part I is simply to lay out systematically what we know about the building blocks, such as who the key actors in electoral reform may be, how they may be motivated, and what opportunities and constraints they face. In Parts II and III, I explore the processes of reform by elite majority imposition and elite–mass interaction by narrowing the study to a detailed analysis of post-war electoral reform in France, Italy, Japan, and New Zealand.

Building blocks

Major electoral reforms occur through the conscious decisions of actors. In discussing the major types of electoral reform above, I have already given some indication of who the key actors are: politicians and citizens. More precisely, these actors may include political leaders, others who hold or seek elected office, party activists, leaders of interest groups such as trade unions and business organizations, activists who mobilize specifically around the issue of electoral reform, and ordinary voters. The first of the building blocks that I consider concerns the goals that these various actors pursue: what is it that they are trying to achieve when deciding how to approach electoral reform? These motivations are the subject of Chapter 2. As I shall argue, they may vary along a number of dimensions. Actors may be concerned with personal or partisan gain or with wider values directed towards the good of the nation as a whole. They may have short or long time horizons. They may pursue objectives in relation not only to electoral systems as outcomes, but also to the nature of the reform process itself and their own role in it.

To argue that social inquiry must proceed through analysis of actors is not, of course, to claim that agency is all-important (cf. Boudon 1986: 29–30; Coleman 1986; North 1990: 5), and such analysis cannot on its own satisfy our curiosity. First, we wish to know why actors attach particular weights to the various possible motivations. Second, we want to understand how actors' motivations are translated into preferences across specific alternatives. Third, we want to know how these preferences translate into outcomes. I begin to consider these three issues in Chapter 3. Regarding the first, the determinants of actors' motivations may include aspects of the wider political and social environment such as the nature of political parties and the party system, historical legacies and traditions, and cultural tendencies. They include also the immediate circumstances in which reform is debated, circumstances that may be shaped, for example, by scandals and crises. And they include features of the actors themselves, such as their positions within the political system and the nature of their career trajectories. Turning to the second issue, the translation of motivations into preferences is complicated by several factors. There may be high uncertainty regarding the effects of the alternatives. Actors may be subject to cognitive constraints that limit the options that they perceive or seriously consider. Actors may also work within legitimacy constraints that limit the courses of action deemed acceptable. Finally, the third issue – the translation of preferences into outcomes – depends above all upon actors' power. Most particularly, we need here to know the institutions through which decisions regarding the electoral system are made.

Chapter 4 completes the overview of building blocks by taking the analysis of motivations and their translation into preferences and then outcomes one stage further. Chapter 3, as just outlined, concerns factors relevant to these three issues that are exogenous to the reform process itself. But endogenous factors may be important too, particularly where the process of electoral reform unfolds over an extended period. I consider these endogenous factors in Chapter 4 under two headings: leadership and path dependence. Individual agents – I call them leaders – may strategize the electoral reform process, seeking to influence any of the building blocks that I have already mentioned. Drawing on the literatures on leadership and policy-making, I explore the wide variety of techniques that such leaders may employ to pursue their ends, and point towards the potential roles that these techniques play specifically in the realm of electoral reform. As to path dependence, meanwhile, several of the mechanisms discussed in Chapter 3 can generate *long-term* path dependence in electoral system trajectories. In Chapter 4, however, I focus on mechanisms generating path dependence *within* the reform process itself: that is, mechanisms that cause early steps in the reform process to have a disproportionate effect upon final outcomes. Such mechanisms can be crucial, I argue, in allowing reform sometimes to occur even when initial support for it is low.

My purpose in Part I is to survey and systematize what we already know about electoral reform. I seek inclusiveness: I allow for the full variety of mechanisms that scholars of electoral reform have thought important to the processes they study. Without an initial broad survey of this kind, the subsequent detailed study of particular cases would be limited, hamstrung by what we see in those cases. I therefore cast the empirical net in Chapters 2 to 4 widely, drawing on the literature on electoral reforms around the world from the end of the nineteenth century onwards. Where appropriate, I utilize relevant theoretical literatures in other subfields of political science too.

For some scholars, cataloguing building blocks in this way is all that we may reasonably hope to achieve: the further step of understanding how the building blocks combine in complex processes is, these theorists contend, beyond our reach. According to Elster (1993: 5), 'Moving from a plurality of mechanisms to a unified theory would mean that we should be able to identify in advance the conditions in which one or the other mechanism would be triggered ... My own view is that the social sciences are currently unable to identify such conditions and are likely to remain so forever.' Elster, Offe, and Preuss (1998: 78–80) apply this approach to the analysis of constitutional choice in Eastern Europe during the transition from communism, identifying various mechanisms underlying the choices made, but avoiding any attempt to explain where each mechanism operated. Similarly, Remington and Smith (1998: 568) find that several motivations ('perspectives') need to be allowed for in order to explain institutional choices in the Russian Duma. They do not reject outright the possibility of modelling the trade-offs among these motivations as Elster does, but they nevertheless argue that our theoretical understanding is not yet at a level where we can do this.

Yet there is a substantial gap between simply identifying mechanisms as they occur without attempting to understand how they may fit into broader patterns and the sort of universalistic project implied by Elster's phrase 'unified theory', and many theorists have sought to occupy precisely this ground. These range from the deductively inclined Merton (1967), who advocates 'theories of the middle range' as a step towards the

development of more general theory, to much more inductive comparative historical analysts, such as Skocpol and Somers (1980) and Mahoney
and Rueschemeyer (2003). As Pierson (2004: 169) puts it, there has been
'a wave of recent work … that seeks to combine sensitivity to causal
complexity and contextual effects with aspirations to draw out implications about social processes that transcend a single social setting' (similarly, see Bernhard 2000: 345). Goodin (1996: 39) contends,

> In discussions of institutional design what we often can do, and all we
> usually ought to be trying to do, is seeking principles that trade on
> 'theories of the middle range' in both empirical and normative realms.
> We can hope to discover, and to embody institutionally, a raft of general-
> izations of reliable validity, at least within a certain (perhaps tightly
> circumscribed) sphere.

In this book, I argue that it is indeed often possible to gain considerable
understanding of how the various building blocks link together in similar
processes that can be observed across multiple cases – to gain understanding of the mechanics of each *type* of reform. The degree to which we
can identify the antecedent conditions of particular mechanisms varies
greatly. In some cases, it is true that we can say rather little. But in others
we can develop considerable understanding.

Reform processes

The chapters of Parts II and III are devoted to elucidating the two key
types of reform process in established democracies that I identified
above: reforms by elite majority imposition and by elite–mass interaction. In the case of reform by elite majority imposition, elected politicians
dominate the process and seek electoral reform to advance their partisan
or personal power interests; reform occurs because the elite majority
have both the will to change the system and the power to impose their
wishes. This type is close to the power-maximization model discussed
above, but I seek to gain traction over a greater range of the complexities
of reform processes falling within this type than previous authors have
done. Two such complexities are particularly important: the multidimensional nature of actors' power interests; and legitimacy constraints,
which limit politicians' capacity to deploy this strategy, even when they
calculate that an electoral system different from the status quo would
advance their interests.

Elite–mass interaction, meanwhile, is characterized, as its name suggests, by a complex interaction between politicians and citizens. It

unfolds by way of a three-stage process. First, a minority of politicians, for various reasons, come to see reform as desirable. Lacking the power to enact change through regular legislative channels, these pro-reform politicians, at the second stage, take the issue to the public. Attempts to spark public interest in the esoteric subject of electoral reform are unlikely in general to succeed. But where the public is angry at the state of the political system and electoral reform can plausibly be portrayed as a (partial) solution to the problems prompting that anger, public pressure for change in the electoral system can be stoked. At the third stage, this pressure forces the reluctant majority among politicians to accept reforms they do not want. This type of electoral reform is very different from the first and implies that reform can occur – though only rarely – even when most politicians do not want it.

Part II analyses reforms by elite majority imposition; Part III does the same for reforms by elite–mass interaction. In each case, I first narrate the core cases and then investigate cross-case patterns and their generalizability.

Conclusions: power, interests, values, and outcomes

Detailed analysis of key real-world episodes of electoral reform is valuable in part simply because of the light it sheds on each of those cases: several of the reforms covered here have had far-reaching effects upon the politics of their respective countries; some have also influenced discourse over electoral system change in other parts of the world. I hope that readers interested primarily in understanding the stories of electoral reform in France, Italy, Japan, or New Zealand will find much of value in the following chapters.

But, as I have argued, such detailed study is useful also because it helps us answer broader questions of more general significance. I began this chapter by identifying three particularly important questions regarding electoral reform: first, who has power to influence electoral system outcomes; second, what interests and what values are served by electoral reform; third, what trends we can expect to observe in the electoral systems chosen. I elaborate answers to these questions in the final chapter, but some brief pointers are in order here.

Power

Whether politicians holding a majority have the power to select their preferred electoral system depends, in the first instance, on whether they want to maintain the status quo or shift to a new system. If their preference is for the status quo, they can almost always achieve it: reforms by elite–mass interaction that force politicians to accept change they do not want are rare events and occur only when there is both widespread anger regarding systemic failure and effective pro-reform leadership. If, by contrast, politicians want to change the status quo, what matters is the extent to which they are constrained by perceptions of illegitimacy. If manipulation of the electoral system for manifest partisan or personal gain is likely to provoke a widespread public backlash – or, even more, if politicians themselves regard it as unacceptable – then politicians are less likely to pursue it. Such constraints are difficult to gauge empirically, but the evidence suggests they can be very real.

Interests and values

The preceding paragraph gives much of the answer also regarding interests and values. Most of the time, the politicians of the majority can maintain their power interests: most of the time, those interests are served by the status quo and the status quo can be preserved. But in two circumstances – those rare cases where reform by elite–mass interaction is possible and those potentially more common cases where politicians are constrained from enacting reforms that are too blatantly self-serving – others' interests or values come to the fore. Additionally, cognitive constraints may limit politicians' ability to *perceive* their interests. The cases considered here suggest cognitive constraints may be high specifically where electoral reform has not recently been prominent on the political agenda.

Two further questions regarding interests and values need also to be considered. First, in cases of reform by elite–mass interaction, does public pressure always effectively serve the public interest or can it be manipulated by individuals to suit their own ends? Which electoral system might best serve the public interest is, of course, endlessly con-testable. Nevertheless, the evidence does support some conclusions, suggesting that self-serving manipulation of the electoral system through this mechanism is difficult.

Second, in so far as values matter, which values are they? There are at least three possibilities. First, values may be rooted in the *longue durée*: traditionally enshrined principles may have compelling weight. Second, they may be subject to change over time, as in the proces-ses of post-materialization analysed by Inglehart (1997). Third, the weight that a value has may be determined primarily by immediate circumstances: values that are seriously threatened at a given time may rise to unusual prominence. There is evidence for all of these patterns.

Outcomes

The final question – concerning the electoral system choices that are made – encompasses a number of important subsidiary questions. The first – how frequently are electoral systems likely to change? – can be answered simply: major reforms in established democracies will be rare events. Though I identify multiple routes through which change can occur, I have also argued that each faces significant hurdles. The paucity of real-world cases is therefore not theoretically surprising.

The second subquestion concerns when we should expect change. One possibility is that change will occur, as Shugart (2001) implies, only when the existing electoral system is 'extreme'. I argue that this is certainly likely to be true of cases of reform by elite–mass interaction, but that it is less clear for elite majority imposition. Another possibility is that electoral reform occurs when the electoral system and the party system become incompatible: when the number of parties rises too high under plurality systems or falls too low under proportional systems (cf. Colomer 2004a: 62–6). I argue that there is indeed a link from the party system to the choice of electoral system, but that it is more complex than the simple equation supposes. Under reform by elite–mass interaction, quite the reverse pattern may hold: a high number of parties may generate problems that encourage reform away from proportionality, while excessive concentration of power may be particularly problematic under plurality systems where there are fewer parties. The conventional relationship is more likely under reform by elite majority imposition, but even here it is mediated by other factors.

The second subquestion leads towards a third, concerning the likely direction of change. Colomer (2004a: 55–62) argues that we should expect to find a general drift towards more proportional systems, and the evidence that he presents for this trend on the global scale is overwhelming. The analysis conducted here suggests that this trend should indeed be expected among new and fragile democracies, but that any such trend among reforms in established democracies should be much weaker. The evidence suggests that in fact there is no clear trend at all towards greater proportionality in established democracies. In the final pages of the book I consider what broad path electoral reform can be expected to take in the coming years.

I do not argue in this book that existing formal or statistical approaches to the study of electoral reform are not valuable: such a view would be absurd in the light of the great insights they have provided in recent years. Rather, my claim is more modest: that more fine-grained comparative analysis provides an important complement to these approaches, generating detailed knowledge of mechanisms that, while not universal, nevertheless apply across a range of cases. The intricacies of processes of electoral reform matter. They are crucial for understanding who has power over the electoral system, which interests or values are served by electoral reform, and what patterns are observable in outcomes.

PART I

Building blocks

We know many things about electoral reform processes. But this knowledge is not very systematic. Much of it is buried in case studies from around the globe. Some surveys have been offered (notably Benoit 2007; Gallagher 2005; Katz 2005), but they have been brief. In order to gain from the knowledge that is already out there, we need to take a step back, survey the terrain, and develop a framework by which we can lay out and comprehend the various crucial elements. This is one of my goals in the following three chapters. In particular, a great variety of motivations has been invoked by scholars studying electoral reforms, but we lack a clear overview. Systematizing knowledge of these motivations is the task of Chapter 2. Likewise, we know many things about the factors that shape these motivations and their translation into preferences and outcomes, and in Chapters 3 and 4 I pull these many strands together.

There are also gaps in the literature on electoral reform. In particular, though the process of changing the electoral system is an instance of policy change, there has been (at least until very recently) little exchange of ideas between policy scholars – who have worked primarily on economic and social policy – and electoral system scholars – whose intellectual backgrounds more commonly relate to elections and parties. Chapter 4 therefore draws extensively on concepts familiar from the policy literature – particularly relating to leadership and path dependence – that have been relatively underexplored in the world of electoral reform.

I thus include a very wide variety of explanatory factors in these chapters. Political scientists sometimes assume that comprehensive lists – 'laundry lists' – of factors and mechanisms are undesirable. But while they can never exhaust our analytical curiosity in themselves, they nevertheless provide an important starting point for further analysis. Once the possibilities have been laid out and structured, we can proceed much more systematically to analysing which of them matter in what ways under what circumstances. Thus, this part of the book will build a picture of the things we need to know about in order to understand electoral reform processes. I then apply these insights to the detailed study of episodes of enacted and attempted reform in the chapters of Parts II and III.

2

What motivates actors?

As I argued in Chapter 1, electoral reform processes may involve a diverse range of actors. The most important actors in the sorts of reform considered here are politicians and citizens: elected officeholders, those seeking office, party activists, interest group leaders, electoral reform activists, and ordinary citizens. Experts can have an important role in defining options too. In understanding how these actors behave in respect of electoral reform, our first task is to analyse what motivates them – what it is that they seek to achieve through their actions. The simplest model focuses on politicians and assumes they are motivated predominantly by narrow partisan concerns. This undoubtedly captures a great deal of truth. But reality is more complex: just what those partisan concerns are is far from straightforward; and many actors – including politicians themselves – may have broader values too. I survey these diverse motivations in the present chapter.

I begin by considering power: assuming that actors do want to maximize their power, what are the issues they think about in relation to electoral reform? I then turn to values: if actors are not out to enhance their own position, but rather seek the wider good, what are the criteria according to which they may judge the many options available? While I use the language of 'power interests' and 'values' to describe these two broad categories of motivation, the first should not straightforwardly be equated with self-interest, nor the second with altruism. Power, as I shall shortly elaborate, can be a means to further ends as well as an end in itself, and those further ends may be wholly other-regarding. Conversely, voters' desire for good governance, say, is likely to rest in significant part on their wish to experience personal security and prosperity. Nevertheless, the labels provide a convenient shorthand that saves us from too much circumlocution.

My purpose in this chapter is simply to survey and systematize the possibilities. In the next chapter I begin to consider the various steps through which these many possibilities can begin to translate into processes of electoral reform.

Power interests

Following Strøm and Müller (1999: 5–9), I conceptualize power-seeking in terms of two elements: the pursuit of office and the pursuit of policy influence. Pure office-seekers strive to win or retain office as an end in itself or for the perks it affords; pure policy-seekers pursue the maximum leverage over public policy outcomes.[1] These two elements will underlie the development of a typology of the ways in which power-seekers think about electoral reform. But they do not in themselves get us very far in building that typology: actors may pursue office either as an end in itself or as a means to their policy goals, and they may advance policy goals either because they believe in them or as a means of attracting votes and thereby gaining office. Whether they are fundamentally office-seekers or policy-seekers therefore gives us few clues on what criteria they will actually use in weighing different electoral system options.

Rather, the typology that I offer disaggregates power-seekers' thinking about electoral reform along four dimensions. In summary, these are the following:

1 *Power-seekers.* We commonly assume that the key power-seekers are political parties: the model developed by Benoit (2004: 373–4), for example, assumes that the key to electoral reform lies in which electoral system maximizes the seat share of the party or parties in power. But parties are not always so unified: they may contain factions, and the individual politicians within them have their own interests. Simplifying somewhat, I allow for two different sorts of power-seeker: parties and individuals.

2 *Actions and outcomes.* It is easy to assume that all that matters about an electoral reform process is its outcome: the electoral system that it generates. As Reed and Thies (2001: 153) and Shugart and Wattenberg (2001c: 577–81) argue, however, things are not always so simple. The electoral system generated by a reform process may clearly influence the power of the various actors involved. But so too may the actions of

---

[1] Strøm and Müller add a third category: vote-seeking. But, as they themselves observe (Strøm and Müller 1999: 9), 'It makes little sense to assume that parties value votes for their own sake. Contrary to office or policy, votes can only plausibly be *instrumental* goals. Parties only seek votes to obtain either policy influence, the spoils of office, or both.' I shall argue that vote-seeking plays an important part in many instances of electoral reform. But it is a derivative objective, not a basic motivation; the dichotomy between policy- and office-seeking is analytically more cogent without it. Benoit (2004: 367–8; 2007: 378–82), in applying the framework to the study of electoral reform, also drops the vote-seeking category.

those actors in the course of the reform process: actors who are seen to try to block a popular desire for reform or those perceived as trying to manipulate the system for their own private ends may suffer a backlash from voters that diminishes their power. Following Reed and Thies's terminology, I distinguish between *outcome-contingent* considerations that relate to the effects of different electoral systems and *act-contingent* considerations that pertain to the effects of an actor's behaviour in respect of reform.

3 *Objectives.* The most obvious ways in which the choice of electoral system can affect actors' power are through what Duverger (1954: 226) called the mechanical and psychological effects: first, the effect of the electoral system on the translation of votes into seats; second, the consequent effect upon strategic voting and the translation of voters' preferences across parties into votes (cf. Amorim Neto and Cox 1997: 152). But the electoral system can have a number of other effects too that may play an important role in thinking about electoral reform: as I discuss further below, it can affect the formation of voters' preferences and it can influence the translation of seats into office and of office and other resources into influence. I thus distinguish a number of intermediary objectives that influence power. In the case of parties, these are voter preferences, votes, seats, office, and influence (cf. Blau 2008: 63–4).

4 *Time horizons.* Finally, actors' time horizons may vary widely. Actors may be concerned simply with the result of the next election. They may have particular objectives for the one or two elections after that. Or they may lay greatest stress on the long-term competitive dynamic that an electoral system encourages. Allowing for varying time horizons is therefore important (Rose 1983: 42–3).

Table 2.1 lays out a typology of power-seeking considerations in terms of these dimensions. Panel (a) assumes the actors are parties, while panel (b) focuses on individuals. Each panel allows for both act- and outcome-contingent considerations and for a range of possible objectives. Time horizons are not explicitly shown, but imply variation for all of the elements in the table. I elaborate upon the content of the table in the paragraphs that follow.

Power-seeking by parties

The first five rows of Table 2.1 analyse the various ways in which a party's power may be influenced by choices made in the electoral reform process.

Table 2.1. *Typology of power-seeking considerations*

(a) *Parties*

	Aspects of reform	
Objectives	Outcome	Act
I Voter preferences	(a) Importance of candidate-, party-, and leader-centred competition	(b) Answering voters' desire for reform (c) Avoiding reforms seen as illegitimate
II Votes	(a) Psychological effect (b) Intra-coalition candidate distribution (coalition effect)	
III Seats	(a) Mechanical effect	
IV Office	(a) Ensuring favourable coalition dynamics	(b) Retaining/securing coalition allies
V Influence	(a) Enhancing party's intra-coalition influence (b) Splitting one's opponents	(c) Securing other policy goals (d) Retaining legitimacy (e) Minimizing transaction costs

(b) *Individuals*

	Aspects of reform	
Objectives	Outcome	Act
VI Re-election	(a) Fit between system and personal resources	(b) Answering voters' desire for reform (c) Avoiding reforms seen as illegitimate
VII Intra-party power	(a) Intra-party power of backbenchers and leaders	(b) Building personal credit within the party
VIII Influence in political system	(a) Reconfiguring the party system	(b) Attracting potential allies in other parties

Row I: voter preferences

The basic seat-maximization model that I alluded to above, founded on Duverger's mechanical and psychological effects, assumes that voters' underlying preferences across parties are exogenous to the electoral system and the process of electoral reform. But this need not be the case. In the first place, different electoral systems push the focus of political competition in different directions: towards individual candidates, party leaders, or parties as programmatically based organizations (I(a) in Table 2.1). To the degree that a party's strength lies, say, in its locally entrenched candidates, it may hope to win more votes under a system that emphasizes these candidates rather than one that directs attention to national party platforms. In South Africa, for example, Gouws and Mitchell (2005: 358) suggest that one reason the African National Congress (ANC) supported PR was that, '[g]iven high levels of illiteracy among many of its likely supporters, it would benefit from a simple system that would focus attention on its most popular symbols and leaders – supporters could, more or less, just "vote Mandela".' During transition from communism, Hungary's Communist Party initially sought a system based on single-member districts, believing its local candidates were more popular than its national brand; only when new information suggested that even local candidates were likely to lose did it shift its strategy in favour of PR (Schiemann 2001: 243–4). According to Pilet (2007: 215–17), a reform of the Belgian district structure passed in 2002 was supported by parties with nationally popular candidates and opposed by those with locally popular candidates. I shall argue in the chapters that follow that thinking of this kind has been central to electoral system choices in France and was also important in the Italian reforms of 2005.

Act-contingent considerations are also widely important. If there is a strong desire among voters or prominent party backers for electoral reform, politicians may fear that they will lose votes at the next election should they fail to respond to that demand (I(b) in Table 2.1). Conversely, politicians may be dissuaded from manipulating the electoral system to suit their own purposes if they fear that popular distaste for such manoeuvres will prompt an electoral backlash (I(c)). As Katz (2005: 75) writes:

> Even when a reform would clearly be costly to the parties in power, they may expect resistance to be even more costly; even when parties have the capacity to tweak the rules to their advantage, the expected benefits may be outweighed by the potential backlash.

Public pressure is central to all cases of reform by elite–mass interaction: the reforms in New Zealand, Italy, and Japan in 1993 and 1994 all emerged from lengthy processes in which public disquiet and elite attempts to respond to it were important (cf. Shugart and Wattenberg 2001c: 572–8). The role of public disapproval in constraining politicians from overt manipulations, meanwhile, was first theorized, to my knowledge, by Quintal (1970: 755) under the label of the 'costs of voter affect': 'The greater the seat bonus which the majority tries to engineer,' he suggests, 'the greater is the danger of turning the next election into a referendum on the new system.' He cites the adoption of the *legge truffa* ('swindle law') in Italy in 1953 as a case where politicians failed to pay heed to this danger and lost votes in consequence (Quintal 1970: 758). I consider these legitimacy constraints in much detail in the next chapter.

Rows II and III: votes and seats

The second and third rows of Table 2.1 can be taken together. Some electoral reforms have clearly been motivated by calculations of party seat shares under alternative systems on the basis of Duverger's mechanical and psychological effects (III(a) and II(a)). In Chile in 1989, for example, the outgoing Pinochet regime, expecting to finish second in the coming elections, engineered what is, to my knowledge, the only electoral system in the world that gives the greatest seat bonus to the second largest party or coalition (Rahat and Sznajder 1998: 430–31; Siavelis 2005: 436–8). Blatant manipulation of the electoral system to enhance the ruling parties' seat shares occurred also in France in 1951 and Greece in 1956: in both cases, different electoral systems were adopted in different parts of the country, corresponding to which system would maximize the seat shares of the parties in government (Carstairs 1980: 180–82; Clogg 1987: 32). Less egregiously, Reilly finds that alternative vote was adopted in Australia and has been considered in the United States because parties saw that it would allow them to avoid vote-splitting and thus win more seats (Reilly 1997b: 3; 2004: 261–2).

The general proposition that electoral systems are determined by parties seeking to maximize their seat shares is widely advanced. Early statements include those of Lipson (1959: 21) and Rokkan (1970: 157). More recently, the proposition has been theorized by Brady and Mo (1992: 406) and Benoit (2004: 373–4). These theorists (explicitly or implicitly) offer narrow accounts of seat-maximization in two senses. First, they assume that, in considering the effects of different electoral systems on their party's seat share, politicians take the distribution of voters' underlying preferences across parties as fixed: that is, they assume away the first row of Table 2.1. Second, they see the translation of those voter preferences into votes and then seats as entirely encapsulated by Duverger's mechanical and psychological effects. This assumption is often accurate. But where parties form pre-election coalitions involving mutual stand-down arrangements, intra-coalition bargaining power may have a further significant role in deciding outcomes (II(b) in Table 2.1). This 'coalition effect' was, as I argue in Chapter 8, a factor in the Italian reforms of 2005.

Row IV: office

A party's power is likely to be strongly influenced by its seat share, but it is not entirely determined by it. Row IV of Table 2.1 considers the next step: the translation of seats into the capacity to hold governmental office.

Where governments are formed by single parties, seat shares may indeed be all we need to know: the party that enters government is the one with the largest seat share. But things are more complex where governments are formed by coalitions (cf. Austen-Smith and Banks 1988: 417). Here one's party must be part of a coalition that is capable of entering government, and so various aspects of coalition dynamics (IV(a)) come into play. For example, analyses by Cox (1997: 194–6) and Bueno De Mesquita (2000: 72) suggest that, where formateur power goes to the largest party, small parties have an interest in bolstering the seat share of their largest ally, even if doing so diminishes their own share. Following alternative reasoning, a party may seek the role of pivotal player in coalition negotiations rather than try to maximize its own size. Proportional representation may give centrist parties this pivotal role, as the Italian and Dutch Christian Democrats demonstrated to good effect during decades of unbroken government office that ended in 1993 and 1994 respectively (Andeweg 1989: 55–6). Curtice (1996: 121) argues that the UK Labour Party agreed to proportional representation for the new Scottish Parliament in the 1990s in part because, as a large centrist party (outflanked on the left, he says, by the Scottish Nationalists), it believed (wrongly, as we now know) that it would be essential to almost any governing coalition. Iversen and Soskice (2006) offer another version: proportional systems, they argue, systematically favour the formation of coalitions of the centre and the left, while majoritarian systems favour the right. Extending this work, Cusack, Iversen, and Soskice (2007) argue that the right will favour PR only where the underlying structure of the economy demands cross-class coalition-building.

On the act-contingent side, meanwhile, parties may be reluctant to endorse reforms that would bolster their own seat shares if doing so appears hostile to the interests of potential coalition partners (IV(b)). In West Germany, for example, proportional representation was not abandoned during the grand coalition of the 1960s in part because neither large party wanted to alienate the Free Democrats, who were potential future coalition partners (Carstairs 1980: 172; Jesse 1987: 435–6). In Israel too, repeated attempts to reduce the proportionality of the electoral system have foundered on the rock of coalition politics (Diskin and Diskin 1995: 36; Rahat 2001: 128, 2008: 15).

Row V: influence

The final step concerns the translation of votes, seats, and office into influence over governmental policy. Again, several issues are important here.

First, a party operating in a coalition will seek to maximize not only its chances of occupying government office, but also its power within the coalition (V(a) in Table 2.1). While such intra-coalition power may principally be a function of the coalition partners' relative vote and seat shares, it depends also on the degree to which each party retains an independent identity and voter base, which can give it added weight in coalition negotiations. As the various coalition partners knew in Italy in 2005, different electoral systems afford parties different degrees of independence.

Second, even where a party does not hope to secure office, it can still increase its influence (or at least reduce its opponents' ability to enact their alternative agenda) by working to keep its opponents divided (V(b)). Bawn (1993: 975–6) argues that West Germany's Social Democrats preferred proportional representation to single-member plurality in 1949 even though the latter would have given them more seats because under proportional representation the Christian Democrats would be able to form a government only in coalition with others. In drawing up plans for the new Scottish Parliament in the 1990s, Labour opted for proportional representation partly to ensure that the Scottish Nationalists would never win an overall majority through which they might secure Scottish independence (Bogdanor 1999: 219–20; Taylor 2002: 56–7). Similar logic mattered in France too in 1985.

Three further considerations relate to act contingencies. First, a party may bargain across issues, agreeing to an electoral reform in order to secure other policy objectives that matter to it more (V(c)) (Benoit 2004: 385; Katz 2005: 62, 66). For example, in the Netherlands in 1917, the Christian Democrats and Social Democrats agreed to the Liberals' demand for proportional representation to secure Liberal backing for a package that also included educational reform and universal suffrage (Andeweg 1989: 45).

Second, the popular legitimacy of an electoral system or an electoral reform may matter not only for the vote-seeking reasons already noted but also for its impact on a government in office (V(d)): as Katz (2005: 72) puts it, 'being seen to have won office by manipulating the rules devalues the victory'. Plant (1995: 12) suggests that the Scottish Parliament needed to use a proportional system so as not to be 'seen as a one-party state'; Laffin (2000: 537) makes the same point for Wales. Lacking such legitimacy, a government may find it harder to pursue its objectives over the medium term.

Finally, electoral reform has an opportunity cost, absorbing time and resources that might have been devoted to the pursuit of other goals; politicians will always be keen to avoid or minimize this cost (V(e)) (Benoit 2004: 386; Colomer 2005: 3; Quintal 1970: 755, 756; Shepsle 2001: 323). This may mean that actors 'satisfice' (Simon 1959) on the electoral system: so long as they find its effects reasonably satisfactory, actors may just not think about electoral reform as a possibility: other matters may always be higher up their agendas. The higher is uncertainty regarding the effects of alternative systems, the greater are the costs involved in developing clear preferences. I discuss the role of uncertainty in electoral reform fully in the next chapter.

Power-seeking by individuals

Panel (b) of Table 2.1 turns the focus from parties to individuals: as I have suggested, parties are composed of individuals, and it is never wise to assume that they always act solely in pursuit of the good of the group. I distinguish three objectives for individuals: re-election, intra-party power, and influence in the wider political system. Which of these matter and how they play out depends crucially on who the key individuals are: party leaders, backbenchers, or party activists.

Row VI: re-election

There can be few concerns dearer to the heart of the average politician than that of securing re-election (VI(a) in Table 2.1). In the absence of further information, individual politicians' re-election prospects rise with their party's expected seat share. But sometimes further information is available. For example, locally popular or otherwise entrenched politicians in systems where such local resources matter will generally oppose reform towards a system where these resources matter less. This was certainly true in Hungary in 1989: even after communist leaders shifted their position towards PR, backbenchers opposed the proposed mixed system and forced a small increase in the share of district-based seats (Schiemann 2001: 245–6). It was also true in Japan, both in the run-up to the successful reforms of 1994 and during an abortive attempt to introduce a similar mixed system in 1973: many backbenchers from the ruling Liberal Democratic Party (LDP) opposed reforms that threatened the relevance of their existing local support organizations.

On the act-contingent side, meanwhile, individual politicians face the same potential pressures from voters as do parties, and they may need to react accordingly (VI(b) and VI(c)).

Row VII: intra-party power

Enhancement of intra-party power relates primarily to the distinction already mentioned between electoral systems favouring candidate-centred, leader-centred, and party-centred competition (VII(a) in Table 2.1). On the whole, we may expect party leaders to favour leader- or party-centred competition, while backbenchers will value candidate-centred competition. Non-professional party activists, meanwhile, will tend to prefer party-centred competition focused upon programmatic appeals.

As for act contingencies, individual politicians may seek to build credit with various constituencies in their party through the approach that they take to electoral reform (VII(b)). This is particularly so where some of the steps that turn out to be crucial to a process of electoral reform appear unimportant at the time. As I shall argue, for example, many leading governing-party politicians in New Zealand in the mid-1980s accepted the deputy prime minister's proposal to create a royal commission on the electoral system simply to save resources for other battles that they thought more important: they had no expectation that it would produce major reform.

Row VIII: influence in the wider political system

The final element in Table 2.1 relates to party system reconfiguration (VIII(a)): as Katz (2005: 62) notes, sometimes actors may seek 'to change the whole format of the party system'. Actors may desire such change for two reasons. One is that they believe that a different format would be better for the country – promoting, for example, better representation or more effective governance. This belongs to the discussion of wider values that I pursue below. The other reason is that certain actors believe that their own power will be enhanced if the parties are reconfigured. This need not be an individual pursuit: a group of politicians may share this objective; a whole party may sign up to the goal of self-dissolution in favour of new parties constructed on new lines. What differentiates these ideas from the considerations outlined in panel (a) of Table 2.1 is that they do not take the existing menu of parties as given. For example, even a small party can favour the adoption of a plurality electoral system if it expects to form a core part of a new, large party in the two-party system that the change induces. I shall argue in Part III that ideas about party system reconfiguration were important in the electoral reforms in Japan and Italy in the early 1990s. Pilet (2006: 7–8) offers a third case, namely the debates over electoral reform in Belgium since the early 1990s: he labels as 'optimists' those who expected that majoritarian reform would serve their long-term interests by reshaping the party system.

This consideration has an act-contingent element too: anyone wishing to reconfigure the party system must retain the confidence of potential allies in other parties (VIII(b)).

Values

So far I have analysed power-seeking, where actors think of electoral systems and electoral reform processes in redistributive terms and pursue the course of action that will maximize their power. For some authors, it seems that these are the only considerations that matter. Riker (1984: 103) contends that 'most actual choices [of electoral systems] have been made with the intention of promoting partisan advantage rather than with the goal of incorporating sound constitutional principles into governmental structure'. Kellner (1995: 23) observes aphoristically that, 'In politics, when principle collides with self-interest, principle tends to retreat with a bloody nose.'

Yet others disagree. Blais and Massicotte (1997: 117) argue that 'politicians sometimes make choices primarily on the basis of their views about what is good, just or efficient'. Katz (2005: 68) concludes that 'it does appear that parties sometimes simply want to do the right, or the democratic, thing'. Furthermore, such wishes can exert great power over outcomes: as Nagel (2004: 530) observes, 'New Zealand's experience suggests that models of electoral choice based on political bargaining are not always applicable, and that reformers who shape their proposals to meet the interests of dominant political actors may ultimately have less influence than those who appear more quixotic'. Two further points add to these observations. First, as I suggested in Chapter 1, even the most self-interested politicians may lay down their short-term power and opt for institutions serving the national good if to do otherwise is likely to engender conflict and instability. Second, as again I have emphasized, politicians are not the only actors involved in processes of electoral reform. Ordinary citizens, activists, and experts are very likely (in so far as they are interested in the electoral system) to be concerned about matters such as the quality of democracy and the effectiveness and probity of governance. Thus, to understand values as well as power interests is imperative.

Various lists of possible values or criteria of evaluation already exist: several, drawn up both by political scientists and by real-world review commissions, are summarized in Gallagher (2005: 569–70). I build on these and others (notably Reynolds, Reilly, and Ellis (2005: 9–15)) in what follows. In Table 2.2, besides distinguishing between outcome- and act-contingent considerations, I group values in several broad categories. The paragraphs that follow elaborate.

Row I: democracy

Elections are among the fundamental institutions of representative democracy. It is therefore no surprise that many of the values that electoral systems and processes of electoral reform can influence relate to democracy. The first five elements in Table 2.2 all concern aspects of representation. The first is fairness in the distribution of seats between parties (I(a)). At a minimum, fairness simply implies equal application of the rules to all candidates or parties (Elklit and Svensson 1997: 35). But often it is taken to mean more than that: to imply proportionality in the distribution of seats and therefore equality in the contribution each vote makes to the outcome (Blais, Dobrzynska, and Indridason 2005: 183; Carstairs 1980: 54, 113).

The avoidance of anomalous election results (I(b)) relates to serious instances of distortion of seat shares compared to vote shares, which Taagepera and Shugart (1989: 227–8) argue should be minimized. The most egregious distortions are what Siaroff (2003) and Shugart (2008) term 'spurious majorities' (also known as 'wrong winner' elections), where a party coming second in votes wins a majority of seats. Siaroff identifies thirteen national elections worldwide between the late nineteenth century and the end of the twentieth century in which spurious majorities occurred. The spurious majorities in New Zealand in 1978 and 1981 were one factor that helped initiate the chain of events leading to electoral reform in that country over a decade later (Renwick 2009b;

Table 2.2. *Values in electoral reform*

Values	Aspects of reform	
	Outcome	Act
I Democracy	(a) Fair distribution of seats	(k) Democratic process
	(b) Avoidance of anomalous	of system choice
	results	(l) Constitutional
	(c) Fair distribution of power	process of system
	(d) Representation of society	choice
	(e) Voter choice	
	(f) Accountability of governments	
	(g) Accountability of individual	
	politicians	
	(h) Checks and balances	
	(i) Encouraging effective political	
	parties	
	(j) Simplicity	
II Stability	(a) Avoidance of inter-group	(b) Avoidance of
	conflict	conflict/deadlock
		over choice of system
III Governance	(a) Efficient decision-making	
	(b) Effective scrutiny of decisions	
	(c) Avoidance of corruption	
	(d) Avoidance of money politics	
IV Policy outcomes	(a) Economic policy objectives	
V Constituency service	(a) Quality of constituency service	
VI Identity	(a) Affirmation of links with	
	national tradition	
	(b) Affirmation of links with	
	favoured states	
VII Practicability	(a) Administrative simplicity	

Vowles 1995: 100). Shugart (2008) also highlights disproportionately lopsided majorities as a potential spur to reform initiation.

Fairness is most commonly associated with proportional distribution of seats in the legislature. Yet as Blau (2004) shows, the meanings of the concept of fairness are many. Most importantly for current purposes, it may also relate to the distribution of power in government (I(c)). Opponents of proportional systems often criticize the undue influence they may give to small parties – the problem of 'the tail wagging the dog' (for discussion, see McGann and Moran 2005). As Blau (2004: 173) puts it, 'fairness in translating votes to seats may lead to unfairness in translating seats to power'.

Another aspect of representation is representation of society, particularly of minorities and women (I(d)) (Reynolds, Reilly, and Ellis 2005: 9). For example, New Zealand's Royal Commission concentrated much effort upon ensuring effective representation for Māori (Royal Commission on the Electoral System 1986: 11, 81–116).

The final aspect of representation concerns voter choice (I(e)). Farrell and Gallagher (1999: 309) find from focus groups that voters stress 'voter choice' when asked to evaluate different electoral systems. This was also a key criterion identified by participants of recent citizens' assemblies that made proposals for electoral reform in British Columbia (British Columbia Citizens' Assembly on Electoral Reform 2004: 2) and Ontario (Ontario Citizens' Assembly on Electoral Reform 2007: 2, 4). Voter choice may mean many things, and some of its meanings overlap with other elements in Table 2.2. It may mean having more parties to choose from, so that the likelihood there is a party that closely represents one's own views is higher. It may also mean having the opportunity to express some of the complexity of one's preferences – either preferences for both a party and an individual candidate or multiple ranked preferences.

Beyond the various dimensions of representativeness, a further core aspect of democracy is accountability: voters should be able to hold both governments (I(f)) and individual politicians (I(g)) to account, voting them out if their performance is inadequate. Concern over inadequate accountability was a major factor in public pressure for reform in Italy in the early 1990s (Katz 1999: 3) and in Austria before the reduction of district magnitudes in 1992 (Müller 2005: 399–400). Andeweg (1989: 48) reports that a major source of pressure for electoral and wider constitutional reform in the Netherlands since the 1960s has been the perception that 'only the most tenuous link exists between the competition for votes and the acquisition of executive power'. Concern over the lack of accountability of individual legislative members has prompted repeated calls for reform of the closed list PR electoral system introduced in South Africa in 1994 (Gouws and Mitchell 2005: 369–70; Reynolds 1995: 93).

Democracy requires not just that voters be able to hold governments to account every three to five years, but also that governments remain subject to ongoing checks and balances throughout their term in office (I(h)). The inadequacy of checks and balances was the major concern of

Geoffrey Palmer, who, as New Zealand's deputy prime minister and (briefly) prime minister, was that country's leading advocate of electoral reform during the 1980s. Shortly before embarking on his political career, he wrote:

> The issue is simple: are there sufficient checks upon the power of the government in New Zealand? My conclusion is that although the power of the executive is not entirely unbridled, it is extensive enough to cause concern. We need to examine how the power of government might be matched with effective, continuing restraints.
>
> (Palmer 1979: 10)

That effective political parties (I(i)) are essential for the healthy working of modern democracy is widely recognized (Finer 1984: 1; Schattschneider 1942: 1; Ware 1996: 1), and Reynolds, Reilly, and Ellis (2005: 12–13) argue that the development of such parties should be a criterion of electoral system design. Indeed, it was an explicit criterion for the commissions in both New Zealand (Royal Commission on the Electoral System 1986: 12) and Fiji (Fiji Constitution Review Commission 1996: 310). The perception that factionalism prevented effective party functioning contributed to the abandonment of the single non-transferable vote system in both Japan in 1994 and Taiwan in 2005 (Reilly 2006: 102–3).

Finally (as regards outcome-contingent criteria pertaining to democracy), electoral systems should, so far as possible, be simple (I(j)). Simplicity has two aspects: simplicity for voters in understanding what choices are available and how they should express them, and administrative simplicity. I consider the latter below, under practicalities. Concern to ensure simplicity for voters was significant in South Africa in the early 1990s, where the ANC apparently concluded that closed-list PR – in which voters need only recognize the party logo or a picture of the party leader – would place least burden on its many illiterate voters (Sisk 1995: 189). Simplicity matters in highly educated societies too. It was a criterion used by the Scottish Constitutional Convention in its early deliberations over the electoral system for a devolved assembly (Brown 2000: 544). Yet Scotland's politicians conspicuously failed in this regard: Scottish voters now face the most diverse range of electoral systems across four levels of government to be found anywhere in the world, apparently contributing to high numbers of invalid ballot papers in the elections of 2007 (Scottish Elections Review 2007).

Belief in democracy amounts to belief in the value of following certain processes. Thus, democrats may be concerned about the process of electoral reform as well as its outcomes. Voters might dissent if they perceive that electoral reform has been imposed against their wishes (I(k)). Modern democracy being a matter of constitutionalism as well as of majority rule (Elster and Slagstad 1988), many actors are likely to want any electoral reform to follow constitutional procedures (I(l)).

Row II: stability

A large part of the literature on designing appropriate electoral systems, particularly for developing democracies, focuses on the avoidance of inter-group conflict (II(a) in Table 2.2) (e.g., Fraenkel and Grofman 2006; Horowitz 1991, 1997; Lewis 1965: 71–4; Lijphart 1985, 2002; Reilly 1996, 1997a; Reynolds 1995). The observation that electoral systems are sometimes chosen to defuse tensions that might otherwise generate violence goes back at least to Rokkan's analysis of the wave of electoral reforms in Western Europe in the late nineteenth and early twentieth centuries (1970: 157). It has been corroborated for that period through case studies (Carstairs 1980) and statistical analysis (Boix 1999: 619–21). Elsewhere, the same mechanism has been observed in Nigeria and Sri Lanka (Horowitz 1985: 636–40) and in much of southern Africa (Gouws and Mitchell 2005: 358; Mozaffar 1998: 89–91; Southall 2003). Fiji's Constitution Review Commission regarded multi-ethnic government as its most important goal (Fiji Constitution Review Commission 1996: 18). In Latin America, the primary cleavage lines have been ideological rather than ethnic, but the divisions have been intense, and the use of electoral and wider constitutional reforms as part of the solution has been the same, as argued by Lehoucq (1995: 27–8) in relation to Costa Rica, Hartlyn (1988: 3–4) for Colombia, and Karl (1986) and Levine (1985) for Venezuela. Of course, such positive responses to crisis are not inevitable (Horowitz 2000), but they are frequently observable in the world.

While actors with concerns about stability are likely primarily to focus on the consequences of electoral systems, it is at least logically possible that they may attend also to the possibility that reform processes may have destabilizing effects if managed unwisely (II(b)). Whether this has ever been a significant concern in practice is moot. There is some evidence to suggest that one of the major parties in the roundtable negotiations in Hungary in 1989 – the Hungarian Democratic Forum – thought in this way: it never voiced any preference regarding the electoral system and intervened only to suggest compromise between other parties' proposals. But whether it did so to expedite agreement and avoid conflict or for other reasons is unclear (Renwick 2005: 999–1000).

Row III: governance

The third set of values relates to governance: elections are fundamental to democracy; but democracy is required only because collective decisions must be made; actors may therefore concern themselves with the effectiveness of such decision-making and of the state.

The perception that governments are incapable of making decisions efficiently (III(a) in Table 2.2) has been an important driver of reform in several cases, notably Israel, where direct election of the prime minister was introduced in 1992 (Katz 1999: 2; Ottolenghi 2001: 109), and Italy in 1993 (e.g., Gambetta and Warner 2004: 240). Opponents of PR frequently invoke the Israeli and Italian examples to illustrate its dangers (Jackson and McRobie 1998: 82). In Hungary, the liberal parties were similarly concerned that a proportional system could lead to multiplication of parties and ineffective government, potentially opening the way to renewed dictatorship (Renwick 2005: 1013).

Easy decision-making, however, is not necessarily effective decision-making: at the opposite end of the spectrum from the previous, actors may wish to ensure that decisions be made only following appropriate scrutiny (III(b)). New Zealand's Geoffrey Palmer wanted greater checks and balances in part, as noted above, on democratic grounds, but also, in part, to promote better decision-making. Complaining that New Zealand has 'the fastest law in the West', he argued, 'Law-making should be a solemn and deliberate business. It ought to permit time for reflection and sober second thought' (Palmer 1979: 94).

In many countries, the principal concerns of electoral reformers have focused on the related issues of corruption (III(c)) and 'money politics' (III(d)). As Reilly (2006: 100–101, 2007: 62) argues, the desire to tackle patronage, vote-buying, and other aspects of corruption and the power of money has been a major factor in the wave of electoral reforms in recent years in the Asia-Pacific region. Corruption scandals were important triggers for reform in Italy in 1993 and in Japan in 1994.

Row IV: policy outcomes

The elements in Row III of Table 2.2 relate to the general process of governance. A growing political economy literature argues, additionally, that electoral systems also have specific policy effects, influencing, for example, levels of government spending and budget deficits (Persson and Tabellini 2005) and price levels (Chang, Kayser, and Rogowski 2008).

Few of these authors have contended that such effects have influenced electoral reforms. But one such argument has been made by Rogowski. He argues that the more dependent a country is upon international trade, the more desirable it is to use PR in national elections: this insulates the state from particularist demands, limits the role of 'pork' and patronage, and promotes policy stability (Rogowski 1987: 207–8). Furthermore, he argues that these facts have shaped electoral system choice: he finds that more trade-dependent countries are indeed more likely to use proportional systems (Rogowski 1987: 212–13) and cites instances in which the mechanisms he identifies have featured in reform debates (Rogowski 1987: 220–22).

Row V: constituency service

Constituency service can be regarded as a form of representation: the representation of the concerns of individual citizens to the state. Yet in so far as constituency service involves the provision of essentially private services by members of the legislature to individual citizens, it does not really form part of the process of democratic control over collective decisions, and so I consider it here separately.

The negative side of constituency service has been seen in many countries in the forms of pork, wedding and funeral money, and other such diversions of resources to private ends (Kitschelt and Wilkinson 2007). But in several countries there is considerable attachment to the positive aspect: the role of the local parliamentarian in intervening on behalf of the ordinary citizen when he or she feels unreasonably treated by the state. The Royal Commission in New Zealand made this one of their criteria for judging electoral systems and argued, 'An important function of individual MPs is to act on behalf of constituents who need help in their dealings with the Government or its agencies' (Royal Commission on the Electoral System 1986: 11). The terms of reference of the Jenkins Commission in the UK, appointed in 1997, included 'the maintenance of a link between MPs and geographical constituencies' as one of the requirements for any new system (Independent Commission on the Voting System 1998: v). As Bogdanor (1997: 93) observes, the single-member district 'has become deeply embedded in the political culture of Westminster' (similarly, Lundberg 2007: 15); Pearse (2005) highlights continued attachment to constituency representation in the UK, Canada, Australia, and New Zealand.

Row VI: identity

All of the considerations that I have discussed so far relate to the *effects* of different electoral systems or of processes of electoral reform. But actors may at times be interested in electoral systems not only for their effects on diverse values, but also for their ability to embody certain values. More specifically, Row VI in Table 2.2 highlights two ways in which the choice of electoral system may allow actors to embody aspects of their identity. The first involves affirmation of links with national tradition (VI(a)). In the Baltic states after the collapse of the Soviet Union, for example, many argued for the reinstatement of the inter-war constitutions in order to express continuity with those systems and assert the illegitimacy of the Soviet takeover (EECR 1992: 3–4; Loeber 1998: 2; Taagepera 1994: 214). Alternatively, actors may pursue examples taken from abroad in order to affirm identity with particular states or broader cultures (VI(b)). In much of East-Central Europe in 1989, the overwhelming desire to 'return to Europe' after forty years of forced detachment from the region's perceived European identity contributed to an eagerness to draw on West European examples in constructing the new democratic institutional structures.

These mechanisms involve more than mere cognitive constraints on the options actors perceive (which I discuss in Chapter 3). Rather, actors may choose positively to espouse certain systems above alternatives because of the values they embody.

Row VII: practicability

The final value I consider is that of practicability. As Reynolds, Reilly, and Ellis (2005: 14) write, 'Elections do not take place on the pages of academic books but in the real world, and for this reason the choice of any electoral system is, to some degree, dependent on the cost and administrative capacities of the country involved.' To my knowledge, the clearest case in which administrative simplicity has been a major consideration in electoral system design has been Papua New Guinea. Having used an alternative vote system during the final years of Australian colonial rule, Papua New Guinea switched to single-member plurality ahead of independence in 1975. The reason was the greater ease of administering the plurality system: the Chief Electoral Officer argued that using alternative vote was complex and time consuming while making little difference to election results (Reilly 1996: 55). Pressure for a return to alternative vote began in the early 1980s (Reilly 1996:

49–50). But worries about administrative capacity remained. Having observed the 1992 elections in Simbu province, Standish (1996: 320) argued that alternative vote 'would be too complex for both the electoral staff in this province and the scrutineers and candidates'. State administrative capacity had declined since independence and political culture had toughened (similarly, see Fraenkel 2004: 130). Even Reilly, whose advocacy of reform contributed to the return to alternative vote in 2002, acknowledged the potential difficulty (Reilly 2002: 253). It was only against this concern that the alternative vote system was reinstated in 2002.

Conclusion

I do not claim that this overview of power-seeking concerns and values is entirely exhaustive. Actors in politics are human beings, and human beings are too complex to contain in a single chapter: a great variety of idiosyncratic concerns may come into play. But the discussion here covers the main ground: it encompasses the various considerations that have had the greatest impact in most cases of major electoral reform around the world in recent decades. It gives an essential starting point in understanding electoral reform processes.

But these lists of motivations are not very useful in themselves: we want also to understand both why actors are motivated as they are (even to predict what their motivations are likely to be) and how any given constellation of actors with certain motivations translates into outcomes. I take several steps in these directions in the next chapter.

3

From motivations to outcomes: exogenous factors

The previous chapter provided the first building block for understanding processes of electoral reform: a wide overview of the power interests and values that actors may pursue. The next stage is to explore the key steps through which these potential motivations come together and translate into electoral system outcomes. I distinguish three such steps. The first concerns the processes that shape particular actors' motivations: of the many considerations laid out in Chapter 2, which do particular actors in fact focus on and what determines the weights they give them? The second relates to the mechanisms through which these motivations translate into specific preferences over the many available courses of action. Here we must consider both which option is objectively best given actors' goals and what constraints their perceptions are subject to. The third addresses how these preferences translate into outcomes.

I begin the task of analysing these mechanisms in the present chapter by considering factors exogenous to the reform process. I pursue it further in Chapter 4 by analysing the internal dynamics of the reform process, focusing especially on leadership and path dependence.

In analysing the three steps in this chapter, I invoke six categories of explanatory factor: history, ideational change, the nature of parties and the party system, state institutions, events and circumstances, and the nature of actors. Most of these are relevant to both the first and second stages. With regard to the third stage, I focus more narrowly upon the role of institutions. I draw together the various roles played by these factors in the conclusion.

My purpose in this chapter is to develop initial propositions regarding the mechanisms that may operate in the course of electoral reform. Some of these propositions are necessarily rather general; others are more specific. They are not rigid hypotheses that could be tested rigorously in the empirical chapters of Parts II and III of the book. In those chapters I will, rather, assess their plausibility and refine them further.

Determinants of actors' motivations

As Chapter 2 shows, actors may be motivated when thinking about electoral reform by an enormous variety of both power interests and values. But which of these do particular actors actually give significant weight to? Indeed, do they give significant weight to any of them, or do they ignore the electoral system entirely? Understanding what factors shape actors' motivations amounts to understanding the determinants of these weights.

I proceed through four steps. The first two steps generate expectations regarding the weights attached to the two broad categories of motivations: power interests and values. The second two steps analyse in turn the relative weights of the various elements within each of those categories

The importance of office-seeking

As I emphasized in Chapter 2, the distinction between power-seeking and the pursuit of values in electoral reform is not the same as the distinction between self-interest and altruism. Some actors may seek power simply because they like it, others because it allows them to achieve further policy goals, which may be entirely other-regarding. Nevertheless, we can say that those who do see power simply as an end in itself – those who are office-seekers – will, unless the stability of the political system is seriously threatened, pursue power interests alone. Thus, an understanding of the distribution of office-seekers and of wider policy-seekers is valuable as a predictor of the importance of values in the reform process.

The key determinant of the degree to which actors are office-seekers or policy-seekers, I propose, is their position in the political system: those who hold or pursue office can be expected to have a greater tendency towards office-seeking – towards seeing office as an end in itself – than those who do not. Even if office is initially viewed as a means towards further ends, it comes, through pursuit, to be seen as its own end. Many aspects of the officeholder's life come to depend on holding office: income, prestige, social contacts, lifestyle. Thus, officeholders have vested interests in retaining office that non-officeholders do not share. As Michels (1962 [1911]: 206) argued almost a century ago, 'It is certain that the exercise of power produces a profound and ineffaceable change in the character' of leaders.

This reasoning is the underpinning of May's law of curvilinear disparity (May 1973), according to which party leaders – those holding office – will be less ideological (more constrained by the desire to retain office) than party activists. May's law is not uncontested (Norris 1995b), but it can ground a tentative proposition: that party activists and other non-politicians are more likely to attend to values than are politicians, who will tend to focus upon power interests.

But two qualifications should be made to this proposition. The first is simply that, even if they are office-seeking to some degree, many politicians retain a strong interest in policy too. As McLean (1987: 34) notes, 'Most politicians who make laws do so because they believe in them, or at least because, among other things, they believe in them.' Thus, at least some level of interest among politicians in values is likely. The second qualification is a little more complex: we can differentiate among politicians. The logic described above implies that those who have not yet attained office, and perhaps those who have only recently attained it, may retain a more policy-seeking focus: interests become vested primarily only once office has been attained; and the psychological shift may take time to embed. Thus, we may expect recent entrants to the class of politicians to approach electoral reform differently from their more seasoned colleagues. Such was the experience in East-Central Europe during transition from communism, when former dissidents often initially retained idealistic ways of thinking (Birch et al. 2002: 69; Renwick 2005). Further, those whose income, prestige, social contacts, and lifestyle are less contingent upon retaining office may also place less emphasis on office-seeking. This may apply above all to those who have attained success and security in a world outside politics and who retain access to that world while pursuing political careers (cf. Lehoucq 2000: 470).

This reasoning suggests three propositions:

P1: Non-politicians – such as citizens, political activists, interest group leaders, and experts – will tend to give greater weight to values than do politicians.

P2: Recent entrants to the class of politicians will tend to give greater weight to values than do more seasoned politicians.

P3: Those politicians whose income, prestige, social contacts, and lifestyle are less contingent upon retaining office will tend to give greater weight to values than do those politicians for whom these are more contingent on office.

Policy outcomes or electoral system values?

Understanding the weight attached to office-seeking gets us some way, but not the whole way, towards understanding the relative weights attached to power interests and to values. To emphasize a crucial point again, even politicians who are not office-seekers may pursue power as a means to their policy ends. And citizens and interest group leaders who are not office-seekers at all may be interested not in the electoral system values analysed in the previous chapter, but, directly, in the concrete outputs of the governing system. In order to gauge the weights of power interests and values, therefore, we need a second step, concerning the importance actors attach to policy outcomes versus electoral system values.

I posit that the main determinant of this is the degree to which the electoral system values are perceived as seriously threatened. In established democracies, most of the time, these values are likely to be seen by many as adequately secured; policy-seekers will tend therefore to concentrate their efforts not upon the electoral system, but upon the activities of the state that more directly influence citizens' lives. Only where the political realm is perceived as suffering from systemic failure or crisis is significant attention likely to be directed towards the values underpinning the electoral system.

Thus it is that, as several analysts have pointed out, electoral reform motivated by values is likely to occur in established democracies only in the wake of sharp trigger events that cause confidence in prevailing governing institutions to falter (Katz 2005: 74; Norris 1995a: 7; Sakamoto 1999b: 421; Shugart 2001: 26–7, 2008; Shugart and Wattenberg 2001c: 577–81). Both Japan and Italy were rocked by severe corruption scandals in the early 1990s. In New Zealand, governments of both main parties pursued radical economic reforms that came as a surprise to those who voted them into office. Thus:

P4:   Values are likely to underpin widespread pressure for electoral reform in established democracies only where crises cause a loss of confidence in prevailing institutions and electoral reform is seen as able to address the sources of the crisis.

The propositions so far can be summed up briefly: most politicians most of the time attend primarily to power-seeking, though there can be exceptions; voters are not power-seekers; but they think about electoral reform only if they perceive the values in Table 2.2 as seriously threatened.

Which values?

Supposing values do matter, which of the long list of values in Table 2.2 do actors focus on? This is again a matter in part of the degree to which particular values are threatened. Where representation is secure but effective governance is imperilled, for example, attention is likely to focus upon the latter. But there may be more basic differences between actors too, and these reflect at least two underlying factors: historical traditions and cultural change.[1]

As Nohlen (1984: 218) observes, 'the options for change are usually limited by the existing principle of representation and its historically strong perseverance'. I shall mention several mechanisms for such perseverance in the course of this chapter. The relevant one for now is the tendency for the values of a society to mould themselves to the system in place. The attachment to constituency service observable in Anglophone countries accustomed to single-member district elections was noted in the previous chapter. A further example is the deeply entrenched belief in the principle of proportionality noted by analysts in countries such as the Netherlands (Andeweg 2005: 508–9; Lijphart 1978: 131–2) and Germany (Jesse 1987: 436). Generalizing, Shugart (2008: 11–13) argues that an electoral system is likely to be perceived as failing where it fails by *its own* criteria: for example, where a plurality system fails to deliver majority power to the plurality party, checked by effective opposition.

But values also change, and such value change may produce strong pressures for electoral reform. Carstairs (1980: 63–4), for example, finds that 'towards the end of the First World War, the climate of opinion in many countries was in favour of PR'. The most prominent argument about value change in the contemporary world is Inglehart's thesis that socioeconomic development is generating a rise in post-materialism (Inglehart 1997). Inglehart and Welzel argue that the post-materialist value shift has underpinned the global spread of democracy in recent decades: 'Rising self-expression values lead people to demand the institutions that allow them to act according to their own choices. Accordingly, self-expression values motivate people to seek the civil and political rights that define liberal democracy' (2005: 152).

Does the post-materialist shift have implications also for choice between alternative democratic institutions? Certainly, scholars seeking

---

[1] A further factor – ideology – has received some attention in recent years (Bowler, Donovan, and Karp 2006; Pilet 2006; Renwick 2005: 1005–6). But findings remain tentative, and I do not consider this possibility further here.

to understand recent trends towards the creation and strengthening of bills of rights have seen post-materialization as a significant factor (Erdos 2009: 25–6; Morton and Knopf 2000: 77–80). McLeay *et al.* (1996) analyse such value change as a precursor to electoral reform, arguing that declining deference towards the notion of the benign state and growing belief in the importance of limited government and protection of citizens' rights have underpinned wide-ranging institutional reforms in New Zealand since the 1960s, including the 1993 change in the electoral system. Post-materialists' focus on 'self-expression values' may generate a desire for a system permitting greater voter choice.

This discussion suggests three propositions:

P5:   Actors' values are shaped by domestic historical traditions.
P6:   Value change also occurs. Post-materialist value change may encourage greater focus on expanding voter choice.
P7:   The more a particular value is perceived as threatened at a particular time, the more salient it is likely to be.

Power-seeking

In so far as politicians pursue power, what shapes the criteria by which they evaluate electoral systems? We will never be able to predict all the factors involved here, but several pointers can be given. In Chapter 2, I identified four dimensions of variation among power-seeking concerns, relating to the identity of the power-seekers, the objectives they pursue, their time horizons, and whether their concerns are outcome or act contingent. For now I focus solely on outcome contingencies: act contingencies can be treated as constraints on politicians' ability to pursue their goals, and so I treat them in depth in the next section. Here, I consider the three remaining distinctions in turn.

The power-seekers who matter may be individuals – party leaders or backbenchers – or parties. Which of them in fact matter depends upon the power of these actors, which is shaped by the nature of the parties and the broader institutional structure. Where parties are centralized, party leaders will control how their backbenchers act and seek to maintain centralism. Where they are decentralized, the interests of individual politicians will matter more, and those politicians will wish to retain their independence. In Japan in the 1970s, for example, reforms that would have bolstered the seat share of the largest party – the ruling Liberal Democratic Party (LDP) – were blocked in part because they threatened backbencher interests; these interests could prevail because of the LDP's factionalism and consensual decision-making. In Italy in 2005, by contrast, reforms that concentrated power in the hands of party leaders were possible because parties were centralized and reform could be pushed through rapidly at elite level with little wider discussion.

The second question concerns which of the various objectives actors are likely to focus on: whether voter preferences, votes, seats, office, or influence in the case of parties, or re-election, intra-party power, or wider influence in the case of individuals. In thinking about this, we should recall that these various objectives all boil down in essence to different ways of pursuing power. They should therefore matter to the degree that they influence actors' power. In the absence of coalitions or the expectation of coalitions, for example, seat shares may largely determine a party's officeholding potential and influence; but where coalitions are a feature of politics, coalition dynamics are likely always to matter. The influence of the electoral system upon voters' preferences, meanwhile, should matter to the degree that parties' resources are strongly skewed towards candidates or policies or leaders. And weakening one's opponents may become more important the less one expects to win power oneself or the more antagonistic one's opponents' agenda is to one's own.

The third question, finally, concerns actors' time horizons. There is no simple, *a priori* way of predicting a politician's time horizons. They may be determined partly by actors' enduring nature: some people may just think more to the long term than others. More usefully for our ability to make predictions, however, it is reasonable to posit that time horizons are also shaped by actors' career trajectories. A politician nearing the end of her career is more likely to have a short time horizon: seeing only one more chance for success, she may put all her efforts into securing the desired result in the next election. By contrast, younger politicians whose careers are on the rise and who aspire to future leadership are likely to have longer time horizons: they may primarily be concerned with their prospects for power one or two elections hence.

The following propositions can be drawn out:

P8:   The degree to which the power-seeking concerns of parties, party leaders, or backbenchers come to the fore depends upon the power these actors are granted by the nature of political parties and the broader institutional environment.

P9:   The weight attached to the various objectives depends upon their contribution to actors' power. This in turn depends on, for example, the salience of coalitions, the degree to which parties are strongly defined in either leader-, candidate-, or programme-centric terms, and the intensity of conflict between parties.

P10: Actors' time horizons are shaped by the point actors have reached on their career trajectories and the duration of their future ambitions.

The translation of motivations into preferences

The next step is to understand how actors' motivations turn into preferences over the different options available to them. Here, we must be concerned both with the objective effects of different options on the achievement of different goals and with various constraints that limit actors' perceptions or ability to pursue their goals. As in the previous section, I divide this task into four elements. First, I consider the objective effects: what can we say, assuming full knowledge, about which electoral systems best serve particular power interests and values? Second, I assess the impact of uncertainty regarding effects. Third, I consider cognitive constraints upon the options that actors perceive as being available to them. Finally, I investigate legitimacy constraints: some options may be recognized but regarded as illegitimate and therefore inadmissible.

How electoral systems affect interests and values

In some cases, the relationship between a given power interest or value and a particular electoral system option is rather straightforward. Where, for example, actors prioritize 'fair' translation of votes into seats in the legislature, we can reasonably expect that they will seek a form of proportional representation. In other cases, however, the effects of different systems remain disputed among scholars. For example, whether countries grappling with severe inter-group conflict are better served by proportional systems that ensure representation of all significant groups (as argued by Fraenkel and Grofman 2006; Lewis 1965: 71–4; Lijphart 1985, 2002; Reynolds 1995) or by alternative vote systems that encourage politicians to make cross-group appeals (Horowitz 1991, 1997; Reilly 1996, 1997a) is still not fully resolved. In the case of accountability, the academic consensus has seen plurality or majority systems as most beneficial (e.g., Gallagher 2005: 572; Powell 2000: 47–68), but several authors have recently questioned this (Curtice 2009; Samuels and Hellwig 2008; Vowles 2008b). It is too early to say whether further research will restore the old consensus or lead to a revised understanding. To the extent that expert opinion contains varying interpretations, it is important that we understand which experts decision-makers listen to and what positions those experts take.

I shall concentrate here, however, upon the translation into preferences of the various power-seeking considerations. The most firmly grounded proposition here concerns seat-maximization: assuming they are seat-maximizers, small parties should generally prefer proportional systems while large parties should seek plurality or majority systems. Put another way, if there are many parties (assuming partisan seat-maximization) proportional systems are likely to be retained or adopted; if there are few parties, plurality or majority systems should be retained or adopted; a change in the number of parties may lead to a change in preferences (e.g., Colomer 2004a: 62–6; Dunleavy and Margetts 1995: 24; Rokkan 1970: 157–8).

We should recall, however, that partisan seat-maximization is not the only power-seeking consideration. The other considerations – relating, most importantly, to individual power, vote-seeking, coalition dynamics, and influence over policy outcomes – are not affected so directly by party sizes. Even a small party may prefer a plurality or majority system if it has locally entrenched candidates, or if the strength of a coalition partner *vis-à-vis* the opposition is thereby enhanced, or if its leaders hope to engineer a reconfiguration of the party system that will increase their prominence. Even a large party may prefer a proportional system if it affords party leaders greater authority over candidates, or if party leaders are so hostile to the agenda of another party as to want to prevent it ever from gaining a majority, or if the party is not large enough to govern alone and must therefore curry favour with potential coalition allies. Thus, though a general relationship between party size and preferences over alternative electoral systems can be expected, we should not be surprised by exceptions. Thus:

P11: Small parties tend to prefer proportional systems, large parties plurality or majority systems. But this relationship is conditioned by other considerations, notably relating to individual power, vote-seeking, coalition dynamics, and influence over policy outcomes.

Uncertainty regarding the effects of reform

Even where the general effects of various electoral systems are well known, their effects in a particular case may be uncertain: politicians and parties may be unsure of their support levels and thus unsure of which system would best serve their power interests. Reforms may also set up unpredictable dynamics: electoral reforms tend to be followed by high electoral volatility (Bartolini and Mair 1990: 152–5). As Shepsle (2001: 324) argues, where institutions have multiple equilibria, institutional reform may precipitate a long process of equilibrium selection the outcome of which cannot be predicted. In relation to electoral reform, for example, a shift to a plurality system can be expected to lead to a concentration of votes on a few parties, but which parties voters coordinate on may not be readily predictable: outcomes depend on chance occurrences and the strategies of many actors. Such uncertainty may generate two mechanisms: either actors recognize it and adjust their preferences to accommodate it; or they fail to recognize it and base their preferences on misperceptions. I consider these in turn.

Recognized uncertainty

Where they recognize that uncertainty is high, actors are likely to pursue one of two approaches to electoral reform: either they adopt very conservative positions, regarding a world under different rules as an unknown black box that they would rather not open; or they follow a logic akin to that of the Rawlsian veil of ignorance, actively seeking the electoral system that will best protect them should things turn out badly (Rawls 1971: 136–42).

Pilet (2006: 8) finds evidence of the first response, observing parties that could benefit from electoral reform but oppose it because of the risks involved. Given uncertainty, of course, their reluctance may be entirely rational: the effects of change may be genuinely unpredictable. Alternatively, it may reflect a 'satisficing' approach, where actors take the existing electoral system as one of the fixed parameters within which they operate and avoid incurring the costs of assessing how far alternatives would advance their goals. The second, Rawlsian, response has, however, received rather more attention in studies of electoral reform: as mentioned in Chapter 1, for example, its role in electoral system choices during the transition from communism in Eastern Europe is well known (Andrews and Jackman 2005; Birch et al. 2002: 19; Przeworski 1991: 87–8). This is, in Rawlsian language, the 'maximin' strategy: politicians seek to ensure themselves a place in the political system even if their popular support turns out to be low (that is, they seek to maximize their minimum return) (Rawls 1971: 152–4).

It is certainly reasonable to expect the second approach in instances of democratization where there is no plausible status quo to which the risk-averse could cling and where uncertainty regarding even the short-term electoral strength of the various parties may be very high. Colomer (2005: 2) suggests it is likely in established democracies too. But where democracy is well established, and particularly in the modern world of relentless polling and focus groups, uncertainty regarding future electoral prospects under the existing electoral system may typically be lower than the uncertainty unleashed by reform, with all the reconfiguring of parties and inter-party relations that that entails. This leads to the following proposition:

P12:   Where actors recognize that they face uncertainty or are highly risk-averse, they will adopt one of two courses: either they seek to preserve the status quo; or they adopt a maximin strategy. The former course is more likely where a viable electoral system already exists and uncertainty regarding voting strengths is low relative to the uncertainty of reform; the latter should be expected where there is no viable status quo and uncertainty regarding voting strengths is higher.

Misperception

An alternative process is generated by uncertainty where actors believe that particular outcomes will ensue, but turn out to be wrong. Such misperception can play an important role in shaping electoral system preferences (Katz 2005: 62). In Poland, for example, the communists believed that the partially democratic electoral system they negotiated in 1989 would allow them to retain power for another four years. In fact, however, they were routed in the election that summer, forcing them to accept the appointment of the Soviet bloc's first non-communist prime minister and helping to catalyse the collapse of communism throughout Central and Eastern Europe (Kaminski 2002).

The precise incidence of misperception is difficult to predict. It is tempting to posit that experience of hegemony fuels hubris: the Polish communist party was a hegemon that had been feeding for too long upon its own rhetoric of popularity; even its opponents found it difficult to imagine that the system that had ruled for forty years would simply collapse. But such accustomed comfort appears not to be a necessary condition for hubris: as I discuss in Chapters 10 and 12, several small parties in Japan supported majoritarian reforms in 1993 and 1994 in the expectation that they would form part of a new, large party that subsequently failed (in the short term) to coalesce. Thus, neither the incidence nor the particular content of misperception appears predictable. All we can do, therefore, at least at this stage, is be alive to the possibility that it may be important to the processes we analyse.

P13:   Given uncertainty, misperception can be important in shaping preferences.

Cognitive constraints

The range of alternatives available to actors engaged in or thinking about electoral reform is, in principle, enormous. In their detail, no two countries' electoral systems are identical, and innovation beyond even this broad set of alternatives is possible. Actors cannot consider all these options when deciding how to act: their thinking about alternatives is necessarily limited by cognitive constraints upon the options they know about or bring to the forefront of their minds.

In some cases of cognitive constraint, actors seem to be entirely unaware of certain options that are, in principle, available. Kamiński (1999: 99), for example, argues that the goals of the Communist Party in Poland in 1989 would best have been served by the single transferable vote (STV) electoral system, and concludes that STV was not considered in all probability because the relevant actors simply did not know about it. In Hungary a few months later, when a bright young spark from the League of Young Democrats (Fidesz) suggested the use of open lists to fellow members of the opposition umbrella organization, he was met with bewilderment by his colleagues: most had clearly never heard of such things, and the discussion quickly moved on to other matters (EKA 1999: 367). In other cases, actors are constrained not so much by their knowledge as by their ability to process information (Simon 1985: 294). Here, actors are likely to focus on those options that are more familiar and discount those that, though known, are less familiar.

We may ask two sorts of question regarding cognitive constraints. First, how limiting are they? Second, in so far as they are limiting, where do the limits lie?

The intensity of cognitive constraints

The degree to which cognitive constraints limit choice can be expected to depend upon the nature of the decision process. At one extreme, some politicians may simply sit down, consider what they know (or think they know), and come up with a plan. At the opposite extreme, they may establish an expert commission that gathers evidence from a wide range of written and oral sources, both domestic and international, deliberates carefully, and offers recommendations. The closer a given case approximates to the second extreme, the more we can expect existing cognitive constraints to be broken down (cf. Birch *et al.* 2002: 13).

The location of cognitive constraints

Three primary factors can be predicted to shape actors' knowledge of and familiarity with different options and therefore determine the location of cognitive constraints: history, geographical proximity, and fashion (cf. Horowitz 2002: 31–3).

I have already discussed two mechanisms through which history may shape electoral system choices: first, some actors may regard the fact that their country has used a particular system in the past as in itself a reason for returning to that system (see Chapter 2); second, a country's past political experience is likely to shape the weights actors attach to different values such as proportionality or constituency service (see the first section of this chapter). Here we have a third mechanism: a system used in the past will be well known, particularly if that experience is not too far distant (Birch *et al.* 2002: 13). If it seems likely to generate desired effects, actors may therefore latch on to it without considering in detail whether an alternative would be even more beneficial.

Broad cross-national surveys have identified correlations between past practice, especially colonial legacies, and current electoral system choices (Lundell 2005: 206–22; Massicotte, Blais, and Yoshinaka 2004: 159), but are less able to distinguish between the different causal mechanisms. A case where the third mechanism has clearly operated is the reintroduction of the alternative vote system in Papua New Guinea in 2002. Advocates of this change could recall how much more effectively electoral politics had operated when that system had previously been used; it was easier to convince others of the merits of a system they knew than to ask them to learn about systems they did not know (Reilly 1996: 49–51).

The Papuan case also illustrates the second general pattern in how actors cope with the multiplicity of options available: that of regional contagion. It is presumably no coincidence that the second and third countries to have adopted forms of alternative vote – Fiji and Papua New Guinea – are close neighbours of the first – Australia (Reilly 2004: 259). Lundell (2005: 206–22) finds that such regional diffusion effects occur widely.

The third factor shaping cognitive constraints is fashion (Katz 2005: 74). Shugart and Wattenberg (2001a: 1) argue that, while '[t]he major electoral reform of the twentieth century was proportional representation', it may well be that '*the* electoral reform of the twenty-first century' will be the mixed-member system. The surge in interest in mixed systems had multiple independent starting points in the late 1980s and early 1990s in Hungary, Japan, New Zealand, and elsewhere. But it subsequently gathered its own momentum: scholarly surveys appeared (Massicotte and Blais 1999; Shugart and Wattenberg 2001b); advice to electoral reformers began to treat the mixed-member system as a major option in its own right (Reynolds and Reilly 1997: 74–5); by 2004, mixed systems of one kind or another were used to elect national lower houses in thirty countries (Reynolds, Reilly, and Ellis 2005: 30).

The discussion in this section yields two propositions:

P14:   Cognitive constraints will be the stronger as the process used when exploring and specifying alternatives is the less systematic.

P15:   The location of these cognitive constraints is shaped by history (including colonial legacies), regional contagion, and fashion.

Legitimacy constraints

Whereas cognitive constraints relate to limits on what actors know or can practicably process, legitimacy constraints refer to limits upon what they are willing to countenance. Benoit (2004: 385) writes,

> Some self-interest-maximizing institutional changes will be excluded from consideration as being simply beyond the pale, according to the limits set by public acceptability, opposition threats to withdraw support for the democratic institutions, or the simple bounds of political propriety.

According to Brady and Mo (1992: 406), 'The range of electoral systems that can be considered is constrained by local political conditions and traditions. If a country has bad experiences with certain electoral systems, they are not likely to be on the table for bargaining.'

These legitimacy constraints overlap with act-contingent considerations. At their most fundamental such constraints may eliminate certain options from all relevant actors' minds without their having to think about it: it is unlikely, for example, that anyone in an established democracy today would even begin to weigh the pros and cons of the party block vote system, as it is just not very democratic.[2] In less extreme cases, however, illegitimacy impinges on politicians' calculations indirectly, by influencing what they can get away with without provoking a voter backlash: that is, by shaping act contingencies.

Two principal questions need to be answered regarding legitimacy constraints. First, where are the boundaries between what is perceived as legitimate and as illegitimate and how strong are these perceptions? Second, to what degree do perceptions of illegitimacy have constraining force? I consider these questions in turn.

Legitimacy perceptions

I posit three factors as likely to shape the location and intensity of legitimacy perceptions: (1) objective values and their relation to proposed electoral reforms; (2) historical experience; and (3) actors' strategies in playing the electoral reform game.

Objective values   Table 2.2 in the previous chapter laid out a series of values that actors may pursue in advocating or opposing electoral reform. As I have argued, actors differ in the weights they attach to these values, but few are likely to disagree that all are good in themselves. These can therefore be considered objective values: values that all reasonable people in democratic societies may be expected to agree upon. We can posit that the further reforms deviate unnecessarily from such values, the more they are likely to be deemed illegitimate.

But these objective values can take us only so far in understanding the location of legitimacy constraints: given that perceptions of legitimacy vary across space and time, we must identify explanatory factors that vary too.

Historical experience   I posit three major mechanisms through which historical experience may influence legitimacy perceptions (though others are also likely). The first is that where manipulation of the electoral system to suit partisan ends has been practised before, it may become an accepted (if not entirely condoned) aspect of the political

---

[2] According to Reynolds, Reilly, and Ellis (2005: 166–73), party block vote is used today in pure form for national legislative elections only in Djibouti. It is also used to fill most of the electoral college that formally chooses the US president. Here too it has many detractors (e.g., Edwards 2004; Longley and Peirce 1999), though, because it is used in this case to elect a winner-take-all executive office rather than a legislature, its principal drawback – extreme disproportionality – is of little relevance.

game, such that the perception of illegitimacy regarding such behaviour is low in intensity. As Knapp (1987: 89) suggests, for example, 'French electoral systems have always been both an element in the rules of the political game and a part of the game itself': voters thus become inured to manipulative behaviour and no longer react to it.

Second, by contrast, where an electoral system is stable over a long period, it may gain a patina of rightness, such that any attempt to tamper with it is viewed dimly. This connects with the tendency, already posited, for an electoral system to be evaluated in terms of the principles that it is itself based on. One mechanism that may underlie such a tendency is that where a stable electoral system is associated with delivery of success – such as rapid economic growth – it comes to be valued on grounds of its effects. I note in Part II, for example, that, in both Germany and Japan, the strengthening of attachment to the prevailing electoral systems in the post-war decades was associated with periods of rapid economic growth, while the delegitimation of Japan's SNTV system in the early 1990s (discussed in Part III) came as the post-war economic bubble began to deflate. Another mechanism is that the electoral system comes to be seen as embodying aspects of the national character. The most prominent example is the Netherlands, where Lijphart (1978: 131–2) thirty years ago observed a deep attachment to a particularly pure form of proportional representation, despite the problems this creates for forming stable governments and holding politicians to account. The recent decision of a citizens' assembly established in 2006 to look into the question of electoral reform to recommend retention of the status quo suggests that the same constraint still survives (Electoral System Civic Forum 2007: 11; Van der Kolk and Thomassen 2006: 125–6).

Third, where an electoral system is associated with positive or negative historical experiences, it may thereby be legitimized or delegitimized. I argue in Part II, for example, that negative experience constrained the reform options considered in Italy between the mid-1950s and the 1980s. Mainwaring (1991: 35) finds the same of electoral system choices in Brazil.

Actors' strategies   The two factors considered so far are exogenous to the electoral reform process. But legitimacy perceptions need not be fixed: they are subject to manipulation by strategic politicians. Reformers will be likely to invoke discourses that legitimize the change, while opponents seek delegitimizing language. Actors' success in using these tools is shaped by the availability of such discourses, influenced by the objective and historical factors already discussed, and by actors' past pronouncements and ideological ties. It is also influenced by the actors' own heresthetical and other persuasive skills (McLean 2002; Riker 1986). I consider such mechanisms in detail in Chapter 4.

The constraining force of legitimacy perceptions

Legitimacy perceptions can exert significant constraining force in either of two circumstances. In the first, actors with the power to enact reform themselves internalize the legitimacy perception and thus regard any violation of it as unacceptable. In the second, those able to enact change (most likely to be politicians) are not internally constrained by the legitimacy perception, but others (most likely to be voters) do think it important and can punish those in power for ignoring it. This latter is the case of constraint by act contingency. Three factors may influence the strength of these mechanisms.

First, the most obvious factor is the intensity of the legitimacy perception itself. The more voters are offended by the idea of pursuing a particular option, the more they are likely to seek means of punishing those willing to follow it. And the stronger perceptions of illegitimacy are in society, the more likely they are to percolate through to politicians themselves.

Second, the more onerous are the institutional hurdles that a reform bill must pass before enactment, the more legitimacy perceptions are likely to weigh. In part, the onerousness of reform procedures relates to the number of veto players (Tsebelis 2002): the more veto players there are, the more hurdles must be got over, and so the more opportunities there will be for public opinion to be aroused. Onerousness applies also to the duration of enactment processes. In Japan in 1956, for example, LDP leaders proposed but later withdrew reform proposals that attracted considerable hostility from the opposition. Those leaders knew that the opposition, though lacking veto power, had the institutional capacity to prolong debate, thereby exposing the government to a lengthy period of hostile publicity through which illegitimacy perceptions could do significant harm.

Third, the most potent instrument of punishment in this context is often the ballot box, but there may be variation in the degree to which citizens are able to use their votes to punish actions that they deem illegitimate. The longer before the next election a reform takes place, the less opportunity will voters have to inflict punishment: by the time the election comes round, other issues are likely to have superseded the electoral system at the top of the political agenda. A further mechanism is suggested by the case of Italy in 2005: where a government already has a reputation for Machiavellian behaviour, it may calculate that those voters whose votes are influenced by such behaviour will already have decided not to vote for it, such that the addition of electoral system manipulation can do it no further harm.

I thus posit that the location and constraining force of legitimacy perceptions are shaped by factors relating to basic values, historical experiences, actors' strategies, the institutions that shape the reform process, and the political calendar. These mechanisms can be summed up as follows:

P16:   Perceptions of legitimacy and illegitimacy are shaped by objective values, historical experiences, and actors' strategies.

P17:   Where legitimacy perceptions are internalized by those in power, they may have direct constraining effect. Where they are not so internalized, their constraining force depends upon the capacity of other actors to punish violations. This punishment capacity depends not only on the strength of the legitimacy perceptions, but also on the nature of the reform process and the availability and proximity of unused instruments of punishment.

The translation of preferences into outcomes

The final stage in the stylized reform process analysed in this chapter is the translation of actors' preferences into outcomes: into whether reform occurs or not, and into the content of any reform that does take place. This translation depends in considerable part upon the type of reform process, as analysed in Parts II and III of this book. It depends also upon the mechanisms of leadership and path dependence that I analyse in Chapter 4. In the present section, I consider one further factor: the role of institutions. Institutions have effects at two principal levels here: at the macro level, they influence the overall likelihood that reform will in fact occur in a country; at the micro level, they influence the degree of power that particular actors have over outcomes. The logic of both of these levels can be described in terms of Tsebelis's (2002) theory of veto players.

At the macro level, the principal institutional factor in the likelihood of reform is the number of veto players. In the simplest case, the electoral system can be changed through a regular majority vote in the legislature. It is no coincidence that both of the established democracies that have undergone major reform by politicians in recent decades – France and Italy – belong to this category. Where, by contrast, the hurdle is higher (there are more veto players), reform is harder. Hungary, for example, has since 1989 required a two-thirds legislative majority for passage of electoral reform; correspondingly, though successive governments have proposed reform, none except a threshold increase has occurred (Benoit 2005: 249–50). In Ireland, the electoral system is constitutionally entrenched, and constitutional amendment requires a majority in a referendum as well as the legislature. Legislation to replace STV with single-member plurality, which would have strengthened the position of the ruling Fianna Fáil party, was passed by the Dáil in 1959 and 1968 but both times was defeated at the subsequent referendum (O'Leary 1979: 58, 69).

At the micro level, meanwhile, besides the general constraining effect of the number of veto players, the crucial issue is who has the power to set the agenda (Tsebelis 2002: 34). In most cases, that role is formally the exclusive preserve of politicians, though citizen-initiated referendums can give it to voters. It is tempting to predict that where politicians hold formal agenda-setting power they will have greater capacity to resist any public reform pressure. But this must be subject to two qualifications. First, formal institutions do not necessarily determine actual agenda-setting power: as I have discussed, act-contingent considerations may force an issue on to the agenda against politicians' will. Second, institutions are themselves subject to change, and the capacity to achieve such change may be an important tool in the hands of skilful leaders. In Thailand in the mid-1990s, reformers succeeded in engineering a wholly new process for constitution-drafting that largely excluded politicians (Connors 2002; Maisrikrod 2002: 190–91). In so far as institutions are manipulable, their causal power over outcomes is impaired. I discuss this further in Chapter 4.

I therefore offer two propositions. The first is a particular case of Tsebelis's theory of veto players; the second is very general and will require further investigation in Parts II and III.

P18: The more veto players there are, the less likely is electoral reform to occur.

P19: The influence of particular actors over the process is a function partly of the degree of their formal agenda-setting power. But this formal power can be overturned either by public pressure or by the strategic actions of individuals.

Conclusion

In the introduction to this chapter, I listed six key factors that underpin the three steps that I have discussed. These were history, ideational change, the nature of parties and the party system, state institutions, events and circumstances, and the nature of individual actors. Some of these are central to just one step, others to two or all three. Discussion of their functions has been sprinkled throughout the chapter. I conclude by drawing these strands together and summing up the roles that each plays.

That history can matter was already apparent in the discussion of values in Chapter 2: some actors regard certain institutions as valuable simply by virtue of their historical provenance (item VI(a) in Table 2.2). As the discussion in the first section of the present chapter suggests, this value is likely to be most prominent where national identity is or has been most threatened, as was true in the Baltic states as they struggled for freedom from the Soviet Union. Historical experience affects the priority actors give other values too: particularly where the status quo is long-standing, actors will tend to emphasize the values that it embodies. In addition, the second section of the chapter suggests that the options actors give most attention are likely to be those with which they are most familiar, and history plays an important part (alongside regional contagion and fashion) in determining such familiarity. Finally, perceptions of legitimacy and illegitimacy are likely to be strongly influenced by historical experience.

Ideas are in significant part products of history, but they are also subject to change. Cultural change, such as the wave of post-materialization in recent decades, may shift the values that actors prioritize. And changing ideas about electoral systems themselves may give rise to waves of fashion in electoral system design.

Parties and party systems matter in a variety of ways. The most obvious and unoriginal point is that small parties tend to prefer more proportional systems while large parties prefer systems based on plurality or majority. This has the further implication that interest in proportional systems should rise with the number of parties. But these relationships are likely to be mediated, I have suggested, by coalition structures, wider inter-party relations, and the nature of individual parties. The number and nature of parties also affect the number of veto players and thus the ease with which reform can be enacted. In turn, of course, parties and party systems are themselves shaped by a whole further layer of factors, including the existing electoral system and the structure of society. These further links are the subject of a vast literature in political science (e.g., Amorim Neto and Cox 1997; Clark and Golder 2006; Duverger 1954: 206–55; Katz 1980, 1997: 147; Lakeman 1974: 173; Lijphart 1994: 96, 102–13, 1999: 165–70; Lipset and Rokkan 1967; Norris 2004: 86–8; Ordeshook and Shvetsova 1994; Rae 1971 [1967]; Riker 1982).

The institutions of the state, meanwhile, are posited to influence the process at every stage. At the first stage, as just noted, the current electoral system helps shape parties and party systems, as well as the values that actors prioritize. At the second stage, the processes used for deliberating alternatives may influence the degree to which choice is subject to cognitive constraints, while more onerous decision-making processes increase the salience of perceptions of illegitimacy and can therefore dissuade actors from pursuing self-serving reforms. At the third stage, finally, institutions structure the processes by which actors with given preferences make decisions and generate outcomes, though in this they are not all-powerful.

A variety of events and circumstances come into play. The degree to which public opinion attends to the electoral system at all depends on whether events raise doubts about the efficacy of the status quo: in particular, I have suggested, in line with Shugart and Wattenberg (2001c: 572), that significant systemic failure is required before strong public pressure for reform is likely to develop. The nature of that failure influences, in turn, the values citizens focus on. Circumstances also influence the levels of uncertainty that attach to alternative courses of action: in particular, uncertainty is likely to be highest during democratic transition. Proximity to elections is a factor influencing the degree to which perceptions of illegitimacy have constraining force.

Finally, I have posited that the nature and position of actors themselves shape their goals and the means by which they pursue them. Whether politicians are new to politics or old hands, whether their income, prestige, social contacts, and lifestyle depend on their continued political career or could survive without it, whether they are leaders or backbenchers, and whether they have ambitions for the future or are approaching the end of their careers are all factors that I have posited as affecting the priority actors give to particular goals. In addition, as I elaborate further in the next chapter, actors' skills in playing the strategic game can importantly influence their ability to achieve their goals and therefore the broader character of outcomes.

So far I have covered only factors exogenous to the reform process itself. While noting the potential for skilful leaders to manipulate these factors, I have not yet analysed in detail how leaders may do this and what effects their actions may have upon electoral reforms. Nor have I considered the dynamics of the reform process itself or how the forces they generate can reinforce seemingly insignificant initial moves. In the next chapter, therefore, I complete the analysis of building blocks by considering two crucial endogenous factors: leadership and path dependence.

4

The reform process: endogenous factors

I have so far treated the factors that shape the process of electoral reform as exogenous: either as fixed or as changing only in response to factors outside the process itself. Yet those factors are often, at least to some degree, amenable to change from within the reform process. Two mechanisms of such endogenous change may particularly be noted. The first stems from the intentional action of participants within the process, through exercise of leadership, the second from the unintended consequences of action, notably through path dependence.

In this final chapter on the building blocks of electoral reform, I analyse in turn these two endogenous factors. I look at the possible strategies of actors who wish to steer the reform process, and at ways in which the process itself takes over and subverts the intentions of its human participants. Unlike in the previous chapter, I do not seek to identify the antecedent conditions of these various mechanisms: by their nature, their incidence is generally unpredictable. Rather, I catalogue the mechanisms in order to give a clear framework for the analysis in Parts II and III.

Leadership

Leadership is a concept that has proved very difficult to pin down, even though everyone knows it exists out there. Bennis and Nanus (1985: 4) claim to find 350 definitions of the term. As I shall use the term here, leadership occurs where actors change how other actors behave, and they do so in intended ways. I thus follow the approach set out by Edinger (1975) in two respects. First, I use a *behavioural* conception, according to which leadership 'is identified with persons who shape the actions of other persons', as distinct from a *positional* conception, where leadership is 'associated first and foremost with the rights and duties of an office or status in a hierarchical structure' (Edinger 1975: 256, 255). Thus, leadership can be exercised by any actor, not necessarily one occupying a position with formally recognized leadership functions. Second, successful leadership occurs only where effects are, at least in significant part, as intended: leadership does not occur where results markedly differ from intentions (Edinger 1975: 258). Such unintended consequences are, of course, an ever-present part of politics, but I leave them to the next section.

My purpose here is to understand how such leadership can influence processes of electoral reform. Many students of electoral reform – most of them very recent – have recognized that the role of leaders or entrepreneurs can be decisive (see, for example, Bowler and Donovan 2008: 108; Flinders and Curry 2008: 385–6; Gaunder 2007: 2–6; Longley and Braun 1975: 127–76; Rahat 2008: 217, 219). To understand how these leaders influence outcomes, we need first to understand what the various things are that leaders can do to shape reform processes. Unfortunately, however, it is widely recognized that we lack any adequate theory of leadership. In oft-quoted words, leadership's most prominent student has observed that 'leadership is one of the most observed and least understood phenomena on earth' (Burns 1978: 2; see also Kellerman 1984a: ix; Rejai and Phillips 1997: 1; Tucker 1995: 11). Certainly, some scholars studying leadership have presented lists of the sorts of things leaders do (e.g., Almond 1973: 19–20; Burns 1978: 43–4; Edinger 1990: 517; Kellerman 1984b: 35–7; Wriggins 1969: 10). Yet none, to my knowledge, has attempted a systematic, cross-national analysis.

In this section, therefore, I offer detailed discussion of the things that leaders do. I certainly do not seek to construct a general theory of leadership, or even of political leadership: I do not, for example, consider the roles of leaders in winning elections, or crafting an overall programme of office, or leading the nation in war. Rather, I focus on how leaders can influence the policy process, and specifically the process of electoral reform. In doing so, I draw widely on the literature on leadership, as well as relevant parts of the literature on policy-making.

Vision and delivery

Perhaps the commonest understanding of leadership is that leaders point the way: they create a vision for how things should be and they seek to mobilize other actors around that vision. According to Burns (1978: 462), for example,

> The function of leadership is to *engage* followers, not merely to activate them, to commingle needs and aspirations and goals in a common

enterprise, and in the process to make better citizens of both leaders and followers.

For Bennis and Nanus (1985: 27–42) a leader must, first, have vision and, second, be able to communicate that vision to others. Among electoral reformers, such leadership may be ascribed to figures such as Nelson Mandela in South Africa (Ebrahim 1998: 31–2) and Sitiveni Rabuka in Fiji (Lal 1998: 100–1), individuals who offered a vision of a new future for their country, much wider than the technical details of electoral systems.

But leadership is about much more than the development and communication of vision. First, even where leaders have a genuine vision of a better future for the country and seek to communicate that, they must typically also engage in hard strategizing and tough politics in order to deliver that vision. As Lord (2003: 24) puts it, 'The exercise of leadership may amount to articulating a "vision," but statecraft properly understood is also about something more – and something arguably more difficult: the ways visions are implemented.' Second, actors may exercise leadership without using a mobilizing vision as an important part of their strategy. Interest groups, for example, may lobby government behind the scenes without seeking to mobilize wider opinion. Third, whereas leadership – at least, ideal leadership – as conceived by authors such as Burns or Hargrove (1998: viii, 2), can be guided by moral purpose, it may also be exercised in pursuit of narrowly partisan or personal goals. For all these reasons, leaders do much more than generate vision: they can influence ongoing policy processes in a variety of ways. I suggest they do so through two broad types of means, which I label persuasion and process manipulation. I analyse each of these in the following two subsections.

Persuasion

The idea that persuasion is central to what leaders do is well established. As Neustadt (1960: 10) famously declared, 'Presidential *power* is the power to persuade.' Similarly, Tucker (1995: 60) argues that 'the need to *persuade* is the phenomenon with which we are most concerned as professional students of politics'. In the political realm, actors can rarely get their way by command; rather, they must convince others of the merits of backing them. They must change others' basic motivations, or change the weights others attach to their various goals, or convince others that a particular course of action is the best means available for pursuing their goals.

Such persuasion can take diverse forms. The first is argumentative persuasion, in which leaders seek to influence others by genuinely laying out their understanding of the matter in hand and engaging in debate. As Checkel (2003: 212) writes, 'Here, persuasion is not manipulation but a process of convincing someone through argument and principled debate.'

Pure argumentative persuasion may at times be observable in the private domain. In the public arena, however, it is likely almost always to shade into a second type of persuasion, in which leaders use rhetoric, heresthetic, and framing as tools to convince others of the merits of their case. Here, leaders do not simply lay out their understanding; rather they adjust their presentation to suit the listener. Riker (1986) developed the notion of heresthetic (or heresthetics) to describe (principally) the process by which leaders manipulate the multidimensionality of issue space to pursue their objectives. That is, where an issue is complex and has implications for a number of dimensions of debate (say, laissez-faire versus dirigiste, liberal versus authoritarian, and nationalist versus internationalist), the skilled heresthetician will emphasize those dimensions on which her or his proposals are most likely to attract majority support and de-emphasize the dimensions where such support is less likely. For Riker, manipulation of dimensions was important mainly where a vote cycle existed. As McLean (2001: 231, 2002: 555) argues, however, whether cycles exist is largely irrelevant: manipulation of dimensions is nevertheless observable where multidimensional space exists or can be created; its potency comes from the impossibility of considering in full all these dimensions simultaneously – that is, from the boundedness of rationality. The idea therefore converges with the concept of framing (Goffman 1975; Snow *et al.* 1986), according to which actors cast their preferred policies in the terms most likely to secure their passage. As Baumgartner (1989: 115) writes, 'policy makers have great leeway in portraying issues according to their interests ... Because different groups of actors are likely to become attracted to issues depending on how they are portrayed, political leaders can attract or avoid particular groups of participants by affecting the way in which people perceive the issue. Leadership is often a matter of rhetoric.'

Framing may play an important role in processes of electoral reform. The electoral system is rarely, in itself, an issue able to catch fire in the public imagination, but if it can be linked to issues that do have strong public resonance, leaders may be able to generate significant pro-reform sentiment. As I argue in Part III of this book, reformers in Japan and Italy in the early 1990s harnessed popular discontent caused by corruption scandals by arguing that electoral reform could help prevent such abuses in the future; New Zealand's reformers similarly picked up citizens' perception that politicians did whatever they wanted without regard for public opinion.

When using rhetoric, heresthetic, and framing, leaders adjust the presentation of their proposals to suit their audience, but they do not adjust the proposals themselves. Under a third type of persuasion, leaders do change the proposals themselves in order to secure support. This is the realm of bargaining, compromising, threats and promises, giving and calling in favours, cajoling, log-rolling, and pork-barrelling (e.g., Cronin and Genovese 2004: 120; Edinger 1990: 517; Kellerman 1984b: 35–7). Here, leaders seek to build a coalition of support that secures the core of their objectives by compromising on certain particulars or by promising others they will lend support for their goals in other spheres. There is no attempt to mobilize belief in the value of the proposed reforms in themselves; rather, leaders seek to understand and accommodate the interests and wider purposes of other actors as they are. This may sound venal, but it need not be: it may involve the positive notion of crafting mutually agreeable solutions in situations where total welfare can be increased but its distribution across actors is contested (cf. Scharpf 1997: 120–1). Leaders using such tactics must understand those whom they seek to persuade; they must also often be creative and versatile in finding solutions that will bring a diverse coalition together without negating their basic purposes.

It is difficult to imagine an electoral reform in which bargaining does not at some level take place. Even where reform is imposed by an elite majority without seeking support from others, the majority itself is unlikely to be wholly of one mind. Intra-coalition bargaining was central to the reforms in Italy in 2005 and France in 1951, for example. Even where non-politicians have sought to win control over electoral reform, the will of the popular majority cannot always prevail entirely: as I argued in Chapter 1, politicians are always involved to some degree and bargaining always occurs. One factor behind the recent popularity of mixed-member systems may be the perception that they can offer compromise between the competing interests of different actors. Compromise over details of the electoral system – such as the number of seats filled by different mechanisms, the level of thresholds, and district magnitudes – is common. Compromise may also occur regarding the process of implementation, as in Papua New Guinea in 2002, where implementation of the new alternative vote (AV) system was delayed until after the follow-ing election to calm politicians nervous about their own re-election (Reilly 2002: 252). Finally, compromises can be made relating not to the electoral system, but to other issues or to politicians' careers. In Italy in 2005, for example, the electoral reform stemmed in part from the need to secure coalition unity on proposals for wider constitutional changes.

A fourth and final strategy for pursuing success in persuading others takes a longer-term perspective. Effective leaders know they will be better able to persuade others to follow them if they are widely trusted; thus, they may pursue a strategy of engendering trust. Such trust may matter for several reasons. First, in a context of bounded rationality and limited time, actors may use their trust in others as an information shortcut (Lindblom 1968: 20): if actor X supports a given measure, they may reason, then, given X's record, it is fair to suppose that the measure is a good thing. This mechanism operates where actors are uncertain as to the effects that the measure is likely to have if implemented – which we may call outcome uncertainty. A second form of uncertainty – implementation uncertainty – underpins a second mechanism. Here, actors are uncertain over how a leader will act or over whether the leader will succeed in implementing the measures they seek. Where a leader has a reputation for consistency and effectiveness, others may feel confident to follow him or her; where the leader lacks such a reputation, others may prefer to hedge their bets. The importance of a strong 'professional reputation' is emphasized particularly by Neustadt (1960: 58–85). But the insight goes back at least to Machiavelli, who argued that the prince must avoid being hated and despised if he is to achieve his ends. He continued, 'What makes him despised is being considered changeable, frivolous, effeminate, cowardly, irresolute' (Machiavelli 1979 [1513]: 136). We would not use all of these words today, but Machiavelli's basic thought endures: leaders are more effective if followers trust them to deliver.

Successful leaders thus strive to engender trust and build suitable reputations. But it should be recognized that leaders can also be priso-ners to reputations that they are powerless to change. Westlake (2000: 163–4) finds that leaders of major transitions tend to have been viewed previously as conservatives. It is this conservative reputation that encou-rages others who are reluctant to accept change to believe that the proposed path really is the best available. Correspondingly, if somewhat paradoxically, committed reformers may be the most hamstrung in achieving change, because they are likely to be viewed as zealots by the cautious, moderate majority.

To summarize, this section has identified four strategies that leaders may deploy in seeking to persuade others to follow them:

S1:   argumentative persuasion;
S2:   rhetoric, heresthetic, and framing;
S3:   bargaining;
S4:   investment in trust and reputation.

Process manipulation

Beyond persuasion, leaders may influence policy outcomes by manipulating in various ways the processes that generate those outcomes. The first strategy of this type involves changing the set of actors involved – changing what Schattschneider (1975 [1960]: 3) calls 'the scope of conflict'. 'The most important strategy of politics', Schattschneider argues, 'is concerned with the scope of conflict.' This strategy may itself be divided into several subtypes.

First, leaders may decide the process of researching policy alternatives: whether to set up a formal inquiry process, whom to appoint as members of a commission, whether to engage international experts, and so on. Though such actors play only an advisory role, these decisions may significantly influence outcomes by shaping the options available and the rhetoric around them.

The second subtype involves changing the set of actors who have formal decision-making power over the matter in hand. For example, an individual or party unable to command a legislative majority on an issue that thinks it has public support may seek a referendum to pass the measure into law (LeDuc 2003: 167; Rahat 2008: 37) – as did de Klerk in deciding to call a referendum in 1991 on ending apartheid in South Africa (Welsh and Spence 2000: 41). Actors may also be changed at a much smaller scale, as when jurisdiction over some matter is switched between government departments (Majone 1989: 102). Banting and Simeon (1985: 16) observe several cases in which 'the issues, concerns and alternatives debated shifted dramatically when constitutional politics shifted from one forum to another'. Baumgartner and Jones (1993: 36) refer to this as 'venue shopping'.

Finally, the third subtype utilizes the importance of act contingencies. It involves mobilizing one group in order to influence the behaviour of another – most usually, appealing to the public in order to influence legislators. Kernell (1986) argues that 'going public' has replaced bargaining in Washington as the dominant presidential strategy: 'In appealing to the public to "tell your senators and representatives by phone, wire, and Mailgram that the future hangs in the balance," the president seeks the aid of a third party – the public – to force other politicians to accept his preferences' (Kernell 1986: 3). Similarly, Hargrove (1966: 2) argues that 'the President must lead and educate public opinion. It is his chief source of power in Washington in his dealings with other holders of power.' Supporters of electoral reform have sought to mobilize public opinion even in cases where the process of electoral system change has involved no formal popular participation through referendum – notably in Japan in the early 1990s (Morita 1991: 80–1) and Thailand a few years later (Wasi 2002: 23). These activists knew the indirect power that popular pressure could exert via politicians concerned to secure re-election. Conversely, opponents of electoral system change successfully blocked proposed reforms in Japan in 1973 by mobilizing public opinion around the issue of manipulation by the ruling elite (Maeno 1974: 55). What is striking about the reforms in France in 1985 and Italy in 2005 is the failure of any public appeal adequately to chasten those seeking reform in pursuit of their own ends.

The last of these subtypes of the strategy of changing the set of actors overlaps with another strategy, namely the manipulation of multi-level games. This concept derives from Schelling's insight that, where an actor bargains in more than one setting simultaneously, weakness in one setting may be a strength in another: 'in bargaining, weakness is often strength, freedom may be freedom to capitulate, and to burn bridges behind one may suffice to undo an opponent' (Schelling 1963: 22). Putnam applied this concept to the setting of international diplomacy: a government that can say that public opinion bars it from accepting certain options may thereby be strengthened at the international negotiating table (Putnam 1988: 440). In some cases, this strategy may involve extending the set of participating actors and thereby opening up a new level of the policy-making game. In other cases, it involves using the techniques of persuasion to change the views of existing participants, thereby limiting outcomes. Such strategies have been widespread in processes of electoral reform. In New Zealand, for example, pro-reform politicians repeatedly signalled to the public their desire to push the issue forward, thereby pressuring their party colleagues, who would not have wanted to create an impression of disloyalty or division, into acquiescing.

A third strategy of process manipulation is, as noted in Chapter 3, to change the institutions through which policy is made. As Majone (1989: 96-7) argues, 'Despite the substantial cost of modifying institutional constraints, experienced actors have always recognized the advantages of influencing policy outputs by such indirect methods.' Changing institutions and changing the set of actors often go hand in hand – for example, in the creation of a commission tasked with proposing alternatives, peopled by certain individuals, and given specified resources and terms of reference. But the two elements can decouple – for example, where decision rules are changed within an existing decision-making venue. In New Zealand, opponents of electoral reform sought late in the day to change the rules of the forthcoming referendum so as to require a majority not only of those voting, but of the whole electorate for passage; the move was, however, blocked by the prime minister, who foresaw a public outcry (Jackson and McRobie 1998: 148-54). In Canada, where the public has been less mobilized on the issue of electoral reform, governments in both British Columbia and Ontario were able to apply 60 per cent thresholds to electoral reform referendums, held in 2005 and 2007 respectively. This had no effect in Ontario, where electoral reform won the support of just 36.9 per cent of voters (Elections Ontario 2007). In British Columbia, however, though the pro-reform vote was higher than in New Zealand – 57.7 per cent compared with 53.9 per cent (Elections BC 2005; Jackson and McRobie 1998: 255) – electoral reform failed. A repeat referendum was held in May 2009, but support for reform collapsed to 39.1 per cent (Elections BC 2009).

The fourth and final mechanism centres on salami slicing. According to Zahariadis (2007: 78):

> A 'salami tactic' basically involves the strategic manipulation of sequential decision making. Entrepreneurs are assumed to have a grand design of the desired outcome. However, because they are reasonably certain their desired solution will not be adopted because it's too risky, they cut the process into distinct stages which are presented sequentially to policy makers. Doing so promotes agreement in steps.

I shall argue in Chapter 12 that New Zealand offers a classic case of such tactics. The role of salami slicing illustrates a dimension of the reform process that I briefly alluded to in Chapter 2: participants frequently think not about final outcomes (alternative electoral systems), or even about the act-contingent implications of the reform process as a whole, but rather about the immediate decision that is before them. They may discount seemingly remote possibilities of major change and focus rather on the day-to-day matters of politics: allowing a colleague some slack in pursuing his pet project in the expectation of receiving slack in return; avoiding upsetting senior party figures on seemingly insignificant matters. Similarly, for voters, the creation of inquiries into esoteric matters may simply pass beneath their radar screens. The implication here is that apparently insignificant acts can have highly significant consequences – a point to which I return in the section below on path dependence. Because actors are generally accustomed to electoral system stability, it does not occur to them that small steps might overturn the status quo. They are thus lulled into a false sense of security – what Rahat (2008: 29) calls 'the tranquility of the guardians of the status quo'. For current purposes, the key point is that strategic politicians can take advantage of such misperceptions to advance their ends.

Most of the strategies that I have described can be used by either supporters or opponents of change. Salami slicing, however, is the preserve of supporters: its whole purpose is the achievement of large shifts through small steps. Opponents of reform may, nevertheless, pursue a strategy that, on the surface, looks very similar – namely, taking small steps in response to large demands. The classic tactic is the establishment of an inquiry into a matter that has gained strong political salience in the hope that, by the time the inquiry reports back, attention will have moved elsewhere, the issue will have dropped back down the agenda, and the findings can be quietly shunted into the sidings. Such appears to have been the hope of Japan's leaders in 1989 when, in response to the first of a series of corruption scandals, they set up several commissions to investigate political reform. Had further scandals not emerged, their strategy might well have worked and reform been avoided. Here again, however, the danger of unintended consequences – of generating momentum for unwanted changes – always lurks.

This section thus yields four further, partially overlapping, leadership strategies:

S5: changing the scope of conflict by (a) changing the process of researching policy alternatives, (b) changing the set of actors who have formal decision-making power, or (c) mobilizing one group in order to influence the behaviour of another;
S6: manipulating multi-level games;
S7: changing the institutions of decision-making;
S8: salami slicing.

Timing

I have discussed various strategies that leaders may deploy in pursuit of their reformist or conservative ends. Effective leaders need not only to be good at using these strategies, however: they need also to understand when and how to apply them. Hargrove (1998: 35) defines 'discernment' as 'the ability to estimate, more or less accurately, the kinds of political action that will be successful in a given historical context'. He insists that 'Discernment is the master skill', involving the capacity to deploy all the other skills wisely. Others make the same point. It is central to the multiple streams literature within policy studies: windows of opportunity for policy change open rather randomly, but policy entrepreneurs have a crucial role in utilizing them in order to advance their purposes (Kingdon 1995; Zahariadis 2003, 2007). For Westlake (2000: 158–61), while successful leaders are people who have good luck, they are also people who use that luck effectively.

Leaders can exert considerable influence over electoral reform processes. But Riker (1986: ix) points out that 'Heresthetic is an art, not a science'; and, heresthetic being merely a subset of leadership, leadership as a whole is *a fortiori* an art too. It can achieve its desired results only with considerable skill, and that skill requires not just knowledge of how to use each of the techniques discussed here, but also understanding of when to deploy them and in what ways. The presence of skilful leaders at any given time and place is far from guaranteed, and each leader is likely to do things somewhat differently. In so far as leadership matters, therefore, outcomes may be impossible to predict on the basis of starting conditions alone.

Path dependence

The concept of path dependence has gained considerable attention over the last two decades, both in economics and in political science. Central to this concept is the idea that small initial events can generate substantial outcomes by steering subsequent developments on to a particular path that it is progressively harder to switch from. Path dependence may shape electoral reform at two levels. First, it may generate patterns of long-term persistence in the electoral system in force in a given country. Second, it can be located within the process of electoral system change itself, causing early events to constrain subsequent developments. I consider these two levels – exogenous and endogenous – in turn. The first takes us away from the core purpose of this chapter, but allows several points made in preceding chapters to be tied together. I begin by reviewing existing accounts of the mechanisms that underlie path dependence.

Mechanisms of path dependence

Arthur (1994: 112) identifies four principal mechanisms of path dependence in the economic world. First, wherever production involves 'large set-up or fixed costs', whichever actor builds up production first and thereby benefits from economies of scale gains an advantage over competitors, from which position it can further consolidate its strength. Second, where users of a product must invest resources to learn how to use it – as in the classic example of the QWERTY keyboard (David 1985) – they will be reluctant, once they have made that investment, to switch to an alternative. Third, where a product is characterized by 'coordination effects' (or 'network externalities'), such that the benefit any user gains from it rises with the number of other users, a version that predominates early is likely to persist, as was true of the battle between the VHS and Betamax video recording systems. Finally, the prevalence of a given product generates an expectation of continued prevalence that becomes self-fulfilling.

Thelen (1999: 392–4) and Pierson (2000: 257–63) argue that these mechanisms are important in the political realm too. But, they continue, these are not the only mechanisms that matter: both argue that power is an additional core aspect of the political world that can generate path dependence. In essence, the actors whom an institution empowers frequently have, by virtue of that empowerment, both the reason and the capacity to block any reform of the institution, even if such reform would benefit the majority of actors (Pierson 2000: 259; Thelen 1999: 394). Mahoney (2000: 517–25) goes still further, arguing that the utilitarian perspective of economics is just one of four approaches that might be taken in unpacking path dependence. Another, the power perspective, corresponds to Pierson's and Thelen's addition. The remaining two are functionalist and legitimacy based. From the functionalist perspective, an institution that is functional (for the system) can expand, thereby enhancing its functionality and allowing it to expand further. 'In the legitimation framework,' finally, 'institutional reproduction is grounded in actors' subjective orientations and beliefs about what is appropriate or morally correct. Institutional reproduction occurs because actors view an institution as legitimate and thus voluntarily opt for its reproduction' (Mahoney 2000: 523).

I adopt Mahoney's approach in what follows, though I do not make use of the functionalist category and relabel Mahoney's legitimation framework as the normative perspective. The three remaining categories – utilitarian, power-based, and normative – provide a useful organizing framework, but the lines between them should not be viewed as impenetrable. In particular, in a world of bounded rationality, utilitarian actors employ norms that may be indistinguishable empirically from those of their more fundamentally normative kin. Trying to maintain a division between them is of no practical value.

Exogenous path dependence

In discussing mechanisms of exogenous path dependence in processes of electoral reform, I deviate from the core purpose of this chapter. But it is useful to tie together, in the light of the preceding theoretical discussion, the various elements of long-term path dependence in the electoral system that have emerged over the preceding chapters. There are five in total.

The first is the central reason for stability in electoral systems: those who benefit most from the status quo and those who have the power to determine whether there will be change or not are typically the same people: even if there are many good reasons for changing the system, those in power are generally likely to block such a move. This fits precisely into the power-based source of path dependence identified by Pierson, Thelen, and Mahoney.

A second mechanism relates to the existence of large set-up costs. Actors – especially politicians – often sink considerable resources into winning by the current rules. Those who have already invested in this way – incumbents – have an advantage over those who have not invested. They will not want to change to a system in which they lose that advantage because their investments carry little value. In Japan, for example, politicians invested heavily under SNTV in local support networks that were configured around the existing electoral system and district boundaries. Many LDP Diet members opposed reform that could reasonably be expected to benefit their party as a whole, because it threatened the value of their existing networks.

A third mechanism, similar to the second, is rooted in learning: actors have generally invested in understanding the existing rules of the game and the best way to play them. By contrast, other rules are unfamiliar, and it may be difficult for actors to foresee their effects. Before deciding to support reform, these actors would have to invest in understanding the alternatives, an investment that may not appear worth while. Thus, they will tend to prefer the familiar status quo to other systems that they know less well.

Fourth, and more generally, path dependence can be seen in the operation of cognitive constraints and legitimacy constraints: as I proposed in Chapter 3, these are strongly influenced by historical factors. Even utilitarian actors need information shortcuts. Arthur (1994: 133–58) suggests that in developing such shortcuts actors tend to focus on early information, causing ideas to lock in that may not be borne out by wider evidence. This fits the argument made in Chapter 3 that an electoral system's positive or negative historical connotations may shape how it is viewed, even when an alternative understanding could better fulfil actors' purposes. Legitimacy constraints may have similar origins: familiarity with particular institutions or practices may breed comfort with the status quo, leading to the perception that it is legitimate while alternatives are less so.

A final form of exogenous path dependence is based solely on the normative perspective. As I suggested in Chapter 2, some actors may favour the reinstatement of a past electoral system precisely because it belongs to the national history: they have an ideological commitment to the maintenance of tradition. To the extent that such ideological commitment shapes preferences, normative path dependence exists.

Endogenous path dependence

The primary purpose of this chapter, however, is not to elucidate the mechanisms of path dependence underlying the long-term trajectory of an electoral system, but to shed light upon the dynamics of the reform process itself. It is typically to the long term that scholars of path dependence have looked. But many instances of electoral reform – particularly those characterized by elite–mass interaction – unfold over an extended period of time. Path dependence can emerge in the course of these processes, with early steps constraining subsequent developments. This can be crucial in allowing reform sometimes to occur even where it initially has few supporters. I propose four mechanisms of endogenous path dependence.

The first is based in Arthur's coordination effect (1994: 112). Politicians facing popular protest over perceived system failure need, for act-contingent reasons, to find a means of responding to that pressure. It may matter more that they find and implement some response than what that response actually is. Thus, they face a coordination problem: they need to coordinate on some response to ensure its passage. Once it becomes clear what response is most likely, actors will flock towards it. Similarly, those who oppose the status quo are most likely to secure change if they all campaign for a single alternative. Yet several alternatives may exist, each with its own supporters. So long as reformers all rank the various alternatives above the status quo, they face a coordination problem: they must decide which alternative to back. In both cases, a proposal that gains early prominence may be favoured, even if others might serve actors' purposes better. I shall argue that these mechanisms were important in Italy, Japan, and New Zealand in the early 1990s.

A second mechanism reflects bounded rationality and the costs of learning. In essence, issues, once aired, can sometimes gain legs. In a world of bounded rationality, actors focus on only a subset of all possible issues at any time. Most of the time in an established democracy, electoral reform is not one of those issues. But if an actor succeeds in placing electoral reform on the agenda, others may think about it and recognize that they too would prefer change. They may also learn about others who share their views, thereby facilitating organization. Through these mechanisms, a pro-reform dynamic may develop even when initial support appears low. I shall argue that such a mechanism influenced developments in New Zealand in the decade before the 1993 reform. Similarly, opponents of reform who hope to defuse pressure for change by establishing a commission to investigate options – as in Japan in 1989 – may find that that very act sets up dynamics that cause them to lose control of the agenda.

The third mechanism falls under the normative heading and stems from the power of public commitments and promises. Once an actor – particularly a politician – has made a promise, she or he may be punished if seen by others to break it. Were it not for this mechanism, New Zealand might never have experienced electoral reform: as I describe in Chapter 11, promises, broken promises, and the fear of the consequences of breaking promises played important roles at several stages during the events that led to the 1993 change. At each stage, politicians made promises without fully realizing the effects they would have, and were subsequently bound either to act contrary to their wishes or to face sharp public opprobrium. A strategic pro-reform politician who understands this mechanism may use it as the basis for deploying salami tactics. Path dependence here is not total: as the UK's Labour government demonstrated after 1997, sometimes a prior commitment on electoral reform can be quietly sidelined. Whether commitments bind depends partly on actors' rhetorical strategies, so is not wholly predictable.

Finally, and again falling largely within the normative category, actors who participate in an extended reform process may develop a commitment to the process and its other participants such that they become progressively less willing to countenance failure. Ebrahim (1998: 189–221), for example, describes vividly the long nights through which South Africa's post-apartheid constitution was negotiated; no one who worked through those nights wanted their efforts to come to naught; thus, a dynamic developed favouring success. Furthermore, as actors work together through lengthy negotiations, mutual trust – even personal friendship – may develop, encouraging each to accept the other's word and inclining them to find ways of accommodating the other's concerns. Lal (2000: 325) argues, for example, that the Fijian reforms of 1997 became possible in part because of the increasingly warm relationship between Prime Minister Rabuka and the leading Indo-Fijian politician, Jai Ram Reddy: as the talks proceeded and trust deepened, scope for compromise increased. Strand, similarly, cites 'rapport among leaders' as a key factor in the negotiations in South Africa (Strand 2000: 95, 131, 166, 252).

These four mechanisms of endogenous path dependence may be summarized thus:

PD1: Where actors need to coordinate, options that are prominent early on can gain particular strength.
PD2: Issues, once aired, can gain legs of their own.
PD3: Promises and other commitments can have strong binding force.
PD4: Extended reform processes can generate commitment among participants to positive outcomes.

Through all these mechanisms, seemingly minor actions can significantly alter policy-making processes, thereby, in some cases, changing outcomes dramatically.

Conclusion

As I suggested in Chapter 1, understanding the *politics* of electoral reform is crucial to full understanding of reform outcomes: we cannot just identify antecedent conditions and predict the end result. This is so in part simply because of the complexity of the reform process: given the great variety of factors that may shape that process – historical, cultural, institutional, contextual, personal – we cannot hope to understand it without understanding the mechanisms through which these background factors interact with each other and shape outcomes. But we need to understand the politics also, more particularly, because some of these interactions generate their own, endogenous processes. It is these endogenous factors that have been the focus of this chapter.

In part, endogenous change in the parameters that generate or fail to generate electoral reform is produced by the strategic action of participants – leaders – who seek to further their own purposes by changing how others act. And in part it is produced by processes of path dependence that are often beyond the control of individual agency, which can generate major unintended consequences from apparently minor beginnings. I have sought in this chapter to set out the various mechanisms involved in these endogenous processes.

In coming to the end of this chapter, we come also to the end of Part I of the book, dealing with the building blocks of electoral reform. The first step in understanding complexity is to lay out the many elements of that complexity. In the remainder of the book, I move to the second step, seeking to understand how these building blocks combine in overall processes of electoral reform.

PART II

Elite majority imposition

Part I analysed the many building blocks of electoral reform. I now consider how these building blocks link together to generate overall reform processes. As I explained in Chapter 1, I focus on two very different types of electoral reform process that have taken place in recent decades in established democracies: here I consider reforms by elite majority imposition; in Part III, I turn to reforms by elite–mass interaction. My focus is on electoral reform and attempts at electoral reform in France, Italy, Japan, and New Zealand since 1945.

Where reform occurs by elite majority imposition, a group of politicians with the capacity to change the system consider that electoral reform would serve their power interests and therefore adopt change. Cases that fall clearly within this type include reforms in France in 1951, 1985, and 1986, Italy in 1953 and 2005, and Japan in 1947. In several further cases – France in 1991–1992, Italy between 1994 and 2001, and Japan in 1956 and 1973 – reforms by elite majority imposition have been attempted or mooted but not enacted. Reforms implemented during regime transformation in these countries – in France in 1945–1946 and 1958, Italy in 1946, and Japan in 1945 – also exhibit aspects of elite majority imposition, though they shade also towards elite settlement or elite–external interaction. Finally, France experienced pressure for bargained reform in 2007–2008, which, had it been successful, would likewise have occupied an intermediate position. I explore all of these episodes in detail in the following chapters.

I begin with three narrative chapters, focusing on the stories of reform by elite majority imposition in France, Italy, and Japan. I then turn, in Chapter 8, to comparative analysis. Simplicity appears on the surface to be the dominant characteristic of electoral reforms of the elite majority imposition type: politicians are the only actors who strongly influence outcomes, and they focus solely on the effects of alternative options on the distribution of power. In fact, however, several strands of complexity are important, and I give particular attention to two of these in Chapter 8.

87

First, though the dominance of power-seeking does simplify the process, still, as shown in Chapter 2, power may be pursued in many ways; we need to understand so far as possible how these various considerations play out. Second, the relative simplicity of reform by elite majority imposition itself needs to be explained. How can a group of politicians impose electoral reform on the basis solely of their power interests, unencumbered by other actors? Though electoral systems rarely set the public imagination on fire, we might expect that the *manipulation* of the electoral system by politicians for manifest personal or partisan gain would spark popular protest from which politicians would recoil. Reform by elite majority imposition can therefore occur (without politicians later regretting it) only where legitimacy constraints on such action are permissive. The location and intensity of such constraints are therefore important.

These first two sources of complexity are the most important for understanding reform by elite majority imposition. But the other building blocks – uncertainty, cognitive constraints, leadership, institutions – matter too, and I consider each more briefly in the course of Chapter 8. I leave out only endogenous path dependence: I find no evidence that it has played any significant role in any of the relatively short processes of reform by elite majority imposition.

5

France: the recurrent game of electoral reform

France has changed the electoral system used for its national lower house at least as often as any other country: Colomer (2004a: 74–6) counts nineteen cases stretching back to 1789, a number rivalled only by Greece. As Pickles (1958: 33) remarks dryly, 'Passing new electoral laws is a traditional pastime of French parliaments.' The two-round system in single-member districts was used for most of the life of the Third Republic, between 1871 and 1940, but was intermittently dropped in favour of various alternatives (Cole and Campbell 1989: 48–71). This chapter encompasses seven episodes of reform or proposed reform since the end of the Second World War, as summarized in Table 5.1.

The adoption of proportional representation, 1945–1946

France emerged from the Second World War under a provisional government headed by General Charles de Gaulle that included all the major political parties. The choice of electoral system over the following eighteen months proceeded in three distinct stages. First, a new electoral system was chosen for a constituent assembly, elected in October 1945. Second, that assembly proposed an electoral system to be used for elections to the future National Assembly, a proposal that lapsed when the draft constitution was rejected by referendum in May 1946. Third, a second constituent assembly, created following the referendum defeat, drafted a somewhat revised electoral system in conjunction with a second draft constitution, accepted by referendum in October 1946. Occurring as they did in the context of redemocratization following a brief non-democratic interlude of five years, these electoral reforms had a somewhat mixed character: they fell close to the elite majority imposition type, but they displayed some features also of elite settlement. (Though referendums took place, the positions adopted by the various parties and politicians dominated the outcomes.)

Table 5.1. *Summary of major electoral reform in France since 1945*

Year of reform or debate	Year of first use	New (or proposed) system
1945–1946		
1945	1945	Closed-list PR in departments
1946	Not passed	Closed-list PR in departments with national pool
1946	1946	Effectively closed-list PR in departments
1951	1951	Paris region: effectively closed-list PR; elsewhere: conditional party block vote
1958	1958	Two-round system with qualified single-member plurality
1985	1986	Closed-list PR in departments with 5 per cent threshold
1986	1988	Two-round system with qualified single-member plurality
1991–1992	Not passed	Consideration of introducing an element of proportionality
2007–2008	Not passed	Consideration of introducing an element of proportionality

Note: See text for sources and details.

The principal parties in de Gaulle's interim government were the Communists (PCF), the Socialists (SFIO), the Christian democratic Popular Republican Movement (MRP), and the Radicals. Gaullists such as Michel Debré and René Capitant were also prominent (the latter was in the cabinet). The Communists, Socialists, and MRP all agreed that the constituent assembly should be elected by proportional representation employing large districts or, at least, a national top-up tier to ensure proportionality. The Radicals wanted to restore the Third Republic system of two-round elections in single-member districts, while Debré and Capitant advocated single-member plurality.

The Radicals' thinking was relatively simple: they had been the dominant party during the first four decades of the twentieth century, and they hoped that the readoption of the system that had existed in those years could deliver them similar results again. Thus, they sought the restoration not only of the old electoral system, but of the whole Third Republic constitution, opposing its abolition in the referendum of October 1945 (Williams 1954: 14). As regards the electoral system in particular, they were the oldest party in France; they had little in the way of a central organization but were strongly entrenched at the local level (Williams 1954: 90); they thus expected to gain more votes – and, therefore, seats – under a single-member-district system that emphasized candidates over parties or leaders (Williams 1964: 311; Wright 1950: 89–90).

The thinking of the other large parties was to some extent the obverse of that of the Radicals: they wanted competition to concentrate not upon local candidates but upon national party labels and platforms. The Communists and Socialists were centralized parties with strong ideological profiles. The MRP was a new party that had emerged from the underground resistance with much collective credit but few well-known leaders (Neumann 1951: 741). These parties therefore expected to win more votes in a system that emphasized party identities and programmes rather than individual candidates. Several further considerations mattered to them too. First, the values of fairness and good governance played a role. The Socialists and Communists had long argued for PR, both because they valued the principle of proportionality (Neumann 1951: 741), and because they believed the single-member districts of the Third Republic favoured the provision of private over public goods: as Williams (1964: 308) puts it, they believed that PR 'would free the deputy from the parish pump, broadening his own horizon and that of his followers'. Second, these politicians also wanted to secure popular legitimacy for the new republic: 'They wanted the new chamber to reflect accurately political opinions so that it could make a new constitution which would enjoy the people's confidence' (Cole and Campbell 1989: 73). Third, all these parties saw PR as allowing them to maintain their pre-electoral independence, whereas the two-round system would force them to form alliances in the second round (Goguel 1952: 59–60). Finally, and, at least in Goguel's view, most importantly, the parties operated from behind a veil of ignorance from where they sought the security offered by PR. Uncertainty was high not only because there had been a five-year break in democracy, not only because the political landscape had been changed substantially by the experiences of war, occupation, and resistance, but also because women were enfranchised for the first time. In these circumstances, PR offered the best guarantee that each party would gain seats in the Assembly and made it unlikely that any opponent would secure an overall majority (Goguel 1952: 60–2).

Gaullists such as Debré and Capitant, finally, advocated SMP on the basis of the value of governability. Debré had proposed it for the constitution that he drafted in the underground in 1943 (Wright 1950: 90). He argued vehemently that proportional representation would generate party system fragmentation, prevent the creation of stable majority governments, favour fragmentary sectional interests rather than the national interest, and cause governments to be formed on the basis not of the popular vote, but of post-election dealing among parties (Debré 1947: 193–8). 'These men', argues Wright (1950: 90), 'contended that no modern democracy could function effectively on a coalition basis, and that the only way to force a dozen parties to fuse into two blocs would be to adopt the Anglo-Saxon system of election by a mere plurality.'

The decision on the electoral system used for the first constituent assembly ultimately lay, however, in the hands of General de Gaulle. De Gaulle was, of course, close to Debré and Capitant; he shared their distaste for political parties and their disbelief in the possibility of effective government based on a coalition of parliamentary parties (e.g., De Gaulle 1959a: 103–4, 130, 252; Hazareesingh 1994: 267). We might therefore expect the General to have joined them in support of SMP. But he did not. Rather, he opted for a system of closed-list proportional representation using small, departmentally based districts of between two and nine members. This was a middle road between the large-district PR system advocated by the Communists, Socialists, and MRP and the SMP system proposed by de Gaulle's allies; but it was rather closer to the former than the latter.

Several considerations underlay the General's decision. De Gaulle himself offered three explanations for his rejection of single-member districts, both in a private letter to Debré (reproduced in Debré 1974: 413–18) and in his memoirs (De Gaulle 1959a: 260–1). First, he had to take account, he told Debré, of the opinions of the parties, and the advocates of PR would not have accepted a non-proportional system (Debré 1974: 70). Second, the pre-war districts were severely malapportioned, and full-scale reapportionment could not be achieved quickly (De Gaulle 1959a: 260–1). Third – and, it appears, most importantly – he feared that a system based on single-member districts risked giving a majority to the Communists, either on their own (in the case of SMP) or in alliance with the Socialists (under a two-round system) (De Gaulle 1959a: 261; Debré 1974: 70). De Gaulle operated behind the same veil of ignorance as the parties; he too preferred a system that would minimize the prospects of a hostile majority in the assembly.

Two additional considerations seem to have mattered. First, de Gaulle, like many others, despised the parish pump politics of the Third Republic and therefore wanted to abolish the 'minuscule constituencies in which parochial local issues and local favorite sons had an advantage' (Wahl 1959b: 50; see also Knapp 2007a: 6). Two committees of the wartime Free France movement that de Gaulle had led advocated PR on this basis (Shennan 1989: 111–18). Second, he seems simply not to have believed that the electoral system could make much difference. His focus had long been upon the role of the statesman who operated above party and parliament in pursuit of the national interest (e.g., De Gaulle 1960 [1932]: 96). He argued in his famous Bayeux speech of June 1946 that 'the rivalry of parties in our country is a national characteristic' (De Gaulle 1959b [1946]: 387), and he apparently believed its ill effects could not be overcome through electoral system tinkering: speaking in 1950, he observed, 'We have experimented, we French, with all possible electoral systems, and none has ever been able to compensate for the harm done by the regime of parties' (De Gaulle 1970 [1950]: 346; Debré 1974: 124). In setting out his proposed structure of political institutions at Bayeux, he did not mention the electoral system. Debré suggests that, in this light, he accepted the will of the majority of politicians: 'He did not want to jeopardize his legitimacy in quarrels he viewed as secondary' (Debré 1981: 4).

By the time of the second phase of discussion over the electoral system – in the first constituent assembly – the circumstances had changed somewhat. First, de Gaulle had resigned as prime minister and played no direct role in the drafting process. Second, an election had taken place, and the uncertainty facing the parties had thus decreased significantly. The results of that election, held on 21 October 1945, are shown in Table 5.2. As can be seen, the Communists, Socialists, and MRP

Table 5.2. *Results of the two constituent assembly elections, 1945–1946*

Party	October 1945		June 1946	
	% votes	% seats	% votes	% seats
Communists	26.1	28.4	26.2	28.0
Socialists	23.8	25.7	21.1	22.0
MRP	24.9	27.0	28.1	30.7
Radicals	11.1	6.7	11.5	7.5
Conservatives	13.3	11.9	12.8	11.9
Others	0.9	0.4	0.4	0.0

Source: Mackie and Rose (1991: 149, 151).

between them won substantial majorities of both votes and seats; all three were well ahead of the Radicals and conservatives. We might expect that, with this new information, these parties would have modified their previous strong support for PR. And to some extent they did: whereas previously they had been disappointed with the low district magnitude imposed by de Gaulle in 1945, now they advocated retention of the same districts. But the principle of proportionality remained: the system proposed by the first constitutional assembly was virtually identical to the system that had been used to elect it.

This decision is fully intelligible in terms of the preferences already described. The advantage that these parties expected to gain over the Radicals from a focus on parties over candidates remained. So too did the principled arguments for proportionality and programmatic parties. Finally, though uncertainty had diminished, still, three large parties existed with roughly equal vote shares; in this situation, a majoritarian system could have produced unpredictable results; and none of the three parties wanted any of its rivals to secure an artificial advantage in seats, much less an overall majority. Thus, PR gave these parties more stable access to power, kept their opponents in check, and fitted their principles.

The constitutional draft produced by the first constituent assembly was, however, rejected in the referendum of May 1946, having been voted through the assembly by the Communists and the Socialists against the votes of all the other parties (Williams 1954: 17). In the second constituent assembly, recognizing the need to secure a wider consensus, the Communists and Socialists negotiated a draft that gained the endorsement also of the MRP. In respect of the electoral system, however, only minor details changed. This is as we would expect: the results of the elections to the second constituent assembly, in June 1946, had been very similar to those of the previous October (see Table 5.2); all three parties therefore retained their preference for limited PR (Williams 1964: 309). Thus, the first National Assembly of the Fourth Republic was elected in November 1946 using broadly the same system as had been introduced in 1945.

The electoral system choices made in France in 1945 and 1946 thus conformed largely to the elite majority imposition type. Politicians dominated. And though those politicians did genuinely consider which institutions would facilitate effective democracy and governance, they always pursued options that they expected would also advance their power interests while hindering the power aspirations of their rivals. In the earliest phase, when uncertainty was highest, most actors sought the maximin option of proportional representation, and the new system – at least, its basic form – thus won broad support across most parties. By the second and third phases, the parties of the majority coalition retained a preference for PR, but grounded this on clearer expectations of their future prospects and, accordingly, no longer pursued PR in very pure form.

Manipulation against the extremes, 1951

The 1946 election proved, however, to be the last to use the departmental PR system in unadulterated form. Between 1946 and 1951 – when the next election was due – two pertinent changes in the political environment occurred. First, the tripartite alliance of Communists, Socialists, and the MRP that governed up to the National Assembly election of November 1946 was disbanded. From May 1947 on, as Cold War hostilities deepened, the Communists were excluded from government, were cast increasingly as an uncoalitionable extreme, and themselves adopted at Moscow's insistence a highly confrontational and isolationist strategy (Bell and Criddle 1994: 177; Naoumova 2007: 179). Government coalitions comprised, rather, the Socialists, MRP, Radicals, and conservatives (for details, see Williams 1954: 436–7). Second, from 1947 onwards, the Gaullists organized themselves as an institutionalized grouping – the *Rassemblement du Peuple Français* (RPF). Initially, 'the General and his supporters earnestly denied that they intended to construct a new party' (Williams 1954: 121): in parliament they formed an 'inter-group' of deputies who retained their existing party affiliations. But this strategy brought little success and was blocked by the parties; by 1951 the General was preparing to run his own Assembly candidates. With a million members by the end of 1947 (Williams 1954: 120), the RPF constituted a considerable threat to the existing parties.

The combined effect of these two changes was that the majority status of the ruling coalition was threatened: the Ministry of the Interior estimated that, using the existing electoral system, the Communists would win 159 metropolitan seats and the Gaullists 146, easily surpassing half the total of 544 (Williams 1954: 317). The broad goal of the coalition parties in pursuing electoral reform in early 1951 – indeed, their broad goal for most of the period between 1946 and 1951 – was to avoid this outcome (Rioux 1987: 151–69). They presented the potential loss of the centrist majority as a threat to the survival of the republic: 'The overt aim ... was to protect parliamentary democracy against the two extreme parties which menaced it' (Goguel 1952: 77). Whether parliamentary democracy was in fact so threatened is open to debate. Both Goguel (1952: 78) and Williams (1964: 314) imply that the situation was indeed dangerous and manipulation of the system to skew the results was justifiable. On the other hand, Cole and Campbell (1989: 84) suggest that, in fact, the ruling parties (except the Socialists) 'would probably have preferred an alliance with De Gaulle's RPF than complete political chaos'. And, indeed, alliance with elements of the RPF is precisely what gradually emerged after the Socialists left the government following the 1951 election. Thus, it may be that the coalition parties used heightened rhetoric to justify a manoeuvre that was motivated more by a desire to retain power by boosting their seat shares (Neumann 1951: 752). Whatever the true mix of motivations, the coalition parties sought an electoral system that would favour parties able to form electoral alliances over those that, while large in themselves, were isolated from other support.

This was their broad goal. But the various coalition parties were divided as to how best to pursue it: in respect of goals other than overall coalition seat share, their interests diverged. The Radicals continued to argue for two-round elections in single-member districts. This system would allow the coalition parties to coalesce in the second round to defeat most Communist or RPF candidates. It also retained the attraction it had always had for the Radicals of favouring parties with strong local candidates. But the MRP remained deeply hostile to this system, for the same reasons as before. It proposed instead a conditional party block vote system: parties would present lists in multi-member districts; alliances among these lists (called *apparentements*) could be declared ahead of the election; in any district where a list or alliance of lists won an absolute majority of the votes, it would win all the district's seats; if no list or alliance won such a majority, the seats would be distributed proportionally among all parties. Such a system would again permit the coalition parties to act together in order to defeat the isolated Communists and Gaullists, but it would also focus attention on parties rather than candidates. The other parties, meanwhile, were more divided (Neumann 1951: 743–7; Williams 1964: 310–11).

The debates over electoral reform that ensued from this situation lasted six months and involved numerous heated parliamentary debates and close parliamentary votes (Browne and Hamm 1996 provide detailed analysis). In the end, the MRP's proposal largely won out. According to Neumann (1951: 749), the MRP's bargaining power was enhanced by the fact that it was more willing than its coalition partners to countenance retention of the status quo and thus more able to play a game of brinkmanship – though not all analysts share this interpretation.

In fact, the system adopted was even more convoluted than the description above suggests, for two different systems were used in different parts of metropolitan France. The system of conditional party block vote described above was used across most of the country, but in the Paris region proportional representation was retained and was made more favourable to smaller parties through a switch in the seat allocation method from highest average to largest remainders. It was in this region that the coalition parties were weakest; they did not want to create the possibility that others could capture all the seats. (For more detailed description of the electoral system, see Cole and Campbell 1989: 79–81; Goguel 1952: 74–6; Williams 1954: 442–5.)

The new system produced the results intended by its proponents: though the Communists and the RPF secured between them 48.5 per cent of the vote in the election of June 1951 and were by some margin the first and second largest parties respectively, they won just 37.5 per cent of the seats, while the four coalition parties, on 51.0 per cent of the vote, secured 62.5 per cent of the seats (Mackie and Rose 1991: 148–51). Yet it achieved this result by such contrived means as to struggle in terms of legitimacy. As Williams (1964: 319) suggests, the system 'seemed to produce blatantly unjust results and so helped to discredit its authors and the regime itself'. Such manipulations, he continues, 'inevitably contributed to the ordinary citizen's disillusionment with politics' (Williams 1964: 319–20).

In the light of this dissatisfaction, the question of electoral reform again rose to prominence in 1955, ahead of the elections that were due by the end of 1956. Once more, reform proposals filled much parliamentary time, but on this occasion they got nowhere. Interpretations vary as to why the reform effort failed. In Cole and Campbell's view, though the parties of the governing coalition agreed on the need for reform, their interests diverged so far that they could not all agree the same reform (Cole and Campbell 1989: 25). Leites (1959: 66, 85–7), by contrast, suggests that in fact the majority in the National Assembly favoured retention of the 1951 system: just as it had bolstered their interests in 1951, so it continued to suit them in 1955. No one was willing publicly to defend that system, however, and so, he argues, the parliamentary debates were merely an elaborate mechanism for blocking reform while seeming to take the matter seriously. Whichever interpretation is closer to the truth, the outcome was that the election of 1956 was held under the same electoral system as had been introduced and used for the first time in 1951.

The foundation of De Gaulle's republic, 1958

In 1958, the Fourth Republic collapsed. The army took control in Algeria and threatened a coup in Paris. To forestall this, parliament appointed the hero of the right, General de Gaulle, as prime minister, with authority to draft a new constitution. In this context, the 1951 electoral system stood little chance of survival. As in 1955, no one was willing to defend it openly (Williams and Harrison 1961: 101). It had been designed in part specifically to hinder the Gaullists, who had 'bitterly criticised' it (Williams and Harrison 1959: 33).

Three principal options were on the table in 1958. The Communists continued to favour PR. They valued proportionality, believed in disciplined, centralized, programmatic parties, and disliked systems that facilitated the rise of local notables. In addition, isolated from other parties and with no prospect, therefore, of forming alliances, PR was their seat-maximizing option. For this last reason, however, PR was unacceptable to the other parties, as it had been in 1951, and in Williams and Harrison's (1961: 102) view, therefore, it had 'no chance of adoption'.

The second option was a two-round version of the party block vote, based on department-level multi-member districts, in which an absolute majority would be required in the first round and only a plurality in the second. This system was pushed by de Gaulle's supporters, who expected that the combined right could secure a plurality in almost every department and thereby virtually sweep the board (Williams and Harrison 1961: 102). Debré, whose role in drafting the new institutional structure was huge (Wahl 1959a: 371–2), was, as noted above in relation to 1945, a keen advocate of SMP, but even he appears to have supported the party block vote system as a short-term measure in 1958 (Williams and Harrison 1961: 102n).

The third option, finally, was the two-round system in single-member districts, with a requirement for absolute majority in the first round and plurality in the second. This option was favoured by the non-Communist left – especially by the Socialists, but even by the MRP, who had been so hostile to it in 1951. By 1958, the Socialist and MRP candidates were better known than they had been in the early stages of the Fourth Republic; now it was the Gaullists who were largely anonymous. Thus, these groups believed that single-member districts 'should enable them to save local pockets of party or personal strength, and should favour prominent, entrenched personalities against the Gaullist political unknowns' (Williams and Harrison 1961: 102).

All available accounts suggest that the choice regarding the new electoral system was essentially de Gaulle's: whereas in 1945 he had been constrained by the self-confident parties and his own political naïvety (cf. Goldey 2007), in 1958, the existing party-led system having collapsed and the General having learnt many lessons, his hand was stronger. Given the distribution of preferences across parties just described, and given that de Gaulle had himself repeatedly backed the departmental party block vote system in the late 1940s (Debré 1974: 122–3; Goguel 1952: 37, 64), it surprised everyone that in fact the General chose the two-round system in single-member districts.

In part, this decision no doubt reflected de Gaulle's well-known distaste for political parties, which the party block vote system could only strengthen (Frears 1977: 179). But the major reason was that many of de Gaulle's supporters were given to zealotry, while the General himself recognized that tough decisions would soon have to be made. As Goldey and Williams (1983: 72) put it, de Gaulle 'had no wish to encumber himself with a Parliament full of rigid diehards over the Algerian question, and hoped to balance them with Socialists and others, who would be critics on some issues but might respond to his appeals over the most crucial problem of all, thus giving him more freedom of manoeuvre' (see also Frears 1977: 179; Wahl 1959b: 51). Williams and Harrison (1961: 96, 100–1) show that containment of his most ardent supporters was part of de Gaulle's strategy from the moment he was invested as prime minister at the beginning of June 1958, visible, for example, in the inclusive composition of his cabinet.

Thus, de Gaulle opted for the two-round system in single-member districts precisely because it would *not* maximize the seat share of his own party in the National Assembly. This seeming conundrum is intelligible if we recognize that de Gaulle was neither a parliamentarian nor a party man: he sought the system that would allow him to exercise the power of presidential office as he wished – above the partisan fray. This case thus illustrates the point, made in Chapter 2, that for most politicians what matters is not simply whether they hold office, but also whether they can do what they want while in office: whether, that is, they genuinely hold power. De Gaulle did not expect to maximize his power simply by maximizing the seat share of his avowed supporters in the National Assembly.

Return to proportional representation, 1985

Several changes to France's electoral system occurred in the two decades following the installation of the Fifth Republic in 1958. The threshold candidates had to reach in the first round of the elections to gain entry to the second round was raised from an initial 5 per cent of the vote in 1958 to 10 per cent of the electorate in 1967 and then 12.5 per cent of the electorate in 1976. More significantly for the character of French politics, the method of electing the president changed from indirect to direct as a result of a referendum called by de Gaulle in 1962.

But these changes do not fall into the category of major reforms of the lower house electoral system covered here. In these terms, the first decades of the Fifth Republic were a period of unusual electoral system stability: only in 1985 was major reform again implemented. De Gaulle – particularly once he had secured the direct election of the president in 1962 – had established the strong extra-parliamentary executive that he wanted, and he did not seek further changes to the assembly. The status quo served the Gaullists and their allies well throughout the 1970s, and they advocated no major reforms.

Electoral reform was, however, on the agenda of the Gaullists' opponents during this period of uninterrupted right-wing government. The Communists' commitment to PR remained constant. As we have seen, they had always believed in proportionality and in centralized, programmatic parties. PR also remained their seat-maximizing option: in 1958, the majoritarian system gave them just 2.2 per cent of the seats on 18.9 per cent of the vote; though they did erode that seat deficit over time, they never entirely closed the gap (Mackie and Rose 1991: 149–55). It might be argued that the two-round system, despite its effect on the PCF's seat share, enhanced the party's power: Duverger (1974: 16) points out that, by encouraging alliance between the PCF and the Socialists, it helped the Communists escape the isolation they experienced under the Fourth Republic and therefore advanced their prospects of securing office. In fact, however, the party placed maintenance of its rigid ideological identity above immediate office (Bell and Criddle 1994: 1). Though it pursued alliance with the Socialists in the mid-1970s, neither party regarded this as more than a marriage of convenience, and, once it became apparent that the alliance was endangering the Communists' future as a strong independent force, the party forced it to an acrimonious end (Brown 1982: 124, 146; Lavau and Mossuz-Lavau 1980). Thus, given its size and desire for ideological purity, the PCF was best served by PR. It vigorously defended this system – while condemning the two-round status quo – in its programme of 1971 (PCF 1971: 131–2). Party leader Georges Marchais pursued the same arguments with even more vigour in a book published two years later (Marchais 1973: 86–7, 111–12).

The Socialists, meanwhile, were more ambiguous. They had backed the two-round system in 1958. Subsequently, they suffered significant seat deficits relative to votes under that system twice, in 1958 and 1968; but in 1962, 1967, and 1978 they gained a bonus (Mackie and Rose 1991: 149–55). Nevertheless, they proposed a mixed-member proportional (MMP) system in their programme of 1972 (PS 1972: 101), they backed PR as part of the 'Common Programme of Government' signed with the Communists later that year (Programme Commun de Gouvernement 1972: 150), and a commitment to PR was part of the programme on which party leader François Mitterrand was elected president of the Republic in 1981 (Mitterrand 1981).

Following his election in 1981, Mitterrand dissolved the National Assembly, secured a majority for the Socialists, and formed a government in coalition with the Communists. Despite all the prior commitments to electoral reform, however, no movement in that direction was forthcoming: for more than three years, the government fell silent on the matter. Only late in the summer of 1984, after the removal of the Communists from the coalition, did President Mitterrand return to the issue,[1] and reform was then formally proposed and rapidly enacted the following spring. The new system was one of PR with closed lists. Proportionality was limited, however, by the use of small districts, a 5 per cent threshold, and the highest average formula for allocating seats (Knapp 1987: 94).

Several considerations fostered the Socialists' decision to implement this reform. Frears (1986: 490, 1988: 212) and Gaxie (1990: 450) suggest that the party's manifesto promise and long-standing commitment to the principle of equity and therefore proportionality were important. They may indeed have played a role, but, given the Socialists' lack of fidelity to that principle in the past and their failure to move on it upon entering office, they were certainly not a major consideration. Mitterrand's aides waited to see the results of the local elections of March 1985 before deciding the precise nature of the reforms,[2] which hardly suggests that principle was paramount. Mitterrand himself, indeed, explicitly argued against viewing electoral systems in terms of fixed principles (Favier and Martin-Roland 1991: 307). Rather, as I suggest in Chapter 8, the main effect of the Socialists' prior commitment to PR was to provide a legitimizing discourse for reforms that were grounded in other considerations.

---

[1] 'Mitterrand Toys with a Change in the Rules', *The Economist*, 15 September 1984.
[2] 'Mitterrand Might Seek Change in Voting Rules', *Washington Post*, 18 March 1985.

Those other considerations centred upon the Socialists' desire to minimize their losses in the elections due in 1986. As Criddle (1992: 111) sums the matter up, their goals 'fell firmly within the tradition of partisan self-seeking'. In part, they simply wanted to maximize their seat share in the coming election (calculated using the Duvergerian mechanisms): the polls suggested they were likely to suffer heavy defeat; PR, by minimizing the exaggeration of vote swings in terms of seat shares, would limit that loss (Alexander 2004: 214; Cole and Campbell 1989: 136), while the limits on proportionality would reduce any erosion of the larger parties' seat shares in favour of very small parties. Thus, projections published by *Le Point* magazine predicted that the Socialists would win 150 seats under the new system compared to 128 under the old.[3] In addition, they saw that a proportional system would give Le Pen's National Front a foothold in the Assembly, thereby splitting the right: the *Le Point* poll projected a seat tally of eighteen for the National Front under the new system. This would make the formation of a stable centre-right coalition government harder and enhance the leverage that Mitterrand could exert from the Elysée Palace (Alexander 2004: 214; Cole and Campbell 1989: 136; Tiersky 2000: 265). Finally, Mitterrand may have hoped that PR would weaken the bipolar logic of the party system, thereby freeing the Socialists from dependence on the Communists as their only significant potential coalition ally and allowing rapprochement with centrist elements among the parties of the centre-right (Cole and Campbell 1989: 136). Governing with the Communists had proved bruising; even before their departure from the government coalition in 1984, Mitterrand had begun to shift policy towards the centre; to pursue that strategy further, he needed new allies.

The interests of the centre-right parties were the mirror image of the Socialists': they expected in 1986 to gain the seat bonus conferred by the majoritarian system on the leading coalition; they did not wish their control of the right to be disturbed by the entry of Le Pen; if anyone among them was interested in switching coalition partners, they did not make their voices heard. Thus, they opposed the reform proposals vehemently, declaring PR 'incompatible with the institutions of the Fifth Republic' (Favier and Martin-Roland 1991: 312).

Opposition came also from two groups within the Socialist Party. One of these was the party's left-wing faction, led by education minister Jean-Pierre Chevènement, which opposed Mitterrand's centrist strategy and

[3] 'France Adopting New Voting Plan', *New York Times*, 4 April 1985.

preferred the bipolarism of left and right that the two-round system enforced.[4] The other group was led by the social democratic agriculture minister, Michel Rocard, who resigned from government over the reforms. Rocard wanted to succeed Mitterrand in the Elysée Palace and thus looked beyond 1986 to the political landscape after 1988. While many saw his resignation merely as a step towards making his presidential bid (Christofferson 1991: 218–19), Rocard's presidential ambitions and genuine belief in social democratic government also gave him reason to oppose the electoral reform: with longer time horizons than Mitterrand, he opposed the adoption of a system that would prevent the Socialists ever again from gaining an overall majority.[5] Despite these dissenting voices, Socialist Party discipline and deputies' interest in minimizing seat losses ensured that the reforms were enacted.

Restoration of majoritarianism, 1986

The new electoral system operated as expected in the National Assembly elections of 1986: the Socialists held on to 35.6 per cent of the seats, though their vote share fell to 31.3 per cent; the National Front, on 9.8 per cent of the vote, won 6.3 per cent of the seats (Mackie and Rose 1991: 153, 155). Nevertheless, the centre-right coalition – comprising, primarily, Jacques Chirac's Gaullists and the Union for French Democracy (UDF), founded by former president Valéry Giscard d'Estaing – did secure a wafer-thin majority. The centre-right parties had vowed to repeal the proportional system in a joint declaration issued before the new law had even been enacted,[6] and they restated this pledge in their joint election manifesto.[7] Following its election, the new government, led by Chirac, moved quickly to implement that repeal. They sought to pass it by government decree, but Mitterrand refused to give his signature, necessitating a lengthier parliamentary process. The new law was finally passed in November 1986 (Cole and Campbell 1989: 141). It was identical to the pre-1985 law, except that an increase in the size of the Assembly that had accompanied the 1985 change was not reversed and district boundaries were consequently redrawn.

[4] 'French Socialists Split on Voting Reform', *Guardian*, 26 March 1985.
[5] 'France Sets Voting Change', *Washington Post*, 4 April 1985.
[6] 'French Opposition to Repeal PR', *Financial Times*, 11 April 1985.
[7] 'French Right's Poll Manifesto Presents a Moderate Image', *The Times*, 17 January 1986.

The reasons for this reform were for the most part the obverse of those that had led the Socialists to introduce PR the previous year: the parties of the centre-right wanted to eliminate the National Front and to shore up their own coalition against the danger of slippage in the centre ground. Chirac looked to 1988, when he hoped to win the presidency. With the two-round electoral system for parliament in place again, he would then be able to dissolve the Assembly and secure a larger majority for his coalition (Cole and Campbell 1989: 142). Additionally, the UDF, more than any other party, was dominated by locally entrenched *notables* (Hanley 1999: 176, 185), who wanted single-member districts, just as the Radicals had done in the 1940s and 1950s.

The 1986 reform was the simplest of all of France's post-war reform episodes. There was some friction within the centre-right coalition in the late summer and early autumn, when some in the UDF feared that the Gaullists were skewing to their own advantage the process of redistricting that was necessitated by the increased chamber size.[8] On the whole, however, the process simply replayed in reverse the events of the previous year, with the centre-right parties supporting the reform while the left and the far right opposed.

The temptation to manipulate again, 1991–1992

In the final two episodes of French politics that I consider, in 1991–1992 and 2007–2008, electoral reform was not enacted, but merely proposed and subsequently dropped. Despite these negative outcomes, both cases cast valuable light upon the nature of reform processes.

Though Chirac's centre-right government reintroduced the two-round system in 1986 in the hope of winning the presidency in 1988, in fact it was Mitterrand whom voters returned to the Elysée that year. As in 1981, he immediately dissolved the National Assembly, but this time the Socialists fell short of an overall majority; they formed a minority government and sought issue-by-issue cooperation from the Communists or the UDF. By 1991 the Socialists' fortunes had plummeted: as Guyomarch (1993: 612) observes, 'By late 1991, … the popularity of the government and the Socialist Party had fallen so low that already many were predicting that only divine intervention could prevent an electoral débâcle for the PS in 1993.' Thus, the situation was very similar to that of 1985, and, correspondingly, Mitterrand gave serious consideration in late 1991 and early

---

[8] 'Map of Contention', *The Economist*, 30 August 1986.

1992 to the adoption either of full PR or of a mixed-member majoritarian (MMM) system.[9] But opposition to the reform within the Socialist Party was stronger this time than it had been in 1985: among others, three of the party's leading figures (and, in normal times, spirited rivals) – Laurent Fabius, Lionel Jospin, and Michel Rocard – united to fight the move.[10] By early April 1992, the reform advocates gave up: the prime minister, Pierre Bérégovoy, announced there would be no reform before the 1993 election.[11]

Mitterrand's reasons for seeking reform were essentially the same as those of 1985. PR was the seat-maximizing option for the Socialists in 1993: the Sofres polling organization projected on the basis of regional election results from March 1992 that the party would win just 112 (of 555) seats under the two-round electoral system, but 138 under PR (Riding 1992). Reintroducing PR would also allow the return of the National Front, which had been cut down to just one Assembly seat by the two-round system used in 1988. Sofres predicted that the parties of the centre-right coalition, which could expect a massive 421 seats under the status quo, would win just 271 seats under PR, marginally denying them an overall majority. Finally, PR was attractive from the perspective of Mitterrand's coalition strategy: this time he sought alliance not only with the centrist parties, but also with the Greens, for whom PR was a key demand.[12]

But the opposition to reform was stronger within the party than in 1985 because the reasons for thinking the change would harm the Socialists were also stronger. In part, the mere fact that the party would be repeating an old trick may have made it harder to execute the manoeuvre without high cost to voter affect: according to Goldey (1993: 293), one factor in the decision not to proceed was the perception 'that tinkering again with the electoral system would discredit the PS more than it would benefit it'.

Other circumstances had changed too. First, the National Front was riding much higher in the polls than it had in 1985: Sofres projected that it could win 77 seats if reform were enacted (Riding 1992). Whereas giving Le Pen a place in the Assembly may have seemed excusable when

---

[9] 'French Socialists Push Ahead with PR Despite Fears that Voting Reforms Will Split the Party', *Guardian*, 21 November 1991; Davidson (1992b).

[10] 'Et Tu, Fabius', *The Economist*, 14 December 1991.

[11] 'France Sets Moratorium on Nuclear Arms Tests', *Washington Post*, 9 April 1992.

[12] 'Et Tu, Fabius', *The Economist*, 14 December 1991; 'Major Shift Expected in French Vote Sunday', *Washington Post*, 20 March 1992.

his support was lower, allowing the far right such substantial representation in the early 1990s would have caused much greater disquiet.[13]
Second, the threat that PR posed to the Socialists' continued domination
of the left appeared greater in 1991 and 1992 than it had done in 1985. In
1985, with the Communists in apparently terminal decline, the
Socialists had no serious left-wing challenger. But by 1992, the Greens,
who had scored an insignificant 1.2 per cent vote in 1986, were drawing
close to the Socialists' support levels: in the regional elections of March
that year the combined vote of the two ecology parties was 13.9 per
cent, compared to 18.3 per cent for the PS.[14] Introducing an electoral
system that could consolidate that rise appeared highly risky to
most Socialist leaders. Finally, Socialist eyes were turning to the
post-Mitterrand era much more than had been the case in 1985. Party
leaders, therefore, were concerned not just with the 1993 election result,
but also with the party's prospects for elections in 1995 and beyond
(Davidson 1992a).

Were we to focus on short-term seat-maximization alone, the opposition to PR within the Socialist Party in 1991 and 1992 would be difficult
to understand. Taking a broader perspective on the ways in which the
electoral system affects politicians' and parties' power, however, it thus
becomes clear why the centre of gravity had shifted in the party on the
electoral reform issue since 1985.

Bérégovoy did seek to save face and mollify the Greens when announ-
cing the abandonment of immediate reform by setting up a multi-party
commission to look into the issue for future elections, and this reported
in February 1993 in favour of electing 10 per cent of National Assembly
members by PR.[15] But when the Socialists were swept away in the
elections the following month – they secured just 67 seats (Machin
1993a: 600) – the idea died. Though the 1993 elections – which generated
higher disproportionality than any previous election during the Fifth
Republic (Machin 1993b: 629) – sparked renewed interest in reform in
many opposition circles (Guyomarch 1993: 624), the centre-right were
by then in power and were not about to change the system that had given
them such a commanding majority. Thus, the issue slipped again from
the agenda.

[13] 'The Politics of Hate in France', *Washington Times*, 10 January 1992; 'France
Fragmented', *Financial Times*, 24 March 1992.
[14] 'Poll Shows Up Divisions in French Right', *Independent*, 24 March 1992.
[15] 'French Urged to Adopt Limited PR', *Financial Times*, 4 February 1993.

'Une dose de proportionnelle'?, 2007–2008

The most recent round of debate concerning electoral reform in France concluded on 21 July 2008, when the National Assembly and Senate, sitting in joint session in the gilded surroundings of the Palace of Versailles, voted through a series of amendments to the Constitution of the Fifth Republic *without* any accompanying reform of the electoral law.[16] These amendments stemmed from widespread unease regarding the operation of France's governing institutions, which had grown in the final years of the presidency of Jacques Chirac. Many had argued that the institutional reforms should include the introduction of an element of proportionality – 'une dose de proportionnelle' – in elections to the National Assembly. These demands were strongly resisted, however, by the new president, Nicolas Sarkozy, elected in May 2007. In securing his constitutional reform agenda – by a margin of just one vote – without needing to concede electoral reform, he ensured that the existing two-round system would survive for the foreseeable future.

A crucial precursor to these events was an earlier constitutional amendment, passed in 2000, which reduced the presidential term from seven to five years (Légifrance 2000). In combination with a further law passed the following year (see Légifrance 2001), this ensured that, under normal circumstances, the legislative elections would follow within months of each presidential election. This synchronization diminishes the likelihood of 'cohabitation', when the president confronts an opposing parliamentary majority, and thus increases the concentration of power in the hands of a single party and president (Levy and Skach 2008: 120–2).

These changes fuelled growing concerns about the development of 'hyper-presidentialism', and calls for further institutional reform became widespread. In the presidential elections of 2007, both the Socialist candidate, Ségolène Royal, and the UDF's François Bayrou gave significant weight in their programmes to reform plans designed to weaken the presidency and strengthen parliament (Royal 2007: 16–17; Bayrou 2007: 10, 14), calling for the creation of a 'Sixth Republic' (Fouchet 2007). Together with all the minor party candidates, both also called for electoral reform designed to reduce one-party dominance (Boissieu 2007). Bayrou argued specifically for the election of half of the National

---

[16] This section draws on very helpful conversations with David Goldey and Andy Knapp, to whom I am grateful.

Assembly by proportional representation (Bayrou 2007: 14). Royal called for the election by PR of an unspecified proportion of deputies (Royal 2007: 16).

By contrast, Sarkozy, who was the candidate of the latest incarnation of Gaullism, the *Union pour un Mouvement Populaire* (UMP), pursued a different agenda. He too gave prominence to institutional reform proposals, but he preferred to consolidate rather than constrain the powers of the presidency (Sarkozy 2007a: 4-6). Throughout the campaign he opposed the adoption of any proportional element for elections to the National Assembly. Following the first round of the election on 22 April, however, even he indicated a willingness to consider an element of proportionality in the hope of thereby attracting Bayrou's centrist voters (Ridet 2007).

Little more than two months after his election, on 12 July 2007, President Sarkozy set out his plans for institutional reform in a major speech at Épinal (Sarkozy 2007b). He announced the creation of a committee, chaired by former prime minister Édouard Balladur and including representatives of the left as well as the right, to propose specific constitutional amendments, and indicated that the committee should consider the introduction of 'une dose de proportionnelle' (Sarkozy 2007b). He repeated this injunction in his letter to Balladur setting out the committee's task (reproduced in Comité de Réflexion ... 2007: 106-9). The committee duly reported in late October. While evincing no enthusiasm for proportional systems, it did suggest that a small proportional element of twenty to thirty seats (around 5 per cent of the total) might be appropriate. It did not indicate whether these should be allocated on a compensatory basis (Comité de Réflexion ... 2007: 69).

Though Sarkozy and the UMP remained hostile to this idea, its prospects for adoption for a period appeared significant. None of the opposition parties was willing to back constitutional reform without it. Furthermore, the Nouveau Centre, which formed from the disintegrating UDF after Bayrou's defeat in the presidential election and which had entered Sarkozy's governing coalition, also backed the measure. The party's leader, Minister of Defence Hervé Morin, said in December 2007 that electoral reform was one of several 'unavoidable' issues that would 'influence' the party's vote on the constitutional reforms as a whole (Morin 2007). He continued to argue in April 2008 that it was a 'duty' to work for such reform (Mandonnet and Vigogne 2008), and the party lodged several amendments to the constitutional reform bill that would have guaranteed 'pluralist' and 'equitable' representation in parliament (Amendments 244 and 357 to the constitutional reform bill: Assemblée Nationale 2008a). The position of the Nouveau Centre was crucial: without it, Sarkozy would be unable to secure the three-fifths majority that passage of his constitutional package required.

Ultimately, however, the reform package passed without provision for electoral reform. While the opposition parties voted almost unanimously against, most of the Nouveau Centre's deputies and senators supported the package (Assemblée Nationale 2008b). The Nouveau Centre had won concessions on other matters, notably citizen-initiated referendums and balanced budget rules, and had decided not to press electoral reform to the wire. This opportunity for electoral reform having passed, another is not likely to emerge any time soon. Rather, at the time of writing, attention is focused on a reapportionment and redistricting bill: districts have remained unchanged, despite repeated Constitutional Council demands, since 1986, and inequalities in populations are huge (Balinski 2008; Conseil Constitutionel 2003, 2005, 2008).

Had electoral reform been achieved in 2008, it would have occupied an intermediate position on the spectrum between reform by elite majority imposition and elite settlement. It would have constituted a bargain in which the major governing party conceded this measure to its small coalition partner in return for the latter's support for its broader agenda. Such bargains have yielded minor electoral reforms in a number of cases, such as West Germany in 1985 (Scarrow 2001: 66) and Norway in 1988 (Aardal 1990: 152–3). Yet the fact that this route did not generate reform in France in 2008 should not surprise us, for international comparison suggests that the odds are stacked against: it is very difficult to find any case of major reform by this path. To an extent, the French case illustrates why. The major party – the UMP – refused to make any more than symbolic concessions. The minor party – the Nouveau Centre – preferred in the end to press other issues where public interest was greater, the danger of appearing self-interested smaller, and the likelihood of UMP movement higher. Similar calculations have been made by small parties holding the balance of power elsewhere too, as the British Liberals during the era of the Lib/Lab Pact in the 1970s (Steel 1989: 134). It is above all for this reason that such bargained reform does not play any significant part in the stories told in this book (see Renwick 2009a: 370–2). There appear also to have been more particular considerations operating in the French case. First, the desire for reform among Nouveau Centre deputies may not have been as great as the party's size alone would lead us to expect. As a successor to the UDF, the Nouveau Centre is largely a party of local *notables* who may prefer single-member districts to larger districts in which their strong local support would be diluted. Second, the Nouveau Centre is exceptionally weak: it was created in order to join Sarkozy's coalition, and without that coalition it would lose its *raison d'être*. It was thus in no position to push its demands to the brink.

6

Italy: the search for stability

Italy does not quite share France's record of electoral system instability. Nevertheless, it does rank among those countries that have seen frequent changes: five major electoral reforms have occurred since the Second World War. One of these changes – the adoption of a semi-compensatory mixed system in 1993 – falls into the category of elite–mass interaction and is therefore discussed in Part III. In this chapter, I narrate the events of the remaining reform episodes: the re-establishment of proportional representation after Fascism and world war in 1946; the adoption of a bonus-adjusted system in 1953; the rapid abandonment of that system and restoration of PR in 1954; and the creation of a some-what different bonus-adjusted system in 2005. I also outline the failure of intense reformist pressure between 1994 and 2001 and, briefly, the failure of a referendum on electoral reform in 2009. Table 6.1 provides an overview.

The origins of proportional representation

Proportional representation was first introduced in Italy, as in many other European countries, in 1919, following the end of the First World War. It was supported by all reformist forces, who hoped it 'would sweep away the corrupt personalised politics of [pre-war] *Giolittismo* and substitute a struggle of principle between disciplined mass parties' (Seton-Watson 1967: 514). But the new system was used in only two elections: Mussolini gained the premiership in 1922, and in 1923 inti-midated parliament into passing a new electoral law. Known as the Acerbo Law, this gave the party winning most votes (so long as that was more than 25 per cent of the total) two-thirds of all the seats (Carstairs 1980: 155–6; Seton-Watson 1967: 635). As it turned out, the Fascists used sufficient violence and voter intimidation in the election the following year to secure 69.9 per cent of the seats without the bonus, thereby rendering the manipulation of the electoral system superfluous

Table 6.1. *Summary of major electoral reform in Italy since 1945*

Year of reform or debate	Year of first use	New (or proposed) system
1946	1946	PR with preferential voting within lists, national pool, and low threshold
1953	1953	Bonus-adjusted PR
1954	1958	PR with preferential voting within lists, national pool, and low threshold
1993	1994	MMM with partial compensation
1994–2001	Not passed	Various schemes to enhance majoritarian character of system
2005	2006	Bonus-adjusted PR
2009	Not passed	Apply bonus to largest party rather than largest coalition

Note: See text for sources and details. For 1993 reform, see Chapter 9.

(Seton-Watson 1967: 648–9). Democracy was not restored until after Mussolini's defeat in the Second World War.

In 1946, proportional representation was re-adopted with little discussion: Einaudi (1946: 903) comments that 'no alternative to proportional representation was really ever contemplated'. All the members of a multi-party committee established to consider the electoral law in autumn 1945 supported PR. Agreement was not total: the Liberals favoured small district magnitudes and the left opposed compulsory voting. But compromise was reached without major dispute (Einaudi 1946: 903–4; Smyth 1948: 220). In a highly divided and uncertain context, all were keen to deny the possibility of an absolute majority to their opponents (Sidoti 1993: 109). The new system contained only weak limits on proportionality: the average district magnitude was high, at 20.3 seats; there was also a national pool of seats allocated to parties winning at least one regional seat and 300,000 votes nationwide (1.3 per cent of the valid votes cast in 1946). In addition, voters were able to express (depending on district magnitude) three or four preferences regarding individual candidates (Seton-Watson 1983: 111–12). This system was used to elect a constituent assembly in June 1946. The first Chamber of Deputies was elected in April 1948. A slightly modified system was used, the effect of which was to reduce the number of seats allocated in the national pool and therefore to limit marginally the proportionality of the system (see Carstairs 1980: 157–8). But the fundamentals were not altered.

The *legge truffa*, 1953

The Christian Democrats secured an absolute majority of the seats in the 1948 elections on the basis of 48.5 per cent of the votes (see Table 6.2). Yet this predominance was short-lived: in local elections held in 1951 and 1952, the party's vote share fell to just 35.1 per cent (Ginsborg 1990: 141). By 1952, the position of the four parties of the centre – the Christian Democrats, Social Democrats, Liberals, and Republicans – appeared threatened by the resurgence of the right (the Monarchists and the

Table 6.2. *Election results for the constituent assembly, 1946, and Chamber of Deputies, 1948 and 1953*

Party	1946		1948		1953	
	% votes	% seats	% votes	% seats	% votes	% seats
Centrists						
Christian Democrats (DC)	35.2	37.2	48.5	53.1	40.1	44.4
Liberals	6.8	7.4	3.8	3.3	3.0	2.4
Republicans	4.8	4.5	2.5	1.6	1.6	0.8
Social Democrats	–	–	7.1	5.7	4.5	3.2
Centrist dissidents						
Popular Unity	–	–	–	–	0.6	0
National Democratic Alliance (ADN)	–	–	–	–	0.5	0
Left						
Communists (PCI)	18.9	18.7	31.0*	22.8	22.6	24.2
Socialists (PSI)	20.7	20.7		9.1	12.7	12.7
Right						
Monarchists	2.8	2.9	2.8	2.4	6.9	6.8
Italian Social Movement (MSI)	–	–	2.0	1.0	5.8	5.0
Others	10.9	8.7	2.4	0.9	1.7	0.5

*Joint PCI–PSI list.
Sources: 1946 and 1948: Mackie and Rose (1991: 269, 271); 1953: LaPalombara (1953: 688).

neo-Fascist Italian Social Movement, MSI) and the continued strength of the Communists (PCI) and their Socialist (PSI) allies. We should remember that these were times of deep ideological conflict in Italian politics: neither the MSI nor the PCI was at all committed to parliamentary democracy; the PSI was also close to Moscow and it seriously considered merging with the Communists in 1951 (De Grand 1989: 121–2). As La Palombara (1953: 683) observed, 'If the trends of these elections were to prevail in 1953, it was obvious that the Parliament chosen under P.R. would be characterized by three power blocs, with the Center just able to muster a majority of the votes. This would mean unstable and disorderly government from which only the extremes could profit' (see, similarly, Piretti 2003: 25).

The situation that arose was thus very similar to that in France in 1951: forces that were not committed to parliamentary democracy threatened the ability of the democratic centre to maintain a stable parliamentary majority; whether they really believed that democracy was in danger, or simply accentuated this possibility in their rhetoric to mask a straightforward attempt to retain power, the centre parties sought a system that would strengthen the centre against the extremes. They opted for a revised version of the Acerbo Law of 1923: any party or coalition winning an absolute majority of the nationwide vote would win 380 (that is, 64.4 per cent) of the 590 Chamber seats; if no party or coalition won a majority, the PR list would operate as before (Pryce 1952: 271–3).

In analysing attitudes among politicians to the new electoral law, we can divide the parliamentary parties into three categories: the Christian Democrats, the other centrist parties, and the opposition parties of left and right. Though some in the Christian Democrats demurred (Grindrod 1955: 82–3; Piretti 2003: 34–5), the position of the party as a whole strongly favoured the majoritarian electoral reform. Indeed, some within the DC proposed a very much more drastic reform than eventually emerged: this would have given a party or coalition securing an absolute majority of the votes *three-quarters* of the seats; even if the largest party or coalition won only a plurality, it would have gained two-thirds of the seats.[1] Such proposals were clearly seat-maximizing for the Christian Democrats: they would allow the party to secure a substantial majority in the Chamber of Deputies even if its share of the vote fell below 50 per cent. On this basis, the scheme would also maximize the

---

[1] Piretti (2003: 34–5, 157); 'Aim of Italian Democrats: Move for Electoral Stability', *The Times*, 6 October 1952.

DC's power: an absolute majority would allow the party to govern with little interference from its smaller centrist allies.

Those centrist allies – the Liberals, Republicans, and Social Democrats – faced a tougher calculation. In terms of the simple Duvergerian mechanical effect, they could expect the bonus-adjusted system to maximize their seat shares: there are very few electoral systems that grant a bonus of seats to small parties, but this system would do just that. This was particularly attractive to the Social Democrats, who wanted to strength their hand *vis-à-vis* the Socialists: the bonus might allow them to surpass the Socialists in terms of seats (Piretti 2003: 64; Quagliariello 2003: 41). The system was also advantageous for these parties in terms of coalition dynamics. By locking the Christian Democrats into coalition with the centre, it would reduce the danger of the Christian Democrats' abandoning their existing allies – most probably the Social Democrats – in favour of an 'opening to the right' including the Monarchists (Kogan 1966: 76; Quagliariello 2003: 42). That this mattered to the smaller parties is indicated by the terms of the electoral cooperation deal signed by the four centrist parties in November 1952, which prevented any local alliances with other parties without the agreement of all four coalition partners.[2] From two other perspectives, however, the bonus-adjusted system was harmful to the small parties' power interests. First, while the new system would increase their seat shares, it would not enhance their power within the governing coalition. Their reasoning here was the reverse of the Christian Democrats': the small parties would be able to exert more leverage if the DC relied on their support for its majority; the new system, by facilitating a single-party majority, would therefore diminish their power. Second, some supporters of the small parties – particularly on the left wing of the Social Democrats – opposed the alliance with the Christian Democrats. By backing the electoral reform and entering into an electoral agreement with the DC, these parties risked blurring their independent identities and losing votes in the coming election.

The small parties therefore bargained hard with the Christian Democrats before agreeing to back the reform. In particular, they sought to reduce the size of the seat bonus and limit its application to a party or coalition winning an absolute majority of votes. Reducing the size of the bonus reduced their own expected seat shares, but it also limited the chances of an overall Christian Democrat majority. The cabinet initially

---

[2] 'Blow to Italian Communists', *The Times*, 17 November 1952.

agreed a scheme in October 1952, under which a party or coalition winning over 50 per cent of the votes would gain 383 (64.9 per cent) of the seats.[3] But the Liberals and Social Democrats remained uneasy and wanted to limit the bonus to between 360 and 370 seats; in agreeing the four-party electoral alliance in November, they extracted a further three-seat concession, and thus the bill took its final form, granting 380 seats to the majority coalition.[4] Even then, some in the small parties refused to back the deal, and the dissidents formed two splinter parties that came to haunt the centrist coalition in the elections of June 1953.

The remaining parties – the Communists and Socialists on the left and the Monarchists and neo-Fascists on the right – all bitterly opposed the reform. The Communists and Socialists labelled the new law 'la legge truffa' – 'the swindle law'. They used every delaying tactic in the book to impede the bill's passage (LaPalombara 1953: 685), and the parliamentary debates at times descended into physical violence.[5] They also called street demonstrations and strikes.[6] And they submitted a petition with over 500,000 signatures urging senators not to pass the bill and calling for a referendum. Citizen-initiated referendums, as we will see in Chapter 9, played a major role in the Italian electoral reforms of the early 1990s. By 1953, however, though the constitution envisaged this mechanism, the enabling legislation had not yet been drawn up, and the petition was therefore purely symbolic.[7] The Communists pressed the case for a referendum in parliament, but to no avail (Piretti 2003: 88).

The reasons for the opposition parties' hostility to the reform are not difficult to discern. Neither the left nor the right had any prospect of gaining the majority bonus for itself; the reform therefore reduced their expected seat shares. The reform was additionally harmful for those among the Monarchists and the Socialists interested in pursuing government office in coalition with the Christian Democrats: by solidifying the centre coalition, it reduced the likelihood of such a development.

---

[3] 'Election Bill in Italy', *The Times*, 20 October 1952.

[4] 'Political Dangers in Italy: New Electoral Law Obstructed', *The Times*, 14 November 1952; 'Blow to Italian Communists', *The Times*, 17 November 1952; LaPalombara (1953: 685n).

[5] E.g., 'Uproar in Italian Chamber: Deputies at Blows', *The Times*, 5 December 1952; 'Italian Reform Bill Passed: Scene of Violence in Senate', *The Times*, 30 March 1953.

[6] 'Italian Chamber's Long Sitting: Pointless Filibuster on Voting Law', *The Times*, 20 January 1953; 'Blow to Italian Communists: Electoral Bill Passed', *The Times*, 22 January 1953; 'Italian Reform Bill Passed: Scene of Violence in Senate', *The Times*, 30 March 1953.

[7] 'Stormy Scenes in Italian Senate: Prime Minister Taunted', *The Times*, 17 March 1953.

Despite all their protests, however, the opposition parties were unable to block the reform. The process of parliamentary passage was long and arduous; both chambers endured all-night sittings; the government's other business was severely disrupted. But the centre coalition held, and on 31 March – just two months before the elections – the president of the Republic signed the reform bill into law.

Repeal of the *legge truffa*, 1954

The passage of electoral reform in 1953 raised enormous passions on both sides and was the dominant item on the political agenda for many months. Yet little over a year later, in June 1954, the Chamber of Deputies voted by near cross-party consensus – by 427 votes to 75 in a secret ballot – to repeal the very same law (Atti Parlamentari 1954: 8964). The repeal of the *legge truffa* has received very little attention from either political scientists or historians. This presumably reflects the fact that it occurred so quietly. From an analytical point of view, however, it is a fascinating case: the composition of the government was in essence the same in 1954 as in 1953; how could the reformers who had struggled so hard to secure their objective one year give it up without a fight the following year?

That change can be attributed to the experiences of the 1953 election and its aftermath. Four principal effects may be noted. First, as Table 6.2 shows, the vote shares of all four centrist parties fell. The DC's reduced support was expected: it had already been clear in the local elections of 1951 and 1952. But the vote shares of the three small parties had held steady in the local elections (LaPalombara 1953: 686), and their losses in 1953 were perceived as directly attributable to the *legge truffa*. Their decline appears to have reflected two mechanisms. Some of their supporters simply regarded the reform as an unacceptable manipulation of the democratic process: the opposition's accusation that this was a *legge truffa* had resonated widely and been a persistent theme in the election campaign (Grindrod 1955: 82, 85, 87; Kogan 1966: 76); as Rich (1953: 478) suggests, 'To those who had followed the Social Democratic leadership because of its idealism and devotion to democratic principles this Machiavellism of [party leaders] Saragat and Romita was difficult to digest.' Others were perturbed, meanwhile, not so much by the principle of the reform as by the practice of coalition with the Christian Democrats. The Social Democrats' party congress in January 1952 had opposed such collaboration; a special congress reversed the decision the following October, but many remained opposed.[8] These two mechanisms caused the small coalition parties to lose votes, either to the existing parties of left or right, or to two splinter parties that emerged from the Liberals and Social Democrats: the National Democratic Alliance (ADN) and Popular Unity (*Unità Popolare*).

Second, while these vote losses were significant in themselves in shifting opinion regarding the 1953 law, they had the further effect of denying the coalition parties the prize of the electoral bonus: the combined vote share of these parties was 49.2 per cent; the combined vote share of the two centrist dissident parties was 1.1 per cent; particularly when defections to other parties are allowed for, it appears very likely that the centrists would have gained an absolute majority of votes without the electoral reform. The significance of this was of course symbolic: without the electoral reform, gaining an absolute majority of votes would have conferred no particular bonus. But the result was widely perceived as signifying the defeat of the electoral law, and the reform's opponents lost no time in highlighting their victory. Prime Minister De Gasperi himself recognized shortly after the election that the failure of the coalition parties to reach the 50 per cent threshold meant that 'the law must be viewed as having fallen into disuse' (Piretti 2003: 214).

Third, the law had been justified as essential in order to protect democracy from imminent danger. But the mechanism introduced by the law did not operate – the majority threshold was not reached – and yet democracy survived. Indeed, the first post-election government was formed by Giuseppe Pella with the parliamentary support (though not the cabinet participation) of the Monarchists. Given these developments, many of the arguments offered in defence of the law during its passage were no longer credible.

Finally, several of the parties began at this time to rethink their coalition strategies. Not only did a limited 'opening to the right' occur in the form, as just noted, of Monarchist support for the Pella government: in addition, the possibility of an 'opening to the left' began also to be taken seriously. The Social Democrats initially refused to support a DC-led government after the 1953 elections without the participation of the PSI; the Socialists had begun to distance themselves from the Communists earlier in the year, and PSI leader Pietro Nenni signalled

---

[8] Grindrod (1955: 83); 'Socialists at Loggerheads: Italian Congress Disunity', *The Times*, 8 January 1952; 'Aim of Italian Democrats: Move for Electoral Stability', *The Times*, 6 October 1952.

his willingness to enter a centre-left coalition immediately after the election. At the time, the PSI's links with the PCI and Moscow meant the DC refused to countenance such a move: it was not until 1963 that the PSI entered the governing coalition (De Grand 1989: 137–8; Grindrod 1955: 99–105). But the future possibility was taken seriously, and the rigid coalition lines assumed by the 1953 electoral law came to seem increasingly anachronistic.

Thus, the repeal in part simply reflected a changed perception among the small centrist parties of the law's impact on their vote-seeking interests, and these parties made abrogation of the law a condition of their participation in the Scelba government formed in February 1954.[9] More widely, however, the law failed to reflect the more fluid coalition possibilities that began – tentatively – to emerge after 1953. And, most fundamentally, any moral defence of the law simply became untenable. The argument that the law was a *truffa* – a swindle – was seen to have won in the 1953 election. The argument that this was a manipulation needed in the defence of democracy – that noble ends justified the dubious means – became unsustainable in the months that followed. The law thus had many vocal opponents and no audible defenders. This circumstance does not, of course, lead automatically to reform: as the failure of reform in France in 1955 shows, a further crucial condition is agreement on an alternative. In Italy too there was some disagreement: the small parties wanted not merely to return to the 1948 law, but to secure a still more proportional system under which they hoped to win more seats (Piretti 2003: 216). This delayed abrogation for a year. Nevertheless, a path forward was found: in June 1954, the *legge truffa* was repealed and the 1948 law restored; at the same time, the government was asked to draw up proposals for a new system based on PR; this was finally passed in 1957, slightly increasing the proportionality of the 1948 system without disturbing its essence (Carstairs 1980: 159; Pryce 1957: 320–1).

Intense debate but no reform, 1994–2001

The most widely discussed electoral reform of the post-war era in Italy – that of 1993 – is analysed not here, but in Part III. Suffice for now to say that in 1993 the PR system was replaced with a semi-compensatory mixed system; slightly different variants were used for the Chamber of

[9] 'New Electoral Law in Italy: Cabinet Consideration', *The Times*, 15 June 1954.

Deputies and for the Senate, but in each chamber 75 per cent of seats were elected through single-member plurality and 25 per cent by closed-list PR. This outcome was a compromise between reform advocates and the majority of parliamentarians: the former wanted SMP or a two-round system in order (*inter alia*) to foster a two-party system (or at least bipolarization), thereby allowing alternation in power, improved accountability and governability, and less corruption; the latter wanted to preserve as much of the status quo as they could get away with (Furlong 2002: 19; Katz 1996: 37).

The reform fulfilled its advocates' expectations to a degree: progressive bipolarization of the party system into two distinct blocs did occur (Bartolini, Chiaramonte, and D'Alimonte 2004); the 2001 election brought clean alternation of governing coalitions for the first time in the history of united Italy (Bellucci and Bull 2002: 29); Silvio Berlusconi in 2006 became the first prime minister to serve a full five-year term since Alcide De Gasperi, who held office for seven years between 1946 and 1953. But the reformers were also disappointed: in the early post-reform years, governments remained just as unstable as ever – indeed, even including the Berlusconi years, the average government duration was just fifteen months (Pasquino 2007: 86); and party fragmentation, despite bipolarization, remained high (Bartolini, Chiaramonte, and D'Alimonte 2004).

Thus, pressure for further change – for the 'completion' of the reforms of 1993 – continued. Every government that held office between 1994 and 2001 pledged such reform, often as part of a wider package of constitutional change. Silvio Berlusconi, during his first stint as prime minister, between April and December 1994, sought a pure SMP system.[10] His successor, Lamberto Dini, who headed a technocratic administration for a year from January 1995, reformed the regional electoral system (Donovan 2000: 53–4),[11] but was toppled from office having failed to enact pure SMP for the Chamber of Deputies.[12] A brief attempt was made in February 1996 by Antonio Maccanico to form another interim government with the explicit purpose of enacting electoral reforms before calling fresh elections, but the bid was abandoned after Maccanico failed to secure adequate parliamentary support (Daniel

---

[10] 'Northern Cool in the Neapolitan Heat', *Financial Times*, 9 July 1994.
[11] 'Italians Vote in Key Test for Parties', *Financial Times*, 24 April 1994.
[12] 'Caretaker PM Sets Out Bold Vision to Reform Italian Politics', *Independent*, 12 October 1995.

Williams 1996). A centre-left alliance under Romano Prodi came to power following the elections of April 1996 promising reform (Gumbel 1996), leading to the creation of a Bicameral Commission on constitutional revision, headed by the leader of the post-communist Democratic Party of the Left (PDS), Massimo D'Alema. The Bicamerale came up with a messy compromise electoral system under which 55 per cent of the seats would have been elected by SMP and 25 per cent by PR, while the remaining 20 per cent would have been awarded to the winning coalition (Pasquino 1998: 49). Yet the deal unravelled in early 1998 after Berlusconi withdrew, apparently because he did not get the judicial reforms he wanted (Fusaro 1998; Köppl 2004: 10–12; Pasquino 2000). D'Alema was one of the keenest advocates of reform among major party leaders: his long-term political strategy depended on the consolidation of the bipolar structure of party competition. Thus, he made electoral reform one of his top priorities when he succeeded to the premiership in October 1998 (Stanley 1998), and in February 1999 his government proposed a system under which 90 per cent of seats would have been filled by a two-round ballot, while the remaining 10 per cent would have been split evenly between the winning coalition and parties belonging to no coalition.[13] Yet this, too, got nowhere. Finally, the successor to the D'Alema government, headed by Giuliano Amato, came close over the summer of 2000 to proposing a system based largely on the German model of MMP, using a 5 per cent threshold to prevent excessive fragmentation in the PR component and giving a bonus for the largest party in order to improve governability (Pasquino 2001: 44–5, 50–1n). Again, however, the idea was abandoned.

In parallel with these processes at parliamentary level, four attempts were made during this period to pursue reform by means of referendum. Referendum petitions were rejected by the Constitutional Court in 1995 and 1997 (Donovan 2000: 57; Graham 1995), but referendums were held in 1999 and 2000. The 1999 vote, sponsored by many of the leaders of the reform campaign of the early 1990s, would have kept the 75 per cent of seats elected by SMP; the remaining 25 per cent, however, would have been awarded region by region to the losing district candidates with the most votes (Donovan 2000: 56). Given the restrictions on the admissibility of referendum questions – they could be abrogative only and could not leave a constitutional vacuum in which the country was left with no

[13] 'Italian Government Proposes Electoral Reform Bill', *Agence France Presse*, 12 February 1999.

operable electoral system – this was the closest the reform campaigners could get to their true goal of SMP. Though 91.5 per cent of those voting supported reform, the referendum failed because the turnout – 49.6 per cent – fell just short of the 50 per cent required. The legitimacy of this result was highly questionable – the electoral rolls 'included many who were either dead or uncontactable' (Donovan 2000: 61) – but a legal challenge failed. The 2000 referendum was in many ways a rerun of the poll one year earlier, and it would have enacted the same electoral reform if passed. Despite a clean-up of the electoral register, however, turnout collapsed to just 32.4 per cent (of whom 82 per cent supported reform). The voters, it appeared, were weary of years of bickering and stalling over the electoral rules, and the momentum behind reform was lost (Fabbrini 2001).

Principled pursuit of values played a role in these events: key advocates of reform from the early 1990s, such as Mario Segni and Marco Pannella, continued to promote referendums and argue for a pure SMP electoral system, even though it was clear by this stage that the bipolarization of the party system after the 1993 reforms had harmed their own prospects of gaining any significant elected office. As I argue in Chapter 12, conventional political careerism was not the primary driver of these individuals' engagement in politics.

Nevertheless, it was the narrow power interests of the various parties that predominated. The most consistent advocates of majoritarian reform in parliament were the post-Fascist National Alliance (AN), led by Gianfranco Fini, and the post-communist Democratic Party of the Left (PDS) under D'Alema. Both parties' predecessors had been excluded from power during the centripetal era of Christian Democratic dominance before 1993, and both parties' strategies post-1994 depended upon bipolar competition between alliances of left and right, within which they could play prominent roles. Among the key opponents of further moves away from PR, meanwhile, were the small parties of the centre. We might expect small parties to prefer PR because it allows them a greater seat share. But this was not, in fact, the main consideration: stand-down deals among the parties within the coalitions meant that the SMP component of the system was 'proportionalized' in its outcomes; most small parties, having high blackmail potential *vis-à-vis* their larger counterparts, in fact gained most of their seats by this route (D'Alimonte 2001, 2005; Sartori 2000: 18–19). Rather, these parties were principally concerned with the dynamics of coalition politics: at the least, they wanted to retain their independence within the coalitions and avoid being swamped by their larger partners; but really they hankered after a return to the centripetal pattern of competition from which they had done so well before 1993.

Berlusconi, meanwhile, changed his position regarding electoral reform over the years. He entered politics in 1994 in order to promote bipolarism, sought further majoritarian reform during his first, brief period as prime minister in 1994, and again campaigned in 1996 on a similar platform. But in February 1998 he declared himself in favour of PR (Blitz 1998), in 1999 he failed to support the electoral reform referendum (Donovan 2000: 60), and in the 2000 referendum he argued explicitly for abstention (Fabbrini 2001: 46). The principal factors in this shift appear to have been manoeuvring over judicial reforms and his need to keep the centrist parties on board in order to return to power. Fabbrini (2001: 49) suggests that Berlusconi's reversal formed part of a broader strategy to reposition his own Forza Italia as 'a Christian social party of the Centre'.

Thus, partisan interests dominated during this period. But the calculation of the Duvergerian effects of different electoral systems upon the parties' seat shares played only a small role. Rather, competing interests in respect of coalition formation dominated. None of the reform efforts succeeded because, at every stage, governing coalitions relied upon the support of parties whose interests diverged on this dimension.

Adoption of bonus-adjusted PR, 2005

Following the elections of May 2001, a new centre-right government came to power under Prime Minister Silvio Berlusconi comprising four main parties: Forza Italia, Fini's AN, the Lega Nord (Northern League) of Umberto Bossi, and a successor to the old Christian Democrats, the Union of Christian Democrats and Democrats of the Centre (UDC).[14] Despite some talk of electoral reform in the course of the electoral campaign,[15] and though some minor reform proposals were made,[16] the early years of the Berlusconi government were a period of calm in the hitherto relentless electoral reform debate. Only in 2004 did the issue of major electoral reform return to the agenda: the UDC demanded a

---

[14] This section draws on research conducted with Chris Hanretty and David Hine. For a more detailed account, see Renwick, Hanretty, and Hine (2009).

[15] 'Key Berlusconi Ally Reveals Secret Governing Pact', *Agence France Presse*, 5 April 2001.

[16] See legislative proposals C. 2712, C.3304, and C. 2620, submitted in 2002 and 2003 (Camera dei Deputati 2002/3).

return to PR as a quid pro quo for the party's acceptance of wider
constitutional reforms (involving federalization and the strengthening
of the office of prime minister) that the other coalition partners were
pushing.[17] Berlusconi initially indicated a willingness to discuss the
matter (Magri 2004), but subsequently, in December 2004, proposed
only a slight adjustment of the existing system.[18]

It was not until June 2005, when the UDC pressed the matter again,
that reform began in earnest. The UDC's initial proposal was to switch
around the existing mixed-member system and elect 75 per cent of the
seats through PR, 25 per cent by SMP.[19] Intensive intra-coalition negotiations followed. On 13 September the government published proposals
for a system based largely on PR, but with the addition of a seat bonus for
the largest party or coalition that would guarantee it 55 per cent of the
seats in each chamber (excluding the eight Chamber seats and six Senate
seats elected by Italians abroad).[20] The bill was signed into law on
23 December having undergone some further amendments in the course
of its parliamentary passage. Of these, two were particularly significant.
First, the bonus, which was originally to go to the party or coalition
winning most seats, in the final law was granted to the party or coalition
winning most votes. This meant that votes cast for parties falling below
the threshold for entering parliament would count towards their coalition's total. Second, in the Senate, reflecting concerns over the constitu-
tionality of the original proposals, the allocation of the bonus was
switched from national to regional level; this had the effect of making a
clear Senate majority for one coalition less likely and has been a major
source of pressure for yet more reform in the years since. Though the new
system has widely been said to restore 'full proportional representation'
(e.g., Barber 2005b; Hooper 2005; Rizzo 2005), this, given the seat bonus,
is wrong. The system does, it is true, allow high party system fragmentation, but it also provides considerable incentives for the coalescence of
parties into rival blocks, and it guarantees the winning coalition a working majority, at least in the lower chamber.

This reform was initiated less than a year before an election that polls
at the time suggested the coalition parties were almost certain to lose, and

[17] 'Il proporzionale che piace ai centristi', *La Stampa*, 11 July 2004; Vassallo (2005: 128–9).
[18] 'Verso le urne – Berlusconi rilancia su legge elettorale e presenze in tv', *Il Sole 24 Ore*,
10 December 2004; D'Alimonte (2004).
[19] Amendments no. 1.5 to 1.13, made by deputies Volonte, di Giandomenico, and Mazzoni
(all UDC) (Camera dei deputati 2005: 39–65).
[20] 'Legge elettorale, la Cdl accelera', *Corriere della Sera*, 14 September 2005.

it was passed into law less than four months before the election against vehement opposition protests. Given these circumstances, it will come as no surprise that the reform was designed with the power interests of the politicians and parties involved firmly in mind. But the range of power-seeking considerations that came into play was enormous, including almost all those, at least on the outcome-contingent side, that were introduced in Chapter 2.

Though some have interpreted the Italian reform of 2005 solely in terms of simple seat-maximization (e.g., Floridia 2007: 3; Mannheimer 2005; Pasquino 2007: 81), this view is not really plausible. Looking at the seat share of the coalition as a whole, various projections published in autumn 2005 suggested that the new electoral system could reduce the centre-left's post-election majority by no more than thirty-eight seats, and under some assumptions it could in fact increase it by fourteen seats. Thus, any seat gain for the centre-right would be small and uncertain. More importantly, while the reform might have *increased* the centre-right's expected seat share somewhat, it certainly did not *maximize* it: given that the governing coalition's prospects of winning the bonus were slim, it would have been better off introducing PR without the bonus. Looking, alternatively, at the seat shares of the individual parties within the coalition, the picture is more complex. The standard Duvergerian mechanisms would lead us to predict that a shift to a more proportional system would benefit the smaller coalition parties: the UDC and the Lega Nord. In fact, however, as noted above, the parties within each coalition agreed detailed stand-down arrangements for the single-member districts before each election, and these were the principal determinants of the intra-coalition distribution of seats. Given the bargaining advantage of the smaller parties, they were significantly over-represented, while Forza Italia was under-represented. Thus, reversion to PR for intra-coalition seat allocation would enhance Forza Italia's seat share, while lowering the shares of the other parties. This may partially explain Berlusconi's endorsement of the reform, but it cannot explain why it was initiated by the UDC and backed by the AN and Lega Nord.

In building a fuller account of the power calculations that were involved in this reform, it is sensible to begin with the initiator of the reform – the UDC – whose goal was to return the electoral system as far as possible to proportionality. Its main concern was unchanged from the late 1990s: as a centrist successor to the Christian Democrats, it wanted to rebuild the centre as an independent force in Italian politics, free of the need to align with either left or right and able to negotiate governing coalitions on its own terms after each election. Seeing the 1993 electoral system as the principal source of bipolarization, it wished to return essentially to the system that had been used before (Massetti 2006: 263).

The other coalition parties were willing to consider the UDC's demands in part because to have done otherwise would have endangered their own constitutional reform plans and the future of the coalition itself (Massetti 2006: 264). Electoral reform was a quid pro quo for the UDC's acquiescence in those wider constitutional changes, and also for the UDC's dropping a demand, deeply opposed by Berlusconi, for primaries to elect the coalition's leader (Pasquino 2007: 81–2).

In addition to this bargaining across issue domains, however, the other parties could also expect to benefit in some ways from a proportional electoral system in itself. First, the positive effect on Forza Italia's seat share has already been noted. Second, PR would enhance the parties' independence from each other, for now they could run candidates nationwide under their own labels, rather than supporting candidates from other parties under the coalition label. Third, past experience suggested that the combined vote share of the centre-right parties was greater when they ran separately rather than as a single bloc: voters loyal to one party may have been reluctant to give their vote to a candidate coming from another, or to endorse the coalition as a whole (Newell 2006: 804; Pasquino 2007: 81). Fourth, negotiating stand-down agreements was a costly process, and was likely to be particularly acrimonious ahead of the 2006 elections in the light of the coalition's diminished expected vote share. Avoiding this process would ease coalition tensions and focus attention instead on competing with the opposition. Finally, the reform was negotiated by a small number of party leaders, whose intra-party power could be enhanced by PR with closed lists.

Yet the UDC's coalition partners, while willing to countenance a system with a substantial proportional element, were not prepared to accept the UDC's original proposals. This was for the simple reason that Forza Italia and, particularly, the AN were wedded to bipolarism and would not accept reform likely to erode it. The maintenance of bipolarism was the primary criterion by which Fini judged possible electoral systems: in autumn 2004, responding to the UDC's first demand for PR, he said, 'we are not against discussing proposals for reform, so long as they maintain democratic alternation in power and the logic of bipolarism' (quoted in Verderami 2004). Similarly, as the debate gathered speed in early September 2005, he said, 'the Alleanza Nazionale is ready to discuss the electoral law … but "the era of bipolarism" cannot be rolled-back'.[21] For these parties, the bonus-adjusted system was ideal: it gave them the aspects of PR, just described, that they liked; but it also ensured that the pressures for bipolar party competition would survive undiminished.

We understand, then, why the UDC initially demanded PR and why the other coalition parties accepted that demand, but with the modification of the majority bonus. But why, then, did the UDC accept this compromise? Having sought reform primarily to escape bipolarism, it ended up accepting an outcome designed precisely to keep bipolarism as before. On the face of things, we come up against a conundrum. The principal dimension of concern among the coalition parties regarding the electoral system was the degree to which it enhanced or hindered the bipolarization of the party system. Different parties within the coalition occupied positions on opposite sides of the status quo in respect of this issue, which should mean, in theory, that alteration of that status quo was impossible. And yet, reform was passed. The answer appears to be that, while the bipolarism dimension was the main one, it was not the only consideration that mattered. The reform roughly maintained the status quo in respect of bipolarism, but the UDC gained, as did the other parties, from the other aspects of PR cited above: in particular, greater intra-coalition independence, greater capacity to garner votes, and greater power within the party for its leaders. While these gains were much less than the party wanted, to have played for more just months before a general election would have been risky.

The Italian reform of 2005 is perhaps the most complex of all the cases of elite majority imposition studied here. Seat-maximization on its own cannot account for it: indeed, at the 2006 election, the party that initiated the change suffered a fall in its seat share despite doubling its vote share because of the loss of its bargaining strength in stand-down negotiations. The main concern of the various parties was the structure of the party system and pattern of coalition building, yet this too can get us only so far in explaining the outcome. Rather, we need also to take account of several further effects of PR – upon the parties' capacity to garner votes, their independence from each other, the costs of coalition management, and the distribution of intra-party power – in order to complete the picture.

The 2005 reform did not generate a stable outcome: the centre-left government that entered office following the elections of April 2006 vowed to replace the law; the new system was denounced even by its

---

[21] 'AN: Esecutivo parte in salita', *ANSA Notizario Generale*, 7 September 2005.

principal author, Roberto Calderoli (Barber 2006). But the centre-left government collapsed in January 2008 having lost its Senate majority: yet another government came and went without delivering a sustainable electoral system. Meanwhile, yet another referendum campaign was launched, and succeeded in gathering sufficient signatures to force a vote.[22] This was held in June 2009. Had it passed, it would have transferred the majority bonus from the largest coalition to the largest party, thereby creating strong pressure not just for bipolarism, but for two-partism (Baldini 2009: 10–12). As in 1999 and 2000, however, though a clear majority (in this case, 77.6 per cent) of those voting favoured the change, turnout (at just 23.3 per cent) fell below the required 50 per cent, and the referendum was therefore invalid (Ministero dell'Interno 2009). Thus, though the desire to 'complete' electoral reform remains strong in Italy, no route to that completion has yet been found. The issue remains high on the political agenda.

[22] 'Electoral Reform Referendum OK'd', *ANSA English Media Service*, 16 January 2008.

7

Japan: the persistence of SNTV

For most of the five decades following the Second World War, the lower house (House of Representatives) of Japan's Diet was elected using the system of single non-transferable vote (SNTV), under which voters cast a vote for one candidate in a multi-member district, and candidates were elected in order of their vote tallies until all the seats were filled. The reform that abolished this system, enacted after years of debate in 1994, took the form of elite–mass interaction, and is therefore discussed in Part III. In this chapter, I focus on four earlier episodes, summarized in Table 7.1. Reform was achieved in two of these episodes (in 1945 and 1947); in the remaining two (in 1956 and 1973), it was proposed but subsequently abandoned. The last three are all cases of actual or putative reform by elite majority imposition; the first, conducted in the immediate wake of the Second World War and heavily influenced by the Allied occupying powers, involved elite–external interaction. I briefly set the scene by describing the origins of the status quo at the time the first of these episodes occurred.

Japanese electoral reforms, 1889–1945

Japan was not a democracy during the early decades of the twentieth century, but it did have a popularly elected lower house whose approval was required – alongside that of the unelected Privy Council and House of Peers – for all legislation. The lower house was initially elected, from 1889, using single-member plurality (SMP). SNTV, combined with districts of up to twelve members, was first introduced in 1900, but SMP was readopted in 1919. SNTV was restored in 1925, this time taking the form familiar from post-war years, based on districts of between three and five seats, and it survived until the Second World War.

SMP appears in 1889 to have been borrowed without much reflection from the United Kingdom (Fukui 1988: 126, 131; Ramseyer and Rosenbluth 1995: 44–6), while the reasons for the change in 1900 have been heavily

Table 7.1. *Summary of major electoral reform in Japan since 1945*

Year of reform or debate	Year of first use	New (or proposed) system
1945	1946	Limited vote with districts of 4–14 seats
1947	1947	SNTV with districts of 3–5 seats
1956	Not passed	SMP in most districts; SNTV in 22 two-member districts
1973	Not passed	MMM
1994	1996	MMM

Note: See text for sources and details. For 1994 reform, see Chapter 10.

disputed (Fukui 1988: 128; Kawato 2002: 181–2; Ramseyer and Rosenbluth 1995: 44–6). In 1919 the lower house was dominated by two large parties, whose interests were well served by the adoption of a more majoritarian system. The oligarchs who dominated the unelected branches of government could also be persuaded to back SMP on the basis of the perceived communist threat in the wake of the Russian Revolution (Ramseyer and Rosenbluth 1995: 46–7). By 1925, however, there were three principal parties, and the continued use of SMP was risky for them all (Ramseyer and Rosenbluth 1995: 49–50). Furthermore, the parties had been forced by public pressure to accept universal adult male suffrage (Quigley 1926: 394), and the quadrupling of the electorate added to uncertainty (Kawato 2002: 183). SNTV combined with what in Japanese parlance are called 'medium-sized districts' would reduce this uncertainty without lowering the threshold so far as to admit the left.

Immediately following the Second World War, in December 1945, however, this system was replaced with a 'large-district' system: district magnitude ranged between four and fourteen seats; voters had two or three votes depending on the number of seats in the district.[1] In the language of international political science, the system was one of limited vote. Given the higher district magnitudes, this system made it easier for smaller parties to win Diet seats.

Three interpretations of the 1945 change exist in the literature. According to one, primary responsibility for the new electoral system

---

[1] In principle, voters in districts with three or fewer seats had only one vote. But no district in fact fell into this category (Kohno 1997: 37).

belonged not to domestic actors, but to Japan's American occupiers, who wanted 'to eliminate vestiges of militarism by breaking the stranglehold of conservative parties' (Woodall 1999: 27; see, similarly, Fukui 1988: 130). The second account attributes similar motivation to domestic bureaucrats. Kawato (2002: 183) claims, 'The commonly accepted view is that there was no intervention from the General Headquarters of the Allied Occupation Forces (GHQ)' and argues that Home Ministry bureaucrats sought 'to undermine the basis of the existing parties and to promote election of popularly supported national notables and newcomers suitable for the new situations'. Finally, the third view emphasizes political parties. Kohno (1997: 34–7) acknowledges that GHQ vetoed the preference of the largest party – the Progressive Party – for SMP, but argues that the Progressives believed the limited vote system would also serve their goal of undermining new parties.

The existence of these multiple interpretations reflects the fact that these were confused and confusing times. The new electoral law was passed by the Diet on 15 December, little more than four months after the bombing of Hiroshima and Nagasaki. The Japanese political scene was in turmoil. The position of the occupation forces was still in rapid flux: GHQ's Government Section, which in February 1946 would draft the basis of Japan's new post-war constitution, had not yet consolidated. Nevertheless, it appears very likely that the steer for the new electoral system did come from the occupying powers. Early American policy focused upon breaking the power of the old militaristic regime (Williams 1979: 14–15). The Japanese government would initially be subject to heavy control by the occupation authorities: a return to representative Japanese government was stated as an 'eventual' rather than an immediate goal (US Government 1949 [1945]: 423). Thus, the primary purpose of the new electoral system was not to guarantee effective government: this would be achieved through diktat from above. Rather, two goals were paramount: first, the development of pro-democratic ideas and values among the Japanese people; second, the fostering of new democratic parties and a new democratic political elite that could, in time, constitute a fully responsible government. As the major statement of US policy in the early phase of occupation stated, 'The Japanese people shall be encouraged to develop a desire for individual liberties and respect for fundamental human rights, particularly the freedoms of religion, assembly, speech, and the press. They shall also be encouraged to form democratic and representative organizations' (US Government 1949 [1945]: 423).

GHQ certainly intervened in the formulation of the new electoral system: specifically, General MacArthur, the Supreme Commander for the Allied Powers, commanded the extension of the franchise to women in order 'to bring to Japan a new concept of government directly subservient to the well being of the home' (MacArthur 1949 [1945]): 741). Replacement of the pre-war medium-district SNTV system with the large-district limited vote system was entirely consonant with the early occupation goals. First, by permitting greater party system fragmentation, it would allow new forces to enter the Diet via Duverger's mechanical effect. Second, the conservatives had become increasingly entrenched over the pre-war period in their secure local bailiwicks, or *jiban*; the enlargement of districts would dilute these *jiban* and weaken their influence over election outcomes (Bisson 1949: 57; Ward 1966: 551). The available evidence does not demonstrate conclusively that the shift to large districts was indeed spurred by the Americans, but it tends in that direction: most specifically, Justin Williams, a senior official in the Government Section, states in his memoirs that the large district system was adopted 'at the urging' of and 'on instructions from' the State Department's arm in Japan (Williams 1979: 176, 225).

As to why this prompting apparently met no significant resistance from the Japanese parties, Kohno's suggestion that the limited vote system in large districts was seen by the Progressives as little different from SMP is implausible: this system would manifestly generate greater party system fragmentation than SMP, as Japanese politicians could well predict from pre-war experience. That the Progressives – who held an overwhelming majority of Diet seats at the time the reform was enacted (Table 7.2) – nevertheless pursued only relatively minor concessions in the direction of SMP (Uchida 1987: 320-1) in large part simply reflects their very weak position *vis-à-vis* GHQ. But it should be remembered also that the political situation was highly fluid. A democratic election based (for the first time) on universal adult suffrage would be very different from the previous, wholly undemocratic election of 1942, and the new party system was still emerging. This uncertain context probably contributed to politicians' willingness to accept a more permissive electoral system.

Thus, the 1945 electoral reform belongs to the category of elite-external interaction: the concerns of both the foreign occupiers and domestic actors are likely to have influenced the reform process and the outcome.

That outcome was not entirely settled by the passage of the new electoral law in December 1945: it still had to gain final approval from GHQ. The

Table 7.2. *Election outcomes and Diet composition in Japan, 1945–1949*

Party	December 1945 % seats*	April 1946 % votes	April 1946 % seats	April 1947 % votes	April 1947 % seats	January 1949 % votes	January 1949 % seats
Progressive Party**	57.9	18.7	20.3	25.0	26.0	15.7	14.8
Liberal Party	9.7	24.4	30.2	26.9	28.1	43.9	56.7
Cooperative Party	5.6	3.2	3.0	7.0	6.2	3.4	3.0
Socialists (JSP)	3.6	17.8	19.8	26.2	30.7	13.5	10.3
Communists (JCP)	–	3.8	1.1	3.7	0.8	9.7	7.5
Independents	10.9	20.4	17.4	5.8	2.8	6.6	2.6
Others	–	11.7	8.2	5.4	5.4	5.2	3.6
Vacancies	12.2						

* Seat shares as at the dissolution of the Diet, 16 December.
** Renamed the Democratic Party in 1947.
Sources: 1945: Uchida (1987: 321); 1946–1949: Stockwin (2008: 273–4).

law's passage coincided with the appointment of a new Government Section head, General Courtney Whitney. With his arrival, primary policy-making power shifted from the State Department to the Government Section, and priorities shifted from slaying the old enemy to building up the new system (cf. Williams 1979: 159). Some in the Government Section wanted to impose American electoral practices, including the SMP electoral system and American-style ballot papers and campaign rules. But Whitney resisted this and allowed the new law to pass (Masumi 1985: 93; Williams 1979: 75–8). It is presumably on the basis of this later episode that Kawato argues GHQ played no important role. This was an impression that GHQ was keen to foster: it knew the new law would gain greater legitimacy if seen as a Japanese creation (Masumi 1985: 93; Whitney 1955: 244). Nevertheless, the Americans' influence earlier in the design process does appear to have been significant.

The readoption of SNTV, 1947

The new electoral system was to survive for just one election. As Table 7.2 shows, three main parties emerged from that election, held in April 1946: the Liberals, Progressives, and Socialists (JSP). But the electoral system also facilitated substantial fragmentation: large numbers of independents were elected, and the Communist Party (JCP) gained representation for the first time. The conservative forces of the Liberal and Progressive parties, who combined to form a governing coalition, were greatly dissatisfied. They wanted a system that would limit fragmentation while still allowing their own distinct parties to survive, and a return to the SNTV system in medium-sized districts suited this purpose well (Kohno 1997: 39–40). Whitney initially rejected this move (Masumi 1985: 139), but Prime Minister Shigeru Yoshida took the matter direct to General MacArthur himself. With the Cold War emerging, MacArthur shared the conservative politicians' desire to contain the left, and he therefore gave his blessing to the change (Kawato 2002: 183–4; Ward 1966: 551–2; Woodall 1999: 26–7). Seeing that the reform was directed against them, independents and left-wing groups bitterly opposed it. The Socialists and Communists both wanted a proportional system and refused all compromise (Kohno 1997: 39). The government finally pushed the bill through the Diet just two weeks before the elections of April 1947 'with the police surrounding the parliament building, ready to enter in the event of a riot' (Kohno 1997: 43).

This was thus an unambiguous case of reform by elite majority imposition: the political majority conceived of the reform as a means to consolidate its own power, and it imposed the new system over the fierce opposition of other parties. The reform had its desired effect. As Table 7.2 shows, party fragmentation fell substantially in the 1947 election. Furthermore, though the JSP's seat share rose considerably, Schonberger (1989: 103) argues that the new electoral system contained that growth, estimating that it cost the party around fifty seats.

The 'Hatomander' of 1956

The reform of 1947 satisfied the power objectives of its proponents. But it also restored perceived ills of the SNTV system that reformers had sought to overcome in 1945. Those ills – which came to play an important role in the process leading to reform in 1994 – were, in summary, that SNTV encouraged money politics and factionalism and hindered the development of programmatic parties and coherent leadership. As Ward (1966: 548) summed it up, 'By fostering campaign abuses, disunity, and internecine warfare within parties, and by placing a premium on local as opposed to national issues and upon considerations of personality rather than of policy, it [SNTV] tends to produce a type and quality of representation in the lower house that is doing serious harm to the national interests.' The adoption of a system of single-member plurality was widely seen as offering a solution to these problems (Ward 1966: 561). Home Ministry officials created a series of research councils to investigate electoral law reforms, and as early as 1951 one of these councils recommended the adoption of SMP (Schuller 1998: 116; Ward 1966: 554).

Initially, no significant reform action was taken at the political level. But the situation changed in 1955. The first ten post-war years were a period of considerable flux in the Japanese party system; 1955 brought that period to a close. First, in October, the two wings of the Socialists, which had been in tension for some time and formally split in 1951, reunited (Neary 2002: 78). Then, recognizing the dangers of division in the face of the Socialists' renewed unity, the two main conservative parties – Liberal and Democratic (formerly the Progressives) – merged in November to form the Liberal Democratic Party (LDP), which went on to dominate Japanese politics, with only one short break, until it was ejected in August 2009 (Neary 2002: 62). With the creation of a two-party system, the adoption of SMP came to serve not only the value of tackling clientelism, but also the power interests of the ruling political elite. Specifically, the LDP could expect such a change to augment its share of the seats in the lower chamber (Ward 1966: 561).

Thus, the government, headed by LDP leader and Prime Minister Ichirō Hatoyama, brought forward proposals for reform. These proposals were based on the recommendations of the latest research council, which, like its predecessors, had argued the case for SMP. But an LDP committee changed the council's recommendations in two respects. First, in addition to 467 single-member districts, the Hatoyama bill made provision for 22 two-member districts in which SNTV would be retained. These were located in areas where single-member districts would threaten the positions of LDP incumbents. Second, the committee changed many district boundaries, again in a manner beneficial to LDP incumbents, thereby earning for the bill the popular title of 'Hatomander' (Ward 1966: 553–4).

As the other of the two parties in the newly founded two-party system, we might expect the JSP to have supported the introduction of SMP, which would protect it from the emergence of smaller challengers. But even after the party's initial vehement protests had led the government to drop the districting provisions, the JSP continued to oppose the bill strongly. It saw no immediate prospect of winning a majority against the united LDP. Its opposition thus derived from a primary focus on its own short-term seat share, which it prioritized over potentially favourable long-term effects upon the development of the party system (Curtis 1999: 146; Ward 1966: 562). Facing strong opposition both in the Diet and from the public, the government allowed the bill to die in the upper house. Under parliamentary rules, the opposition had considerable capacity to deploy delaying tactics if it wished; with other important matters on its legislative agenda, and fearing for its future popularity, the government decided this was not a fight that it was in its interests to wage (Curtis 1999: 146; Ward 1966: 554).

Tanaka's reform bid, 1973

The reform issue simmered throughout the 1960s. The start of that decade saw the upgrading of the research councils that had looked into electoral law during the 1950s, and the first of a series of Electoral System Advisory Councils (*Senkyo Seido Shingikai*) reported in 1961 (Schuller 1998: 116). These Councils discussed a variety of alternatives to the status quo, including pure SMP, MMM, and MMP; but little genuine progress was made (Reed and Thies 2001: 159–61). Some observers did see the beginnings of movement by the mid-1960s (Farnsworth 1966; Ward 1966: 562–7). But it was not until 1973 that a further serious reform attempt was made, when the government of Kakuei Tanaka proposed the introduction of MMM.

The LDP's vote share had by this time slipped at every election since 1958; in 1972 it was more than 10 percentage points below its peak. The prime minister and some other party leaders saw MMM as a way of shoring up the party's Diet majority in the face of this seemingly inexorable decline. Under their proposal, 310 seats were to be elected using SMP and around 200 by PR (Maeno 1974: 55; Reed and Thies 2001: 161–2).

This time, however, the reform proposal met staunch opposition not only from the opponents of the Hatoyama bill in 1956 – JSP, press, and public – but also, widely, from within the LDP itself (cf. McElwain 2008). This dissent had three main sources. First, SNTV had encouraged LDP Diet members to build personal support organizations (*kōenkai*) that were sunk investments in the status quo; they did not relish the prospect of fighting under new rules and in new district boundaries. Second, some party leaders were also unconvinced. As Curtis (1999: 147) points out, the opposition had become more fragmented since 1956. 'LDP leaders', he continues, 'were no longer enthusiastic about adopting a system that would encourage opposition parties to consolidate and confront the LDP with a single candidate in districts where the LDP currently won seats because of competition among the opposition parties.' The reform proposal was tweaked to accommodate this concern: voters would have one vote rather than two, in order to prevent opposition parties that wanted to run independent PR lists from running joint candidates in the single-member districts (Reed and Thies 2001: 162). But this was insufficient to persuade all doubters. Finally, many within the party 'blanched at the prospect of fierce confrontation with the opposition that passage of the bill would require' (Maeno 1974: 55). This trepidation intensified after the opposition succeeded in mobilizing mass rallies against the change, rallies that 'attracted the participation of 321,000 people in all 47 prefectures' (Masumi 1995: 145; see also Reed and Thies 2001: 162). Faced with all these doubts, Tanaka backed down.

Thus, while the adoption of SMP would have enhanced the LDP's seat share in the short term, the proposal was felled by three types of consideration. First, it was contrary to the perceived interests of many well-established individual LDP Diet members. Second, its long-term impact on the structure of party competition and therefore the LDP's future capacity to win seats could be negative. Third, the act of reform itself would have created acrimonious debate, potentially harming the government's wider agenda and having a negative impact upon voter affect. It would take more than twenty years for these hurdles finally to be overcome. The story of the reform of 1994 is taken up in Chapter 10.

8

Elite majority imposition: comparative analysis

Armed with the case knowledge developed in the preceding chapters, I now seek to analyse the elite majority imposition type of electoral reform in greater depth. The defining features of enacted reforms falling into this type are that politicians dominate the reform process and that those politicians primarily seek to advance their own power. Though these features imply that reforms by elite majority imposition are simple compared to those involving elite–mass interaction, still they contain complexities that raise important analytic questions. Two are particularly important, and I devote most time to them. The first relates to politicians' goals: what are they, and what shapes them? Are they dominated by the maximization of short-term seat shares, or are other considerations also important? Second, why is it possible for reforms of this type to occur at all? What determines whether manipulation of the electoral system for personal or partisan gain is seen as legitimate (or at least tolerable) rather than illegitimate? What determines whether perceptions of illegitimacy constrain politicians' actions?

I also address the other building blocks surveyed in Part I. How far are actors' preferences shaped by uncertainty and misperception? To what degree are their preferences constrained by cognitive limits on the alternatives that actors perceive, and what determines where these limits lie? How far can skilful leadership by key individuals change outcomes? What is the role of institutions in translating preferences into outcomes? The only building block that I leave out is endogenous path dependence: in contrast to the prolonged processes of elite–mass interaction that I discuss in Part III, I find no evidence that endogenous path dependence significantly shaped the much shorter processes of elite majority imposition discussed here.

I frame the discussion in terms of the propositions developed in Part I. I do not test them formally: the evidence and, in some cases, the nature of the propositions do not permit this. Rather I seek to refine them and assess their plausibility in the light of the evidence from the cases covered.

Actors' goals and the factors that shape them

The first point to note is that, as expected, where the political majority controls electoral reform, power calculations predominate: with the possible partial exception only of the French left's attachment to the principle of proportionality in the Fourth Republic, politicians were in all cases guided overwhelmingly by power-seeking considerations. This fits proposition P1 from Chapter 3. The propositions pertaining to those rare politicians who do focus primarily on non-power-seeking concerns (P2–P7) therefore do not figure. As I posited in Chapter 2, however, the cases covered here suggest that politicians pursue power in many ways. I analyse this diversity along three dimensions: who the relevant maximizers are (individuals or parties), what particular power objectives they pursue, and what their time horizons are. I focus at this stage primarily on outcome contingencies and turn to act contingencies (at least, those relating to vote-seeking) when discussing legitimacy constraints below.

Who are the maximizers?

The first question concerns whose power interests dominate: parties', party leaders', or party backbenchers'. I posited (proposition P8) that this depends upon the power these actors are granted by the nature of parties and the broader institutional environment.

Of all the cases studied here, the one where the interests of backbench parliamentarians were most important appears to have been the aborted reform in Japan in 1973, where consensual decision-making procedures allowed ordinary LDP Diet members considerable negative (if not positive) influence over outcomes. Many saw their personal re-election prospects (VI(a) in Table 2.1, Chapter 2) as determined not primarily by their party's prospects nationwide, but by the strength of their own local support organization (*kōenkai*), and they therefore opposed reforms that would limit the significance of the *kōenkai* or shift district boundaries such that they no longer corresponded to the *kōenkai*'s area of strength.

Where individual leaders have considerable power, by contrast, that power can clearly extend to influencing the electoral system in pursuit of their own power interests (VII(a)). To some extent this power may derive from the presence of strongly centralized party structures. In Fourth Republic France, for example, leaders particularly of the Communists and the MRP could, given their parties' centralized structures, pursue systems of (essentially) closed-list PR.[1] Leaders' power depends not just on formal institutional structures, however, but also on leaders' personal standing. De Gaulle's power in 1958 to select the electoral system that suited his purposes against the wishes of his avowed supporters derived from dominance not of a party, but of the nation as a whole. Mitterrand in 1985 could shrug off the challenge to his reforms from Michel Rocard because he knew that strong party discipline would ensure those reforms' passage, but by 1991 he was clearly in the twilight years of his rule, his party colleagues were looking to a future without him, his power over the party was consequently waning, and he was unable to get his way.

Thus, the relative salience of parties, leaders, and backbenchers is fluid: it is influenced by formal institutional structures, individual personality, and circumstance.

Which objectives?

The next question concerns which power-seeking objectives actors pursue and what determines their strategies. I begin by surveying the evidence regarding the incidence of the various objectives before assessing the propositions on explanatory factors. This evidence is summarized in Table 8.1, using a slightly simplified version of the classification developed in Chapter 2 (Table 2.1). Any such rough schematization inevitably misses much of the complexity of reality and should be treated with caution. In most of the cases, the interests of parties dominated or were largely consonant with those of individual leaders and backbenchers. Though the table includes both partisan and individual objectives, I therefore focus upon the former.

The evaluation of electoral systems according to the degree to which they allow parties to present their most favourable face – candidates, party, leader – to the public (I(a) in Table 8.1) has been a major consideration in France. Most clearly, in 1945–1946 and 1951, while the Radicals wanted a system that focused attention on their popular local candidates, the MRP preferred structures emphasizing national party programmes and images. Similarly, in Italy in both 1954 and 2005, the coalition partners believed that a system allowing them to present their own party images to the electorate, rather than a single coalition image, would enhance their capacity to garner votes.

---

[1] The system adopted in France in 1946 included partial list openness, but the conditions required for this to operate were onerous and never triggered (Williams 1954: 315).

Table 8.1. *Actors' objectives in electoral reform*

Objectives	France 1945–1946	France 1951	France 1958	France 1985	France 1986	France 1991–1992	France 2007–2008	Italy 1946	Italy 1953	Italy 1954	Italy 1994–2001	Italy 2005	Japan 1945	Japan 1947	Japan 1956	Japan 1973
I Voters' preferences																
(a) Outcome-contingent	xx			x	x		x		x	xx	x	x				
(b)/(c) Act-contingent						xx			x	xx					xx	xx
II–III Votes and seats																
(a) Duverger	xx			xx	xx	xx	xx	xx	xx		x	x	x	xx		xx
(b) Coalition effect											x	x		xx		xx
IV–V Office and influence																
IV(a)/V(a)–(b) Outcome-contingent	x	xx	xx	xx	xx	x			xx	xx	xx	xx				
IV(b)/V(c)–(e) Act-contingent							xx				xx	xx				

(cont'd)

Table 8.1. (*cont.*)

Objectives	France 1945–1946	France 1951	France 1958	France 1985	France 1986	France 1991–1992	France 2007–2008	Italy 1946	Italy 1953	Italy 1954	Italy 1994–2001	Italy 2005	Japan 1945	Japan 1947	Japan 1956	Japan 1973
VI–VII Individual power																
VI Re-election				x	x		x									xx
VII Intra-party power	x	x									x	x				
VIII Influence in system			xx	x	x	x										

Key: xx = major factor; x = significant contributing factor. Row labels refer to those used in Table 2.1.
We can assume that individual re-election prospects are always a consideration for politicians. They are marked in the table only where they influenced electoral reform processes in a manner that diverged from party-level considerations.

Short-term seat-maximization (given vote shares) (II–III) appears to have been the main consideration in Japan in 1947 and 1956. Modified by Rawlsian thinking in the context of high uncertainty, it was also important in the adoption of proportional systems in France in 1945–1946 and Italy in 1946, and may have contributed to politicians' acceptance of a more proportional system in Japan in 1945. In the case of the French electoral reform of 1951, simple seat-maximization based on the Duvergerian mechanisms explains the broad thrust of the changes that were enacted – the centrist coalition parties wanted to bolster their share against the Communists and the Gaullists – but not the prolonged tussle among the coalition partners over how to achieve this end: these disagreements were based on other considerations. Similarly, seat-maximization explains the decision to reform in Italy in 1953, but not the insistence of the Christian Democrats' small coalition allies upon reducing the size of the bonus that they themselves expected to share in. Short-term seat-maximization has been important in France since 1985, though an account based solely on this factor would oversimplify the thinking of the actors involved. Short-term seat-maximization was far from being the only obstacle to 'completing' reform in Italy between 1994 and 2001; in its conventional form, based on the two Duvergerian effects (II(a) and III(a)), it was marginal to the enactment of reform in Italy 2005. Nor can it account for opposition to reform from within the LDP in Japan in 1973 or the Socialist Party in France in 1991–1992. In France in 1958, General de Gaulle deliberately chose a system that would *not* maximize the representation of his avowed supporters.

Longer-term concerns regarding seat shares are observable in several of the cases. Opponents of reform within the Socialist Party in France in 1985 and 1991–1992 and the LDP in Japan in 1973 were all concerned that the reforms that their leaders sought could limit their parties' long-term seat-winning capacity: in France, Rocard and others feared that with PR the Socialists would never again regain the majority position they secured in the National Assembly in 1981; in Japan, some in the LDP were concerned that SMP would encourage unity among the fractious opposition parties, allowing them to pose an enhanced future threat.

Table 8.1 distinguishes non-Duvergerian seat-maximization from the more usual Duvergerian form. This mattered in Italy both in the 1990s and in 2005. Coalition parties' seat shares were influenced not just by their shares of voter preferences and the translation of these into outcomes via the mechanical and psychological effects, but also by the coalition effect (II(b)): that is, by pre-election stand-down agreements among the parties.

The goals of winning government office and influencing policy outcomes (IV–V) were often important. The tactic of seeking to split one's opponents (V(b)) was most clearly evident in France in 1985, when Mitterrand hoped the arrival of the National Front in the National Assembly would split the right sufficiently to prevent formation of a majority centre-right government. He entertained similar thoughts in 1991–1992. Considerations of coalition dynamics (IV(a)), meanwhile, have been especially prevalent in Italy since 1994, where the dominant debate has been between those wanting to cement the shift towards bipolarism and those wishing to return to the centripetalism of old. The enhancement of intra-coalition influence (V(a)) was manifest in several cases in the desire to maintain party independence *vis-à-vis* coalition partners. It was crucial to the wariness of the small centrist parties towards reform in Italy in 1953 and to their insistence upon repeal a year later. It mattered also in France in 1945–1946 and 1951 and Italy in 2005.

I shall consider act-contingent effects upon voters' preferences (I(c)) below, when analysing legitimacy constraints. The other act-contingent concerns in Table 2.1 also figured. The desire to secure coalition allies (IV(b)) or other policy goals (V(c)) were both important in Italy between 1994 and 2001 and again in 2005. Berlusconi's unexpected shift in favour of PR in 1998 was probably prompted in part by his wish to improve his relations with the centrists. The UDC's allies in government in 2005 responded positively to its demand for electoral reform partly because they wanted to secure the wider constitutional reforms that they had been pursuing for years, which required UDC acquiescence, and because they did not want to endanger the stability of the coalition so close to the 2006 election. Equally, it was in large part for coalition reasons that the Nouveau Centre chose not to press electoral reform in France in 2008.

What explains these patterns? I suggested several factors in Chapter 3, including the salience of coalitions, the degree to which parties are strongly defined in either leader-, candidate-, or programme-centric terms, and the intensity of conflict between parties (P9).

The incidence of a strong focus on voters' preferences (I(a)) is relatively straightforward: as expected by P9, this occurred where parties' resources were unusually skewed in a particular direction. The Radicals in France in the 1940s and early 1950s were a disparate collection of locally entrenched *notables*, whereas the MRP lacked well-known personalities but had strong group appeal given their Resistance past and moderate, modernizing policy stance. In Italy in 2005, the previous, mixed-member electoral system had given the parties unusually clear evidence of the relative strength of party and coalition appeals: where voters had been able to cast two votes, one for a party list and one for a coalition candidate, the coalition's combined share of the former had been higher than their share of the latter.

P9 also suggests that the degree to which actors focus on seat-maximization (II–III) will depend upon the structure of the party system: where parties form or hope to form single-party governments, seat share is the principal determinant of their power. This was clearly the case in Japan in both 1956 and 1973: seat-maximization was the major concern of LDP leaders who wanted to ensure that their party would be able to continue governing alone even as its share of the vote declined. Closely related to this, where existing coalition boundaries are well entrenched, the same logic may lead to seat-maximization across the coalition as a whole. This counted in France in 1951 and Italy in 1953, where the existing centrist coalitions sought to protect their parliamentary majorities. Similarly, the Japanese conservative parties sought in 1947 to protect themselves against minor parties, independents, and the left. As I discuss below, seat-maximization also predominates when – as in France and Italy immediately after the Second World War – uncertainty regarding future election results is high.

To the degree, by contrast, that coalitions are needed to form governments and coalition boundaries are contentious, the capacity to participate in a coalition with governing potential and to have significant influence within that coalition becomes key. This has been clearest in Italy. In 1953, the small coalition parties forced a reduction in the size of the majority bonus in order to reduce the danger of domination by the Christian Democrats. In 1954, the same consideration (among others) led to that reform's abandonment. Since 1994, some parties have been most likely to gain power and influence where the logic of party competition is bipolar, others where it is centripetal, and they have approached the electoral system issue accordingly. Similarly, in France in 1985 and 1986, Mitterrand wanted to undermine the existing bipolar structure of coalition possibilities, while Chirac wanted to strengthen it, reflecting differing calculations as to how they could best secure power and pursue their agendas.

Time horizons

According to proposition P10 actors' time horizons are shaped by the point those actors have reached on their career trajectories and the duration of their future ambitions. Evidence regarding time horizons is available in several cases, and supports this proposition. In France in 1985, Mitterrand held the presidency but had very uncertain prospects of re-election in 1988. He therefore focused primarily upon the immediate future, and upon minimizing the chances that he would have to work with a strong centre-right government after the National Assembly elections of 1986. Rocard, by contrast, was driven by ambition for the future: he wanted to capture the presidency, in 1988 or later. Knowing that the Socialists' down-swing would reverse in due course, he wanted a system that would allow the party to take full advantage of changed fortunes (preferably on the back of his own presidential victory) and secure a stable governing majority in the Assembly for itself. By 1991–1992, the limits of Mitterrand's ambitions were even clearer: there was no prospect of his running again for the presidency in 1995. Thus, he again focused on the immediate future, seeking the most pliant Assembly possible. But Rocard was no longer alone within the Socialist Party in looking to the post-Mitterrand future. With other aspirants to presidential office also concerned about the effects of PR on their party's longer-term prospects, Mitterrand was forced to back down. Similarly, in Italy in 2005, Berlusconi – who was approaching the age of seventy – knew his political career would not go on for ever. Recognizing that the collapse of his coalition could jeopardize his chances of securing top office again, he placed particular emphasis on keeping his fractious allies on board by reconciling their various policy objectives. Other leaders of the centre-right coalition, however – notably Gianfranco Fini of the AN and Marco Follini and Pier Fernando Casini of the UDC – had ambitions for the post-Berlusconi future. They therefore placed particular emphasis upon the long-term dynamics of the Italian party system and the coalition possibilities within it.

We have always known that politicians' motivations when thinking about electoral systems are complex. This section has shown that we can gain an empirical handle on that complexity. First, we can identify which motivations matter when for whom across the various cases studied. Second, we can explain much of that variation in terms of the nature of parties and the party system and the positions of individual politicians. Some factors – such as the return of de Gaulle in France in 1958 – remain sui generis. But many of the mechanisms underlying politicians' electoral system preferences are generalizable.

So far, however, the picture remains incomplete: I have discussed neither the translation of motivations into preferences, nor that of preferences into outcomes. The first of these translations is shaped by legitimacy constraints as well as by uncertainty and cognitive constraints. Given the centrality of legitimacy constraints to any understanding of reform by elite majority imposition, I analyse them in detail in the following section.

Legitimacy constraints

Electoral reform by elite majority imposition involves deliberate manipulation of the electoral system for personal or partisan purposes. We might expect such behaviour to be subject to legitimacy constraints. As I suggested in Chapter 3, a legitimacy constraint exists where two conditions are present: first, certain actions or options are perceived as illegitimate; second, these perceptions exert constraining force upon politicians in power, either directly, because the politicians internalize them, or indirectly, because others (most likely, voters) are able to punish politicians who violate them. I offered two broad propositions regarding these two conditions. The first related to perceptions of legitimacy and illegitimacy: these are shaped by objective values, historical experiences, and actors' strategies (P16). The second focused on the constraining force of such perceptions: where they are internalized by those in power, they have direct constraining effect; where they are not so internalized, their constraining force depends upon the capacity of others to punish violations, which depends, in turn, on the strength of the legitimacy perceptions, the nature of the reform process, and the availability and proximity of unused instruments of punishment (P17).

In order to evaluate these propositions, we need first to identify legitimacy perceptions and the constraining force they exert. This is no small task in itself. I pursue it for twelve of the cases of reform or attempted reform outlined in the preceding chapters (I exclude the four transitional cases in 1945–1946 and 1958, when legitimacy constraints were less relevant). I add two further cases from (West) Germany, where legitimacy constraints have forestalled reform on at least one, possibly two, occasions. In some cases it is possible to locate legitimacy constraints quite clearly; in others, the evidence is more ambiguous. I then turn to consider the factors posited to shape these constraints.

Before embarking, I should first clarify that the discussion of legitimacy constraints here represents only a subset of the subject as a whole. I discuss the matter solely in relation to how perceptions of legitimacy constrain (or fail to constrain) electoral reform by elite majority imposition. The absence of legitimacy constraints can permit not only reforms that would elsewhere be thought impermissible, but also the survival of a status quo that would not be deemed acceptable in other cases. The gerrymandering practised in some states in the US, for example, would be unthinkable in a country like the UK, with its tradition of independent boundary review. But the UK's highly disproportional electoral system – in which the Labour Party in 2005 secured 55.0 per cent of the seats on just 35.2 per cent of the vote (Fisher 2006: 1283) – would, equally, be seen as wholly unfair in a country such as the Netherlands in which the principle of proportionality is highly valued. Thus, the discussion here of apparently lax legitimacy constraints in some countries where electoral reforms by elite majority imposition have occurred does not imply that the political cultures of these countries are necessarily less wholesome than those of countries in which such reforms would be thought, in Benoit's (2004: 385) words, 'beyond the pale'.

The location and intensity of legitimacy constraints

Cases of enacted, proposed, or mooted electoral reform by elite majority imposition can be divided into three categories: those where reform is not enacted; those where it is enacted but is seen as illegitimate, leading to negative consequences for those who enacted it; and those where it is enacted and its sponsors suffer no negative consequences stemming from perceived illegitimacy (see Table 8.2). In the first category, we can identify the location and intensity of legitimacy constraints *if* it can be shown that such constraints contributed to the decision not to proceed. The second category may offer precise information on legitimacy constraints. The third category may seem to allow us to say only that legitimacy constraints

Table 8.2. *Legitimacy constraints and electoral reform*

Reforms proposed but not enacted	Reforms enacted and reformers punished	Reforms enacted but reformers not punished
France 1991–1992	Italy 1953	France 1951
(France 2007–2008)		France 1985
(Italy 1994–2001)		France 1986
Japan 1956		Italy 1954
Japan 1973		Italy 2005
West Germany 1966–1969		Japan 1947
Germany 2005		

are absent (or at least, lie somewhere beyond the reforms enacted); but in fact I suggest that the information they offer can be more subtle. I consider these three categories in turn.

Reforms proposed but not enacted

The cases narrated in the preceding chapters in which reform was proposed but not enacted are those of France in 1991–1992 and 2007–2008, Italy between 1994 and 2001, and Japan in 1956 and 1973. As already outlined, the failure in Italy between 1994 and 2001 to complete the reforms of 1993 was due primarily to the lack of shared interests among the many relevant political parties: there was no question regarding the legitimacy of such reform. The French case of 2007–2008 was similar. Thus, I do not consider these cases further here. In the three remaining cases, however, some analysts at least have suggested that one factor in the decision not to proceed with reform was the fear that it would be seen by voters as illegitimate and that politicians would be punished at the polls in consequence. The *Financial Times*'s correspondent in France in 1992 suggested that some in the Socialist Party were 'resisting full proportional representation, for fear that it should look too much like bare-faced electoral engineering' (Davidson 1992c; see also Goldey 1993: 293). In both Japanese cases, particularly that of 1973, the proposals met a hostile public response that viewed them as self-serving for the LDP. Ward (1966: 553–4) reports that the 1956 reform attempt met opposition from other parties, the press, and the public, and that opponents 'objected vehemently and used every possible tactic – including violence – first to stall the bill's progress and then to kill it'.

The available sources suggest that these legitimacy perceptions played a causal role in politicians' decisions to pull back in the two Japanese cases; there is, however, no clear evidence of this in France. Ward (1966: 554) notes of Japan in 1956 that 'a group of leaders within the LDP became worried about the longterm consequences of forcing through so unpopular a measure'. In 1973, as I have argued, there was more significant opposition to reform from within the LDP; nevertheless, Maeno (1974: 55) argues that, with the opposition parties organizing unprecedented joint rallies and demonstrations against the measure, fear of the effects of a prolonged fight also contributed to the decision to back down. In France in 1991–1992, however, sources focus overwhelmingly on opposition to Mitterrand's plan from within the Socialist Party.

Further evidence can be gleaned by expanding the case set to include the experiences of (West) Germany. Following the Second World War, West

Germany adopted what is now the world's oldest MMP electoral system. Though this system did not cause a proliferation of parties, it did allow the survival of the Free Democrats (FDP) and, in more recent years, has permitted the rise of the Greens and the Party of Democratic Socialism (PDS)/Left Party. Germany's large parties – the Christian Democrats (CDU/CSU) and Social Democrats (SPD) – might therefore have been expected to prefer a more majoritarian alternative. Electoral reform indeed appeared on the agenda at the formation of Germany's first post-war grand coalition, in 1966, and it was mooted also by some commentators at the formation of the second grand coalition in 2005. Both in the late 1960s and in 2005, however, the project got nowhere. Writing of the late 1960s, Jesse acknowledges that the SPD had some tactical reasons for backing away from electoral reform, but argues, 'However important the tactical considerations of the parties may be, they are probably not decisive. Of greater significance is the fact that the existing system of proportional representation has become tantamount to an "established right"' (Jesse 1987: 436). He suggests that at least some major-party politicians had internalized that belief, viewing deviation from proportional representation as unacceptable in principle (Jesse 1987: 436–7). Helms (2006: 59) makes the same point, even more bluntly, of 2005: 'Neither of the two major parties even dared to touch the issue, which would have been considered by many as little short of an assault on democracy itself.'

   That reforms that would depart significantly from the prevailing level of proportionality and whose manifest purpose would be the elimination of the smaller parties were widely viewed as illegitimate in both German episodes is clear, and in 2005 it appears that they did act as a causal constraint: electoral reform never even seriously reached politicians' agendas. Whether they had meaningful constraining power in the 1960s is, however, ambiguous, because the SPD and some in the CDU – as both Jesse and Helms acknowledge – had tactical reasons for opposing majoritarian reform too, which Pulzer (1983: 99–102) analyses in detail. Whether reform would have occurred in the absence of the taint of illegitimacy therefore cannot be known.

Reforms enacted and reformers punished

The clearest case in which reform was implemented and those who promoted it were subsequently punished for their violation of legitimacy constraints is that of Italy in 1953. This change became indelibly marked with the label of '*la legge truffa*' – 'the swindle law' – and the ruling coalition appears to have lost votes in the following election in direct consequence. Certainly, the politicians of that coalition *felt* they had been punished: the acrimonious parliamentary debate surrounding the law's passage did them no good (La Palombara 1953; 685), and in repealing the law they recognized that it was harming their interests (Katz 2005: 68–9). Furthermore, the law had a lasting impact: the effect of its perceived illegitimacy, according to Pasquino (2007: 85), 'was that an entire generation, and more, of politicians became marked with a proportional mentality. The equation "PR = democratic regimes" meant that for decades anyone who proposed revising the electoral law came to be considered an enemy of the democratic regime.' This perception arose from the troubles that the 1953 law had visited upon its instigators. The 1953 reformers did meet a legitimacy constraint that, with hindsight, they probably wished they had heeded from the start.

Reforms enacted but reformers not punished

In all the remaining cases, the reformers succeeded in imposing change without suffering adverse electoral consequences. Yet in at least three of these cases, a perception of illegitimacy does appear to have been widespread; the evidence suggests simply that this perception exerted no significant constraining power upon politicians. The French reform of 1951, for example, was 'the subject of much criticism' (Pickles 1958: 33) and was labelled the 'thieves' ballot' by its parliamentary opponents (Williams 1964: 314). As noted in Chapter 5, Williams (1964: 319–20) contends that the blatant manipulation 'inevitably contributed to the ordinary citizen's disillusionment with politics'. Yet this perception of illegitimacy appears not to have brought the reform's instigators direct punishment. In the view of Neumann (1951: 752),

> In the United States and England, an attempt of this kind would have resulted in an outcry of rage all over the country, in hundreds of protest meetings, in thousands of indignant letters to the Members of Congress or of Parliament and to the editors of the leading newspapers. But in France, the 'gerrymandering' on a massive scale and by a variety of methods ... was met only with monumental indifference.

Williams (1964: 314) finds no evidence of a voter backlash on election day: 'Although critics – including de Gaulle – had warned that disgusted voters would stay at home, there was no evidence that they did' – turnout was in fact slightly up on the previous election, in 1946. And the manoeuvre, as we have seen, produced the results that were intended.

Similarly, it would be wrong to say that Mitterrand's reform of 1985 violated no norms. We can see this from the rhetoric used by the opposition parties in speaking against the bill: they appealed to a number of norms – that it was unacceptable to change the rules mid-game,[2] that in waiting for regional election results before deciding the detail of the reforms the government was brazen in pursuing partisan advantage,[3] that Mitterrand placed 'his personal interest above the national interest'[4] – clearly believing these norms had resonance. Yet the government did not see these norms as constraining. According to one journalist at the time, 'The Government anticipates a major outcry from the Opposition but coldly calculates that this will die down before the Parliamentary elections next year' (Housego 1985). Thus, though the reform was not seen as entirely appropriate, the government did not expect to be punished for it. As Elgie (2005: 134) finds, 'There is always an outcry when governments propose any such reform [in France], but the electorate never seems to punish the government when a reform is introduced. The government's popularity is much more closely linked to economic issues than to institutional engineering.' The outcry occurred largely among politicians themselves; the public, it seems, while hardly approving (Knapp 1987: 92), did not disapprove enough to regard the reform as a major issue (Frears 1986: 490).

We can say the same of Italy in 2005. The reform – particularly as originally proposed – did attract criticism as an unacceptable attempt to secure partisan advantage (notably, Sartori 2005). Opposition politicians, as in France in 1985, appealed to several norms in denouncing the change: Romano Prodi, the centre-left coalition's candidate for prime minister, for example, declared,

> A few months before the elections, a governing majority which knows it no longer enjoys the country's confidence, which has lost all the electoral tests of recent years, which is divided and fragmented on the inside and incapable of leadership on the outside, is about to strike the definitive blow at our constitution.
>
> (Quoted in Barber 2005a)

Yet Berlusconi and his colleagues appear to have been right to calculate that the reform would do them no great harm at the ballot box: it was not

---

[2] 'Mitterrand Takes to the Hustings', *Washington Post*, 2 February 1985.
[3] 'It's Election Year, All 12 Long Months of It, for France', *The Economist*, 2 March 1985; 'Paris to Detail Polling Reforms within 2 Weeks', *Guardian*, 22 March 1985.
[4] 'France Sets Voting Change', *Washington Post*, 4 April 1985.

a major issue in the electoral campaign; and the centre-right coalition in fact gained support in the months between the reform and the April 2006 elections, coming very close to pulling off a surprise victory.

Turning to Japan, the reform of 1947 certainly caused uproar among opposition politicians (Fukui 1988: 130; Kohno 1997: 43). But the available accounts focus entirely upon politicians and the occupying powers: they give no indication of any popular reaction. Whether the reform – enacted, recall, just two weeks before the election – was widely seen as illegitimate therefore remains unclear.

Only in the two final cases – Chirac's reversal of Mitterrand's reform in France in 1986 and the Italian centre parties' abandonment of their own *legge truffa* in 1954 – is it clear that reform met no widespread perception of illegitimacy. Both governments were merely restoring a system that had been abolished or amended by tactical manoeuvre the previous year. The Chirac government was elected on a manifesto that gave prominence to the reform, and it moved immediately to enact it. The public, having opposed the 1985 change, supported its reversal in 1986 by more than a two-to-one margin.[5] The *legge truffa*, as we have just seen, was universally derided, and its passing was mourned by no one. In these cases therefore, the absence of a legitimacy constraint was due not only to the absence of constraining force, but also to the absence of significant perceived illegitimacy.

In all but one of the cases (Japan in 1947), clear evidence is available regarding the perceived legitimacy or illegitimacy of the (putative) reforms, and in all these cases except Italy in 1954 and France in 1986 perceptions of illegitimacy were widespread. We can also say that those perceptions varied in intensity. They were strongest in Germany, particularly in 2005, where they had been internalized by politicians themselves, and they had wide resonance in Italy in 1953 and in Japan too. In Italy in 2005, by contrast, and in France throughout the period investigated, it has been possible for politicians to enact reforms without sparking much interest except among politicians and professional political observers.

In some of the cases where reforms were not enacted (particularly Germany in the late 1960s and France in 1992) we cannot be confident that these legitimacy perceptions had constraining force, for it is unclear

---

[5] A poll conducted in mid-June 1986 found 56 per cent of respondents supported the reform while 25 per cent opposed: 'Why Chirac Promised Paris a Long Hot Summer: French Political Reforms', *Guardian*, 1 August 1986.

to what extent politicians backed away from reform because of legitimacy problems or for other reasons. But in the remaining cases the evidence is clearer: in France in 1951, 1985, and 1986, Italy in 2005, and Japan in 1947, politicians correctly calculated that they could manipulate the system for their own ends without incurring substantial costs; in Italy in 1953, politicians believed they could get away with the reforms but were, at least to a degree, disappointed; in Japan in 1956 and 1973 and Germany in 2005, politicians balked at reform in part because they expected to be punished for proceeding or because they themselves regarded such action as unacceptable.

Thus, though some ambiguities do remain, we can gain a reasonable empirical picture of where legitimacy constraints lie and how strong they are. The foundation therefore exists to explore propositions P16 and P17 further.

Factors underlying legitimacy constraints

Legitimacy perceptions

Proposition P16 posits three factors that may drive legitimacy perceptions: objective values, historical experiences, and actors' strategies. I consider these in turn.

Objective values   There is some evidence that reforms are more likely to be viewed as illegitimate the further they deviate from generally agreed values for democratic electoral systems such as those outlined in Chapter 2. In Japan in both 1956 and 1973, for example, perceived illegitimacy arose from the fact that SMP or MMM would deliver *highly* disproportional results: projections suggested in 1973 that the proposed mixed system could deliver 80 per cent of all seats to the ruling LDP with considerably fewer than half the votes (Reed and Thies 2001: 162).

Yet there is also much contrary evidence. The French law of 1951 was introduced in circumstances very similar to those in Italy in 1953, involved a much more drastic redesign of the electoral system, and, in contrast to the Italian case, had large and problematic effects upon the election result. Yet it was the Italian law that proved more damaging to its instigators: unpopular though the French law was, it did not generate equivalent troubles. In Germany by 2005, meanwhile, it appears that even moderate deviation from proportionality was unacceptable. Thus, objective values are clearly far from telling the whole story.

Historical experiences   I suggested in Chapter 3 that historical experiences can shape legitimacy perceptions through three principal mechanisms. First, where the electoral system has been manipulated to suit partisan ends before, such behaviour may become an accepted (if not entirely condoned) aspect of the political game, such that the perception of illegitimacy regarding such behaviour is low in intensity. This mechanism has been clearly evident in France, where the tendency of both politicians and voters to accept that electoral reform is a weapon that majorities will use when it suits them was widely noted in the 1950s (Neumann 1951: 752; Pickles 1958: 33) and the 1980s (Cole and Campbell 1989: 3; Criddle 1992: 110; Frears 1986: 489; Knapp 1987: 89; Laponce 1980: 369).

The second, contrasting, mechanism is that where an electoral system is stable over a long period, it may gain what I called a patina of rightness, such that any attempt to tamper with it is regarded with distaste. This is backed by evidence from Germany and Japan, where periods of rapid post-war economic growth were associated with strengthening attachment to the prevailing institutional structures (Conradt 1996: 82–7; Curtis 1999: 147). The delegitimation of Japan's SNTV system in the early 1990s (discussed in Part III) came as the post-war economic bubble began to deflate.

Under the third mechanism, an electoral system that is associated with positive or negative historical experiences may thereby be legitimized or delegitimized. The readoption of SNTV in Japan in 1947 may have been smoothed by the fact that this system was associated with Japan's previously most democratic period, between the mid-1920s and early 1930s. Negative historical experience, meanwhile, was a major factor in Italy in 1953, and is likely to have been a major source of the difference noted above between this case and the French reform of two years earlier. The Acerbo Law of 1923 was clearly associated with the onset of Fascism. The 1953 law was not identical to it, but it was sufficiently similar for the connection to resonate widely, and the law became untenable: as Carstairs (1980: 159) observes, 'The measure differed only in detail and not in principle from the Fascist measure which was adopted in 1923, and was for this reason widely discredited and opposed.' These associations rendered any similar reform attempt impossible for decades after. Over time, however, memories faded and past associations weakened. Bonus-adjusted systems began to be advocated seriously during the 1980s (e.g., Pasquino 1987; Ruffilli 1987). The idea that they were inappropriate began to undergo re-evaluation, and they were implemented at local and regional levels during the 1990s (Chiaramonte and Di Virgilio 2000). Thus, by the time of the 2005 reform, the majority bonus in itself attracted little negative voter reaction.

Evidence exists also for two short-term historical mechanisms. Though repeated manipulation may over time spawn complacency, a reverse mechanism may also operate in the short term, whereby voters willing to put up with some manipulation object if it is repeated too quickly. Such may have been the case in France in 1991–1992, where Socialists doubted they could get away with playing the same trick again so soon after playing it in 1985. The cases of Italy in 1954 and, even more, France in 1986 suggest a final mechanism: reforms that merely overturn recent unpopular changes may be protected from perceptions of illegitimacy, even if, as in France, they are in themselves no less self-serving than the changes they reverse.

Actors' strategies   Actors on both sides of the electoral reform debates covered here certainly tried to influence legitimacy perceptions through their rhetoric, though whether these efforts had much effect is harder to judge. I have already given examples of the discourse used by opponents of reform in France in 1985 and Italy in 2005. Different discourses are available to different actors. In France in 1985, for example, the Socialists could justify the switch to PR by pointing out that their manifesto had promised such a move since 1972 and by appealing to the principles of equality and justice.[6] The following year, the centre-right government led by Jacques Chirac could invoke Gaullist values of strong central authority when it restored the two-round system that had been in place since 1958. Strategic manipulation can go beyond mere discourse. In Japan, during both failed reform drives covered here, opposition parties were skilful in deploying the various tactics available to them – Diet boycotts, media campaigns, mass demonstrations – to hinder the government's plans.

Constraining force

Perceptions of illegitimacy were strongest in Germany: here, in 2005, the issue of electoral reform barely even surfaced, because politicians themselves had internalized the view that for the two main parties to use a period of grand coalition to manipulate the electoral system to their own advantage would be an unacceptable abuse of power. This is the only case where such internalization is evident.

---

[6] E.g., Laurent Fabius, quoted in 'Les réactions', *Le Monde*, 5 April 1985.

Proposition P17 suggests that where legitimacy perceptions are not fully internalized by politicians themselves, their constraining force is determined not only by their intensity, but also by the capacity of others, especially voters, to punish norm-violating behaviour. First, the more onerous are the procedures that must be gone through before a reform can be passed, the more opportunity there will be for opponents of reform to arouse public opposition, and so the more likely will punishment be. In Chapter 3, I cited the case of the abandoned Japanese reform of 1956: though the LDP had the power to impose whatever system it wished, it could have done so only through lengthy Diet proceedings that would have damaged its standing, and its leaders chose to back down. Similarly, in Italy in 1953, La Palombara (1953: 685) expressed surprise at the fact that the Christian Democrats and their allies proceeded with reform, despite the protracted and acrimonious process of parliamentary approval; and the centrist parties did subsequently suffer negative consequences. By contrast, Mitterrand and his government were able to whip electoral reform very rapidly through the French parliament in April 1985; there was a brief period of intense discussion, but subsequently the issue quickly subsided. The same was true in Italy in the final months of 2005.

Second, voters are able more effectively to punish misdeeds when an election is imminent and where the issue is able to shift how citizens vote. Politicians have sought in most cases not to leave reforms until the last minute even though, abstracting from voter affect, it would be optimal for them to do so in order to gauge more precisely the various parties' likely strengths at election time. Mitterrand enacted reform in April 1985, almost a year before the election was due the following March; the reform discussion in 1991–1992 took place around the same point in the legislative cycle. By contrast, the failure of the Italian government to enact reform until just months before the election of 1953 – though it had begun to consider the idea in early 1952 – is likely to have contributed to the continued salience of the issue as voters cast their ballots. But proximity to the next election clearly does not explain entirely the ability of electoral reform to shift votes. The French reform of 1951 was finalized even closer to the following election than that in Italy two years later. In Japan in 1947, the speed of social and political change may simply have been too great and its scope too wide for many voters to accord electoral reform much attention. The Italian reform of 2005, meanwhile, suggests that a government with an established reputation for Machiavellianism may be able to enact reforms with impunity in the months before an election: the manipulation of the electoral system told voters little about the government that they did not know already; it therefore gave them little reason to change how they intended to vote.

Legitimacy constraints have been widely acknowledged by political scientists, but less frequently analysed. The reason is clear: saying anything precise about them is very difficult. The preceding discussion offers some conclusions, but they are tentative. There is evidence to support all the elements in the propositions made in Chapter 3. Of the various factors identified, those pertaining to history appear to have had greatest effect. Prevailing institutions came to be associated with post-war success in Germany and Japan (though this later eroded in Japan), such that tampering was viewed with hostility; in Germany, the principle of proportionality became deeply entrenched. By contrast, the Italian reform of 1953 was tainted with the memory of 1923, making it easy for its opponents to construct a delegitimizing discourse around it. Manipulation of the electoral system was just too much part of the game in France for its perpetrators to meet serious harm. The key mechanism in Italy in 2005 was similar: a history of adjusting a variety of rules for his own purposes meant that little attention was paid when Berlusconi applied the same tactic to the electoral system.

Uncertainty, cognitive constraints, leadership, and institutions

The building blocks just discussed – actors' motivations and legitimacy constraints – are the features most central to the nature of reform by elite majority imposition. Successful reform of this type, indeed, can be defined as reform imposed for power-seeking reasons by the politicians in power largely unconstrained by the opinions of others. But it is important also to consider how the other building blocks of the reform process line up, and I do this briefly now. I attend, in turn, to uncertainty, cognitive constraints, leadership, and institutions.

Uncertainty

I offered two propositions regarding uncertainty in Chapter 3. One (P13) stated simply that uncertainty may lead to misperception. I cast that proposition in the broadest terms because it was not clear what factors could be adduced that might allow us to predict the incidence or content of misperception. The cases discussed here shed no further light. Misperception of the effects of new electoral systems (that is, of the outcome-contingent effects of reform) is in fact barely evident: in all the cases of enacted reform, these effects were in the intended direction, if not always as great as their proponents hoped. Where significant misperception did occur, it related to act contingencies. This was clearest in Italy in 1953, when the coalition parties believed wrongly that electoral system manipulation would do their public image no harm. It was present also in Japan in 1956 and 1973: had the prime ministers in each case foreseen the reaction their reform plans would elicit, they presumably would never have initiated them. That hubris played a role in these miscalculations is possible: the main parties behind each reform occupied a dominant role in government at the time. But the evidence for any such pattern is very weak. Misperceptions remain beyond the limits of our theoretical knowledge.

Proposition P12, meanwhile, posited that actors who recognize they face uncertainty or are highly risk-averse will adopt one of two courses: they will seek to preserve the status quo; or they will adopt a maximin strategy. The former course, P12 continued, is more likely where a viable electoral system already exists and uncertainty regarding voting strengths is low relative to the uncertainty generated by reform; the latter should be expected where there is no viable status quo and uncertainty regarding voting strengths is higher.

The evidence supports this proposition. Actors responded to uncertainty with a maximin strategy precisely in those cases where there was no viable status quo and where uncertainty regarding voting strengths was highest: that is, in the transitional choices immediately following the Second World War in France and Italy, and to an extent also in Japan. These cases, indeed, moved further than any others towards the elite settlement type of reform. By contrast, there is no evidence that this strategy played any significant role where a viable status quo was already in place. Of the cases analysed here, only those in France in 1985 and Italy in 1954 clearly involved reform towards greater proportionality. By contrast, the reforms in France in 1951, 1958, and 1986, in Italy in 1953, and in Japan in 1947 reduced proportionality, while the effects of the Italian reform of 2005 upon proportionality, at least in the lower house, were minimal. Use of the maximin strategy appears, therefore, to have been limited to the transition context.

Proposition P12 also suggests that where a viable electoral system exists and the salient political actors are used to competing by its rules, the most likely response to uncertainty is conservatism. Testing this proposition is not possible on the basis of the sample of cases used here: the proposition predicts non-reform, whereas I look only at cases where reform was

enacted or at least attempted. I shall, however, offer evidence for this
mechanism in Part III, in relation to reforms by elite–mass interaction.

Cognitive constraints

Given the nearly infinite variety of possible electoral systems, actors
cannot consider them all; rather they focus their attention on some
subset. In order to understand electoral reform processes, we need to
know how limiting these constraints are and which subset of electoral
systems actors home in on. Chapter 3 offered two propositions: that
cognitive constraints will be the stronger as the process used to explore
alternatives is the less systematic (P14); and that the location of these
cognitive constraints is shaped by history (including colonial legacies),
regional contagion, and fashion (P15).

The first of these propositions may imply that where electoral reform
occurs by elite majority imposition cognitive constraints will be strong:
such reforms tend to take place quickly and are controlled by politicians
who seek to restrict debate to a close circle of colleagues; thus, extensive
processes of searching for alternatives are unlikely.

At the broad level of electoral system types, the cases studied here
support this expectation: in all three countries, discussion of reform proposals was largely confined to alternatives that had already been on the
table in that country before. In Italy, most clearly, all the cases of reform by
elite majority imposition have involved a return to variants either of the
1919 system of proportional representation or of the bonus-adjusted system first introduced in 1923. In France, the major alternatives – PR, the
two-round system in single-member districts, and party block vote – had
all been used under the Third Republic (Cole and Campbell 1989: 48–71).
The SMP system proposed in Japan in 1956 had already been used in the
late nineteenth century and again between 1919 and 1925. The MMM
system proposed in 1973 had not previously been used in Japan, but it had
been recommended multiple times by the advisory councils and was
apparently first advocated by a political science professor in the course of
the discussions leading to the 1956 bill (Ward 1966: 564). Thus, the options
considered remained within the confines of the existing national debate.

On the other hand, once we dig below the level of electoral system
types, considerable innovation occurs in the details. The French system
of 1951 was an intricate creation incorporating novelties such as the rules
on *apparentements* and the different provisions between Paris and the
rest of the country. The Italian system of 2005 was innovative, *inter alia*,

in its complex thresholds, the size of the majority premium, and the rules on how the premium could be won. In Japan in 1956, the basic idea of SMP was adjusted by adding a small number of two-member districts. Thus, once the broad framework of the electoral system options has been set, actors can play rather freely with the details. While politicians may not readily hear advisors who propose grand schemes they cannot relate to, they may find it easier to deal with proposed tweaks to schemes that, in broad measure, they do understand.

Turning to the location of cognitive constraints, proposition P15 posits three main determinants – historical experience, foreign models, and fashion. As the preceding paragraphs indicate, where cognitive constraints have been strong in the cases studied here, the factor determining which alternatives actors considered has overwhelmingly been their own country's historical experience. While the initial choice of PR in countries such as France and Italy may have been influenced by pan-European trends, there is no evidence of substantial international diffusion since then. Japan also returned to its pre-war electoral system in 1947. These cases suggest that foreign influence is likely to be strongest at the time of founding democratic elections; thereafter, the debate in any country tends to crystallize around particular broad options that rarely change. Reforms by elite majority imposition appear to involve insufficient jolt to the system to cause this path to be broken.

Leadership

Though the role of leadership is more limited in reforms by elite majority imposition than in cases of elite–mass interaction, nevertheless, leaders can shift outcomes in these cases by at least two mechanisms: first, by constructing pro-reform coalitions at the elite level; second, by manipulating legitimacy constraints. I have already addressed the second of these above, focusing on the careful use of rhetoric and framing (S2 in Chapter 4). I turn now to the first.

Where government is composed of a single cohesive party and electoral reform requires no more than a simple parliamentary majority, the construction of a pro-reform coalition may require very little in the way of leadership. In France in 1985, for example, the combination of a parliamentary majority, party cohesion, and the fact that most Socialist deputies saw the reform as favourable to their interests ensured that Mitterrand could get his way without a struggle. By contrast, if the governing majority comprises a diverse coalition of parties with different electoral interests, securing unanimous support for a specific reform may be enormously difficult. Such circumstances prevented the completion of the shift to plurality in Italy between 1994 and 2001.

On paper, we might have expected the Berlusconi coalition to have faced impossible hurdles to securing agreement in 2005. It was only through complex bargaining across multiple dimensions – the structure of the party system, the vote-seeking potential of the various parties, the intra-party power of party leaders, and so on – and across multiple policy domains – the electoral system itself as well as the wider constitutional reforms and the future leadership of the coalition – that those hurdles were overcome. Though the bargaining process underlying this episode remains a closed book, its outcome was not predictable in advance and is likely to have depended heavily on the skills, strategies, and chemistry of the individual leaders involved.

Similar difficulties were faced by the ruling parties in France in 1951, and in this case considerable evidence does exist in the public domain that supports the view that the deliberate – sometimes ingenious – leadership strategies of certain key individuals were crucial to the outcome. Goguel (1952: 73) argues that 'It required all the political skill of Henri Queuille, who returned as Premier, to persuade the National Assembly to pass the bill.' Browne and Hamm argue that 'the eventual resolution of the reform issue depended heavily upon strategic interventions at critical moments in the decision-making process' (1996: 194). They cite, most notably, the declaration of the president of the National Assembly, Édouard Herriot, that, though the reform bill had been defeated at second reading, it could return to committee rather than die (1996: 190). That decision had a dubious basis in the parliamentary standing orders; it was a creative institutional innovation without which the reform attempt might have failed. These cases thus involved a mixture of bargaining among coalition partners (S3) and manipulation of institutional processes (S7).

Institutions in the translation of preferences into outcomes

Chapter 3 stated two propositions regarding the role of institutions in the translation of actors' preferences into outcomes. The first was that electoral reform is less likely the more veto players there are (P18). The second posited that the influence of particular actors over the process is a function partly of their formal agenda-setting power, though such formal power can be overturned by public pressure or the strategic actions of individuals (P19).

The evidence discussed in this chapter supports the first of these propositions: all these reforms occurred in contexts allowing reform to be imposed by simple legislative majority, an arrangement minimizing the pro-reform coalition that had to be constructed. Nevertheless, the number of *institutional* veto players does not determine the number of veto players *tout court*: this depends also upon partisan veto players (Tsebelis 2002: 2). Reform was blocked in Italy between 1994 and 2001 by the internal diversity of each successive government majority. In France in 1991–1992 and Japan in 1973, it was blocked, at least in part, by the factional nature of the ruling parties. It was achieved in France in 1951 and Italy in 1953 and 2005 only after prolonged and acrimonious intra-coalitional bargaining. The more veto players there are, the more leadership is likely to be needed before change can occur.

Clearly, all governments have the power to place electoral reform on the political agenda. The interesting aspect of P19 concerns, rather, the role played by other actors. The evidence from the cases discussed here is limited, but what evidence there is does not support the suggestion that formal agenda-setting rules are a major determinant of other actors' power. The Italian reform of 2005 was imposed by politicians, voters having failed to use their power to initiate referendums to secure change. In Japan, hostility from opposition parties and the public helped block reforms, despite these actors' lack of any formal power. While institutions are important, they do not determine outcomes.

Conclusion

Compared to the reforms by elite–mass interaction that I shall turn to shortly, electoral reforms by elite majority imposition are simple affairs: politicians dominate and are overwhelmingly concerned with pursuing power; these reform processes tend to last months rather than years. Yet complexity remains. Two dimensions of that complexity – concerning how actors pursue power and where legitimacy constraints lie – are fundamental. Several others – concerning uncertainty, cognitive constraints, leadership, and institutions – are also important. In this chapter I have sought to gain a hold on this complexity, identifying patterns across cases and exploring further the causal relationships proposed in Part I.

The findings suggest two principal conclusions. First, reforms even of the elite majority imposition type are difficult to predict. Just where legitimacy constraints lie may not be clear, even to the actors on the ground. Whether leaders can broker agreement may depend on their

Table 8.3. *Reform by elite majority imposition and the number of parties*

More proportional		Neutral		Less proportional	
Reform	ENPV	Reform	ENPV	Reform	ENPV
France 1945–1946	4.52	Italy 2005	6.32	France 1951	4.65
France 1985	4.13			France 1958	6.09
Italy 1946	–			France 1986	4.65
Italy 1954	4.18			Italy 1953	2.95
Japan 1945	–			Japan 1947	7.78
Average	4.28		6.32		5.22

Note: ENPV is given for the election preceding the reform. Italy and Japan had no post-war elections before introducing the electoral systems of 1946 and 1945 respectively. For France in 1945–1946, ENPV is given for the second constituent assembly election, held in June 1946.
Source: ENPV figures are drawn from Gallagher (2007).

skills, on their mutual relations, and on sheer luck. Second, the various elements of complexity have significant effects on the generalizations we can make concerning who has power over the electoral system and what direction reforms are likely to take. Just how limiting legitimacy constraints are in general is impossible to judge from the evidence here, but we have certainly seen that they are important in some cases. This implies that the political majority is not always able to impose its will and advance its interests. Regarding the direction of reform, the findings of this chapter contradict Colomer's claims (2005) that electoral reform is closely related to the number of parties and that it tends towards greater proportionality.

The evidence on this final point is summarized in Table 8.3, which categorizes each of the enacted reforms analysed in these chapters in terms of whether they led to more or less proportional systems and shows in each case the effective number of parties in terms of votes (ENPV)[7] in the election preceding the reform. As is clear, there is no evidence of the patterns that Colomer predicts: there is no trend towards greater proportionality; nor is it the case that reforms towards proportionality occur

[7] $ENPV = 1/(\Sigma v^2)$ where v is the vote share of each party (Laakso and Taagepera 1979).

when the effective number of parties is high while reforms in the opposite direction take place when the effective number of parties is low. This evidence supports the contention that the many considerations that may disrupt a simple relationship between the number of parties and the choice of electoral system are important and need to be taken into account. Indeed, the evidence of Table 8.3 is rather stronger that I anticipated in proposition P11: among these cases, the effective number of parties is in fact higher prior to moves *away* from proportionality than towards it. Clearly, however, the sample is small and doubts could be cast on the relevance of the data in particular cases. I explore these matters further in the concluding chapter.

PART III

Elite–mass interaction

The process of reform by elite–mass interaction comprises three stages. First, a minority of politicians espouse reform. They initiate the reform process, but they have insufficient strength by themselves to impose reform through normal legislative channels. They therefore go above the heads of other politicians and take the issue to the people, and this popular mobilization around reform constitutes the second stage of the process. But public opinion on its own cannot generate a new electoral system. Rather, at the third stage, public pressure forces politicians to acquiesce in reforms that, on the whole, they still do not want. The reforms in New Zealand and Italy in 1993 and Japan in 1994 all followed variants of this pattern.

Important questions can be asked of each of the three stages. At the first, where a minority of politicians initiate reform, the key question is why those politicians become interested in the issue. I find there are no universal patterns, but that politicians' genuine beliefs in democratic and other values do typically matter. At the second stage, the most important question is what causes popular mobilization to occur around such an esoteric issue as reform of the electoral system. I argue we need to allow for three factors: inherent weaknesses in the prevailing system; contingent crises that focus attention on these weaknesses; and strategic leadership. At the third stage, finally, we need to understand why politicians bow to popular pressure. Much of the answer lies in act contingency: politicians fear that they will lose votes at the next election if they ignore voters' demands for change. But the cases suggest other factors matter too: in particular, experiences gained during an extended reform process may change politicians' own preferences.

As in Part II, I begin by laying out the story of reform in each case: Chapters 9 and 10 fill in the gaps left in Part II in the electoral system histories of Italy and Japan; Chapter 11 then lays out the case of New Zealand. Finally, I draw out comparative findings in Chapter 12.

9

Italy: diluting proportional representation

The story of electoral reform in Italy that I told in Chapter 6 was incomplete: it left out the most significant of all of post-war Italy's reform episodes. In 1993, Italy became the first (and, to date, only) established democracy to replace a proportional electoral system with one based primarily upon single-member plurality (SMP). More precisely, the new law described a semi-compensatory mixed-member system, or, in Shugart and Wattenberg's terms, a mixed-member majoritarian (MMM) system with partial compensation (2001b: 15–16). Seventy-five per cent of seats were allocated by SMP and 25 per cent by PR. Though this distribution would generally be sufficient to provide full proportionality, linkage between the tiers was based on votes rather than seats, and it is for this reason that the system is classified as MMM with partial compensation rather than full mixed-member proportional (MMP). Somewhat different variants of this model were used in the two chambers. For the lower house (Chamber of Deputies), voters cast two votes. PR seats were allocated nationally subject to a 4 per cent threshold using largest remainders after deducting from each party's vote total the number of votes that had been required for victory by that party's winning district candidates (that is, after deducting, for each single-member district (SMD) in which the party's candidate had won, the number of votes won by the second-placed candidate plus one). In the Senate, voters cast just one vote, for an SMD candidate, which was valid also for the party's PR list. PR seats were allocated regionally with no legal threshold using the d'Hondt formula after deducting the votes won by successful SMD candidates (for further details, see D'Alimonte 2005: 256–61; Katz 2001: 115–17).

Not only did this reform violate Colomer's expectation (2004a: 5) that electoral reforms will generally move towards proportionality; it did so when the number of parties was high and rising and when rapid flux in the party system was generating exceptional uncertainty regarding the parties' future electoral prospects – precisely the circumstances in which conventional theories of electoral system choice would expect any move towards plurality to be least likely. The reform was part of a wide-ranging period of 'crisis and transition' in the Italian political system (Bull and Rhodes 1997): besides the collapse of the party system that had existed since the 1940s, there was also exceptional turnover in the membership of parliament (Morlino 1996: 17), and corruption scandals rocked the political establishment. While early talk of the founding of a Second Republic (e.g., Mershon and Pasquino 1995) proved overblown, still, the jolt to the system was severe, and this context was crucial to the electoral reform. But the story of that reform begins much earlier.

The development of reform pressure

Following the hiatus of the *legge truffa* in the 1950s (described in Chapter 6), Italy's proportional electoral system was unquestioned for several decades (Pasquino 2007: 85). But dissatisfaction with the operation of Italy's democratic system grew: Allum (1973: 242) argues that attacks upon the system, though rare, were already 'symptomatic of a wider malaise'. The lack of alternation in government was seen as hindering accountability and fostering corruption; governments were weak and lacking leadership; the system was characterized by *partitocrazia* – the dominance of party machines – to the detriment of democratic control (Hine 1981: 63, 1993a: 1–7; Pasquino 1989: 282–4). In Spotts and Wieser's well-known phrase, Italy was 'a difficult democracy' (Spotts and Wieser 1986). Calls for institutional reforms designed to tackle these problems reached the top of the political agenda in 1976, when Bettino Craxi, newly elected as leader of the Socialist Party (PSI), called for a *Grande Riforma* of the constitutional structure (Bull and Pasquino 2007: 672). In 1983, a Bicameral Commission (the Bozzi Commission) was established to propose changes (Köppl 2004: 3–6; Pasquino 1986).

During these early years, the most prominent reform proposals related not to the electoral system but to the broader constitutional structure. Craxi's main demand (at least, before he became prime minister in 1983) was for the direct election of the head of government (Pasquino 1986: 123). The final report of the Bozzi Commission contained just four pages (out of eighty) on the electoral system, and Furlong (1991: 58) argues that this marginal position 'reflected the priorities of the politicians and their scepticism about the real weight of electoral systems'. Another reason for the Bozzi Commission's silence, however, was not a dearth of thinking on the subject, but rather a surfeit: multiple proposals for electoral reform were put to the Commission, and it proved impossible to achieve even a modicum of consensus among them (Hine 1988: 221).

Several notable proposals had already been made by the early 1980s (Bartolini 1982: 214–15). Submissions to the Bozzi Commission included schemes for bonus-adjusted PR from both the reformist leader of the Christian Democrats, Ciriaco De Mita, and the political scientist and independent leftist senator Gianfranco Pasquino. These differed from both the 1953 *legge truffa* and the 2005 law in that they spread the bonus seats more widely (for details, see Gilbert 1995: 91–3). The Communists advocated MMP, while most of the smaller parties opposed any major reform (Hine 1988: 220).

The Bozzi Commission having come to nothing, reformers sought change by other means. Two parliamentarians stand out in particular as having kept the electoral reform cause alive during the late 1980s. One was Marco Pannella, the leader of the Radical Party. Though his own party was tiny, Pannella saw alternation between single-party governments as the only way to improve Italian governance and constrain corruption. As Gilbert (1995: 93) remarks, Pannella 'never ceased to inveigh against an electoral system that allowed a party as mercurial and oddball as his own to maintain a parliamentary presence'. The other prominent parliamentarian was the free-thinking Christian Democrat deputy Mario Segni. His motives for pursuing the reform agenda have been the subject of some speculation. Bull and Newell (2005: 50–1) suggest that he saw electoral system change as the best means to force the DC to reform itself and meet the challenge of the rising Socialists. According to Donovan (1995: 48), he wanted to reconfigure the party system to facilitate alternation in power at least in part so that he could serve as prime minister in a centre-right government dominated by the DC. As I argue at greater length in Chapter 12, however, both Segni and Pannella were motivated in large part by the genuine belief that Italy's political system was not working and that electoral reform could deliver better governance.

Segni and Pannella initially pursued a primarily parliamentary path to electoral reform (Pasquino 1992: 10). They established the *Lega per il collegio uninominale* (League for Single-Member Districts) in October 1986 with other politicians and academics, and rapidly gained the support of approaching two hundred parliamentarians from across most of the parties (Gilbert 1995: 94; McCarthy 1992: 15). Segni launched a reform manifesto calling for the adoption of the French two-round system that was signed by thirty 'luminaries of Italian culture, science and industry' (Wyles 1987). He created the *Movimento per la riforma elettorale* in April 1988, hoping to pressurize parliamentarians into acting.

It rapidly became clear, however, that the parliamentary route to reform would be blocked: as had been widely predicted (LaPalombara 1987: 234; Spotts and Wieser 1986: 119), the majority of politicians – including, most importantly, the leaders of the DC and the PSI – saw the proposals as violating their power interests and therefore opposed them. De Mita, who had become prime minister in 1988, was replaced as DC leader in early 1989 by the arch-conservative Arnaldo Forlani, signalling a return to the strategy of managing and maintaining existing power structures (Bull and Newell 1993: 207–8). Forlani's fellow conservative Giulio Andreotti replaced De Mita as prime minister later the same year and successfully kicked reform into the long grass (Pasquino 1991: 49–50; Pasquino and Hellman 1992: 3). On the Socialist side, meanwhile, interest in electoral reform had quickly waned as the party's position in the governing coalition had consolidated: like the leaders of the DC, Craxi sought to maintain the existing power balance and saw the prevailing electoral system as a means to that end (Pasquino 1992: 12). With the parliamentary route to reform closed, advocates of change sought another approach.

The referendums of 1991 and 1993

Thus, Segni and other reformers turned to the people. Italian law allows for citizen-initiated referendums, and so, in early 1990, a committee comprising individuals from various political parties and civil society organizations was established to collect the 500,000 signatures required (Pasquino 1992: 11). But such referendums can only be abrogative: they can only annul existing laws or parts of laws; they cannot enact new provisions. Thus, the reformers had to find ways of eliminating phrases from the existing law such as to change the system in the direction they desired. They gathered signatures in relation to three questions. The first would replace the PR system for the Senate with a system much like that finally adopted in 1993, in which 75 per cent of seats would be elected by single-member plurality and 25 per cent by PR (see Katz 2001: 99–101 for an explanation of how removing just one line of the electoral law could effect this radical change). The second would extend the majoritarian electoral system already used in large communes to all communes. The third would reduce the number of preference votes that voters could cast within party lists for elections to the Chamber of Deputies from three or four (depending on district magnitude) to one (Pasquino 1992: 14). This final question reflected the perception that the preferential voting system had become an instrument of corruption, especially in the south.

After some initial difficulties, the signature threshold was met by August 1990 (Gilbert 1995: 99). In early 1991, however, the Constitutional Court ruled against the first two questions (on technical grounds), allowing only the third to proceed. Though the issue directly addressed by the referendum that followed in June 1991 was thus relatively minor, voters and politicians understood it as offering the chance to express a wider view on the state of Italian democracy: a 'yes' vote was implicitly a vote for wholesale electoral reform (Pasquino and Hellman 1992: 4). Thus, the positions taken by the various parties in the course of the referendum campaign reflected their views on the broader issue. The only large party to advocate a 'yes' vote was the Democratic Party of the Left (PDS). This was the successor to the old Communist Party (PCI), having changed its name after the fall of the Berlin Wall in 1989. Party leader Achille Occhetto sought a realigned party system comprising two blocs on left and right, with the PDS forming the core of the left. For this purpose, he argued for a two-round majoritarian electoral system, hoping it would deliver results similar to those seen in France after 1958 (Calise 1993: 549; McCarthy 1992: 14–15, 23). Socialist leader Bettino Craxi, meanwhile, urged voters to ignore the referendum and 'go to the seaside', hoping thereby that turnout would fall below the 50 per cent required for the result to stand. DC leaders, recognizing that such public expressions, coming from widely disliked politicians, might only encourage voter participation, sought to maintain silence on the issue and starve the referendum of publicity (McCarthy 1992: 17; Parker 1996: 41).

Given the technical nature of the referendum question and the attempts to limit publicity, the referendum's supporters feared and opponents hoped that citizens would treat the vote with indifference – as they had done the previous year, when three referendum questions failed by some margin to reach the turnout threshold (Uleri 2002: 864). But the results decisively confounded such expectations: on a turnout of 62.5 per cent, 95.6 per cent of those voting supported the change (Parker 1996: 42). Any idea – voiced most famously just four years earlier by LaPalombara (1987: 8, 89, 165) – that perennial complaints about the state of Italian politics were merely rhetoric, part of a game that high-spirited Italians rather enjoyed, was shattered. Some accounts of the crisis that engulfed Italian politics in the following years date its beginning precisely to the referendum vote of 9 June 1991 (e.g., Gundle and Parker 1996a: 2).

Segni appears initially to have hoped that the moral weight of the resounding referendum result might be sufficient to compel politicians to accept more far-reaching reform.[1] Indeed, many parties did have their own reform blueprints: the PDS, as previously, advocated the two-round system; even the DC played with the idea of a bonus-adjusted system. But the parties' proposals were highly diverse, the Socialist leadership remained trenchantly opposed to reform, and, in any case, the conversion of many politicians to the reform cause was clearly half-hearted at best (McCarthy 1992: 23). The largest tremors in Italy's political earthquake were yet to come, and so the complacent belief that the status quo could hold won the day. The parliamentary route to reform remained blocked.

Signature collection for a second referendum therefore began in autumn 1991 (Pasquino and Hellman 1992: 4–5), and by January 1992 well over a million signatures had been gathered.[2] The referendum question of principal concern for current purposes was a rerun of one of the disallowed questions from 1991, on the creation of a mixed-member system for the Senate with 75 per cent of seats elected by SMP and 25 per cent by PR. With the wording of the question suitably clarified, the Constitutional Court this time gave it its blessing. The referendum was held – encompassing twelve questions in all – in April 1993 (for the detail of the questions, see Newell and Bull 1993).

Two developments profoundly changed the context of Italian politics between the first and second referendums. First, the *Tangentopoli* corruption scandal, which was to engulf the political class over the following years, first broke in February 1992 with the arrest in Milan of Socialist politician Mario Chiesa (Parker 1996: 24–5). The *mani pulite* (clean hands) investigation conducted by Italy's independent-minded judges was to end the careers of many of the leading figures in Italian politics, including Andreotti, Forlani, and Craxi, and served as the backdrop against which subsequent developments played out (Gilbert 1995: 126–54).

Second, the party system, which had been remarkably stable for over forty years, began to unravel. The seeds of this transformation were sown in the 1980s, first with the emergence of Umberto Bossi's *Lega Lombarda* and other northern leagues pushing for greater autonomy from Rome, and second with the collapse of the Berlin Wall and the beginnings of communist realignment. By early 1991, the transformation of the PCI into the PDS had been completed and the unreconstructed *Rifondazione*

---

[1] 'No to Cheats, Yes to Change', *The Economist*, 15 June 1991.
[2] 'Referendum Ad Infinitum', *The Economist*, 18 January 1992.

Table 9.1. *Elections to the Italian Chamber of Deputies, 1987 and 1992*

	June 1987		April 1992	
Party	% votes	% seats	% votes	% seats
Christian Democrats (DC)	34.3	37.1	29.7	32.7
Communists (PCI)	26.6	28.1	–	–
Democratic Party of the Left (PDS)	–	–	16.1	17.0
Communist Refoundation (RC)	–	–	5.6	5.6
Socialists (PSI)	14.3	14.9	13.6	14.6
*Lega**	1.3	0.2	8.7	8.7
Italian Social Movement (MSI)	5.9	5.6	5.4	5.4
Republicans (PRI)	3.7	3.3	4.4	4.3
Liberals (PLI)	2.1	1.7	2.8	2.7
Greens	2.5	2.1	2.8	2.5
Social Democrats (PSDI)	3.0	2.7	2.7	2.5
La Rete	–	–	1.9	1.9
Radical Party (*Lista Pannella*)	2.6	2.1	1.2	1.1
Others	3.8	2.3	5.1	1.0

*In 1987, the *Lega Lombarda* and *Liga Veneta*; in 1992, the combined *Lega Nord*.
Sources: Mackie and Rose (1991: 273, 275); Ministero dell'Interno (1992).

Comunista (Communist Refoundation, RC) had broken away; mean-while, the northern leagues had combined to form the *Lega Nord* (Morlino 1996: 7). The general election of April 1992 generated the highest electoral volatility since the 1940s: the vote shares of the DC and the PSI both fell; the combined share of the PDS and RC was significantly below that of the PCI in 1987; the principal beneficiary was the *Lega Nord*, whose share rose from just 1.3 per cent in 1987 to 8.7 per cent (see Table 9.1; Bull and Newell 1993: 218, 215). The premier-ship was eventually taken not by Craxi, as had been expected before the election, but by the relatively unknown Socialist professor Giuliano Amato, and the majority of the new cabinet's members were newcomers (Hine and Della Sala 1992: 367). In the months thereafter, the old parties – especially the DC and PSI – went into freefall.

These developments had two effects upon the process of electoral reform. First, it became almost impossible for any party to resist the public pressure for reform of some kind. The existing system was dis-credited. Furthermore, the fall of the Berlin Wall and transformation of the communists meant that reforming the system to achieve alternation between left and right no longer frightened the majority of Italians (Sidoti 1993: 112). In the referendum of April 1993, the Christian Democrats, Socialists, PDS, and *Lega Nord* all supported a 'yes' vote, as did many of the smaller parties; only the neo-Fascist Italian Social Movement (MSI), RC, the Greens, and a small Sicily-based anti-corruption movement, *La Rete*, campaigned against (Newell and Bull 1993: 610, 612). As Donovan (1995: 57) observes, 'This was a clear case of that old adage: "if you can't beat them, join them" being put into play.'

Second, the parties worked increasingly hard to formulate their own reform proposals. Some, such as the PDS, did so because they believed that systems other than the status quo would better serve their purposes. Others, such as the DC, probably did so because they knew they could no longer maintain the status quo, and therefore sought to steer the inevitable reform so as to limit the damage it did them (Newell and Bull 1993: 611). As Katz (2001: 106–7) shows, the reform proposals emanating from the parties during this period were many and diverse; in some cases, multiple, markedly differing proposals came from the same party.

The referendum result in April 1993 was unsurprisingly decisive: 82.7 per cent of voters supported reform on a turnout of 77.1 per cent (Katz 2001: 96; Uleri 2002: 864). The reasons for the voters' unambiguous rejection of the status quo have been widely discussed and stemmed from the processes that I have already described: as Gambetta and Warner (2004: 240) put it, voters 'wanted fewer parties, government alternation, more government stability and effectiveness, closer links between parliamentarians and their constituency votes, as well as reduced opportunities for corruption in the electoral process'; 'it is undeniable', they observe, 'that the Italian public was truly enthusiastic for some kind of electoral reform'.

Parliamentary response

The immediate consequence of the referendum was that Italy had, in effect, a new electoral system for the Senate while the system for the Chamber of Deputies remained unaltered. In legal terms, legislators had almost complete freedom in how they responded to this situation: they could leave the new status quo as it was, or they could adopt almost any alternative to it; the only thing they could not do was readopt the system that citizens had voted down. In practice, however, they were more constrained. First, Italy is unique among established democracies in having virtually perfect bicameralism: the two chambers have almost equal powers, and, crucially, governments depend upon the confidence of both (Diermeier, Eraslan, and Merlo 2007: 3). In this context, to elect the two chambers by markedly differing electoral systems was seen as untenable (Donovan 1996: 144; Hine 1993b). Thus, retaining the new status quo was impossible: parliament would have to enact further reform.

Second, the popular will could not be ignored. In voting 'yes' to the electoral reform question in the 1993 referendum, voters clearly did *not* declare that of all possible electoral systems the one that they most preferred was the one that the 'yes' vote established: that this was the option on the table was mostly an accidental reflection of the drafting of the electoral and referendum laws. Nevertheless, the discourse that surrounded the referendum left no doubt that voters did want major change towards majoritarian democracy: an outcome that reproduced broad proportionality in a new guise would not be acceptable.

Within these parameters, the large parties pursued the electoral system that would best serve their perceived power interests. One key issue concerned the choice of formula in the single-member districts: plurality or two-round majority. The PDS continued to advocate the latter. They believed it would foster the emergence of multi-party coalitions of left and right (Katz 2001: 112), which would allow them to end their isolation from power without giving up their separate identity. The DC, meanwhile, remained vehemently opposed to this. Having to choose between majoritarian formulas, they preferred SMP: 'the risk that they wished to minimize was the formation of electoral alliances from which they would be excluded. Their hope was to maintain the dominance of a pivotal center, albeit a center with reduced representation' (Katz 1996: 37). Once this debate had been resolved in favour of SMP, the next major issue concerned the relative sizes of the SMP and PR tiers. The DC appears initially to have sought to eke out as large a share for the proportional component as politicians could get away with without igniting further public anger: the initial proposal from the DC rapporteur of the Constitutional Affairs Committee, Sergio Mattarella, allowed for a 30 per cent PR component. The MSI and RC, meanwhile, suggested a 33.3 per cent share (Katz 2001: 105, 108, 112). Katz (2001: 109) suggests that a primary reason for the final shift to 25 per cent was the perception that this was the maximum permissible in the light of the referendum result. The sponsors of the referendum themselves wanted to go still further: Segni suggested a 10 per cent PR component, while Pannella still called for pure SMP (Katz 2001: 109). But these ideas did not gain wide support.

It is tempting to argue that, within the constraints imposed by the referendum and given the large number of parties and ongoing collapse of the old party system, legislators simply sought the most proportional system that they could get away with. Under circumstances of high uncertainty and no tenable status quo, indeed, that is what P12 in Chapter 3 would predict. This interpretation is supported by the maintenance of the substantial PR tier and the use, in the Chamber of Deputies, of the largest remainders method of seat allocation. On the other hand, however, parliament also introduced a 4 per cent threshold for the lower house (cf. Gilbert 1994: 6), and the linkage between the tiers, particularly in the lower house, was only partially compensatory. The thinking that underlay these provisions remains unclear.

The new electoral systems for the Chamber of Deputies and the Senate were finally enacted into law in August 1993. They were passed on the votes largely of the Christian Democrats, the Socialists, and the *Lega Nord*, while the PDS abstained and most of the small party representatives either abstained or voted against (Katz 2001: 114).

In the process that led to this enactment we can see the outline of the type of reform that I label elite majority imposition. At first, only a minority of politicians adopted the electoral reform agenda, while the majority, calculating effects upon their power interests, resisted. The pro-reform minority therefore mobilized public support in their cause, latching on to growing public disaffection with the operation of Italian democracy in order to reach over the heads of the incumbent political elite. In consequence, the anti-reform majority of politicians were forced to change their stance. Legally, they were not required to do so: they could have responded to the 1993 referendum by introducing new variants on the proportional model. But they knew that to do so would risk severe punishment from voters who were already in a mood to cast off their old voting habits. Thus, constrained by public opinion and thinking of self-preservation, legislators enacted a reform that many rightly feared could only harm their prospects of re-election. They were not entirely supine in doing so: they did tweak the new system in significant ways to preserve the advantages that they gained from the old. Nevertheless, it was public revulsion with the state of Italian politics, mobilized by reformers around the issue of electoral system change, that primarily drove the outcome. Thus was it possible for majoritarian reform to be adopted in a most inhospitable context.

10

Japan: the abandonment of SNTV

In March 1994, just months after the enactment of reform in Italy, Japan's Diet passed into law its own electoral system change, replacing single non-transferable vote (SNTV) with a straight mixed-member majoritarian (MMM) system. Under the new system, there were 300 seats elected by single-member plurality (SMP) and 200 seats elected by PR from closed party lists in eleven districts, with no compensation between the two parts. The same system survives today, except that the number of PR seats was reduced in 1999 to 180. As in Italy, the gestation of the reform was long and involved pressures both from groups within the political elite and from the public. The process can be divided into four phases, corresponding to the tenures of the four principal prime ministers to hold office during the period: Noboru Takeshita (together with his short-lived successor, Sosuke Uno), Toshiki Kaifu, Kiichi Miyazawa, and Morihiro Hosokawa.

Phase 1   Reform talk under Takeshita and Uno, 1988–1989

As Chapter 7 discussed, replacement of SNTV with an electoral system based wholly or largely on SMP was the subject of continuous, if generally low-intensity, discussion from the founding of the modern party system in 1955 until Prime Minister Kakuei Tanaka's aborted reform proposal in 1973. The hostility that met Tanaka's proposal, however, forced most reform enthusiasts to retreat. The seventh Electoral System Advisory Council, which reported in December 1972, was not replaced when its term ended. Though Tanaka's successor as prime minister, Takeo Miki, was a prominent reformer, his support base within the ruling Liberal Democratic Party (LDP) was very weak (Reed and Thies 2001: 162–3). Thus, the issue slid from prominence.

Curtis (1999: 148), indeed, goes so far as to suggest that 'the issue of electoral-system change disappeared from the political agenda, not to surface again until seventeen years later'. This is not wholly accurate.

First, the LDP's own Election Research Council reported in October 1976, in the wake of the major Lockheed corruption scandal. It advocated a mixed system of SMP and PR for lower house (House of Representatives) elections and reform of part of the system used for elections to the upper house (House of Councillors) (Hrebenar 1977: 987). Second, that report's recommendations regarding the upper house were enacted in 1982. Previously, the House of Councillors had been elected entirely through SNTV, though with two types of district: prefectural and national. Now, the seats in the national district (fifty at each election) would be elected by closed-list PR (Stockwin 1983: 223).[1] Nevertheless, at no time between 1974 and 1988 did any senior LDP politician seriously urge reform of the electoral system for the lower house. In part, no doubt, this was because the LDP's continuous slide in the polls between 1958 and 1976 was reversed thereafter (Inoguchi 1990). Additionally, the upper house reform may actually have reduced prospects of reform for the lower house: the change failed to cut the expense of campaigning, as its promoters had said it would (Jain 1993: 81), and was unpopular with voters, who, for part of the election, could now vote only for a closed party list, not for an individual candidate. In Curtis's view at the time (1988: 189), the change in the electoral system for the House of Councillors 'contribute[d] to a general decline in public interest in issues of political reform'.

Nothing in 1987 or 1988 suggested that this pattern was about to change. Certainly, there were concerns about 'money politics' and corruption (e.g., Kōsaka 1988; Uchida 1988), but these were perennial debates in Japanese politics, and no one in power proposed electoral reform as the solution. Rather, the LDP pursued minor changes to the rules on campaign finance.[2]

Over the second half of 1988, however, the largest corruption scandal to engulf Japanese politics since Lockheed in 1976 – the Recruit scandal – gradually unfolded. Numerous politicians were revealed to have received discounted shares in the Recruit Cosmos real estate company, which they subsequently sold at considerable profit (Curtis 1999: 74). Prime Minister Takeshita responded in his New Year address at the beginning

---

[1] The House of Councillors is elected by halves. Thus, in total, 100 of its 242 seats are filled by this method.
[2] 'LDP Panel Approves Package to Limit Political Fund-Raisers', *Japan Times* (hereinafter *JT*), 16 April 1988.

of 1989 by promising 'a year of political reform',[3] and in the weeks that followed he appointed both an Advisory Council on Political Reform that reported directly to him and a Political Reform Committee within the LDP (Shiratori 1995: 83). In May 1989, the latter body reported, advocating a range of reforms to campaign finance and the electoral system, including a reduction in the total number of seats and a shift to a system based on SMP combined with some element of PR (LDP Political Reform Committee 1989; Shiratori 1995: 83–4). By this time, however, Takeshita had himself been implicated in the Recruit scandal and forced to resign. His successor, Sosuke Uno, survived in office for just two months before succumbing to the effects of his sexual adventures and the LDP's defeat in elections to the House of Councillors. He simply batted the reform proposals off for further discussion by establishing, after a seventeen-year break, an eighth Electoral System Advisory Council (Babb 1996: 156–7; Shiratori 1995: 84).

This first phase of the electoral reform process was important for placing the issue of reform on the agenda. It is not clear, however, that much serious reform intent existed. Press commentary at the time suggested that Takeshita and Uno were simply temporizing – playing the age-old tactic of responding to immediate pressures by establishing inquiries in the hope that, by the time the inquiries reported back, feelings would have subsided and politics would continue as normal.[4] As Woodall (1999: 35–9) notes, scandals had repeatedly prompted reform talk among Japanese politicians, but had never generated anything more than minor changes to political financing laws or district boundaries. With the scandal beginning to subside following Takeshita's resignation, most LDP politicians hoped that this tactic would indeed succeed once more in allowing them to ride out the storm.[5]

Phase 2   Thwarted reform under Kaifu, 1989–1991

Following the brief Uno interlude, the second phase in the process began with the election in August 1989 of Toshiki Kaifu as LDP leader and prime minister. Kaifu held office for slightly over two years and during that time made the first serious attempt at enacting electoral reform.

---

[3] 'Takeshita Vows to Make 1989 a Year of Political Reform', *JT*, 14 January 1989.
[4] 'Level of Voter Tolerance Reached', *JT*, 11 March 1989; 'Voters Demonstrate Disenchantment', *JT*, 8 April 1989; 'Punishment at the Polls', *JT*, 12 August 1989.
[5] 'The Voters Hold the Card', *JT*, 8 July 1989.

The eighth Electoral System Advisory Council reported in April 1990, arguing for an MMM system and against mixed-member proportionality (MMP). Specifically, it proposed a lower house of 501 members, of whom 301 would be elected by SMP and 200 by closed-list PR in eleven districts (Shiratori 1995: 85). The Political Reform Bill that the cabinet eventually submitted to the Diet in July 1991 differed from the Council's recommendations only in detail, proposing that 300 seats should be elected by SMP but only 171 by PR (Shiratori 1995: 86).

The balance of forces that developed around the electoral reform issue over these two years differed from that during Takeshita's tenure in several respects. The most obvious was the different identity of the prime minister. Kaifu was chosen for this office in the wake of the Recruit scandal because he had a clean image, just as 'Mr Clean' Miki had been chosen in the face of scandal in 1974. Indeed, Kaifu belonged to the LDP faction that Miki had founded and shared Miki's belief that electoral reform was needed to weaken factions and fight corruption (Curtis 1999: 151; Wolfe 1992: 774). He would later form a reform group within the LDP (Daimon 1993), and in November 1993 he violated the official party line by abstaining in (rather than opposing) an electoral reform vote in the lower house.[6] He left the LDP in 1994 and became leader of the New Frontier Party (*Shinshintō*, NFP), a new party combining several non-LDP groups (Reed 2003b: 32–3). He eventually returned to the LDP fold in 2003.

Kaifu was not, however, the most important player: coming from the smallest LDP faction, he depended on the triumvirate of leaders at the head of the largest faction – the Takeshita faction. These were Takeshita himself, together with Shin Kanemaru and Ichirō Ozawa. Ozawa was secretary general of the LDP; in Otake's words (1996: 283), the cabinet 'was run as if Ozawa was the de facto prime minister'. Two pro-reform groups within the LDP that were to play roles throughout the subsequent phases of the reform process and beyond crystallized in the course of Kaifu's premiership. One was focused upon Ozawa. The other consisted of 'young reformers' – first- and second-term Diet members who were disillusioned with the engrained practices that they saw as suffocating Japanese political life.

By 1993, Ozawa would be Japan's most aggressive advocate of electoral reform. He published a book that year in which he argued for change across all aspects of Japanese life. "'Japanese-style democracy'", he

---

[6] 'LDP Suspends 13 Who Voted with Gov't', *JT*, 29 November 1993.

argued, 'is no longer able to respond adequately to the changes taking place at home and abroad ... We must reform our politics, our economy, our society, and our consciousness, to bring them into greater currency with the rest of the world' (Ozawa 1994 [1993]: 11). His first goal was to 'establish political leadership', which, he argued, was needed if Japan was to play its proper role on the world stage (Ozawa 1994 [1993]: 12, 21–3). Leadership would be impossible without changes in the party system and processes of policy-making in the LDP and the Diet, and these changes required, *inter alia*, electoral reform. The problem with the existing electoral system, he wrote, was 'the overemphasis on proportional representation'. He argued for a system based on single-member plurality, acknowledging also the need to include a proportional component to ensure some minority representation (Ozawa 1994 [1993]: 24–9, 66–8).

Ozawa's belief in the need for electoral reform was long-standing. We might even say that it was in his blood: his father had been a leading advocate of SMP in the 1950s and 1960s (Schlesinger 1997: 176; David Williams 1996: 279); his 'political father', meanwhile, was Kakuei Tanaka, promoter of reform in 1973 (Schlesinger 1997: 172). Less speculatively, we know that he had begun to press for electoral reform by 1989 (Gaunder 2007: 97; Samuels 2003: 328–9). He travelled to Europe for an electoral system study trip in 1990 (Schlesinger 1997: 205), and New Zealand's Geoffrey Palmer recalls discussing electoral reform with Ozawa while playing golf in both Japan and New Zealand during Palmer's tenure as prime minister between 1989 and 1990: 'He was interested in electoral reform. He wanted to change the LDP' (Palmer 2006). Ozawa's belief in the need for reform was further boosted by the experience of the Gulf War in early 1991: he wanted Japan to contribute troops to the coalition against Saddam Hussein, but was unable to persuade his colleagues (Desmond 1995: 125–7; Schlesinger 1997: 258). This experience solidified Ozawa's view that Japan could play its proper role in the world only with an electoral reform that would catalyse transformation of the political system.

Thus, Ozawa was the most powerful advocate of electoral reform during Kaifu's term as prime minister. He was aided in pursuing this goal by his (then) most loyal acolyte, Tsutomu Hata, who was in charge of the process of devising the new system.

The second group within the LDP seeking change in the electoral system was the group of 'young reformers' centred on Masayoshi Takemura. Mostly elected for the first time in 1986, the young reformers were sharply critical of money politics, reflecting 'something approaching a consensus among many younger politicians both in the LDP and in the parties in opposition that systemic change is needed' (Stockwin 1991a: 6). In September 1988, as the Recruit scandal began to emerge, Takemura formed the Utopia Political Research Group, comprising thirty-seven Diet members, committed to seeking solutions to the dominance of money and corruption in Japanese politics (Wolfe 1995: 1065–6). The young reformers were thus present during the Kaifu administration. While they played a major role in the later phases of the electoral reform process, however, there is little evidence to suggest that they exerted significant pressure at this early stage.

Beyond the LDP, important support for reform came also from industry and trade unions. *Keidanren* (the Federation of Economic Organizations, the chief business association) pressed the reform case as early as the summer of 1989.[7] The main trade union confederation, *Rengō*, also actively pursued the cause. Its goal was to create a united opposition force that could challenge LDP power: in the 1989 House of Councillors elections, for example, it sponsored joint candidates of the four main non-communist opposition parties. It argued for 'political reform legislation that would dramatically restructure the Japanese electoral system' (Carlile 1994: 615); specifically, it called for SMP to encourage two-partism, though it suggested that a proportional element would also be required (Tokumoto 1990).

Though various sources of pro-reform pressure thus existed within the Japanese political elite during this period, still the advocates of change were in the minority: a survey conducted in the spring of 1990 found that only 31.4 per cent of Diet members were willing to back the adoption of single-member districts.[8] It might be imagined that LDP members would jump at the prospect of SMP. As noted in Chapter 7, it had long been recognized that the LDP, as by far the largest party, would greatly benefit, in terms of seat share, from such a system: projections from the mid-1980s suggested that the party would win 89 per cent of seats under pure SMP and 79 per cent even with a mixed system (Hrebenar 1986: 47). Nevertheless, the prospect of reform met considerable opposition among the party's Diet members: as one commentator put it at the time, Kaifu's 'job of selling electoral reform to his colleagues in the Diet' was 'a task similar to unloading Florida swampland on market-wise real estate investors'.[9] Two principal

---

[7] 'Keidanren, LDP Agree to Cooperate on Reform', *JT*, 8 July 1989.
[8] 'Kaifu Vows to Implement Reform of Election System', *JT*, 7 May 1990.
[9] 'Kaifu Continues Push for Electoral Reform', *JT*, 21 May 1990.

considerations underlay this conservatism. First, many individual Diet members saw considerable personal costs in reform. They had invested heavily in campaign organizations suited to the needs of the status quo and did not want to face new rules of competition. Faction bosses too had 'thrived' under a system that forced LDP candidates into competition with each other (Masuzoe 1991: 4). Second, the uncertainty associated with change was high. Recent electoral history had reminded LDP Diet members of the high volatility that SMP can allow: the *Yomiuri Shimbun* newspaper calculated that under an MMM system of 301 single-member districts and 200 PR seats the LDP would, on 1990 lower house election figures, have increased its seat tally from 275 to 390. But using voting data from the House of Councillors election of 1989, in which the LDP had suffered major losses, the party would have slipped to just 123 seats, compared to 334 for the Japan Socialist Party (JSP) (Hrebenar 1992: 47). Those in the LDP who wished simply to maintain the LDP's perennial position in power did not see that such a reform could do any good.

Hostility towards the reforms proposed by the Kaifu government was at least as strong among the opposition parties. A case could be made for expecting the JSP to have greeted a system based on SMP with enthusiasm. Though the JSP was the second largest party, there was good reason to think that, without major upheaval, it would never gain government office under the prevailing electoral system. First, SNTV encouraged party system fragmentation (Hrebenar 1986: 37; Reed 1990) and thereby led to a tendency for the opposition parties to nominate more candidates than would maximize their collective seat share (Johnson 2000: 14). Second, the system favoured incumbents: electoral success was significantly dependent upon generous campaign funds and provision of pork; those in power were more likely to attract business donations and could demonstrate effective delivery of pork more readily (Stockwin 1988b: 35). Third, the system made growth beyond the JSP's size (typically around 20 per cent of the seats in the lower house) towards majority status very difficult. In most districts, the JSP ran one candidate (and, in most, that candidate was elected) (Stockwin 1992: 91). To win a majority, however, the party would have had to run at least two candidates in three-member districts and at least three candidates in four- or five-member districts. Yet in the event that its vote share grew less than hoped, this strategy would spread those votes too thinly and thereby lead to seat losses. Thus, the seat-maximizing interests of the party as a whole and, even more, the re-election interests of incumbents encouraged the party to play safe (Reed and Bolland 1999: 212–18). Precisely this happened in 1990: despite winning a majority victory in the House of Councillors elections the previous year, the JSP fielded just 148 candidates in the House of Representatives elections of 1990, far too few to have any hope of securing a lower house majority (Stockwin 1991a: 4).

These problems might have been overcome by the introduction of SMP, but the party was not willing to countenance that option. One reason may have been that it simply lacked the ambition to govern: with little prospect of gaining power in the near future, the party was unable to recruit ambitious candidates and contented itself with the mild influence and perks that the political system accorded the largest opposition party (Curtis 1988: 123; Stockwin 1988a: 15, 1991a: 2; Yayama 1991: 33). Some analysts, however, have questioned the view that the JSP lacked ambition (Babb 2007; Johnson 2000: 15–18). A further reason for caution was the sheer uncertainty engendered by reform. It was widely expected that SMP would promote a two-party system, but it was far from certain that the JSP would form the core of the second party. Ozawa's plan at this stage, after all, was that the LDP's victory in the first SMP election should be so overwhelming as to eliminate the JSP as a serious contender, and that the LDP should subsequently split to create a system of two conservative parties (Desmond 1995: 127). While it may have been easy for the officials of *Rengō* to take such a risk, it was much harder for the elected politicians of the JSP to follow suit: the latter, but not the former, would thereby be putting their own careers on the line.

Thus, the JSP consistently opposed electoral reform (Hrebenar 1986: 47; Morita 1991: 81). As in the LDP, many of the JSP's newest Diet members were anxious to press for change. Following the 1990 elections, twenty-nine of them established the New Wave Society, which was 'dedicated to reforming the party and its policies along social democratic lines' and sought to turn the JSP into 'a party in contention for national power' (Stockwin 1991a: 4). It advocated MMP in a policy document issued in June 1990, but this met opposition from the party leadership (Stockwin 1991b: 294), and the group's influence was short-lived. Unsurprisingly, the smaller opposition parties all also opposed an SMP-based system. Most would have accepted reform only towards greater proportionality (Landers 1991: 1; Morita 1991: 83–4).

Public pressure for reform during this period, finally, was limited. As one commentator observed, 'Although the public in Japan is seen to be furious about corruption among politicians, it has shown little interest in changing the political system itself. The public furor that was kicked up during the Recruit stock-for-favors scandal in the spring of 1989 petered out after a year or so' (Fukuoka 1991: 9). A poll conducted after the Kaifu government had presented its bill to the Diet found that only 21 per cent of respondents readily expressed a preference between single-member districts and proportional representation (Landers 1991: 6). There was no need, therefore, for politicians to agree to reforms on act-contingent grounds.

Given this alignment of forces, it surprised no one that Kaifu's reform attempt failed. On 30 September 1991, LDP power-brokers agreed with the opposition parties to scrap the political reform bills without a vote. Shortly thereafter, Kaifu announced he would not seek re-election as LDP president.[10]

Phase 3   More reform talk under Miyazawa, 1991–1993

Kaifu was succeeded as LDP president and prime minister by Kiichi Miyazawa. Ozawa was instrumental in his appointment (Masaki 1991). Yet in accepting Miyazawa as prime minister, Ozawa seems also to have accepted that electoral reform would not occur, at least for the time being, for Miyazawa was no reform enthusiast (Curtis 1999: 86; Reed and Thies 2001: 165–6). Thus, in the early months of his premiership, Miyazawa showed no sign of taking the issue forward. All changed in early 1992, however, with the emergence of fresh corruption scandals: first the Kyowa scandal, then the much larger Sagawa Kyūbin affair.[11] As in previous scandals, these involved allegations that senior politicians had received large illegal donations from companies seeking political favour. Coming when the Recruit affair remained fresh in many minds, these renewed scandals generated an impression of systemic malaise. One editorial asked, 'Is Japanese party politics corrupt to its core? The question can no longer be dismissed as excessive or radical. Without root and branch reforms that slash the costs of Diet elections and political activity, the public will remain unpersuaded by claims by politicians that all is well in Japan's democratic corridors.'[12]

Miyazawa responded by promising reforms, focusing on changes to the rules on political finance.[13] It appears, however, that such words

---

[10] 'Kaifu Suffers Setback, Diet Rejects Reform Bills', *JT*, 7 October 1991; 'Kaifu Abandons Hope for Re-Election', *JT*, 14 October 1991.
[11] Masaki (1992); 'Nightmare in Nagata-cho', *JT*, 24 February 1992.
[12] 'Rotten to the Core', *JT*, 27 January 1992.
[13] 'Getting Serious about Political Reform', *JT*, 27 January 1992.

were, as before, intended to do little more than enable the government to ride out the storm. Fresh impetus came in autumn 1992 when the LDP's legendary king-maker Shin Kanemaru, having admitted his failure to disclose a ¥500 million ($4 million) donation from the Sagawa Kyūbin trucking company, was fined just ¥200,000 ($1,600). There was widespread outrage at this perceived leniency, and public pressure for genuine reform intensified (Curtis 1999: 87). This time Miyazawa responded by proposing electoral reform. Specifically, his government submitted a bill on 31 March 1993 for a pure SMP system with 500 single-member districts (Shiratori 1995: 87).

The constellation of forces that fought over electoral reform in the first half of 1993 was an evolving form of the constellation that had existed during the Kaifu administration. Having failed to gain control over the Takeshita faction in the aftermath of Kanemaru's resignation in October 1992, Ozawa, with Hata and thirty-four followers, formed a new faction, nominally headed by Hata, but in practice dominated by Ozawa (Curtis 1999: 88–92). They lobbied for SMP with renewed vigour (Kitazume 1993a; Ozawa 1993 [1992]: 11), but they no longer operated at the heart of the LDP power structure. The young reformers within the LDP, meanwhile, had established a new group, the Group of Young Diet Members Committed to Reform, in December 1991, which worked hard to mobilize public opinion in order to advance the reform cause (Wolfe 1995: 1066–7).

On the opposition side, hostility towards majoritarian reforms remained high (Washio 1993: 28), but there was also growing recognition of the fact that rising public pressure for some kind of change could not be ignored. Satsuki Eda, leader of the Social Democratic League (*Shaminren*), the smallest party in the lower house, formed a new group, called Sirius, in November 1992, with members from the JSP and *Rengō* as well as his own party. He argued for abolition of SNTV, saying it was 'a major cause of the political system's rigidity', and proposed MMP in its place (Eda 1993: 38). On 8 April 1993, the JSP and *Kōmeitō* (Clean Government Party) jointly proposed an MMP system comprising 200 single-member districts and 300 seats filled by closed-list PR in twelve regions (Reed and Thies 2001: 166).

Despite the wide gulf that separated the proposals, various groups worked hard for agreement. A group of businessmen, scholars, and labour leaders released a plan on 17 April for a compromise system that, they argued, would keep party strengths roughly as they were. The proposal was for an MMP system under which 300 seats would be elected by SMP and 200 by PR in forty-seven districts (Kitazume 1993c). *Kōmeitō*, *Shaminren*, and the small Democratic Socialist Party (DSP) all voiced support for the proposal (Kishimoto 1993), and Ozawa also pressed for compromise.[14] But the JSP remained hostile (Kishimoto 1993). Some sources suggest that Miyazawa wanted to compromise (Kohno 1997: 138; Woodall 1999: 39), but other senior LDP figures refused to budge. In fact, it appears that many LDP leaders had never been serious about reform. They knew they had to be seen to respond to public unhappiness with the state of politics. Taking advantage of the LDP's minority position in the upper house – which meant reform would need opposition support – LDP leaders quite deliberately proposed a reform that would never gain such support: projections suggested that under the pure SMP plan, the LDP could win 458 of the 500 seats.[15] They stuck rigidly to that plan in order to ensure that no reform would occur (Curtis 1999: 93–6; Kōsaka 1993: 49; Reed and Thies 2001: 166).

The forces pressing for reform during this period were stronger than they had been either in 1989 or in 1991. Young Diet members' genuine unease over the nature of politics intensified as each new corruption allegation broke. So too did public pressure. Having been forced to take an independent course after losing control of the Takeshita faction, Ozawa was freer to advocate the reform cause. Yet still opposition to reform within the political elite remained strong enough to block it. The conservatism of many LDP Diet members – particularly party leaders – was undiminished. Curtis (1999: 93) suggests that a further factor was personal animosity towards Ozawa and the desire not to hand him victory. On the opposition side, meanwhile, there was strong hostility towards any reform that could facilitate LDP dominance. Despite increased public disquiet, these opponents of reform continued to believe that they could safely ignore it (Schlesinger 1997: 251).

Thus, the reform bill fell. A vote of no confidence in the government was called for 18 June and, with the Ozawa–Hata faction voting against the government, it was carried. That night, ten of the LDP's young reformers, led by Masayoshi Takemura, left the party, three days later forming *Shintō Sakigake* (New Party Harbinger).[16] Then, on 23 June, the Ozawa–Hata faction left the LDP too, forming *Nihon Shinseitō* (Japan Renewal Party).[17] In the lower house elections that followed on

---

[14] 'Ozawa Threatens to End Support for Miyazawa', *JT*, 31 May 1993.

[15] 'Reform Plan Would Keep LDP Holding Sway in Diet: Kyodo', *JT*, 7 June 1993.

[16] 'Desertions Eat Away at LDP Power: Disgraced Miyazawa Calls Election', *JT*, 28 June 1993.

[17] 'Hata, LDP Defectors Form New Party', *JT*, 28 June 1993.

18 July, the LDP fell short of an overall majority and the thirty-eight years of uninterrupted LDP rule were ended.

Phase 4   Reform achieved under Hosokawa, 1993–1994

Though the LDP lost its lower house majority in 1993, it remained the largest party (see Table 10.1). The non-LDP seats were divided among eight parties: the pre-existing opposition parties (the JSP, JCP, DSP, Kōmeitō, and Shaminren); the two breakaways from the LDP (Sakigake and Shinseitō); and the Japan New Party (Nihon Shintō, JNP), a party formed outside the Diet in 1992 by prefectural governor and former LDP upper house member Morihiro Hosokawa. After some uncertainty, a coalition government comprising all the non-LDP parties except the

Table 10.1. *Elections to the Japanese House of Representatives, 1986–1993*

	July 1986		February 1990		July 1993	
Party	% votes	% seats	% votes	% seats	% votes	% seats
Liberal Democratic Party (LDP)	49.4	58.6	46.1	53.7	36.6	43.6
Japan Renewal Party (*Nihon Shinseitō*)	–	–	–	–	10.1	10.8
New Party Harbinger (*Shintō Sakigake*)	–	–	–	–	2.6	2.5
Japan New Party (JNP)	–	–	–	–	8.0	6.8
Japan Socialist Party (JSP)	17.2	16.6	24.4	26.6	15.4	13.7
Clean Government Party (*Kōmeitō*)	9.4	10.9	8.0	8.8	8.1	10.0
Democratic Socialist Party (DSP)	6.4	5.1	4.8	2.7	3.5	2.9
Social Democratic League (*Shaminren*)	0.8	0.8	0.9	0.8	0.7	0.8
New Liberal Club	1.8	1.2	–	–	–	–
Japanese Communist Party (JCP)	8.8	5.1	8.0	3.1	7.7	2.9
Independents	5.8	1.7	7.3	4.1	–	–
Others	0.2	0	0.1	0	–	0

Note: Japanese party names are given only where these are commonly used in English-language writings.
Source: Stockwin (2008: 276–9).

communists was eventually formed. Hosokawa, who ably projected an image of moderation and freshness, became prime minister, though Ozawa, as ever, exerted considerable influence behind the scenes.

Voters had clearly spoken out for change in the elections: the three parties most reticent about reform (the LDP, JSP, and JCP) all lost seats relative to the previous election, while the three new parties were the principal gainers (Lin 2006: 122; Reed 1997, 2003a: 12–13). The shift in power wrought other changes too. The LDP's self-assurance was punctured: most of the party's Diet members now recognized the need to fight for public support, a realization that contributed to the choice of Yohei Kōno (who had led an earlier defection from the LDP following the Lockheed scandal in 1976) as the party's new president (Curtis 1999: 109–10). The parties of the new coalition government, meanwhile, having been elected on the promise of a new style of politics, had to deliver on this promise if they were to retain any credibility (Reed 1999: 190). Furthermore, 'they agreed on little else than the necessity of enacting reform' (Reed 2005: 280), and so needed to achieve reform to hold the coalition together.

Thus, reform had to happen. That reform focused primarily on the electoral system not because there was public clamour specifically for change in this arena – in fact, 'the Japanese electorate did not specifically demand a new electoral system and certainly did not hold clear preferences with respect to the most desirable kind' (Reed 1999: 183; see also Sakamoto 1999a: 183–4, 1999b: 425–6). Rather, two factors played a greater role. First, the events of the previous four years had developed momentum. A 'willingness to change the electoral system had become the litmus test of serious reform' (Reed 2005: 279). It had become standard currency among political commentators to blame SNTV for the prevalence of money politics and corruption (Curtis 1999: 145). Much of the thinking for a new electoral system had already been done, whereas devising any alternative plan would have delayed progress and sparked accusations of broken promises. Second, many in the new coalition – not least Ozawa – wanted electoral reform for their own purposes, irrespective of the state of public opinion (Reed 2005: 280).

Though there was agreement on the need for electoral reform, however, the coalition parties differed widely in their views of what system should replace SNTV (Thies 2002: 94–5). They lined up into two broad camps (cf. Curtis 1999: 114–15; Otake 1996: 274–5; Stockwin 1996: 273). One sought a two-party system and therefore advocated maximally majoritarian reform. Ozawa's *Shinseitō* was the most obvious representative of this view, but it was increasingly shared by *Kōmeitō* and the DSP. Though these parties were small, they had adopted a strategy of party system realignment according to which they would join with *Shinseitō* to form one of the two major parties, thereby enhancing their prospects for future power (Curtis 1999: 104; Reed 1999: 180–1). The other camp, meanwhile, wanted multipartism and therefore advocated greater proportionality. At his first press conference as prime minister in August 1993, Hosokawa criticized two-partism and argued that 'building a coalition government centered on a few parties is the best way to give voice to the diverse values of the public' (Hosokawa 1993: 31). *Sakigake* also favoured greater proportionality. While still in the LDP, the young reformers had, as discussed above, campaigned for a system based on SMP. But they changed their stance after leaving. They had long been sceptical of Ozawa's intentions (Kitazume 1993b). They genuinely wanted to clean up Japanese politics, whereas Ozawa had a reputation as a supreme Machiavellian who was lucky to have escaped the corruption scandals largely unscathed (Schlesinger 1997: 267). As Curtis (1999: 115) observed, 'Takemura saw Ozawa as representing precisely the old style of boss-dominated factional politics that he and his Sakigake colleagues wanted to eliminate.' Thus, *Sakigake* had no desire to be subsumed into a block dominated by Ozawa and favoured at least a significant element of proportionality (Otake 1996: 275; Reed 1999: 180). The JSP, finally, was split. Many continued to view the adoption of any system with a substantial majoritarian component as 'a form of political suicide' (Reed and Thies 2001: 171). But some of the party leaders had ties to Ozawa and had begun to support the goal of realignment. *Rengō* too continued to press for the realignment option.

From these various preferences, the coalition parties distilled an initial compromise proposal for a mixed-member majoritarian system comprising 250 seats elected by SMP and 250 elected by closed-list PR in a single nationwide district. At the same time, the LDP, recognizing that it too had to be seen to support reform, produced a rival MMM proposal, with 300 seats elected by SMP and 171 by PR in forty-seven prefectural districts (Curtis 1999: 156; Reed and Thies 2001: 167–8). Facing dissent from within the JSP, Hosokawa (presumably with Ozawa behind him) sought to bring the LDP on board by adjusting the mix of seats in the government's proposal to 274 SMP and 226 PR. But the LDP continued to oppose. The government bill was endorsed by the House of Representatives in November 1993, but was defeated in the House of Councillors in January 1994 after seventeen Socialists voted against

(Kawato 2000). Hosokawa again turned to the LDP and this time agreement was reached: 300 seats would be elected by SMP and 200 by PR in eleven regional districts. The new system passed into law on 4 March 1994 (Curtis 1999: 156–60).

Thus, after three years of bitter arguments, party splits, and a change in government, the reform that was finally enacted was virtually identical to the one that had been proposed by the eighth Electoral System Advisory Council in 1991. The processes that unfolded over these years mirrored those already described in Italy. In the early phases, several groups of politicians, for differing reasons, pursued electoral reform. But they remained in the minority, and public interest in the issue was insufficient to force other politicians to join them. As the succession of political scandals developed, however, unhappiness over the state of politics gradually intensified, both within the political class and in the public at large. Advocates of electoral reform succeeded in portraying attitudes to electoral reform as the key test by which politicians' willingness to tackle corruption was judged. Electoral reform increasingly seemed inevitable, and, in the end, the great majority of politicians fell into line (cf. Christensen 1994: 590–1). Thus, as in Italy, the three basic steps of reform by elite–mass interaction can be observed.

11

New Zealand: MMP in a Westminster setting

As I argued in Chapter 1, the electoral reform in New Zealand in 1993 has a good claim to being the most momentous of all the reform episodes studied here: over eighty years' uninterrupted use of single-member plurality (SMP) were ended in favour of mixed-member proportional representation (MMP), a form of PR never previously used in the Westminster world. In no other case of post-war electoral reform has such a long-standing system been so comprehensively overturned.

The process that led to this change was, as two of its leading students observe, 'long and winding' (Levine and Roberts 1997: 25). A Royal Commission reported in favour of replacing SMP with MMP in 1986 (Royal Commission on the Electoral System 1986), but its recommendation did not initially spark wide enthusiasm, and the proposal could easily have been shelved. Only an improbable combination of factors – the strategic actions of certain key individuals and groups, the miscalculations of others, the dynamics set up by the Royal Commission, and growing public dissatisfaction with a political class that was perceived as having pursued radical economic reforms without regard to the wishes of the electorate – kept the matter on the agenda. In the end, two referendums were held. The first, in September 1992, asked voters two questions. One question simply asked whether the existing electoral system should be retained or changed. The other question offered four alternatives to the status quo and asked voters which they would choose supposing that reform did take place. As detailed below, the first question yielded an overwhelming 'yes' vote, the second a resounding endorsement of MMP. This result set the stage for the second referendum, held in November 1993, which offered a straight choice between MMP and SMP. This time the result was much closer, but still MMP prevailed. Thus began New Zealand's experiment with PR.

The early years: Geoffrey Palmer and the creation of the Royal Commission

The prime mover in the early stages of the long reform process was Geoffrey Palmer. Having been elected a Labour MP at a by-election in 1979, Palmer, previously a professor of constitutional law, quickly took on a prominent policy-making role. He wrote the party's constitutional policy for its 1981 election manifesto – its so-called 'Open Government Policy'. This included, for the first time, a commitment to establishing a royal commission that would consider, *inter alia*, 'whether proportional representation or some other variant from the existing, first-past-the-post, system should be introduced' (New Zealand Labour Party 1981: 3; cf. New Zealand Labour Party 1978: 18; see also Daniell 1983). But the policy received little coverage during the campaign. By the 1984 election, Palmer was the party's deputy leader; the manifesto included an identical commitment on establishing a royal commission (New Zealand Labour Party 1984: 9), and this time it was more widely noticed.[1] Indeed, Labour leader David Lange described the party's policies on the style of government, which included the electoral system policy, as its 'most effective vote-catcher'.[2]

Labour won the 1984 election, Palmer became deputy prime minister, and the Royal Commission on the Electoral System was created. Palmer ensured that the Commission had broad terms of reference, allowing it to recommend whatever changes to the electoral system it saw fit (Royal Commission on the Electoral System 1986: xiii–xiv). He chose as commissioners individuals who he believed were independent-minded and able to weigh the pros and cons of different systems, and excluded serving or former MPs on the basis of their vested interests (Palmer 2006). Thus, he gave the Royal Commission both the freedom and the capacity to draw its own conclusions, in contrast, for example, with the Jenkins Commission in the UK in the late 1990s (Dunleavy 2001: 19; Farrell 2001: 537–8).

Three principal factors explain Palmer's interest in electoral reform and the willingness of his party to accommodate him. The major consideration for Palmer himself was the extreme lack of checks and balances in New Zealand's political system. With a unitary governing

---

[1] E.g. 'Labour Eyes Study of Vote System', *New Zealand Herald* (hereinafter *NZH*), 8 May 1984; 'Spring Clean for House under Labour Govt', *NZH*, 5 July 1984.
[2] 'Leaders Assess the Campaign', *NZH*, 13 July 1984.

structure, a unicameral legislature, no written constitution, no bill of rights, no constitutional court, a plurality electoral system, and a two-party system, New Zealand offered the extreme case of centralized power among democratic states (Lijphart 1984: 16–20, 216–17). In a book published just before he entered parliament, Palmer quipped that New Zealand had 'the fastest law in the West' (1979: 77). He argued that 'although the power of the executive is not entirely unbridled, it is extensive enough to cause concern' (1979: 10), and he proposed a broad range of reforms to address this, of which electoral reform was only one. Palmer was not alone in this view (e.g., Minogue 1976). Widespread concerns were raised in particular by the actions of the prime minister at the time, Robert Muldoon, whom many saw as dangerously keen to expand his own powers.[3]

The second factor is that in the general elections of both 1978 and 1981 Labour came first in votes but the National Party won the absolute majority of seats (see Table 11.1). Several authors highlight this as a key source of reform impetus (e.g., Rydon 1987: 62; Vowles 2000: 681). There is no evidence that the 'spurious majorities' had much impact on Palmer's own views: his belief in strengthening checks and balances and improving the quality of political discourse and, therefore, of legislative outcomes had begun to crystallize at least by 1975, when he was one of the original signatories of a statement condemning Muldoon's style of leadership (Clements 1976; Palmer 2004: 171). Rather, the principal effect of the spurious majorities was to encourage a degree of receptiveness towards the idea of electoral reform in Labour and the wider Labour movement (for further details, see Renwick 2009b). Some Labour politicians mention it as a factor that influenced their thinking (Northey 2006; Wilson 1989: 112; Woollaston 2006). The party conference instructed the policy committee to give 'serious and favourable' attention to adopting proportional representation (Dykes 1979). The Federation of Labour passed remits calling for PR to be explored at its 1979 and 1982 conferences (New Zealand Federation of Labour 1979: 96, 1982: 139–40; Foulkes 2006). Polls suggested rising interest in PR among Labour supporters (though whether this was due to the election results or adverse perceptions of the governing system under Muldoon was unclear).[4]

---

[3] Gustafson (2000: 9); Marshall (1989: 234–42); Palmer (2004); 'Labour Yet to Emerge from Shadows', *NZH*, 30 October 1978.

[4] 'Challenge to First-Past-Post System', *NZH*, 11 March 1982.

Table 11.1. *Elections to the New Zealand Parliament, 1978–1993*

Party	Nov. 1978 % votes	Nov. 1978 % seats	Nov. 1981 % votes	Nov. 1981 % seats	July 1984 % votes	July 1984 % seats	Aug. 1987 % votes	Aug. 1987 % seats	Oct. 1990 % votes	Oct. 1990 % seats	Nov. 1993 % votes	Nov. 1993 % seats
National Party	39.8	55.4	38.8	51.1	35.9	37.9	44.0	41.2	47.8	69.1	35.0	50.5
Labour Party	40.4	43.5	39.0	46.7	43.0	60.0	48.0	58.8	35.1	29.9	34.7	45.5
Social Credit	16.1	1.1	20.7	2.2	7.6	2.1	–	–	–	–	–	–
Democratic Party*	–	–	–	–	–	–	5.7	0	1.7	0	–	–
Values Party	2.4	0	0.2	0	0.2	0	0.1	0	–	–	–	–
Green Party**	–	–	–	–	–	–	–	–	6.8	0	–	–
New Zealand Party	–	–	–	–	12.3	0	0.3	0	–	–	–	–
Mana Motuhake	–	–	–	–	0.3	0	0.5	0	0.6	0	–	–
NewLabour	–	–	–	–	–	–	–	–	5.2	1.0	–	–
Alliance***	–	–	–	–	–	–	–	–	–	–	18.2	2.0
New Zealand First	–	–	–	–	–	–	–	–	–	–	8.4	2.0
Others	1.3	0	1.4	0	0.7	0	1.4	0	2.8	0	3.7	0

*Social Credit renamed itself the New Zealand Democratic Party in May 1985.
**The Green Party emerged from the remnants of the Values Party in 1990.
***The Alliance, formed in 1991, comprised NewLabour, the Greens, the Democratic Party, Mana Motuhake, and the Liberals.
Sources: Levine and Roberts (1994: 247); McRobie (1991: 165); Mackie and Rose (1991: 353, 355).

On the other hand, there is no evidence that the spurious majorities prompted significant rethinking among the Labour elite: leading Labour politicians, as well as the Federation of Labour's president, generally blamed the electoral failures of 1978 and 1981 either on disadvantageous district boundaries,[5] or on the party's own inadequate strategizing (Lange 2005: 127, 143; Moore 1987: 85). Thoughts of major electoral reform were far from most Labour leaders' horizons (Hunt 2006). Furthermore, the majority of Labour MPs remained opposed to electoral

[5] New Zealand Federation of Labour (1982: 25); '"Unfair" Electoral Boundaries Catch Blame for Labour Loss', *NZH*, 18 December 1981; McRobie (1980: 97).

reform (Daniell 1983: 162), and Labour's own submission to the Royal Commission in 1985 called unambiguously for the retention of pure SMP (New Zealand Labour Party 1985: 15–24). The disquiet in the rank and file did influence party policy. But for most of the party elite a third factor was also required. This was the expectation that the creation of a royal commission would lead nowhere: no one expected the Royal Commission to propose radical reform, far less that such reform would be enacted. Given this, and given that Palmer was widely respected in the party, his colleagues were willing to give him some slack to pursue what was known to be his pet project (Mulgan 1989: 119). Furthermore, once Labour entered office it began quickly to pursue a programme of wide-ranging reforms that eventually transformed New Zealand's economy and society. With a heavy workload, cabinet members tended to pursue their own agendas rather than engage in depth with those of their colleagues.[6] In the light of all these factors, a proposal to establish a royal commission on the electoral system was not an issue on which many would have chosen to pick a fight.

The Royal Commission on the Electoral System

The Royal Commission on the Electoral System was created in February 1985 and reported in December 1986. It had five members, chosen for their impartiality and intellectual grasp: its chair, John Wallace, was a senior judge; the four ordinary members included a law professor, a political scientist, a statistician, and a Māori representative. Its terms of reference, as already indicated, were broad: the Commission was asked to consider 'whether the existing system of Parliamentary representation … should continue or whether all or a specified number or proportion of Members of Parliament should be elected under an alternative system or alternative systems, such as proportional representation or preferential voting' (Royal Commission on the Electoral System 1986: xiii). The Commission was not given set criteria by which to judge alternative systems: rather, it devised its own criteria in the course of its delibera-tions (Royal Commission on the Electoral System 1986: 11–12). It took written and oral submissions and conducted a study trip to Australia, Canada, West Germany, Ireland, and the UK.

---

[6] Malone (2008: 30) quotes cabinet minister Mike Moore as saying that ministers 'didn't have time [in] the first couple of years of government to consult most of the cabinet, let alone the caucus, let alone the country'.

The Commissioners placed significant weight upon the proportion-ality of seat shares to vote shares: they rejected not only SMP, but also the mixed-member majoritarian system (MMM, known in New Zealand as 'supplementary member') on this basis (Royal Commission on the Electoral System 1986: 43). They seriously considered two possible proportional systems: MMP and STV. They chose the former on the basis primarily of two factors: first, they concluded that MMP would offer better representation for Māori; second, particularly after their visits to Ireland and West Germany, they were concerned that STV, by encouraging intra-party competition, would foster pork-barrel politics and limit the effectiveness of political parties (Royal Commission on the Electoral System 1986: 51-2, 59-62; Keith 2006; Mulgan 2006; Wallace 2006). Thus, they concluded that MMP was the best system for New Zealand and that a referendum should be held in order to allow the public to decide (Royal Commission on the Electoral System 1986: 64-5).

The recommendation of MMP reflected the independent judgement of the five Commissioners. Some have suggested, contrariwise, that the result was dictated by Palmer. National Party MP Murray McCully, for example, argued that Palmer 'appointed individuals [to the Royal Commission] who he could be confident would make exactly the recommendations he wanted' (McCully 1990: 3; see also Hunt 1998: 3, 23–32). But this claim does not stand up to analysis. Palmer had argued in 1979 for an MMM scheme first proposed by two political scientists in 1971 (Alley and Robinson 1971: 5–7), not for MMP (Palmer 1979: 155–7), and there is no evidence that he changed his view before the Commission reported. It is true that Palmer chose the Commissioners to suit his purposes: for example, he was clear that he did not want to appoint New Zealand's leading academic defender of SMP, Robert Chapman (Palmer 2006; Chapman 1999 [1979]). But his purpose was not to achieve a pre-ordained outcome, but rather to set in motion a thorough and open-minded review of New Zealand's electoral system and possible alternatives to it. This was evinced by the broad terms of reference and the choice of Commissioners: four of the five apparently had no firm pre-existing views on electoral systems (Jackson and McRobie 1998: 104–7; Keith 2006; Nagel 1994: 526; Wallace 2006); the fifth, Richard Mulgan, had criticized Palmer's approach to the electoral system in print (Mulgan 1980: 174–5); he had voiced scepticism regarding PR, but nevertheless indicated a willingness to consider some reform (Mulgan 1984: 77–81).

Politicians react

The initial response of the political class to the MMP recommendation was largely hostile. Palmer himself endorsed the report, but had to make clear this was only his personal view, not the government's.[7] He was unable to persuade his party colleagues to accept the recommendation of a referendum: the most that he could extract was a commitment in Labour's 1987 election manifesto to send the report for consideration to the Parliamentary Select Committee on Electoral Law, following which a Labour government would 'seek to improve New Zealand's electoral system' according to several stated principles (New Zealand Labour Party 1987: 70; Hill 1987).

Then came a surprise: in the course of a live televised debate during the 1987 election campaign, the prime minister, David Lange, stepped beyond his party's official policy and pledged that if re-elected the government would conduct a referendum on electoral reform.[8] Why Lange – who was no fan of MMP – made this pledge has been oft debated: he may have misread his briefing notes, those notes may have contained a mistake, or he may have seized an opportunity to score short-term debating points without thinking of the long-term consequences (Jackson and McRobie 1998: 47). Some suggest that Lange's remarks were crucial to the chain of events leading to reform (Jackson and McRobie 1998: 46), but others doubt this (Vowles 2008a: 178). Whatever the long-term implications, Lange's words certainly had immediate consequences. Palmer pounced on the opportunity they created (Palmer 1992: 178), moving rapidly following Labour's election victory to implement the referendum promise.[9]

But Palmer was almost as rapidly stamped upon by cabinet colleagues, who refused to allow preparations for the referendum to proceed.[10] The Royal Commission's report was duly sent to the Electoral Law Select Committee. Reporting in December 1988, the committee rejected MMP, called for retention of the existing number of single-member districts, and proposed merely an indicative referendum on introducing a limited form of MMM (Electoral Law Select Committee 1988: 21). Yet even this

---

[7] 'Mr Palmer for Electoral Plan', *NZH*, 8 January 1987.
[8] 'PM Promises Electoral Referendum', *NZH*, 10 August 1987.
[9] 'Vote May Take in Maori Seats', *NZH*, 26 August 1987; 'Heavy Load Ahead', *NZH*, 7 October 1987; 'Electoral Poll May Be Held in Two Years', *NZH*, 13 October 1987.
[10] 'Tension on Poll Plans', *NZH*, 5 November 1987.

plan was too much for most members of Labour's parliamentary caucus: after months of behind-the-scenes discussion, Palmer announced in April 1989 that there would be no referendum on the electoral system after all, admitting that lack of support among Labour MPs was the cause. He commented, 'MPs take an interest in the electoral system far deeper and more vigorously than many other subjects. It is quite difficult to persuade them to make great changes to it' (quoted in Armstrong 1989: 1). A further attempt to revive the referendum was made towards the end of the year, after Palmer replaced Lange as prime minister, but it was quickly abandoned, again because the required caucus support was lacking.[11] Thus, the promise that Lange had made to voters was breached.

The next chapter in New Zealand's electoral reform story may appear just as surprising as Lange's 1987 promise: in April 1990, during the pre-campaign ahead of that year's election, the National Party leader, Jim Bolger, announced the formation of a special caucus committee to investigate proposals for electoral and wider constitutional reforms and let it be known that he expected a commitment to holding a referendum on electoral reform to be one of its proposals (Armstrong 1990a). The committee delivered on Bolger's wishes (New Zealand National Party Electoral Law Reform Caucus Committee 1990: 11) and the party adopted the referendum pledge (New Zealand National Party 1990a: 3).

That promise may seem surprising, yet in fact it was very different from Lange's promise three years earlier. Lange had acted on the spur of the moment without prior calculation; National's promise, by contrast, was deliberate and calculated. It has generally been interpreted simply as reflecting short-term electoral calculation. During its six years in office, Labour had pursued an agenda of radical economic reform that had diverged from party tradition and often violated manifesto commitments; many New Zealanders were angered by these 'broken promises' and became disillusioned with their political system. By promising political reform, National could exploit Labour's failings and simultaneously offer voters a positive solution to their growing unhappiness with the political system (Jackson and McRobie 1998: 81; Levine and Roberts 1997: 29; McRobie 1994: 105; Mulgan 1990: 8; Nagel 1994: 526; Vowles 2000: 683).

Such considerations were certainly important to National's thinking. As I have argued in greater detail elsewhere (Renwick 2007), however, short-term electoral considerations were not all that mattered. The three

[11] Collins (1989); 'Referendum Put Aside', *NZH*, 12 December 1989.

main authors of the party's constitutional policies shared a long-standing and apparently genuine interest in reforming New Zealand's constitutional structure in order to reduce the concentration of power in the executive. Bolger had argued for the addition of an upper house at least as early as 1984,[12] and he pursued the idea, despite a lack of popular interest, in the late 1980s and subsequently.[13] Murray McCully, who chaired the caucus committee mentioned above, backed the upper house proposal, arguing it 'would provide some welcome constitutional safeguards against abuse of executive power' (McCully 1988), and campaigned for looser parliamentary whipping (e.g., McCully 1989b). Doug Graham, who would steer the referendum process as Justice Minister in the early 1990s, also supported the creation of a second chamber (Graham 1988: 9) and was a long-standing advocate of introducing a bill of rights.[14] Bolger always supported retention of single-member plurality and opposed electoral reform.[15] Both McCully and Graham, however, while opposing MMP, did criticize the existing electoral system and argued for the MMM system that the Royal Commission had labelled supplementary member (Graham 1988: 4, 2006; McCully 1989a, 2006). McCully rejected the idea that electoral reform was needed to promote fairness, but did support it as a means of reducing excessive executive power.[16] Graham argued that both the perceived unfairness of SMP and excessive executive power needed to be tackled.[17]

Thus, the three key figures within the National Party all wanted to pursue constitutional reform. In doing so, they reflected a long tradition in the party of opposing undue concentration of power: many had acquiesced in the abolition of the old upper house in 1950 only because they were led to believe that a more effective chamber would be created in its place (Jackson 1972: 186–7); constitutional reform had been a significant plank in the party's platform in the 1960s (New Zealand

---

[12] 'Another Look Suggested at Upper House', *NZH*, 30 October 1984.
[13] 'Upper House Bolger Aim', *NZH*, 23 March 1988; 'Repeat Call for Upper House', *NZH*, 19 April 1988; 'Bolger Puts Case for Upper House', *NZH*, 27 March 1990.
[14] 'Storm Clouds Gathering over Bill of Rights', *NZH*, 16 January 1985.
[15] E.g., Armstrong (1990b); Bolger in *New Zealand Parliamentary Debates*, 4 September 1990.
[16] E.g., McCully in *New Zealand Parliamentary Debates*, 30 May 1990.
[17] In 'Minutes of a Meeting of the Electoral Reform Committee held on 30 May 1990 at 3.00pm', McCully Papers, Archives New Zealand, Agency ABWM, Series 7361, Accession W5295, Box 1, File: '1990 Minutes [Electoral Law Reform Caucus Committee], Election Night Stats, US Visit', 3.

National Party 1960: 27A); and Muldoon's political style had sparked widespread unease among his colleagues (Gustafson 2000: 9).

With the deficiencies of the electoral system already on the agenda, it was impossible to pursue constitutional reform without mentioning electoral reform. Besides, both McCully and Graham wanted limited electoral reform. No one at the time believed that a referendum on electoral reform would in fact deliver radical change: it was the received wisdom that New Zealand's voters would not countenance such a move (Boston 1987: 112; McRobie 1989: 404; Mulgan 1995: 93); senior National politicians believed that once the unpopular Labour government had been removed from power and the case against MMP had been made, the Royal Commission's proposal would be defeated (Birch 2006; East 2006; McKinnon 2006). For Bolger, McCully, and Graham, therefore, the referendum promise was, at least in part, a step towards the mild constitutional reforms that they sought. For most others in the National Party caucus, it was probably primarily no more than a short-term manoeuvre designed to discomfit Labour and harness popular dissatisfaction, a manoeuvre that, they believed, carried little risk of bringing adverse long-term consequences. Both elements are needed to understand why the promise was made.

The referendums

As we now know, those who believed in 1990 that New Zealanders would never vote for radical electoral reform miscalculated. The referendum results are summarized in Table 11.2. In the first referendum, held in September 1992, 84.7 per cent of those voting rejected the status quo in the first question; in the second question, which offered four alternatives to SMP, 70.5 per cent voted for MMP (Levine and Roberts 1993: 162). In the second referendum, in November 1993, which offered a straight and binding choice between MMP and SMP, 53.9 per cent of voters backed MMP over the status quo (Levine and Roberts 1994: 245).

Voters were unexpectedly bold in 1992 and 1993 because their anger with politics had grown to a degree that no one had predicted. The Labour government had become deeply unpopular during its second term (1987–1990) because, having promised a return to core Labour values in the 1987 election campaign,[18] in fact it pursued an ever more radical free-market agenda, and because global recession hit New

---

[18] 'New Sentence for "Hard Labour"', *NZH*, 18 May 1987.

Table 11.2. *Electoral reform referendum results in New Zealand*

September 1992	Turnout: 55.2%
Part A: keep or change status quo	
For change	84.7%
For status quo	15.3%
Part B: preferred alternative if change to be considered	
Supplementary member (MMM)	5.5%
Single transferable vote (STV)	17.4%
Mixed-member proportional (MMP)	70.5%
Preferential voting (AV)	6.6%
November 1993	*Turnout: 85.2%*
Change to MMP	53.9%
Keep status quo	46.1%

Sources: Levine and Roberts (1993: 162, 1994: 245).

Zealand's economy hard.[19] But it was still possible for voters to believe that the problem was with Labour rather than the political system as a whole. Yet after the 1990 election the new National Party government repeated Labour's sins: elected on a promise of a return to 'a decent society' (New Zealand National Party 1990b), in fact in office it advanced Labour's economic restructuring still further. Most potently, having promised to abolish a tax on pensions (superannuation surcharge) intro-duced by Labour, it instead increased the tax in the budget of 1991. Ministers could argue that the public finances were in a much more parlous state than Labour had admitted before the 1990 election, but the public was not prepared to listen: it appeared to most that the whole political class was beyond public control and that systemic change was required to bring it back into line (Aimer 1999: 147; Ingle 1995: 78–80; Mulgan 1995: 83). Anger was fuelled by continuing recession and rapidly rising unemployment;[20] by 1993, 71.6 per cent of survey respondents reported that they had been 'angry' 'sometimes', 'often', or 'always' with the government's handling of the economy, while only 15.6 per cent said

---

[19] The economy contracted in both 1987/8 and 1988/9 (Economist Intelligence Unit 1994: 10). Unemployment rose by 61.7 per cent between 1988 and 1990 (Statistics New Zealand 2003: Table 3.01).

[20] The economy shrank again in 1990/1991 and 1991/1992 (Economist Intelligence Unit 1994: 10). Unemployment rose by a further 53.8 per cent between 1990 and 1992 (Statistics New Zealand 2003: Table 3.01).

they had 'never' or 'seldom' been angry (New Zealand Election Study 1993).

The public mood was channelled specifically towards electoral reform and MMP by two factors. First, electoral reform was already on the agenda. It was not alone in that respect: Bolger and a few others, as we have seen, were keen to advance the cause of creating a second chamber. But the second chamber idea, unlike that of electoral reform, necessarily entailed an increase in the number of politicians – the very people who were seen as causing New Zealand's problems – and it therefore never gained public acceptance (Long 1990; Vowles and Aimer 1993: 220; Vowles et al. 1995: 183). Second, a highly effective lobby group, the Electoral Reform Coalition (ERC), worked hard to harness popular dissatisfaction in favour of electoral reform. Though its members had previously advocated a variety of reform options, it recognized that the Royal Commission's decision to recommend MMP would serve as a focal point, and it therefore pushed hard for MMP over all alternatives (Aimer 1999: 152; Mackerras 1994: 38; Saxby 2006).

In the light of the public mood, it may have been tempting for senior National politicians to row back from their referendum promise. Bolger (who was now prime minister), however, refused to countenance such a move: he had broken one promise (on the superannuation surcharge) and had suffered a considerable loss of public goodwill in consequence; he was not willing to do the same on the referendum (Birch 2006; Bolger 2006; Jackson and McRobie 1998: 129).

Nevertheless, there were persistent accusations that National did seek to skew the referendum process against reform. Having originally promised that 'The referendum will be held prior to the end of 1992 to ensure that any changes to the Electoral Act required by its result can be made before the next General Election' (New Zealand National Party 1990a: 3), in fact the second, conclusive referendum was held only in conjunction with the 1993 election. Some saw this delay as reflecting a desire among politicians to avoid a result that they feared would limit their power (Palmer 1992: 193; Temple 1995: 235). Furthermore, many saw the decision to offer four alternatives to the status quo and to require majorities in two separate referendums before change could occur as designed to create barriers to change: Nagel (1994: 526) saw the former as an 'attempt at divide-and-conquer'. Finally, many believed that the details of the MMP system that was devised as an alternative to SMP ahead of the second referendum were designed to make that option less attractive to voters. In particular, the MMP system on offer would require an unpopular increase in the number of MPs from 97 to 120, while the total would remain unchanged if SMP were retained (Electoral Reform Coalition 1993: 1; Levine and Roberts 1994: 243; McLeay 1996: 12–13).

Yet there were plausible other reasons for all these decisions besides any desire to rig the referendum result. Advice from the Justice Department and from external advisors was that 'Changing the electoral system is a complex matter, and the obstacles to implementing reform in time for the 1993 election are insurmountable' (McCully and Eagleson 1991: 3). While offering multiple alternatives to the status quo may have looked like divide and conquer, it was also unavoidable. Given the Royal Commission's report, it would have been impossible not to offer the option of MMP. But both McCully and Graham, as we have seen, wanted MMM, while another prominent National Party figure, Winston Peters, had been pressing for alternative vote.[21] Thus, inclusion of at least three options was necessary. Why the fourth option – STV – was added by the Electoral Law Select Committee relatively late in the process is less clear, but the explanation of the Select Committee – that it reflected public submissions – is plausible (Electoral Law Select Committee 1991: 8; Armstrong 1991: 3). There was also good reason to think that MMP would not work effectively without increasing the number of MPs. It was generally agreed that an MMP system with fewer than sixty single-member districts would create unhealthily large districts, particularly in rural parts of the South Island. The Electoral Reform Coalition and others therefore argued for a system with sixty single-member districts and forty seats elected from national lists (Electoral Reform Coalition 1993: 2). Yet while this might have ensured proportionality, it would have created problems for the political parties: Graham had long argued for a mixed system as a means of allowing senior MPs to focus on national rather than constituency work (Graham 1988: 4); but a detailed report by the Department of Justice suggested that MMP with a small proportional tier would prevent this because of large fluctuations from election to election in the number of list seats won by each party (Department of Justice 1993: 10). Finally, one possible attempt to skew the referendum outcome was clearly rejected by the government. Late in the day, Peter Shirtcliffe, who was one of New Zealand's leading businessmen and head of the anti-reform Campaign

[21] Stickley (1990); 'MP Casts Doubt on Bolger's Pet Plan', *NZH*, 22 June 1990.

for Better Government, pressed for a change in the referendum bill to require a majority not just of those voting, but of all registered voters, before any reform could pass (Jackson and McRobie 1998: 149). The government, however, refused to back the move: such a breach of faith with the electorate would have been an electoral millstone and would have violated Bolger's personal sense of honour (Bolger 2006; Jackson and McRobie 1998: 151–3).

In fact, it seems likely, as Jackson and McRobie (1998: 148) argue, that politicians from all parties made 'a genuine attempt ... to develop a robust and broadly acceptable MMP structure' and that there was little manipulation of the process. By this stage politicians had lost control of the issue, and they knew that any attempt to wrest it back would only do them further harm. Similarly, whereas in 1992 many politicians campaigned against reform (see the contributions collected in McRobie 1993), by 1993 most recognized that doing so only added to voters' desire for change, and therefore kept quiet.

Throughout the process of electoral reform in New Zealand, the majority of MPs opposed change. Even of those who backed reform, only around half supported MMP (Laugesen 1992). That those MPs nevertheless devised an MMP system and put it to the people in a referendum reflects the three-stage process that is characteristic of electoral reform by elite–mass interaction. At the first stage, a minority of politicians pursued reform. In the early years Geoffrey Palmer was the most important actor; given his position within the Labour Party, he was able to set the reform process in train even though few senior politicians shared his objectives. With the great majority of politicians viewing reform as hostile to their own power interests, it was only through mobilization of public opinion that progress could be made. As I argue in greater detail in the next chapter, Palmer himself was unable to achieve such mobilization while in office. Rather, it was the combination of growing public anger with the operation of the political system and the successful efforts of the Electoral Reform Coalition to harness that dissatisfaction in the cause of electoral reform that proved crucial. In 1990, National Party leaders made their initial promise on holding an electoral reform referendum in part in response to public opinion, but in part also because of a genuine belief in the need for some constitutional reform. Politicians subsequently acquiesced as they lost control of the referendum process because to have done otherwise would have courted the full wrath of a public incensed by their own impotence in the face of years of broken promises.

Coda: another referendum by 2011?

New Zealand's MMP electoral system has now been used in five general elections. Its first outing, in 1996, sparked great unease: the new government was formed only after two months' negotiations and was based on a coalition that had not been expected by voters (Vowles 1997: 261). Since then, its operation has mostly been smooth, but it has not yet entirely consolidated: many National Party politicians have continued to express their dislike for the system, and their party has entered each of the last four elections promising a referendum on whether to keep it.[22] After nine years in opposition, National returned to the government benches in 2008. It does not have a majority, but two of its three partners in government – the small ACT and United Future parties – mirrored National's referendum plans in their election programmes (ACT 2008; United Future 2008: 2–3), while the third – the Māori Party – offered tacit acceptance (Māori Party 2008).[23] The referendum policy was included in the Speech from the Throne that set out the government's programme for the new parliamentary session in December 2008 (New Zealand Government 2008), and in September 2009 the government announced it had begun to consider the form the referendum should take.[24]

National's election policy stated that the referendum, to be held 'no later than 2011', 'will give people a choice between retaining MMP without any further consideration, or having a further vote on MMP alongside another electoral system or systems' (New Zealand National Party 2008). National Party leader John Key indicated during the campaign that he expected voters would opt for change but not for a return to SMP. He stated his own preference as 'leaning towards Supplementary Member' – that is, the MMM system that was advocated by leading

---

[22] 'A Chance to Dump MMP', *The Dominion*, 24 November 1999; 'National Pledges Vote on MMP', *The Dominion*, 1 December 2001; 'Poll on MMP Promised if National Wins Election', *Dominion Post*, 14 January 2005; New Zealand National Party (2008).

[23] The ACT Party emerged in 1994 from the Association of Consumers and Taxpayers (ACT), which had been founded to defend the neo-liberal economic reforms of the late 1980s. It retains a strong free-market orientation (see Reid 2003). United Future is a centrist, broadly Christian democratic party formed in 2000 through the merger of two earlier splinter parties (see Aimer 2003). The Māori Party was created in 2004 and is the most successful to date of a series of parties seeking to represent Māori interests (see Smith 2006).

[24] 'Cabinet Preparing for MMP Referendum: Key', *New Zealand Herald*, 7 September 2009.

National Party figures around 1990 (Travett 2008). Polling figures must be treated with great caution: the issue has not been high on voters' agendas in recent years. For what they are worth, however, they suggest that there is much to play for: respondents are roughly evenly split, with 45 per cent supporting the status quo and 42 per cent change.[25]

That the National Party should support such a referendum is not surprising: as one of New Zealand's two large parties, the great majority of its members opposed MMP when it was introduced, and many have remained unreconciled to it since then. What is at first blush more surprising is the support of the small parties. In fact, the Māori Party's position can readily be understood: this party wins all its seats through the reserved Māori districts, not from proportional lists, and therefore has little interest in MMP. United Future, meanwhile, has focused on what it sees as the iniquities of separate Māori representation rather than any flaws in MMP itself (e.g., Dunne 2008). That it is relaxed about opening a debate over the whole system presumably reflects the fact that it is now little more than a vehicle for its leader, Peter Dunne, who won the party's only seat in 2008 in a single-member district.

ACT, on the other hand, elected four of its five seats in 2008 from the proportional lists, and its position thus needs more explaining. Its official policy stated simply that a referendum would give voters a 'long-overdue say on how they like MMP' (ACT 2008). This stance was popular with potential ACT voters, who generally believed (like most New Zealanders) that a further referendum had been promised when MMP was introduced. ACT is a party of free-market liberalism and small government, and its supporters dislike the government interventionism they associate with MMP's first dozen years (Nicholle 2009). ACT has not, however, decided whether it will support a particular system in the referendum. Opinion within the party is divided. Some support the principle of single-party majority government, believing it more likely to encourage small, decisive government than a system requiring compromise with particular interests. Others value ACT's independent voice and recognize this would be endangered by any move away from proportionality (Boscawen 2009; Nicholle 2009).

The story of electoral reform in New Zealand may therefore not yet be over. Events over the coming years will be watched eagerly by analysts around the world.

---

[25] 'MMP Vote Not Clear', *New Zealand Herald*, 12 September 2009.

12

Elite–mass interaction: comparative analysis

In at least two of the three countries discussed here, highly respected analysts argued in the late 1980s that major electoral reform was very unlikely (on Italy, see LaPalombara 1987: 234; Spotts and Wieser 1986: 119; on New Zealand, see Boston 1987: 111–12; Lijphart 1987: 102–3). They all did so on the basis of the same logic: the politicians controlled the decision-making process; and the majority of those politicians opposed electoral reform because it would harm their power interests. Yet in all three cases reform did occur, and it did so because popular pressure forced politicians to concede changes that they would not have supported had they been left to their own devices. In this chapter, I analyse the dynamics of the elite–mass interaction reform type in greater detail.

Given the greater complexity of the process of reform by elite–mass interaction than that of elite majority imposition, this chapter is struc-tured somewhat differently from Chapter 8. I begin by analysing in turn each of the three phases, looking at the processes that operate within them and that lead from one phase to another. Only after that do I focus in on the building blocks of the reform process identified in Part I and the propositions that I offered regarding them.

The dynamics of the three phases

We have seen in the preceding chapters that the same three basic phases characterized reform in all three countries: first, a minority of politicians became interested in electoral reform but were unable to persuade the necessary majority of their colleagues to enact change; second, reform advocates therefore sought to rally public opinion behind the reform cause; third, popular mobilization having proved successful, the majority of politicians acquiesced in reforms that they had not previously wanted. Of the first phase, I ask what motivated the pro-reform minority, what factors shaped their preferences, why the majority of politicians opposed reform, and how far reform was able to gain a footing on the political agenda. Of the second phase, the key issue concerns the relationships among three principal factors that may have prompted popular mobilization around the cause of electoral reform: inherent problems in the electoral system; short-term political circumstances that fostered disquiet with the status quo; and the strategic manipulation of opinion by politicians and other leaders. Of the third phase, I am principally concerned to understand the mechanisms through which popular pressure came to influence politicians' behaviour so decisively.

Phase 1   Initiation of reform

I look at the first phase of reform in two stages. First I look at the various politicians involved: what motivated them to support or oppose reform and where they came from. Then I assess briefly how far the issue of electoral reform was able to penetrate the political agenda and how it got there.

Reformers and conservatives

Those politicians who advocated electoral reform in the early phase of the reform process did so for a variety of reasons: no single motivation underlay their stance. Nevertheless, it is notable that most focused, at least in significant part, upon general values rather than their own power. This is clearest in the case of New Zealand's Geoffrey Palmer. As Chapter 11 described, Palmer was appalled by the poor quality of legislation and by the ability of the government in power – and a strong prime minister – to dictate policy without serious consultation. Electoral reform was one institutional change of many that he believed would slow the legislative process down, encourage greater deliberation, and modify New Zealand's political discourse (Palmer 1979, 1992: 195–7). There is no evidence to suggest that his party's power interests played any significant role in his thinking. He was, as Jackson and McRobie (1998: 46) contend, 'a genuine and committed reformer'.

Though some have contended that Mario Segni in Italy saw some prospect for gain either for his party or for himself personally in pursuing the cause of electoral reform, he in fact appears to have been motivated largely by the genuine belief that Italy's corrupt politics could be cleaned up and the policy-making process rendered effective only if politicians faced the accountability and discipline of bipolarism and the alternation of governing majorities. As Gilbert observed when the referendum movement was at its peak, 'Segni's political past has been characterized by earnest dedication to changing the rules of the game' (Gilbert 1993: 18): he had supported various reform moves since the late 1970s. By the late 1980s, he was working with Marco Pannella and others to pursue electoral reform through cross-party alliance (Gilbert 1995: 93–5).[1] Then, ahead of the 1992 election, he formed a Radical Alliance of candidates from across parties who shared little besides a desire for electoral reform.[2] These coalitions were not embryos of a new party that Segni putatively hoped to lead: they were too diverse for that. That he had no clear plan for how he might position himself personally in the new political order created by electoral reform was apparent after the 1993 referendum, when he failed to build any cogent organization around himself – despite the considerable popularity his campaigns had generated – and failed to develop any serious alliance-building strategy (Gilbert 1994: 5–8; Pasquino 1994: 112). That he was concerned with more than just personal power was indicated in the late 1990s, when he campaigned hard to replace the mixed electoral system with one based on pure SMP (or something close to it) in order to consolidate the bipolarization of politics, even though he had by that stage been marginalized politically precisely because he had failed to find his own place in the bipolar pattern of competition.[3] He continues to pursue the same cause today, and was a leading supporter of the referendum of June 2009.[4] A similar story can be told of Marco Pannella, leader of the tiny Radical Party. Though majoritarian electoral reforms could never boost his party, still, Pannella consistently supported them, arguing relentlessly for single-member districts in the 1980s and participating in the referendum movements of both the early and the late 1990s.

The young reformers in Japan were similar to the reform leaders in Italy. They wanted to change the nature of Japanese politics, ending its reliance upon money and clientelism. They believed that electoral reforms that reduced intra-party competition and enhanced the likelihood of alternation in government would serve this objective (Wolfe 1995). While their switch from advocating SMP to supporting PR after they left the protective environment of the LDP to form the independent *Sakigake* party can be interpreted as reflecting a simple self-interest

---

[1] 'Italian Politicians Plot to Go British', *The Times*, 10 May 1987.
[2] 'Italian Parties Pledge to End PR', *The Times*, 20 March 1992.
[3] 'Italy's Reformers Thwarted', *The Economist*, 24 April 1999.
[4] 'Referendum Bid Gets Green Light', *ANSA English Media Service*, 28 November 2007.

calculation (Otake 1996: 275; Reed 1999: 180), it was also consistent with their broader aims: to support two-partism after the 1993 election was to support competition between the LDP and a block led by Ichirō Ozawa; neither of these options was attractive to anyone genuinely concerned to clean up Japanese politics.

The case of Ozawa himself is more complex. As I suggested in Chapter 10, he believed that Japan should become a 'normal' country on the world stage; to achieve this it needed strong leadership, and the SNTV electoral system was, he believed, one barrier to the achievement of such leadership. These are all general goals relating to Japan's national interests. Furthermore, Ozawa's interpretation of the situation mirrored that of many analysts. While there have been two principal views of the locus of power in Japan in the late twentieth century – one emphasizing concentration in the hands of the bureaucracy (Johnson 1995: 13), the other highlighting dispersal across a broad range of politicians and interest groups (Muramatsu and Krauss 1990: 303; on the distinction between these approaches, see Campbell and Scheiner 2008: 91–4; Hayao 1993: 7–12) – both agree on the limited capacity of political leaders to direct policy. The prime minister was constrained by factional politics within the LDP: Hellman (1979: 96) observed that the need for factional consensus 'imposes serious restraints on the Prime Minister's capacity for leadership'. And once the LDP had lost its secure majority in both houses of the Diet (in the lower house, temporarily, in 1976; in the upper house, enduringly, in 1989) the prime minister also had to negotiate with the opposition (Krauss 1982). Analysts agreed on the difficulties this created for Japan on the international stage (Stockwin 1991a: 6; Van Wolferen 1986/1987: 290–1).

Yet the reform of Japanese politics that Ozawa pursued was also conspicuously consonant with his own power interests. Otake (1996: 290–1) argues that 'while Ozawa's leadership was based on "principles," these were more self-satisfying than realistic and were characterized by a marked lack of consideration for the general public'. Ozawa was a ruthless political strategist who enjoyed holding and exercising power (Curtis 1999: 88). Though, as an LDP king-maker, he could exercise considerable influence over who moved up and who moved down, he was frustrated in his desire to influence real policy decisions, most notably in relation to the deployment of Japanese troops abroad (Christensen 2006: 506–7). Ozawa's is thus a case in which various goals merge into one another. He wanted power for himself and he believed that party system realignment that encouraged the development of strong, centralized parties free of factional dealing would boost his power. But he also believed that the existence of such strong leadership would further Japan's interests in the world. He saw his own advancement as serving Japan's as well as his own interests.

The belief that reform would enhance their power influenced some of the reformers in New Zealand and Italy too. In so far as the New Zealand Labour Party's two electoral defeats in 1978 and 1981 fostered an interest in electoral reform in the party, they did so because some individuals came to see the SMP system as biased against them and thought that an alternative would advance their interests – and the policy concerns of the left – further. In Italy, Achille Occhetto pursued a strategy of party system realignment that was not dissimilar to Ozawa's: he calculated (correctly, as it turned out) that electoral reform would foster straight left–right competition in which his ex-communist PDS would play a prominent role. Thus, the motivations of reform advocates across the three countries were diverse.

But the majority of politicians in all three countries opposed reform at this stage. They did so because they did not believe electoral reform would serve their power interests. Here again, however, as in the cases of reform by elite majority imposition, a mix of considerations came into play. Seat-maximization was a major factor (Rows II and III in Table 2.1): in New Zealand, for example, the adoption of PR would make it very unlikely that either of the two major parties would be able again to secure an absolute parliamentary majority. Seat-maximization allied with uncertainty mattered too: while majoritarian electoral reforms *might* have benefited the Japan Socialist Party and *might* have freed Italy's Christian Democrats from the need always to negotiate with the Socialists and their other coalition partners, there was no guarantee in either case that it would be these parties rather than some other that would reap the rewards of the new system. Proposition P12 in Chapter 3 posited that where uncertainty regarding the effects of electoral reform is high and there exists a viable status quo, politicians will generally support the status quo unless it clearly and persistently disadvantages them, and the evidence here supports that.

But short-term seat-maximization was not all that mattered. In Japan, projections suggested that, at least in the short term, the LDP would increase its seat share to 89 per cent with pure SMP and 79 per cent with a mixed system (Hrebenar 1986: 47). In part, as in 1973, legislators focused on their individual interests rather than their party's, and preferred to maintain the existing system, in which they had invested heavily (VI(a) in Table 2.1). Faction leaders also had interests that did not always coincide with their party's (VII(a)). Similarly, the leaders of the coalition parties in Italy enjoyed a cosy coexistence in which seat shares were not all that mattered: the Christian Democrats, for example, were also concerned to ensure the maintenance of the centripetal competitive structure (VI(a)) that had given them a permanent place in government for approaching fifty years.

All of this means that there is no clear dividing line in terms of motivations between reformers and anti-reformers: we cannot say that the former all had the interests of the nation at heart while the latter were concerned only with their personal or partisan interests. Nevertheless, in all three countries, some reformers were unusual: they were unlike most politicians, in that their primary motivation for pursuing reform related to general values rather than their own or their party's power interests. Palmer, Segni, and Pannella all pursued reforms that ran counter to their own power interests; that Japan's young reformers went this far is not clear, though their genuine belief in the importance of reform for Japan's interests cannot be doubted. These politicians were thus policy-seekers before they were office-seekers, and they were policy-seekers who laid particular emphasis on the nature of the political system itself.

I posited in Chapter 3 that politicians are more likely to place policy-seeking above office-seeking when they are new entrants to the political game (P2) and when their income, prestige, social contacts, and lifestyle do not depend on their political careers (P3). These propositions are supported by the evidence from all three cases. In two of the three cases, the reformers were new to the political game: Palmer began his campaign for political reform just before his election to parliament; Japan's young reformers were identified precisely by the fact that they were first- or second-term Diet members. In all three cases, the reformers were already secure in their life-worlds. Palmer, indeed, never entirely left the life-world that he occupied before entering politics. He had been one of New Zealand's most successful constitutional lawyers, holding professorships in both New Zealand and the United States, and he readily returned to that world after leaving parliament in 1990. According to David Lange, prime minister from 1984 to 1989, 'He was a lawyer first and, some way behind, a politician' (2005: 151). Jim Bolger, prime minister from 1990 to 1997, goes further, saying that 'Palmer and politics didn't really mix' (1998: 27). James (1990: 83) described him as a 'non-politician'. Segni was a lawyer too. Indeed, he consciously delayed his entry into politics in order to secure his legal career first (Gilbert 1993: 18). The son of a former prime minister and president of the Republic, his place in Italy's political elite did not depend upon the success of his political career, and he has been well able to pursue his political interests since leaving the Italian parliament in 1996. Finally, the young reformers in Japan were mostly *nisei* Diet members: that is, in a parallel to Segni, they were the sons or grandsons of former Diet members, and they had inherited their predecessors' support bases. Otake (1996: 277) suggests that their comfortable backgrounds gave them space to be relaxed about the electoral game: 'Many inherited large fortunes and could afford comfortable living without working as Diet members. They shared an "I can always quit" easy-going attitude.' They had entered politics without having to fight for it; 'Their desire to be politicians had never been strong.' Similarly, Curtis (1999: 77) suggests that, as the children of former Diet members, the young *nisei* had parachuted into the political world without being socialized into its ways, and were consequently dismayed by what they found there.

Clearly, not all recent political entrants and not all those whose political careers were identifiably unnecessary to their personal security gave office-seeking (as an end in itself) low priority: in Japan, for example, around 40 per cent of the LDP members in the 1990 lower house were *nisei* (Fukai and Fukui 1992: 30), but only a minority actively pursued the reform cause. Nevertheless, the evidence supports the proposition that those politicians who do favour policy over office tend to be relatively fresh to the political game and/or have strong identities and personal security not contingent on their political careers.

How reform reaches the agenda

Electoral reform became a live issue on the political agenda in the three countries during this first phase of the reform process. But it did so to differing degrees and by differing routes. In New Zealand, the primary impetus came from a small group of reformers (Palmer above all), while others within the Labour elite merely acquiesced. Labour placed the issue in its manifesto in 1981 and the Royal Commission on the Electoral System was formed in 1985. In Japan, by contrast, the reformers seem not initially to have needed to work hard: conservatives established a series of review committees, culminating in the eighth Electoral System Advisory Council of 1989, seeing them as a means to temporize in the face of scandal while in fact unintentionally giving reform its first momentum. Italy's reformers made least progress in the early years: electoral reform ideas were discussed by the Bozzi Commission during the mid-1980s, but the Commission focused its recommendations elsewhere. Despite much effort from reformers, the key party leaders did not budge on the issue, and, hence, no formal review focusing on the electoral system occurred before popular mobilization began.

These differences largely reflect differences in the act-contingent conditions facing opponents of reform in the three countries. In New Zealand, public interest in reform in the early 1980s was present, but weak. Labour certainly saw votes in its programme of governance reform, but its proposed review of the electoral system received limited attention. The primary act contingencies related, rather, to intra-party dynamics: Palmer's senior colleagues allowed him to pursue his project of establishing a royal commission to look at the electoral system because sparking a fight over a proposal that they never believed would lead to change would have wasted time and caused needless tension within the party and the government. In Japan, by contrast, act contingencies relating to the public did matter: the Recruit scandal in 1988–1989 required a response. Both Takeshita and Uno, neither of whom ever showed evidence of actually wanting reform, therefore established commissions to investigate electoral reform in the hope that they could thereby ride the scandal out. In Italy, finally, the lack of progress at this stage reflected the relative weakness of both of these mechanisms: Segni lacked the standing that would have allowed him to prevail via the mechanism seen in New Zealand, while the political leadership became fully aware of public feelings only after the second phase of reform had begun.

Phase 2   Popular mobilization

During the second phase of reform by elite–mass interaction, the scope of conflict broadens from politicians (and ever-fascinated political scientists) to include the wider population. The work of Shugart (2001, 2008) and Shugart and Wattenberg (2001c) suggests three types of factor whose presence is required before public pressure for electoral reform is likely to develop.[5] First, there must be *inherent* problems in the status quo: the electoral system must have a natural tendency to generate problematic consequences of one sort or another. Second, these underlying problems must generate specific *systemic failures* that lend them immediate salience and trigger pressure for change. Third, there need to be

---

[5] Norris (1995a: 7) offers a similar perspective.

contingencies that allow that pressure to gain sufficient force to generate actual reform. I begin by considering the first two of these factors. With regard to contingencies, I focus in particular on the role of strategic leadership.

Inherent factors and systemic failures

The cases analysed here, as Shugart (2001) and Shugart and Wattenberg (2001c) contend, fit the claim that both inherent problems and specific systemic failures must be present before reform is likely. Beginning with the former, New Zealand's SMP electoral system, particularly in the context of New Zealand's wider political structure, generated tendencies towards both extreme concentration of power and disproportional (sometimes anomalous) election results. As I have argued, it was concentration of power that was the more important factor in spurring reform: not only was it Palmer's primary concern; it also underlay the growth of public disquiet in the late 1980s and early 1990s. The Italian system was highly proportional; given the nature of the Italian political universe (particularly the strength of the uncoalitionable extremes), this prevented alternation of power, thereby hindering accountability and fostering corruption. Japan's SNTV system, finally, imposed high levels of intra-party competition, particularly in the majority LDP; given traditional methods of political competition in Japan, this facilitated the maintenance of clientelism and growth in the role of money in politics.

These inherent tendencies generated specific systemic failures that helped trigger reform in all three cases. Corruption scandals engulfed politics in both Italy and Japan in the early 1990s, and the potency of the allegations was enhanced by the context of sharp economic downturn, which heightened perceptions that dirty politics harmed the quality of governance. In New Zealand, the primary trigger for popular mobilization was not corruption, but the perception that successive governments, of both major parties, had broken manifesto promises and imposed radical economic and social reforms that the people had not voted for; again, economic downturn after 1987 strengthened the perception that these abuses harmed the public good.

Can we draw broader inferences regarding the nature of the systemic failures that may trigger reform? What sorts of event have the power to spark public mobilization? How powerful does the shock need to be? The evidence suggests that the shock must be severe. Three sources of such evidence can be highlighted.

First, no case of reform by elite–mass interaction has occurred without widespread public anger at the performance of the political system as a whole. It may also be significant that no case has occurred without a backdrop of economic recession, suggesting that voters need to feel the failures of the political system are directly damaging their material interests.

Second, milder shocks in the countries studied here did not spark sufficient reform pressure in themselves to generate reform. The two spurious majorities ('wrong winner' elections) in New Zealand in 1978 and 1981 prompted some public reaction, but this would not have led to reform without the further impetus of economic restructuring a decade later. In Japan, opponents of reform managed to ride out the first corruption scandal in 1989, and by 1991 the cause of electoral system change appeared defeated. It might well not have risen again had renewed scandal not rapidly engulfed the system.

Third, evidence from cases other than those studied in detail here suggests again that, without public anger over systemic failures, public pressure for electoral reform will not be strong enough to force change. Siaroff (2003) finds that of nine countries to have experienced 'wrong winner' legislative elections, only two have subsequently seen electoral reform. One was New Zealand, where, as I have argued, the 1978 and 1981 results were contributing but not sufficient causes of reform; the other was Malta, where reform was dominated by elites (Hirczy de Miño and Lane 2000: 186). Additionally, three Canadian provinces (British Columbia, Prince Edward Island, and Ontario) have recently held referendums on electoral reform. In all three, the existing electoral system – SMP – was extreme in Shugart's sense (Shugart 2001: 30–2). Furthermore, both British Columbia and Prince Edward Island experienced potential triggering events: both saw elections that generated huge swings in seat shares and gave overwhelming majorities to single parties; British Columbia also witnessed a 'wrong winner' election (Cousins 2004: 281; Cross 2005: 78–80; Ruff 2004: 236). But in two cases (Prince Edward Island in 2005 and Ontario in 2007), change was backed by little more than a third of voters (Elections Ontario 2007; Elections PEI 2005). In British Columbia in 2005, there was a 57.7 per cent 'yes' vote (Elections BC 2005), but opponents of reform had been able to insert a 60 per cent threshold. A repeat referendum was held in May 2009, but the pro-reform vote share collapsed to just 39.1 per cent (Elections BC 2009). Further evidence comes from the aftermath of the Bush v. Gore controversy in the United States in 2000. Long-standing critic of the electoral college Neal Peirce observes, 'as disgusted as most Americans were by the electoral process that played out before their eyes, the massive public outcry many of us had anticipated failed to erupt' (Peirce 2004: x).

These cases support the proposition that anomalous election results on their own are unlikely to provide sufficient impetus to trigger reform by elite–mass interaction. They may trigger reform discussion (Shugart 2008), but they appear not to generate the sort of public pressure that will lead to actual change. They may excite political scientists and commentators, but not, on the whole, the wider public. Rather, for the public to become engaged in the issue of electoral reform, the failings of the status quo need to be seen as impacting upon their lives more directly.

Leadership

Shugart and Wattenberg (2001c: 571–81) argue that inherent problems and specific systemic failures are insufficient in themselves to explain the incidence of electoral reform: contingent factors too have a crucial role as events unfold. Our three cases suggest one particularly important such contingency: namely, the deliberate exercise of leadership designed to encourage voters to link the problems that concern them to the electoral system. In none of the three cases was it inevitable that the public would latch on to electoral reform as the main solution to the problems in the governing system; in all three, reform advocates worked hard to make that connection. Without that work, electoral reform might well not have occurred.

I argue for these claims in two steps. First, I show that electoral reform was not an inevitable solution to the problems that the three countries faced. Second, I show that leaders indeed actively promoted electoral reform as the best option in all the cases.

Regarding the lack of inevitability of specifically electoral reform, there were good reasons to doubt that the particular reforms proposed would have the effects that voters hoped they would, and these doubts were recognized by at least some analysts at the time in all three countries. Furlong (1991: 59) suggested when Italy's reform process was still in its early stages that, while the electoral system was one source of Italy's governing woes, it was not the primary one: 'there is no convincing reason to believe that a more dynamic, less rigorously proportional electoral system would resolve the problem of government instability in the absence of reforms of parliamentary procedure and government organisation'. Gambetta and Warner (1996) have since identified five ambitions that underlay the 1993 reforms and argued that all were misplaced or at least highly contingent on other processes. The reformers' hopes were indeed at best only partially fulfilled following the passage of reform (Katz 2006).

In Japan, reformers argued that electoral reform would weaken factions, reduce money politics and corruption, encourage the emergence of two-partism, and strengthen prime ministerial leadership. Certainly, SNTV's tendency to reward corruption and factionalism had long been recognized: it was already well known when SNTV was restored in 1947 (Bisson 1949: 57); some argue it was understood even when the system was first adopted in 1900 (Ramseyer and Rosenbluth 1995: 45; but cf. Kawato 2002: 181–2). But while the electoral system was seen as one factor promoting these practices, it was certainly not viewed as the only one (Baerwald 1979: 38–49), and commentators such as Matsuzaki (1989: 26–9), Satō (1991: 28), and Nishibe (1991: 26) doubted that adoption of single-member districts would have much effect. Curtis (1999: 142–4) and Jain (1995: 421–2) have since made similar arguments. Stockwin (2008: 175) argues that the personalistic nature of campaigning was not a necessary product of the electoral system, but 'was heavily influenced by the patterns of social interaction in rural Japan, where a deep-rooted sense of mutual obligation helps pork-barrel methods secure' votes. Schuller (1998) shows that, throughout the twentieth century, those seeking to clean up Japanese politics had pursued a variety of reforms other than change to the electoral system. Indeed, problems of factionalism, corruption, and money politics were deeply rooted in the Japanese political tradition before SNTV with medium-sized districts was introduced in 1925 (Schuller 1998: 61–2). The power of factions did weaken following the reforms (Cox, Rosenbluth, and Thies 1999; Ehrhardt 2006; Stockwin 2008: 192), but was not eliminated (Köllner 2004; Park 2001), and factions appear to have regained some of their former prominence since prime minister Junichiro Koizumi left office in 2006 (Takenaka 2007: 12–13). Clientelism, corruption, and money politics remain strong (Carlson 2007; Scheiner 2007, 2008; Woodall 2007). Two-partism has gradually emerged, but it took fifteen years – until the elections of August 2009 – for a strong opposition party to take power from the LDP. Central leadership certainly strengthened under Koizumi (Kabashima and Steel 2007; Mishima 2007), but its foundations remained uncertain (Köllner 2006: 254; Mulgan 2002) and it has weakened under Koizumi's successors. Furthermore, as I suggested in Chapter 10, building on Curtis (1988: 188–9), that an electoral system based partially on closed lists would come to be seen as offering hope for change was particularly unlikely in Japan in the late 1980s: the adoption of closed-list PR for the national constituency in the Diet's upper house in 1982 had only strengthened money politics (because of the competition to secure high list places) and had proved highly unpopular with voters.

The claim made in New Zealand that MMP would prevent any single power clique in a single party from riding roughshod over parliament and public opinion was certainly plausible, and has been borne out by the period of coalition government since MMP's introduction in 1996 (Boston, Church, and Bale 2003: 12; Malone 2008: 232). But equally plausible arguments regarding the likelihood that MMP would muddy the accountability of governments to voters were made by opponents of the reform (e.g., Birch 1993 [1992]; Clark 1993 [1992]; Lange 1993 [1992]; Upton 1993 [1992]) without gaining much traction. Given voters' hostility towards both politicians and parties,[6] we might have expected them to prefer STV over the closed-list version of MMP proposed by the Royal Commission. Yet four times as many voters opted for MMP as chose STV in the 1992 referendum (Levine and Roberts 1993: 162). Palmer (1992: 195–7) argued that MMP would change the style of political debate in New Zealand, making it less adversarial and more conducive to careful deliberation. Yet parliamentary behaviour is just as raucous as it always was and the tribalism of National and Labour continues (Harris 2002: 233; Stockley 2004: 132).

That electoral reform – and the particular reform enacted in each case – was not an inevitable response to the problems that assailed each country left space for the exercise of leadership to link the two. The existence of such leadership is observable. As Christensen (1994: 598) writes of Japan, 'The most important tactic in the struggle for electoral reform was the linkage of political realignment with anticorruption in the debate that surrounded the various proposals.' Ozawa himself recognized the need to win over public opinion as early as 1990: he said, 'The biggest point is whether we can get the public behind us. Reform won't be possible unless public opinion is aroused' (Morita 1991: 80–1, quoting an interview with Ozawa conducted in June 1990). Otake (1996: 288–9)

[6] According to the 1993 New Zealand Election Study, just 13.5 per cent of voters supported state funding for parties, while 60.2 per cent opposed it (New Zealand Election Study 1993: question D2). According to data collected for the World Values Survey in 1998, just 6.1 per cent of New Zealand respondents had 'a great deal' or 'quite a lot' of confidence in political parties, while 93.9 per cent had 'not very much' or 'none at all' (Perry and Webster 1999: 47).

suggests that, indeed, Ozawa did successfully orchestrate media support for reform (see also Gaunder 2007: 50, 94). Wolfe (1995: 1067) emphasizes the impact of the young reformers. As I noted in Chapter 10, the Japanese public never pressed specifically for electoral reform (Reed 1999: 183; Sakamoto 1999a: 183–4, 1999b: 425–6). But the reformers succeeded in making electoral reform the 'litmus test' of whether a party or politician was serious about tackling the deficiencies of Japanese politics (Reed 1999: 189), and this was sufficient to carry reform forward.

In New Zealand, Geoffrey Palmer sought to bring public pressure to bear upon his colleagues in parliament. Most notably, he sought immediately to capitalize on Lange's unscripted promise of a referendum on the electoral system in the 1987 election campaign by backing Lange's words publicly.[7] He has written, 'I ... went on television the next day and backed him up. After that it was difficult for other people to deny the intention, so they had to keep quiet' (Palmer 1992: 178), and he makes clear this effect was deliberate (Palmer 2006). But Palmer was unable while in office to orchestrate sufficient public pressure in favour of reform to push his colleagues into acquiescence. Such public pressure might have been raised by linking the electoral system to the perceived infidelities of the Labour government. But this linkage strategy was not available to Palmer: he was deputy prime minister and later prime minister of that very government. Thus, he ultimately failed in moving New Zealand decisively from the first to the second phase of the process of reform by elite–mass interaction. As Mulgan (1989: 119) observed at the time, assuming that the reform cause was probably lost, 'Palmer's career provides an excellent illustration of how much, and also, perhaps, ultimately how little, one determined reformer can achieve.'

Rather, the primary agents of linkage during the second phase of reform in New Zealand were extra-parliamentary groups. The most important was the Electoral Reform Coalition (ERC). Others included trade unions and the Women's Electoral Lobby. The ERC was led by the irrepressible Phil Saxby and Rod Donald. Saxby worked primarily behind the scenes: he was 'a relentless organizer' (Aimer 2006) and lobbied MPs hard; Donald, meanwhile, was the Coalition's main public face. In their submissions to the Royal Commission, future ERC activists had advocated a variety of forms of PR, including the pure list system (Aimer 1985) and STV (New Zealand Democratic Party 1985: 3–8), as well as MMP (Saxby 1985). But they recognized the need to unite on a single proposal and, in the light of the Royal Commission's recommendations,

---

[7] 'PM Promises Electoral Referendum', *NZH*, 10 August 1987.

there was little dispute that this should be MMP (Aimer 1999: 152; Saxby 2006). In the run-up to the 1992 referendum, the ERC largely monopolized public debate over electoral reform: though some politicians spoke in favour of the status quo, they were sufficiently discredited for the public to pay them little heed. The success of the ERC's strategy was shown in the overwhelming referendum vote both for change and specifically for MMP. By 1993, the reformers' message was countered by the pro-SMP Campaign for Better Government, headed by businessman Peter Shirtcliffe. The more balanced public debate that resulted is likely to have contributed to the closer vote in the second referendum, held that year.

In Italy, the mobilization of public opinion encompassed two tasks. First, as in the other two cases, the link had to be made in the public mind between the governance crisis and the electoral system: a range of reform proposals had previously crowded the agenda, notably Craxi's plan for direct election of the head of government; through relentless campaigning, Segni and others focused attention specifically on the electoral system. Second, the reform strategy pursued in Italy, based on citizen-initiated referendums, required more active participation by the electorate than in either Japan or New Zealand: each referendum could be called only by gathering 500,000 signatures. Particularly in 1991, when reform pressure was still emerging, this required organization and leadership: 'if it had not been for the efforts of the parties, of political leaders and of activists the goal of half a million signatures would not have been reached' (Pasquino 1992: 17; similarly, Donovan 1995: 54). As McCarthy (1992: 14) puts it, the army of public opinion needed generals.

Given how few cases of reform by elite–mass interaction we have to work with, general conclusions must be stated tentatively. Nevertheless, the evidence analysed here suggests that public mobilization around electoral reform requires three conditions. First, the public must be angry about the performance of the political system and political class and feel that these failings are directly damaging their interests. Second, inherent weaknesses in the existing electoral system must make it plausible to link that system to the issues of direct public concern. Third, that link must be made by strategic leaders, who may have to work hard against alternative interpretations, rival schemes, and entrenched interests.

Phase 3   Politicians' response

In all three cases, public opinion had force not because it carried legal weight, but because politicians chose to change their behaviour in response to it. Japan's politicians responded without a formal referendum. In New Zealand, politicians designed an essentially unbiased mechanism by which the public could decide the issue. In Italy, the referendum results did have legal force to the extent that politicians could not simply re-enact the old provisions; but politicians went far beyond what was legally necessary in accepting sweeping electoral system change.

The principal mechanism through which public opinion exerted this force was the act-contingent vote-seeking behaviour of politicians (I(b) in Table 2.1): politicians knew that to deny the public the reforms they wanted or to fail to be seen to take public concerns over the health of the political system seriously would mean a loss of votes and therefore power at the next election. Closely related to this, politicians also wanted to retain the support of their principal institutional backers: Japan's *Rengō* trade union federation, for example, sponsored only pro-reform candidates in the 1993 election (Carlile 1994: 618). These mechanisms have been discussed in earlier chapters and well documented by others, and it is not necessary to go into further detail.

But the cases suggest three further mechanisms through which politicians may re-evaluate their original opposition to electoral reform when the matter becomes a major issue on the public agenda. First, one source of politicians' initial conservatism on electoral reform is the fact that they satisfice: so long as the existing electoral system serves them adequately well, they do not expend much energy considering whether an alternative would be better. Once the issue of electoral reform has entered public debate, however, information regarding alternatives to the status quo becomes widespread and the assessment of whether reforms might serve their purposes comes to be less costly for politicians. Calise (1993: 551), for example, suggests that when Italy's *Lega Nord* switched from opposing to supporting majoritarian electoral reform in autumn 1992, it merely came to recognize a 'basic assumption of electoral system theory: that in the absence of a structured two-party system, the plurality rule strongly favours territorially concentrated forces'. Thus, the *Lega's* leaders came to see that an alternative electoral system would better serve their existing electoral strategy.

Under the second mechanism, by contrast, politicians change their electoral strategy. Some strategy shifts – such as Occhetto's decision to drag the Italian Communist Party from the ghetto and realign it as a force of the moderate left – occur for reasons exogenous to the process of electoral reform. In other cases, however, politicians appear, at least in

part, to respond to the growing inevitability of reform by reconceptualizing how they may best play the political game. Thus, the leaders of several
of the small parties in Japan – *Kōmeitō*, the DSP, and *Shaminren* – moved
in 1993 to support MMM over MMP because they hoped that the
upheaval of reform would spark the emergence of a new political force
to rival the LDP in which they could play prominent roles. In normal
times, a strategy of seeking party system realignment (VIII(a) in
Table 2.1) generally appears too risky: the outcome of such flux is highly
unpredictable. But once major change to the electoral system appears
unavoidable, upheaval may appear unavoidable too, and this strategy
thereby becomes less costly.

Third, engagement with the issue of electoral reform as it gains
prominence on the political agenda may cause some politicians to
develop an interest in the topic that transcends their own power interests.
In New Zealand, two of the three politicians who presented Labour's oral
submission to the Royal Commission – Richard Northey and Margaret
Wilson – later became prominent advocates of reform. Both cite their
engagement with the Royal Commission as important in making them
rethink issues that previously they had taken for granted (Northey 2006;
Wilson 2006). As I argued in Chapter 11, on the side of the National
Party, Murray McCully and Doug Graham both participated in the
discussions of electoral reform in the Electoral Law Select Committee
in the late 1980s (chaired by Northey), and both increasingly engaged
with institutional effects and possible institutional reforms in consequence. All of these politicians became caught up in arguments about
the relative merits of different systems and ceased to view the electoral
reform issue solely through the lens of power.

In these ways, processes of electoral reform may develop their own
momentum: the very fact that debate intensifies releases mechanisms
that enhance reform prospects. Such mechanisms generate endogenous
path dependence within the reform process, and I consider them further
in the section on building blocks below.

Building blocks

The three phases of the process of reform by elite–mass interaction offer
one angle from which to analyse the process as a whole. The building
blocks identified in Part I of this book offer another angle. In this section
I tie together the evidence regarding each of the building blocks scattered
across the three phases and analyse the propositions developed in Part I.

Actors and motivations

The principal actors in processes of reform by elite–mass interaction are politicians and citizens. Politicians initiate the process, play an important role in mobilizing public opinion, and create the mechanisms through which change can finally occur. Citizens are vital in generating the pressure for reform that causes the majority of politicians to accept change. Other actors can matter too. Interest and pressure groups helped mobilize public opinion in all three countries: the Electoral Reform Coalition, backed by trade unions, in New Zealand; the *Rengō* trade union federation in Japan (Carlile 1994; Wolfe 1995: 1070–1); a range of organizations including *Confindustria* and the Catholic church in Italy (McCarthy 1992: 21). Experts were also involved in every case, particularly in developing and selecting alternatives.

As the previous section makes clear, a wide variety of motivations contributed to the reform processes. In keeping with the proposition stated in P1 (Chapter 3), publics generally backed reform because of their exasperation with the state of their polities. This qualitative finding is backed by more detailed survey research conducted in New Zealand. Lamare and Vowles (1996) test hypotheses regarding the factors that influenced whether New Zealand voters supported or opposed MMP in 1993. Some of these hypotheses posit that voters pursued partisan interests – in particular, that 'Party supporters will support the electoral system which will most support the political success of their party' (Lamare and Vowles 1996: 329) – others that they pursued wider values, measured by their location on scales of post-materialism, authoritarianism, and populism. Lamare and Vowles find evidence for both sets of hypotheses, but this is more consistent in the case of the second set than the first (Lamare and Vowles 1996: 330, 336).

Lamare and Vowles's evidence supports the argument of McLeay *et al.* (1996: 27) that New Zealand's electoral reform was underpinned by a fundamental shift away from deferential attitudes towards politicians and acceptance of a benign state, and towards greater belief in the need for a limited state and protection of civil and group rights. That such cultural change can foster reform over the long term was proposed in proposition P6. The main conclusion suggested by the discussion above of how the public can come to mobilize around electoral reform was, however, that they need to feel their interests are harmed by the status quo. They focus on those values that appear responsible for that threat: the lack of checks and balances in New Zealand; corruption in

Italy and Japan. These findings confirm P4 in Chapter 3 – that ordinary citizens think about the electoral system only in exceptional times – and P7 – that the salience of a given value depends on how far it is seen as threatened. Much less evidence appears, however, in support of P5, on the importance of historical traditions. Certainly, New Zealanders were concerned to maintain the tradition of local district representation and constituency service, and lower public support for reform on the South Island appears to have stemmed from fears that this would be threatened by the new system. In other respects, however, the principal values that voters espoused were in no sense particular to the countries in question. Thus, the threat factor appears to take precedence over history.

Politicians, meanwhile, pursued the full range of goals analysed in Chapter 2. The majority of politicians were principally concerned with their own power (whether as an end in itself or as a means to further ends), as P1 predicts, and on this basis initially opposed reform. As discussed above, the exceptions to this rule support the propositions contained in P2 and P3, that new entrants to the political class and those whose lifestyles do not depend on their survival in office may be less focused on office-seeking than others. In conformity with P12, it is clear that most politicians just did not think about the electoral system very much: so long as it delivered adequately satisfactory results, they took it as fixed and pursued the strategy that would maximize their prospects given the parameters of competition that it set. In so far as they did think about the electoral system, seat-maximization clearly mattered, but they also took account of a variety of considerations beyond the Duvergerian mechanisms, relating particularly to personal re-election prospects (VI(a) in Table 2.1) and coalition dynamics (IV(a)). As in the earlier episodes discussed in Part II, the importance of backbench interests in Japan stemmed from the structure of the LDP (P8), while coalition dynamics and the desire to weaken opponents mattered most where coalitions mattered most: in Italy (P9). There is insufficient evidence, finally, to assess P10, concerning actors' time horizons.

I have already analysed the factors that shaped politicians' change of stance in response to public pressure in all three cases. These related principally to vote-seeking act contingencies (I(b)), though the decline of transaction costs (V(e)), change in electoral strategies (VIII(a)), and development of genuine interest in the values attached to reform also mattered.

Uncertainty and misperception

Some of the issues regarding uncertainty have already been discussed in preceding sections. Many politicians were initially reluctant even to think about the electoral system: so long as the status quo appeared acceptable, they stuck by it, as P12 in Chapter 3 would expect. This was true particularly in New Zealand, where major change to the electoral system had not been on the agenda for decades and where politicians' unfamiliarity with alternatives and their implications for the nature of political competition was therefore greatest. As the reform processes unfolded, the majority politicians in all three countries were forced to engage with the issue. There is evidence that some – notably those seeking to maximize the proportional element of the mixed systems in Italy and Japan – adopted risk-averse strategies in doing so. But others – small-party advocates of substantially majoritarian systems in both Italy and Japan – were remarkably willing to accept risk.

Proposition P13 noted no more than that misperception may matter. In the context of reform by elite–mass interaction, it comes in two important forms: first, actors may misperceive the effects of their actions in the course of the lengthy reform process; second, they may misperceive the effects of different electoral system options. Regarding the first of these, for example, Lange did not foresee that his spontaneous referendum promise in 1987 would help keep the idea of electoral reform alive and perhaps contribute to its flourishing in the early 1990s; Takeshita did not recognize that by allowing the idea of reform on to the agenda he would risk eventually losing control of the process. Such misperceptions matter, in general, because actions that seem small turn out to have large effects. They do so via path dependence, which I analyse below.

As in the cases discussed in Part II, politicians foresaw very accurately the effects of different electoral systems on their power in New Zealand. Misperception of the second type was, however, a significant factor in Japan. The advocates of MMM within the Hosokawa government of 1993–1994 believed that this system would foster the rapid development of a two-party system in which they would form the bedrock of the new, powerful alternative to the LDP. In fact, however, a strong second party did not initially materialize: a long series of acrimonious splits and fragile mergers dogged the non-LDP parties. In August 2009, the Democratic Party of Japan (DPJ), which had been led until he was felled by scandal in May 2009 by none other than Ichirō Ozawa, won a decisive – indeed, potentially historic – victory in elections to the lower house. It is possible that two-partism has finally arrived. Nevertheless, this party, founded only in 1996 and built up through subsequent mergers, remains divided by differences of both policy and personality, and its future success is not guaranteed. As I suggested in Chapter 8, it is unlikely that such misperceptions are predictable.

Cognitive constraints

Cognitive constraints, as proposition P14 in Chapter 3 suggests, should be the stronger as the process used when exploring and specifying alternatives is the less systematic. This is borne out by the evidence. The most thorough investigation of possible reform options was conducted in New Zealand, where the Royal Commission laboured for approaching two years and drew extensively on political science research and both domestic and international experience. It offered conclusions on thirteen distinct alternatives to the status quo, several of which themselves contained multiple variants (Royal Commission on the Electoral System 1986: 28–38). Through all this work, the Commission recommended (and New Zealanders eventually accepted) a system that had never before been used in New Zealand, never been used in the wider Westminster world or in the Asia-Pacific region, never been publicly advocated in New Zealand, and was not yet fashionable in the world at large. Certainly, the criteria by which the Commission evaluated different options – notably that on 'effective representation of constituents' (Royal Commission on the Electoral System 1986: 11) – were shaped by New Zealand tradition. But the Commission was open in its thinking and active in its pursuit of new ideas to an exceptional degree.

Investigation of alternatives was rather less thorough in Japan. The Electoral System Advisory Council that reported in 1990 did consider four alternatives to the status quo: the MMM system that they advocated, together with MMP, pure SMP, and pure PR (Yomiuri Electoral System Study Group 1990). But it was a much more limited operation than the New Zealand Royal Commission. And it is noteworthy that inquiries in Japan returned repeatedly to the same mixed-member majoritarian option: having first been advocated in 1956 (Ward 1966: 564), this option was considered by the Advisory Councils from 1962 onwards (Reed and Thies 2001: 160–1) and formed the basis of the Tanaka bill in 1973. It could be that MMM simply remained the most plausible response to Japan's particular needs throughout these decades: after all, clientelism was already a key concern in the 1950s, and lack of alternation was apparent by the early 1970s. But Curtis for one contends that the repeated advocacy of the same solution also reflected cognitive constraints upon how actors conceived of the various options. Indeed, he argues that the roots of the reforms enacted in 1994 reached back still further than the 1950s: belief in the curative effects of single-member districts originated in the debates of the 1920s and derived from a desire to replicate an idealized version of British democracy. This belief, he argues, 'has become frozen in time in Japan, and it has led many people to believe with what can only be described as a kind of religious conviction that introduction of a kind of single-member-district system would cause the advent of policy-oriented, party-controlled, inexpensive election campaigns and a two-party format' (Curtis 1999: 163).

The Italian case, finally, is unusual: an artificial constraint was imposed by the rules regarding abrogative citizen-initiated referendums and the wording of the existing electoral law, which severely limited the options that could be placed before the people. Subsequently, considerations of legitimacy constrained politicians from enacting any system significantly less proportional than the one created (for the Senate) by the second referendum.

As to P15, on the factors that shape cognitive constraints, only the Japanese case offers relevant evidence. As in Chapter 8, and as will be clear from the preceding paragraphs, it suggests that the major factor is the history of domestic debate on the subject.

Legitimacy constraints

The primary role for legitimacy perceptions in cases of reform by elite–mass interaction is in constraining politicians to respond to public demands for change. National Party leaders in New Zealand did not impose a turnout threshold on the referendum of 1993 because to have done so would have been seen as an illegitimate attempt to skew the result. Italy's legislators limited the proportional component of the new electoral law to 25 per cent of the seats because to have done otherwise would have seemed to treat the expressed will of the people lightly. I have already discussed this fundamental mechanism, and it needs no further elaboration.

Legitimacy constraints can also, independently of public pressure, limit the reform options that are considered. In New Zealand, for example, the Royal Commission considered several bonus-adjusted systems (under the heading of 'supplementary seats'), but dismissed them quickly, concluding that such arrangements would 'be perceived as an artificial interference with the system' (Royal Commission on the Electoral System 1986: 33). This instance is, however, unusual and minor: such considerations played only a marginal role in these cases.

Institutions

Institutions have contributed in several ways to the story so far: for example, by shaping historical traditions and influencing the strength of cognitive constraints. Propositions P18 and P19 in Chapter 3 focus on the role of institutions in shaping the final outcome of the reform process, and I turn to this now.

At the broad level, the institutions for decision-making appear to have made little difference in the cases studied here: public pressure was potent whether a referendum was held or not and whether that referendum was formally initiated by citizens or by politicians; no particular institutional arrangement is required before reform by elite–mass interaction can occur. In a sense, P18 is correct: reform becomes possible through elite–mass interaction because public pressure sweeps away all other veto players. But institutions do not determine whether this occurs.

There is more support for P19: differences in the institutional arrangements in the three countries do correlate with differences in the relative power of politicians and citizens. Specifically, the clearer was the preference that voters were able to express (the more precisely they could define the agenda), the more constraining was their will upon politicians. In Japan, where voters were able to express at the ballot box only a general demand for reform, politicians had considerable freedom to negotiate the precise content of that reform in pursuit of their own purposes. Politicians were more constrained in Italy: the referendum results limited the final electoral system they could adopt. But they still had substantial flexibility, for the referendum rules meant that the particular option presented to voters had in large part been randomly generated. That legislators finally chose a system very similar to the one created for the Senate by the referendum was the outcome of competing elite interests and the power of the referendum system as a focal point, not of the power of specific popular wishes. In New Zealand, by contrast, where voters could select from among four alternatives to the status quo, politicians could do little but implement the system that voters had chosen. The version of MMP that was on the table at the time of the first referendum was the one proposed by the Royal Commission, and parliament barely deviated from it in working up a detailed proposal ahead of the second referendum. There were two significant changes, but neither signified power in politicians' hands. One – the raising of the electoral threshold from 4 to 5 per cent – was in any case accepted by the chair of the Commission, John Wallace, in his evidence to the select committee (Wallace 2002: 60). And the other – retention of separate Māori seats – ran against the preferences of the party in power and reflected the will of Māori representatives (Jackson and McRobie 1998: 218–29).

But the New Zealand case also highlights a further major qualification to the conclusion that institutions matter: those institutions are subject to change. That the referendum took the form it did reflected a long series of moves over the previous decade, not a pre-existing institutional constraint.

Leadership

I have discussed in some detail the role of leadership in the second phase of the reform process, in linking the electoral system to matters of public concern and mobilizing public opinion. In the language of Chapter 4, leaders during this phase use the strategy of expanding the scope of conflict (S5), in some cases also manipulating multi-level games (S6), in pursuit of their ends; in connecting electoral reform to issues of direct public concern, they make extensive use of framing (S2) and genuine argumentative persuasion (S1). Here, I focus on leadership in the first and third phases.

The key tasks during the first phase are to push electoral reform on to the political agenda and identify specific alternatives to the status quo. In Japan, as I suggested above, little leadership was required from pro-reform politicians at this stage: Takeshita raised the profile of electoral reform by forming his two commissions in response to the Recruit scandal in early 1989; Uno took it further later the same year with the eighth Electoral System Advisory Council. It is possible that even at this stage Ozawa was active behind the scenes in persuading Takeshita to take up the electoral reform issue: certainly, he was close to Takeshita, and he did serve on the personal advisory council that Takeshita established in January 1989 (Etō 1993: 19). But the extent of Ozawa's backroom role at this time cannot be known.

In Italy and New Zealand, by contrast, the role played by leadership at this stage was vital. In Italy, Segni worked hard to raise interest in majoritarian electoral reform within the parliamentary and wider elite. His principal tactic was to build a cross-party coalition for reform that could channel efforts and thereby exert influence within parliament and beyond: as Parker (1996: 44) observes, 'Segni's role was to be a determinate [*sic*] one because of his ability to link together such unlikely personalities as the leader of the Italian Greens, Francesco Rutelli, the veteran Liberal Alfredo Biondi, the PDS secretary Achille Occhetto and the Catholic historian and constitutionalist Pietro Scoppola.' In doing this, he probably employed a mix of argumentative persuasion (S1), framing (S2), and bargaining (S3). New Zealand's Geoffrey Palmer, by contrast, deployed rather different tactics. He made repeated use of salami slicing (S8), seeking to advance the reform cause in small steps that his more sceptical colleagues could hardly object to. Thus, the relevant section of Labour's 1984 manifesto – written by Palmer – pledged only the formation of a royal commission, while the 1987 manifesto said only that the commission's proposals would be considered by select committee. He recalls of the second of these instances, 'I pushed as far as I thought I could get, which was to keep the thing alive rather than have it dead' (Palmer 2006). In forming the Royal Commission, defining its terms of reference, and selecting its members, he used the tactic of institutional change (S7) in order to generate the process that he wanted. Without Palmer's efforts at this stage, it is quite possible that electoral reform would not have occurred.

Turning to the third phase, though politicians have by this stage to a considerable extent lost control of the process, still, as we have seen, they are not entirely impotent: at least in Italy and Japan, they retained significant capacity to influence the outcome. The deployment of leadership tactics to mould the final electoral system is particularly clear in Japan in the months after the 1993 election. Hosokawa and Takemura publicly announced immediately following the election that they would form a coalition only with parties willing to accept their proposal of an MMM system comprising 250 single-member districts and 250 list seats (Kohno 1997: 140). In doing so, they were playing Putnam's two-level game (S6): by limiting their own capacity to climb down from their publicly stated position, they forced other parties to acquiesce. Initially, this tactic paid off, and the government's first proposal incorporated precisely the 250:250 split. Over the following months, however, the ratio of single-member districts to list seats was changed, first to 274:226 and then, following the defeat in the House of Councillors in January 1994, to 300:200. In this, we must presume that Ozawa – who wanted the most majoritarian outcome he could get – was instrumental. The parts of the governing coalition that were most favourable to PR – *Sakigake* and the JSP – were progressively marginalized, while the defeat in the House of Councillors became an opportunity to open towards the LDP and accept its more majoritarian agenda. In all of this, intense inter-party bargaining across multiple issues (S3) occurred. Bargaining between parties was similarly important in determining the final outcome in Italy.

Overall, then, the role of leadership in cases of reform by elite–mass interaction is considerable. Most striking is the role of pro-reform politicians in mobilizing public support. Beyond this phase, considerable leadership skill may be required to engineer electoral reform on to the political agenda in the first place in a context where the majority of politicians oppose it, and various leadership tactics may be used by both supporters and opponents of change to shape the final outcome.

Path dependence

The final building block relates to path dependence: the capacity for what may initially appear to be small moves to generate large effects by setting off increasingly irreversible chains of events. In Chapter 4, I identified mechanisms of path dependence at two levels: long-term path dependence in the electoral system itself, and endogenous path dependence within processes of change. The preceding sections allude to various forms of long-term path dependence via satisficing, cognitive constraints, and the power of vested interests. Processes of reform by elite–mass interaction are also open to endogenous path dependence: they are prolonged and unfold over multiple stages involving complex interactions among many actors. Chapter 4 identified four mechanisms of such endogenous path dependence, and there is strong evidence for three of these in the cases analysed here.

The first mechanism (PD1) arises from the need to solve coordination games. Where such games exist, a focal point is typically sought and may thereafter gain unstoppable momentum (Schelling 1963). In the context of reform processes, the first option on the table may often have greatest potency as a focal point. As I have argued, for example, Italy's parliamentarians were not legally required to adopt an electoral system modelled closely on the one created for the Senate by the 1993 referendum. But their overwhelming imperative was to give Italy a workable electoral system, and, in responding to that shared need for quick action, the electoral system created by the referendum offered the most prominent focal point around which agreement could coalesce (cf. Hine 1993b). The same mechanism was clear in New Zealand. The Royal Commission's recommendation of MMP dominated the debate, even though the public, not sharing the Commission's belief in the importance of strong political parties (Royal Commission on the Electoral System 1986: 12), might, in a neutral context, have preferred STV. That the public focused on MMP reflects the decision of the pro-reform lobbyists, including the Electoral Reform Coalition, to do the same. They did so knowing that reform was much more likely if a single reform option were advanced, and that the Royal Commission's proposal would carry more weight than any alternative (Aimer 1999: 151–2; Saxby 2006).

Under the second mechanism of path dependence (PD2), issues, once aired in a context of bounded rationality, can gain legs: attention paid to an issue breeds further attention. By placing an issue on the agenda, a politician may encourage others to take an interest in it; this interest may rapidly become self-generating, and the politician who started the process loses control. Takeshita hoped reform talk could allow him to ride the effects of the Recruit scandal and that interest in reform would subside once the scandal began to fade. Indeed, interest did subside. But when fresh scandals emerged under Miyazawa, the electoral reform option was already on the table, and anti-reform politicians had little alternative but to pick it up again. In New Zealand, the Royal Commission and subsequent select committee inquiry sparked or strengthened interest in issues of institutional reform among politicians such as Northey and Wilson from Labour and Graham and McCully from National. It was also crucial in the development of the wider reform movement. Some groups, such as the Women's Electoral Lobby, engaged with the issue of electoral reform only as a result of the impetus the Commission provided (Preddey 2003: 110–16; Ryan 2006). Without the Commission, the Electoral Reform Coalition might well never even have formed: one of the ERC's initiators, Louis Ehrler, reviewed all the submissions to the Commission and contacted those who had advocated some form of PR; from this circle the ERC emerged (Saxby 2006); it was the Commission's inquiry that allowed these widely dispersed individuals to connect with each other and organize their efforts. Media attention also stemmed from the Royal Commission's work: the *New Zealand Herald* came out in support of the Royal Commission's recommendations,[8] having previously paid the issue scant regard.

---

[8] 'A Price on Fairness', *NZH*, 19 December 1986.

Third, public commitments and promises can bind (PD3). More precisely, once a commitment or promise has been made, the cost in terms of voter affect of subsequently breaking it may be high. Reed (1999: 190) argues that the power of promises was fundamental in all three cases studied here:

> The basic dynamic is produced by the pressure to keep popular promises after winning an election ... In each of these cases of political reform, parties got caught in bidding wars, competing to be the true reformers, and sooner or later found they had painted themselves into a corner. They could not avoid keeping their promises, because the electoral costs of breaking the promise had unexpectedly outgrown the costs of enacting the reform.

Curtis (1999: 154) gives the particular example of the decision by the JSP and *Kōmeitō* to propose an MMP system in April 1993:

> They now had put themselves on record unequivocally as supporters of a mixed system in which voters would cast separate ballots for candidates in single-member districts and for parties in proportional-representation districts. In the future, they might argue about the balance between single-member districts and proportional representation, but they could not claim to be opposed to the principle of a mixed or 'parallel' system. The die for an eventual compromise had been cast.

More broadly, having been elected in 1993 on a reform ticket, it was imperative for the parties of the Hosokawa coalition that they deliver. Similarly, in New Zealand, Lange discovered that broken promises could be fatal; Bolger, having experienced this cost with regard to the super-annuation surcharge, refused to countenance it again over the electoral system, even as his earlier hopes that popular disquiet could be tamed were dashed. Commitments may bind even where they are not explicitly given. Having established a royal commission, for example, Palmer could argue that the Labour government was bound at least to give its recommendations serious consideration, even though its manifesto had contained no explicit commitment to do so.

The final mechanism of endogenous path dependence identified in Chapter 4 concerns the tendency for actors engaged in extended reform processes to develop commitments over time to the success of the process and to other participants within it (PD4). Certainly, we can see that actors such as Segni and Pannella in Italy and Saxby and Donald in New Zealand invested enormous time and effort in the reform processes. But there is insufficient evidence to say there was strong path dependence in their engagement. None of the cases discussed here involved the long rounds of negotiation seen in the course of constitutional reform in countries such as South Africa and Fiji.

Conclusion

Electoral reform by elite–mass interaction is rare. There are just three cases in established democracies in recent decades. This is so because it requires an unusual combination of events: a significant core of politicians must come to advocate reform; events must cause public anger regarding the state of politics (and not merely regarding the politicians of one party) to run high; inherent features of the electoral system must allow reformers to make a plausible case that the existing electoral system is a major cause of the problems; and reform leaders must play their hand skilfully. Reform can thereby occur over the heads of politicians whose power interests it violates, even where those politicians formally have the final say in whether any changes are enacted. The old dictum that electoral reform will never occur unless the majority of politicians conclude that an alternative to the status quo would better serve their power interests may be true most of the time, but it is not true always.

Two further questions can be asked. First, if electoral reforms by elite–mass interaction involve substantial public participation, can we for that reason suppose that they serve the public interest? This is an issue that I explore further in the concluding chapter. But the preliminary evidence from this chapter is encouraging: in all three cases, the impulse for reform came, at least in part, from politicians who were genuinely concerned to improve the operation of the governing system rather than feather their own nests.

Second, do the outcomes of reforms by elite–mass interaction tend in any particular direction? The cases studied suggest that they do not. Two of the three cases involved reform away from proportionality (marginally in the Japanese case, substantially so in Italy), but the third case – that of New Zealand – involved a decisive shift towards proportionality. As Shugart (2001) argues, any pure electoral system can generate problems that can incite pressure for reform. I pursue this issue further in the concluding chapter.

13

Conclusions and implications

The chapters of Part I contained detailed analysis of particular aspects – building blocks – of electoral reform. The chapters of Parts II and III analysed major instances of electoral reform in established democracies since the Second World War. In this chapter, I return to the big picture. I begin by outlining the conclusions that emerge from the previous chapters regarding the nature of electoral reform processes. I then consider the implications of those conclusions for the major questions that I asked in the first chapter, concerning who has power over electoral system outcomes, whose interests or which values those outcomes serve, and what patterns outcomes are likely to exhibit. Finally, I hazard a look at the future: should we expect the patterns observable in recent decades to remain the same in the years ahead, or might the politics of electoral reform take on new shape?

The nature of electoral reform in established democracies

Processes of electoral reform, I have argued, can take many forms. In established democracies, two types predominate: reform by elite majority imposition and by elite–mass interaction.

The factor that most obviously differentiates these types from each other and from non-reform is the attitude of the public. Where the public actively pushes for change in the electoral system, then reform by elite–mass interaction becomes possible. The evidence analysed in preceding chapters suggests, I have argued, that this can occur where a major crisis generates public anger at the state of the political system as a whole, where a plausible case can be made that electoral reform could alleviate the causes of that anger – where there are inherent problems in the electoral system itself – and where pro-reform leaders actively make that link between the crisis and the electoral system. Skewed election results are not enough: the troubles in the political system must be seen by voters as impacting on their lives directly. It is the nature of those troubles that primarily determines which values voters seek to advance through electoral reform. Though tradition does matter – voters in New Zealand, for example, were dubious about any reform that would hinder traditional constituency representation – and though value change can ease the passage of certain measures, voters in all three cases of reform by elite–mass interaction sought primarily to restore basic values of good democratic governance that they saw as lacking in the political systems as they stood.

Reform by elite majority imposition becomes possible, meanwhile, where publics are not only uninterested in pushing for reform, but also unwilling or unable to punish manipulation of the electoral system by those in power. In this circumstance, legitimacy constraints are low. This is most likely to occur because citizens have been inured to electoral system manipulation by historical precedents. Even if a reform is widely viewed as illegitimate, its enactors may escape unpunished if they can push it through quickly well ahead of elections or if they already have a reputation for Machiavellianism anyway.

Whether reform occurs at all and what form it takes also depend on politicians' motivations. This applies to reforms by elite–mass interaction just as it does to reforms by elite majority imposition, for, as I have argued, leadership, including the leadership of politicians, is crucial to the enactment of reform by this route. Many of the leading reformers in these cases – in Italy, Japan, and New Zealand – have manifestly been motivated not by the desire to increase their own power, but rather by the belief that reform could, in various ways, improve the operation of the political system. In established democracies, however, the majority of politicians in all cases of both types think of electoral reform primarily in terms of its effects on their personal power or the power of their party. This fact has often been noticed, but the complexity of its implications has not always been adequately acknowledged. Electoral reform may influence power in many ways. It may affect a party's power by affecting voters' preferences across parties, or the translation of those preferences into votes and then seats, or parties' chances of holding office, or their influence over policy outcomes. It may affect individual power in terms of prospects for re-election, intra-party power, and influence in the wider political system. The outcomes of electoral reform processes can affect all these constituents of power; so too may actions taken during the reform process itself. Which of the constituents of power actors prioritize is not always predictable. But it relates fundamentally to which elements influence power most, and this depends in turn on such factors as the internal structure of political parties, their size and number, and the dynamics of inter-party coalitions. Actors may vary also in their time horizons, depending on the stage they have reached in their career trajectories. Whether the interests of individual politicians or of parties matter more depends on the established structure of power in parties and the wider political system.

The motivations of politicians and the wider public are important in processes of electoral reform, but they do not determine outcomes. Several factors shape how motivations translate into preferences. Besides the legitimacy constraints already mentioned, actors face cognitive constraints and limited information. Cognitive constraints limit the options that politicians and other actors consider. Where extensive review processes are used, these constraints can be lifted considerably: New Zealand's Royal Commission on the Electoral System assessed a very wide range of alternatives to the status quo. But the range of options considered is generally limited. The evidence analysed here suggests that in established democracies it is limited primarily by domestic history, to options used or extensively debated in the country in the past. Outside New Zealand, there is little evidence in cases of either reform type that foreign borrowings played much role.

Limited information can mean that, even where an option is considered, actors are uncertain of the effects it will have, either because they are uncertain of its effects in general, or because they do not know how its effects will play out in their own case. I suggested in Chapter 3 that in established democracies where the existing electoral system remains viable actors will tend to respond to uncertainty by favouring the status quo. Evidence in subsequent chapters, particularly from the early stages of the reforms by elite–mass interaction, supports that. Limited information can also spawn misperceptions, which, as I discussed in Chapter 3, have led to well-documented surprises following electoral reforms in some democratizing countries. There are some instances of misperception in the cases of reform in established democracies considered here too: hopes for the effects of reforms driven by public pressure were often too rosy; in several other cases, those who pushed for change to further their own power underestimated the backlash their actions would unleash. On the whole, however, misperceptions have been limited. In all the cases of enacted reform discussed in Part II, except that of Italy in 1953, the reformers' expectations were broadly in line with subsequent outcomes. Even in the cases of reform by elite–mass interaction, though expectations were always overblown, many of the expected effects did ensue in part.

Motivations and the constraints of legitimacy, cognition, and information all feed into actors' preferences for electoral systems. In order to
understand how those preferences translate into outcomes, we need also,
I suggested in Chapter 3, to consider institutions. As Tsebelis (2002)
argues, a greater number of veto players – whether institutional, partisan,
or intra-partisan – makes reform harder. Thus, all the cases of major
reform in established democracies except the 1993 reform in New
Zealand have occurred where such reform could be passed by simple
parliamentary majority. By contrast, where special majorities or majorities in multiple arenas are required – as in Ireland, where the basics of
the electoral system are constitutionally entrenched and can be changed
only by referendum – reform efforts have been blocked. Reform attempts
have also failed where governing coalitions have been complex, as in Italy
between 1994 and 2001. Yet the impact of the number of veto players
should not be exaggerated. First, lengthy bargaining and skilful leadership allowed reform to occur despite diverse coalition interests in France
in 1951 and Italy in 1953 and 2005. Second, strategic action can change
the effective number of veto players: successful pressure for a referendum
effectively removed the parliamentary veto player in New Zealand in
1993; in Japan, pressure by anti-reformers in 1956 and 1973 granted
effective veto power to public opinion. Institutions also have an important but not determinative role in identifying agenda setters. Formal
rules allowed citizen-initiated referendums to push the agenda in Italy
in 1991 and 1993, but the absence of equivalent rules did not prevent
public opinion from pushing events in Japan and New Zealand around
the same time. Thus, while institutions matter, they can also be changed
or subverted, particularly where leaders are skilful or public opinion is
aroused.

The empirical examination of electoral reform processes in France,
Italy, Japan, and New Zealand since the Second World War thus yields
much valuable understanding of how those processes unfold. Clearly, it
would be desirable to test the propositions developed here against
broader evidence. But such broader testing must lie outside the bounds
of the present book, for it is, in itself, no easy task. First, many of the
propositions offered above do not lend themselves readily to statistical
operationalization. I have argued, for example, that reform by elite–mass
interaction occurs when a crisis that directly affects the public can
plausibly be blamed, at least in part, on the electoral system, and pro-
reformers seek to utilize this opportunity to press for change. I have
shown that no case of reform by elite–mass interaction has occurred in

the absence of these conditions, but full testing requires also that we know whether all instances where these conditions are satisfied have generated reform. Yet that is not straightforward: how do we identify *ex ante* criteria for the existence of crisis or the presence of strategic leadership? Second, no matter how sophisticated our identification of antecedent conditions may be, it can only ever generate probabilistic models: the importance of endogenous factors relating to leadership and path dependence introduces an irreducible element of unpredictability. The combination of probabilistic models and small sample sizes makes it very difficult for quantitative analysis to generate firm conclusions. Thus, it is no trivial matter to develop quantitative tests of the propositions developed here. While such quantitative testing should certainly be pursued, further detailed qualitative analysis of particular cases will also be required.

Power, interests, and values

I now turn to the implications of this analysis for the three broad questions with which I began the book. The first two of those questions – who has power to determine outcomes and whose interests or which values are served – are sufficiently intertwined for it to be useful to consider them together. The first point to note in answering them is that, most of the time, reform does *not* occur. Most of the time, politicians retain control and choose not to initiate reform. This makes it seem that, generally, politicians hold the power and outcomes serve their interests. Indeed, that will often be the case: as many analysts have pointed out, those who win under the existing system are typically favoured by it and will therefore want to retain it.

But, for three reasons, non-reform does not always imply that politicians' interests are maximized. First, politicians may be constrained by institutional barriers: though the majority may want reform, the minority may possess either formal veto powers or the capacity to make the passage of reform too time-consuming or conflictual to be worth while. Non-politicians can have veto power too, if amendment of the electoral law requires a referendum. Second, as I emphasized above, politicians are subject to legitimacy constraints. Maintenance of the status quo may signify not that politicians find the status quo conducive to their interests, but rather that they fear that any attempt at change would damage their standing with voters, or that they themselves believe such manipulation of the system to be inappropriate. Just how widely legitimacy constraints matter is impossible to judge on the evidence presented here, but I have discussed cases where they were evidently important. Third, politicians often satisfice: particularly where electoral reform has not been enacted or seriously considered for many years, politicians' knowledge of options and (particularly) how those options will affect their power is likely to be hazy; most will prefer to focus on issues that appear more pressing and that gain more attention from voters. Thus, the status quo can survive even when politicians retain full power and an alternative would better suit their interests.

Cases where reform *does* occur, meanwhile, have been evenly divided in the last three decades between those – France in 1985 and 1986 and Italy in 2005 – in which politicians retain control and seek to advance their power and those – Italy and New Zealand in 1993 and Japan in 1994 – where they lose control to voters, who pursue conceptions of the public interest. Whether the objectives sought will in fact be served by reform outcomes can never be certain *ex ante*: in all cases, misperception is a possibility and cognitive constraints or bargaining among different groups may generate suboptimal outcomes (Horowitz 2000: 270). Nevertheless, as I have just argued, particularly in reforms by elite majority imposition, misperception has been limited. On the whole in these cases, politicians have been able to advance their purposes, even if not always to the greatest degree possible.

With regard to reform by elite–mass interaction, the key question concerns whether public pressure acts genuinely to serve the public interest or can be manipulated by elites in pursuit of their own purposes. Certainly, as I have argued, politicians and other elite actors have an important role to play in mobilizing popular opinion around electoral reform. Furthermore, none of the cases of reform by elite–mass interaction has produced the full benefits that their supporters hoped for. Nevertheless, as I argued in Chapter 12, there is little evidence to suggest that popular opinion can be manipulated far by strategic actors pursuing private ends: even in Japan, where that charge is most plausible, reform could reasonably be presented as offering a (partial) solution to matters of genuine and legitimate public concern. This conclusion accords with much recent research, which suggests that referendums are less manipulable than has often been supposed (e.g., Lupia and Matsusaka 2004). The values that motivate voters are related in part to national traditions and the long-term dynamics of value change. Most clearly, however, voters seek to defend generic values of good democratic governance that they perceive as threatened under the prevailing system. The values that voters espoused in New Zealand, Italy, and Japan – limited and clean government – reflected such immediate concerns. They were not culturally alien, but nor were they peculiar to particular historical traditions or cultural perspectives.

Patterns in reform outcomes

This detailed understanding of the processes that lead (or do not lead) to change in electoral systems is all very well, but what does it tell us about the patterns that we should expect to find in electoral reform outcomes across space and time? Political scientists have advanced a variety of generalizations regarding the frequency with which electoral reform is likely to occur in established democracies, the circumstances in which it is likely to occur, and the electoral system choices that are likely to be made. In this section I analyse these three issues, considering in relation to each, first, what expectations the approach developed here generates and, second, what the available evidence suggests about what occurs in the real world.

The frequency of major electoral reform

The first issue can be dealt with quickly, for it is already addressed by the preceding sections. Numerous political scientists – mostly famously, Nohlen (1984: 217–18) – have argued that major electoral reform in established democracies is likely to occur rarely, and the analysis presented here agrees with this expectation. Though in arguing for an appreciation of the complexity of politicians' motivations I have emphasized various considerations that might lead some to favour electoral reform, I have also offered multiple reasons to expect stasis: politicians typically satisfice; they face legitimacy constraints and other act contingencies; strong popular mobilization around electoral reform requires an unusual combination of circumstances. Though major electoral reform has occurred more frequently in established democracies in the quarter century since Nohlen wrote than it had in the quarter century preceding, still it remains rare: major reform of national lower house electoral systems has occurred just six times in established democracies in the last fifty years.

The circumstances of reform

Shugart (2001, 2008) argues that major reform in established democracies is most likely when the prevailing electoral system is 'extreme' on either the inter-party or the intra-party dimension. The approach here suggests that, indeed, reform by elite–mass interaction is very unlikely without such a background: for such reform to occur, it needs to be plausibly arguable that the electoral system is a source of some significant governance failure, and that is more likely where the electoral system is extreme in Shugart's sense. It is also plausible that the chances of elite majority imposition are greater in this circumstance: an extreme system is more likely to be perceived by politicians as so violating their interests as to justify reform; and reform of such a system is more likely to be sellable to a sceptical public without hitting legitimacy constraints.

In fact, if we focus on the six cases of reform in the last thirty years, when democracy has clearly been consolidated, we find that, while all three cases belonging to the elite–mass interaction type fit this expectation, only one of the cases of elite majority imposition – France in 1985 – does so. The cases of France in 1986 and Italy in 2005 may deviate, however, in part because the systems they overturned had been in place for such short periods: those whose interests had been served by the previous system sought to reintroduce it; electoral system issues were on the agenda and cognitive constraints were low, so the hurdle to reform was reduced; legitimacy constraints were weak too, particularly in France. Thus, reform by elite majority imposition can occur in the absence of an extreme electoral system, but the cases where this has occurred have been unusual ones. The evidence in general supports Shugart's proposition.

An alternative proposed generalization, formalized by Benoit (2004: 374) but present more or less explicitly in many other writings, is that electoral reform will occur (subject to constraints relating to transaction costs and legitimacy) if and only if a group of politicians who are strong and cohesive enough to implement change believe that an alternative system would give their party (or parties) a greater share of the seats in the legislature than the status quo.

As will already be clear, the approach that I advance here does not see this as the only possible route to reform. The majority of politicians may be swayed by other power-seeking considerations, and politicians may lose substantial control to the electorate. Nor does my approach see the condition stated above as sufficient to necessitate reform. First, again, other power-seeking considerations may dominate politicians' view. Second, while Benoit (2004) and others allow for various constraints on the rational pursuit of power, they leave them on the sidelines. These constraints, I have argued, are highly salient and deserve greater attention.

The empirical cases analysed here support this argument. In none of the three cases of reform by elite–mass interaction – Italy and New Zealand in 1993 and Japan in 1994 – was it reasonable to expect that the electoral reform would enhance the seat share of the single governing party or the shares of all the coalition parties. Of the reforms that followed processes of elite majority imposition, straightforward seat-maximization does not alone account for the Italian reform of 2005; nor does it adequately capture the thinking underlying the change in France in 1985 and its reversal the following year. Similarly, the failure to implement reform in Japan in 1973 and in France in 1991–1992 cannot be understood if only short-term partisan seat-maximization is allowed for.

A related claim concerns the impact of the party system upon electoral reform. Colomer (2005: 1) contends, challenging Duverger, that 'it is the number of parties that can explain the choice of electoral systems, rather than the other way round'. In making this case, he follows a long tradition that began with the work of Grumm (1958) and Lipson (1959). The proposition builds on the premise that partisan seat-maximization, coupled with a measure of risk-aversion, is the major driver of electoral reform: where there are few parties, those parties can maximize their seat share through majoritarian electoral rules; where there are many parties, such a strategy becomes highly risky, and the parties tend to favour proportionality.

The approach that I have advocated here also expects the party system to have a strong influence over the choice of electoral system. But the link is more complex. In cases of reform by elite majority imposition, considerations of seat-maximization are likely to play some role, and the number of parties will be a relevant factor. But a second aspect of the party system – namely, the pattern of possible coalition arrangements – matters too. Even where there are many parties, a group of parties may decide to pursue majoritarian reform if they expect that they can form a coalition together while their opponents cannot – as happened in both France and Italy in the early 1950s. And different electoral systems may facilitate the formation of different coalitions, with different implications for the governing potential of different parties. This consideration was a major factor in Italy in 2005 and a lesser one in France in 1985. Finally, these party system considerations sit alongside others relating, particularly, to the nature of parties in themselves. Whether parties base their appeal primarily on candidates, leaders, or policies influences the number of votes they will win under different electoral systems. How far power is centralized in a party influences the degree to which the interests of its leaders or its ordinary legislators come to the fore.

In cases of reform by elite–mass interaction, meanwhile, where the status quo is single-member plurality and the perceived problem with that system is disproportionality in the results it generates, then a rise in the effective number of parties can indeed be expected to lead to demands for a more proportional system. On the other hand, if the perceived problem with single-member plurality is its tendency to facilitate excessive concentration of power, then, if anything, a fall in the effective number of parties may make reform more likely. In New Zealand, the issue that captured the public imagination was at least as much the ability of governments to do as they pleased once elected as it was any perception of disproportionality in election results. Where the status quo is a system of proportional representation, the most commonly perceived problems – instability, difficulties in government formation, lack of accountability – become more acute as the number of parties rises; thus, a greater number of parties would be expected to enhance the likelihood of reform by elite–mass interaction *away from* proportionality. The adoption of a more majoritarian system in Italy in 1993 did indeed follow a rise in the number of parties. Japan also adopted a somewhat more majoritarian system (Gallagher 1998: 217) when the effective number of parties was rising.

All of this means that the links from the party system to choices regarding the electoral system vary depending on circumstances and the nature of the reform process. A weak relationship of the form Colomer proposes is possible, but we should not be surprised if there are many exceptions.

In fact, as I showed in Chapter 8 (Table 8.3), among cases of reform by elite majority imposition, the effective number of parties in terms of votes (ENPV) has been higher prior to reforms *away from* proportionality than towards it. The same is true also of the cases of reform by elite–mass interaction analysed in Chapter 12. Using as our measure of party system fragmentation ENPV at the election preceding the enactment of reform, New Zealand adopted PR when the effective number of parties was 2.77 – lower than in all UK elections since 1970. Even if we take ENPV in the election held simultaneously with the 1993 referendum, at 3.52 it was lower than in any of the last five Canadian elections, and lower than the most recent election in the UK (Gallagher 2007). Italy, meanwhile, moved away from PR with ENPV at a (then) post-war high of 6.63; Japan shifted marginally towards greater disproportionality with ENPV at 5.29, its highest value since the post-war election of 1946.

This evidence can legitimately be questioned, however, on two grounds. First, the sample size is limited. Second, some of the cases in Table 8.3 are not relevant to the question in hand: our focus is upon

Table 13.1. *Electoral system changes in established democracies since 1962*

		Direction of reform			
More proportional		Neutral		Less proportional	
Reform	ENPV	Reform	ENPV	Reform	ENPV
Austria 1971	2.29	Austria 1992	3.16	Belgium 2003	10.28
Costa Rica 1962	3.57	Italy 2005	6.32	France 1986	4.65
Denmark 1964	3.81			Israel 1973	3.63
France 1985	4.13			Israel 1991	5.03
Germany 1985	3.22			Israel 2004	7.05
New Zealand 1993	2.77			Italy 1993	6.63
Norway 1988	3.63			Japan 1994	5.29
Norway 2003	6.19				
Sweden 1970	2.29				
Average	3.64		3.91		6.08

Sources: Lijphart (1994: 55); EJPR (1992–2007); ENPV data are taken from Gallagher (2007) and relate to the election immediately preceding reform.
Additional sources used in classifying some cases: Austria 1971: Carstairs (1980: 133); Austria 1992: Müller (2005: 399–400); Belgium 2003: De Winter (2005: 425); Hooghe, Noppe, and Maddens (2003); Germany 1985: Scarrow (2001: 66); Israeli cases: Rahat and Hazan (2005: 337); Japan 1994: Gallagher (1998: 217); Norway 1988: Aardal (1990: 153); Sweden 1970: Särlvik (1983: 129–31). The Israeli case of 1992 is classified excluding the effect of introducing direct election of the prime minister.

patterns of reform in established democracies, whereas some of the cases in that table occurred during democratic transition or consolidation. In Table 13.1, therefore, I present alternative evidence that seeks to address these problems. First, I employ a more generous definition of what counts as significant electoral reform than I have done previously, namely, Lijphart's definition (Lijphart 1994: 55), which includes all changes of electoral formula and all changes of at least 20 per cent in district magnitude or legal threshold.[1] Second, I include only cases in established democracies, defining established democracies, as throughout this book, as those that were consolidated democracies by 1962 and have remained so since. Again, the same pattern appears: ENPV is higher before shifts away from PR than towards it.

---

[1] Lijphart also allows for substantial changes in assembly size, but I do not include that here.

These figures clearly contradict Colomer's expectations. Indeed, they are even more striking than I expected myself: that there are mechanisms that generate pressure for reform towards proportionality when there are many parties and away from it when there are few seems beyond dispute. I argued only that many other mechanisms of reform exist too.

The overall picture is thus much messier than parsimonious theory would suggest. Of course, no parsimonious modeller has ever claimed anything different: models are avowedly simplifications of reality. What the evidence presented here suggests is that the complexity of electoral reform must be regarded as part of the main action, not as inconvenient noise on the sidelines. Understanding it is necessary if we are to understand the broad patterns that exist in electoral reform outcomes.

The direction of reform

This analysis leads on to a second major claim by Colomer: that 'strategic party choice of electoral systems leads to a general trend toward proportional representation over time' (2005: 2). The logic underlying this is closely related to the logic underlying his first claim: given the assumptions of uncertainty and mild risk-aversion, the circumstances in which seat-maximization favours proportionality will occur more often than those in which it favours majoritarianism. Colomer clearly demonstrates, furthermore, that, across the globe and the whole modern era, the general tendency has been towards greater proportionality.

As I have argued, uncertainty regarding future electoral prospects can indeed generate a tendency towards greater proportionality, especially where there is no viable status quo to fall back on. This is evident in the adoption of proportional systems in France and Italy and a system generating greater proportionality than its predecessor in Japan in the immediate wake of the Second World War, when uncertainty was unusually high. In fragile democracies, a need for inclusiveness may generate a similar tendency. And in new democracies, the genuine desire to create a new political order that is open and free may sometimes carry significant weight and favour the adoption of proportional arrangements. Thus, the global tendency towards greater proportionality can be readily understood given that the great majority of cases of electoral system choice happen in democratizing or recently democratized countries.

In established democracies, however, the effects just described are weaker. First, uncertainty regarding future electoral prospects is lower: elections have already been held, so parties know their general pattern of performance; opinion polls add further information. Second, it is normally the case in established democracies that the status quo electoral system remains a viable option. In these circumstances, as I have argued, the likeliest response to uncertainty, particularly at the individual level, is maintenance of that status quo. Third, the complexity of politicians' motivations means that the range of circumstances in which they are likely to favour more majoritarian systems is wider than Colomer supposes. Colomer contends that 'it can be expected that only in situations in which a single party is institutionally dominant and expects to obtain or maintain most voters' support, will restrictive rules based on majority requirements be chosen or maintained' (2005: 3). The cases that I have discussed show this not to be true: smaller parties may seek a more majoritarian system in order to shape coalition dynamics in their favour; large parties in danger of decline may cling to the hope of revival and fear the consequences of appearing defeatist. Fourth, and turning now to the world of reform by elite–mass interaction, values around which public opinion may be mobilized are various. The many values that I outlined in Chapter 2 (Table 2.2) support diverse electoral system choices.

Thus, I expect no general trend in the direction of reforms that occur via processes of elite–mass interaction. Among all cases of reform occurring in advanced democracies, I expect at most a weak trend towards proportionality among cases of reform occurring in advanced democracies more generally.

The evidence fits these expectations. Among the six cases that have been my primary focus, two (France 1985 and New Zealand 1993) increased proportionality, three (France 1986, Italy 1993, and Japan 1994) reduced it, and one (Italy 2005) left it roughly as it was (at least in the lower house). Among the wider set of reforms summarized in Table 13.1, similarly, there are nine cases of reform towards greater proportionality and seven in the opposite direction. Despite the global trend, therefore, there is no clear evidence that major electoral reforms tend towards greater proportionality in established democracies.

The future of electoral reform

I have focused on electoral reform over the last six decades in established democracies. It is useful, in reaching the end of the book, to look beyond those confines. One extension would be to look at new and fragile democracies, but that is a large task that I cannot pursue here. An alternative extension considers likely patterns of electoral reform in

established democracies in the future. As I have suggested, the importance of factors such as leadership and endogenous path dependence
means that accurate prediction of reform outcomes in specific countries
will remain beyond our abilities. But it is useful to formulate expectations
of likely general patterns.

One point we can be sure of is that electoral reform will remain a live
topic. Though major reform is rarely enacted, it is widely discussed, at
least in elite circles. In the months before this book went to press, lively
debate over electoral and other institutional reforms topped the political
agenda in the UK, referendums on electoral reform were held in Italy and
British Columbia, and a government committed to a reform referendum
entered office in New Zealand. Even in the United States, where significant electoral reform at the federal level is generally assumed to be far
from the political agenda, legislation that would effectively abolish the
electoral college and establish direct election of the presidency has been
passed in one or other house of nineteen state legislatures since 2006
(National Popular Vote 2009). Further cases will no doubt arise. Thus,
we can be confident that electoral reformers will continue to keep us
busy.

I have argued that reforms in established democracies have fallen into
two basic types – elite majority imposition and elite–mass interaction –
which have occurred with roughly equal frequencies in recent decades.
Are these patterns likely to continue in the future? One view would hold
that the most reliable prediction for the future is that it will resemble the
recent past. But there is also reason to expect change. In particular,
Dalton (2004: 181) argues that 'a growing number of contemporary
citizens are disenchanted with the political parties, and these sentiments
are generating support for reforms to improve the system of representative democracy. This creates fertile ground for elites and other political
actors to suggest institutional reform and experimentation.' He demonstrates that voters across established democracies increasingly distrust
governments and parties and believe that politicians are out of touch,
self-serving, and uncaring (Dalton 2004: 29–30). These arguments spark
two hypotheses: first, that reform by elite majority imposition may
become harder; second, that reform by elite–mass interaction (and
even mass imposition) may become easier.

There are at least two reasons for thinking that declining public
support may make it harder for politicians to pursue electoral reforms
designed to enhance their personal or party power. First, if voters are less
inclined to give politicians the benefit of the doubt, they may be more

attuned to – and more ready to punish – self-serving behaviour on the part of politicians, leading to an intensification in legitimacy constraints. Second, at least in some cases, there is a growing perception that questions of constitutional reform should not be decided by politicians alone, but must be put to the people in a referendum. LeDuc (2003: 20–2) and Scarrow (2003: 47–54) chart the growing use of referendums, a trend that has spread beyond the original referendum hotspots in Switzerland and the American states. Thus, politicians' hands may increasingly be tied both by strengthening legitimacy constraints and, in some cases, by a rise in the number of effective (if not formal) veto players. The enactment of reform by elite majority imposition may, in consequence, become harder.

By contrast, prospects for reform by elite–mass interaction (or mass imposition) may be enhanced. Three mechanisms can be hypothesized. First, the growing disconnect between politicians and voters may lead some politicians to believe that reform would be desirable on principled grounds, as a means of restoring democratic engagement. Second, politicians may be more inclined to include electoral system review procedures as part of packages of political reform in their election platforms: they may be more likely to believe that there are (act-contingent) votes to be gained in raising the idea of electoral reform as an issue. Third, when voters are given the chance to vote on electoral reform, they may be more inclined to look upon it favourably: the circumstances needed to induce voters to back change may be less extreme than they have been to date.

The electoral reforms of the 1990s might be taken as already providing evidence for this shift: no major reform by elite–mass interaction had occurred before 1993; then three cases occurred in rapid succession. Clearly, as I have argued, all these cases were spurred by deep public anger at the state of their political systems. It may be that the development of such anger was facilitated by long-term shifts in voters' attitudes towards politics.

The question for the future is whether the degree of crisis required before voters can be moved to vote for electoral reform is falling. Evidence can be sought from recent experiences in Canada. Referendums on establishing more proportional systems were held in British Columbia in 2005 and 2009, Prince Edward Island in 2005, and Ontario in 2007; major reviews have also occurred in New Brunswick and Quebec; there have even been pro-reform rumblings at the federal level (Massicotte 2008: 116–34). In no case were these events preceded by a public outcry. Rather, their backdrop was the sort of trend decline in public confidence in politics that Dalton

(2004: 29–30) highlights. In British Columbia, Premier Gordon Campbell was genuinely committed to reform as a means to tackle public apathy (Carty 2004: 176): Carty, Blais, and Fournier (2008: 141–2) note that he 'spoke about the need to "re-establish the critical link between our democratic institutions and those they are supposed to serve"'. In Ontario, the commitment of political leaders was weaker; rather, the Ontario Liberals saw votes in a platform of political reform (Pilon 2004: 253, 256). Massicotte (2008: 116) places these events in the context of declining political trust and falling turnout. 'Such developments', he argues, 'led scholars and activists to argue that PR would restore public confidence and increase turnout.'

Yet, though these processes have generated much interest in reform, still, no change in any Canadian electoral system has followed. As I noted in Chapter 4, the referendums in Ontario and Prince Edward Island gained the support of little more than a third of voters: in both these cases, clear majorities continued to prefer the security of the status quo. British Columbia appeared different: here, in 2005, 57.7 per cent of voters backed change (Elections BC 2005). Yet even here, the intensity of support for reform was low: a 60 per cent supermajority requirement was added by politicians opposed to reform; voters accepted this, even though it prevented the reform that a majority had supported (Nordic Research Group 2005: 5). A rerun of the referendum was held in May 2009, and the pro-reform vote fell to 39.1 per cent (Elections BC 2009). While disillusionment with politics may weaken support for established institutions, it may also increase apathy, and apathetic voters may be unlikely to exert the active pressure required to overcome politicians' hostility towards reform. Reform by elite–mass interaction remains difficult. Dalton may be right to argue that it is becoming less difficult, but the evidence so far is not conclusive. Ongoing research will be important

To summarize, there are theoretical reasons for believing that reform by elite majority interaction may be getting harder and reform by elite–mass interaction easier. There is some empirical support for both propositions, but it is not yet conclusive. If these propositions do prove correct, however, they suggest that the power of politicians to determine the electoral system will decline, as will the importance of politicians' power interests in determining outcomes. Conversely, ordinary citizens will become more important and conceptions of the public interest will tend more often to prevail.

Conclusion

Understanding processes of electoral reform is important: electoral systems are fundamental institutions of democracy; we need to know where they come from and where they are heading. In developing such knowledge, we should deploy a full methodological toolkit – including formal analysis and statistical research, but also including the detailed comparative process tracing that has been pursued here.

I have argued that electoral reform processes are complex, but that they do not lie beyond our comprehension. They belong to multiple types, some of which are likely to occur only in new or fragile democracies while others can develop in long-established democracies too. Two primary types can be identified in established democracies: elite majority imposition and elite–mass interaction. Through careful historical and comparative analysis, we can say a great deal about how each of these types operates. We can see how the building blocks identified in Part I – actors, motivations, constraints, knowledge, institutions, leadership, path dependence – play out. We can see how the factors underlying these building blocks – history, ideas, institutions, events, features of individuals, and others – exert their influence.

In this final chapter I have sought to show that the detailed understanding that comparative process tracing can provide is of more than mere historical interest: it is needed if we are to understand the big picture too. The general trends in electoral reforms that are observable over recent decades are not as straightforward as some have suggested and can be made sense of only if we recognize and engage fully with the multiple factors involved in determining whether electoral reform occurs and what form it takes. This complex understanding is needed equally if we are to have any hope of foreseeing the future. While electoral systems have until now often been controlled by politicians pursuing their own power interests, politicians have not had complete control. Furthermore, there is reason to believe that politicians will increasingly be constrained by voters and, indeed, that voters may increasingly force reform on politicians who do not want it. Electoral reform is certain to remain a lively topic of study in the years ahead.

APPENDIX: GLOSSARY OF ELECTORAL SYSTEM TERMINOLOGY

additional member system (AMS)   See *mixed-member proportional system (MMP)*.

alternative vote (AV)   A majoritarian system using preferential voting and typically based on single-member districts. Voters rank candidates in order of preference. If no candidate gains over 50 per cent of first preferences, the last-placed candidate is eliminated and the second preferences of his or her supporters are distributed; this is repeated until a candidate passes 50 per cent. In Australia and New Zealand, this is known as the preferential voting system. In the US, it is known as instant runoff voting (IRV).

block vote (BV)   A plurality system using multi-member districts. In a district electing m members, voters can vote for m candidates. Votes for candidates are added up and the m top candidates are elected. For a variant, see *party block vote*.

bonus-adjusted system (BA)   Any system in which the distribution of seats determined by the main electoral system is adjusted by the allocation of a bonus to one or more parties. This bonus may constitute a fixed proportion of the total seats or it may be a variable number designed to ensure, for example, that the largest party secures a specified minimum overall share.

Borda count (BC)   A preferential system in which candidates score points according to their position in voters' rankings. In the simplest form, supposing there are four candidates, a voter's first-choice candidate receives four points, their second choice three points, and so on. Points are then tallied and the candidate with most points wins. Modified versions are also possible using different points distributions.

closed list   See *list system*.

constituency   See *district*.

cumulative vote (CV)   A plurality system using multi-member districts. Voters have multiple votes (typically, as many votes as there are seats available). They can distribute their votes across candidates or cumulate them on a single candidate.

d'Hondt   A system used for the allocation of seats in list proportional representation; the basic form of the highest average method. In order to calculate which party should win the next seat to be allocated, each party's vote total is divided by the number of seats the party has already won plus one, and the seat goes to the party for which this number is highest. In other words, the party vote total is divided by the series of divisors 1, 2, 3, ... as it wins more seats.

district   A territorial unit within which candidates or parties stand for election, votes are counted, and seats are distributed. Various other terms are used in different countries, including constituency (the UK), electorate (Australia and New Zealand), and riding (Canada).

district magnitude   The number of members elected in a district, often denoted by M.

Droop quota   A quota of votes frequently used in the largest remainders form of list proportional representation and in single transferable vote (STV). It is defined as $[v/(m + 1)] + 1$, where v is the number of votes cast in the district and m is the district magnitude. It is an alternative to the *Hare quota*.

effective number of parties (ENP)   A measure of how many parties there are in a party system, weighted by their size. ENP can be calculated on the basis either of votes cast in elections (ENPV) or of seats held in the legislature (ENPS). ENPV = $1/(\Sigma v^2)$ where v is the vote share of each party. Similarly, ENPS = $1/(\Sigma s^2)$ where s is the seat share of each party (Laakso and Taagepera 1979).

electorate   See *district*.

first past the post (FPTP)   See *single-member plurality (SMP)*.

Hare quota   A quota of votes sometimes used in the largest remainders form of list proportional representation and in single transferable vote (STV). It is defined as v/m, where v is the number of votes cast in the district and m is the district magnitude. It is an alternative to the *Droop quota*.

highest average system   A family of formulas used for determining the distribution of seats in a system of *list proportional representation*. The basic principle is that the average number of votes needed to win a seat should be roughly the same for all parties. The basic system is known as *D'Hondt*. Variants are called *Sainte Laguë and modified Sainte Laguë*.

Imperiali   A system of list proportional representation using largest remainders, where the initial distribution of seats is completed using the Imperiali quota: $v/(m + 2)$, where v is the number of votes cast in the district and m is the district magnitude. This is one of the least proportional systems of PR.

instant runoff voting (IRV)   See *alternative vote*.

largest remainders system   A family of formulas used for determining the distribution of seats in a system of *list proportional representation*. In the first instance, a quota of votes needed to fill a seat is calculated. This is generally done using the Droop quota or the Hare quota. The quota is then subtracted from the vote total of each party as many times as possible, each time allocating a seat to the party. Remaining seats are then allocated to whichever parties have the largest vote remainders.

limited vote (LV)   A plurality system using multi-member districts. It differs from *block vote* only in that the number of votes each voter can cast is less than the number of members elected from the district. Where voters can cast just one vote, the system is known as *single non-transferable vote*.

list proportional representation (list PR)   A form of proportional representation. Parties present lists of candidates for election. There are many versions. In some, voters vote for a party, with the order of the candidates on the list decided by the party (closed list). In others, voters vote for one or more candidates, and these votes determine the order of the list (open list). Further variants exist between these extremes. In all cases, the number of votes for each party or its candidates is summed, and this is used to calculate the total number of seats won by the party. Various formulas can be used for this calculation, which are generally variants of the principles of *highest averages* or *largest remainders*. The party's candidates are elected from the top of the list until all its seats are filled.

majoritarian system   Any system in which candidates must obtain an absolute majority of votes to be elected. There are two principal variants: *alternative vote* and the *two-round system*.

mixed-member majoritarian system (MMM)   A mixed system in which members are elected typically by two methods: some by a list system, others by a single-member plurality or majoritarian system. The two parts run independently of each other (or, in some cases, partially independently). This system is therefore sometimes called the parallel system.

mixed-member proportional system (MMP)   A mixed system in which members are elected typically by two methods: some by a list system, others by a single-member plurality or majoritarian system. The two parts are linked: the list seats are distributed such that the overall distribution of seats across the two parts is broadly proportional. In the UK, this system is known as the additional member system.

mixed system   Any system in which different members of the chamber are elected through different mechanisms. The principal variants are the *mixed-member majoritarian (MMM)* and *mixed-member proportional (MMP)* systems. *Bonus-adjusted systems* may be thought of as variants too.

open list   See *list proprotional representation*.

parallel system   See *mixed-member majoritarian system (MMM)*.

party block vote (PBV)   A majoritarian system using multi-member districts. Voters cast their ballot for a party list. All the seats in the district go to the list winning most votes.

plurality system   Any system in which the m candidates securing most votes are elected, irrespective of how many votes that is, where m is the district magnitude. Principal variants are *single-member plurality (SMP), block vote*, and *limited vote*.

preferential voting   See *alternative vote*.

proportional representation (PR)   Any system designed to ensure rough equality between parties' vote shares and their seat shares. Variants are *list proportional representation* and *single transferable vote (STV)*.

riding   See *district*.

Sainte Laguë and modified Sainte Laguë   Systems used for the allocation of seats in list proportional representation; variants of the highest average method. Sainte Laguë is in essence the same as the *d'Hondt* system, except that the series of divisors used is 1, 3, 5, ... rather than 1, 2, 3, ... Modified versions of Sainte Laguë adjust the divisor series further. Sweden and Norway use 1.4, 3, 5, ...

single-member district (SMD)   A district electing one member. Commonly used in plurality, alternative vote, and two-round systems.

single-member plurality (SMP)   A plurality electoral system using single-member districts. Voters cast their ballot for a candidate. Whichever candidate wins most votes is elected. This system is widely known as first past the post.

single non-transferable vote (SNTV)   A plurality system using multi-member districts. Voters cast a single vote for a candidate. In a district electing m members, the m candidates winning most votes are elected.

single transferable vote (STV)   A form of proportional representation using preferential voting and multi-member districts. Voters rank the candidates in order of preference. The number of votes required for election (the 'electoral quota') is defined. Generally, this is the Droop quota: $[v/(m + 1)] + 1$, where v is the number of votes cast in the district and m is the district magnitude. Candidates securing this quota on first preferences are elected and their surplus votes (votes over quota) are redistributed to second-preference candidates. If the number of candidates elected by this means is fewer than the number of seats in the district, the last-placed candidate is eliminated and his or her votes are transferred to second-preference candidates. This process is continued until all the seats in the district have been filled.

threshold   In list systems, the threshold defines the number of votes below which a party cannot win any seats. Many systems define a legal threshold in order to keep out very small parties. Even without a legal threshold, there is an effective threshold, defined by the district magnitude and the distribution of votes. Though the effective threshold thus varies depending on how votes distribute, Taagepera (1998) argues that it can best be approximated by the equation $T' = 75\%/(M + 1)$, where T' is the effective threshold and M is the district magnitude.

two-round system (TRS)   A plurality or majority system using single-member districts. Voting takes place in two rounds; typically, voters cast a single ballot for a candidate. Any candidate winning an absolute majority of the votes in the first round is elected. If no candidate wins an absolute majority, a second round is held, entry to which is typically restricted (for example, to the top two candidates, or to all candidates passing a certain vote threshold). The candidate winning the plurality of votes in the second round is elected. Two-round systems are often called majoritarian. Strictly, this is correct only where the second round is limited to two candidates, such that the winning candidate is guaranteed an absolute majority of votes. Where entry to the second round is restricted, but the rules of restriction can permit more than two candidates to pass through, the system is one of qualified plurality.

BIBLIOGRAPHY

Aardal, Bernt 1990. 'The Norwegian Parliamentary Election of 1989'. *Electoral Studies* 9: 151–8.

ACT 2008. 'Constitutional Framework'. Party policy statement. Accessed at www.act.org.nz, 12 December 2008.

Aimer, E. P. 1985. Written submission to the Royal Commission on the Electoral System, no. 641 (untitled). Mimeo. Papers of the Royal Commission on the Electoral System, Archives New Zealand, Agency AAYI (RCES), Accession W3047, Item 1, 4 – Submissions.

Aimer, Peter 1999. 'From Westminster Plurality to Continental Proportionality: Electoral System Change in New Zealand'. In Henry Milner (ed.), *Making Every Vote Count: Reassessing Canada's Electoral System*. Peterborough, Ontario: Broadview Press, 145–55.

2003. 'United Future'. In Raymond Miller (ed.), *New Zealand Government and Politics*, 3rd edn. Melbourne: Oxford University Press, 293–302.

2006. Interview. Auckland, 12 August.

Alexander, Gerard 2004. 'France: Reform-Mongering between Majority Runoff and Proportionality'. In Colomer 2004b: 209–21.

Alley, R. M., and A. D. Robinson 1971. 'A Mechanism for Enlarging the House of Representatives'. *Political Science* 23: 2–8.

Allum, P. A. 1973. *Italy: Republic without Government?* London: Weidenfeld & Nicolson.

Almond, Gabriel A. 1973. 'Approaches to Developmental Causation'. In Gabriel A. Almond, Scott C. Flanagan, and Robert J. Mundt (eds.), *Crisis, Choice, and Change: Historical Studies of Political Development*. Boston: Little, Brown, 1–42.

Amorim Neto, Octavio, and Gary W. Cox 1997. 'Electoral Institutions, Cleavage Structures, and the Number of Parties'. *American Journal of Political Science* 41: 149–74.

Andeweg, Rudy B. 1989. 'Institutional Conservatism in the Netherlands: Proposals for and Resistance to Change'. *West European Politics* 12: 42–60.

2005. 'The Netherlands: The Sanctity of Proportionality'. In Gallagher and Mitchell 2005: 491–510.

Andrews, Josephine T., and Robert W. Jackman 2005. 'Strategic Fools: Electoral Rule Choice under Extreme Uncertainty'. *Electoral Studies* 24: 65–84.

Armstrong, John 1989. 'Govt to Hold Ballot on 4-Year Term'. *New Zealand Herald*, 17 April.

　　1990a. 'National Set to Promise Binding Referendum'. *New Zealand Herald*, 12 April.

　　1990b. 'Senate Promoted'. *New Zealand Herald*, 10 July.

　　1991. 'Fourth Option in Vote System Poll'. *New Zealand Herald*, 13 December.

Arthur, W. Brian 1994. *Increasing Returns and Path Dependence in the Economy*. Ann Arbor: University of Michigan Press.

Assemblée Nationale 2008a. 'Amendements déposés sur le texte no. 820'. Accessed at www.assemblee-nationale.fr, 23 December 2008.

　　2008b. 'Séance du 21/07/2008: Scrutin public sur le projet de loi constitutionnelle de modernisation des institutions de la Ve République'. Accessed at www.assemblee-nationale.fr, 23 December 2008.

Atti Parliamentari 1954. 'Seduta di Mercoledì 9 Giugno 1954'. *Atti Parliamentari, Camera dei Deputati, Legislatura II, Discussioni*, 8921–75.

Austen-Smith, David, and Jeffrey Banks 1988. 'Elections, Coalitions, and Legislative Outcomes'. *American Political Science Review* 82: 405–22.

Babb, James 1996. 'The Origins and Nature of Japanese Electoral Reform'. *Representation* 33: 155–61.

　　2007. 'The Statics and Dynamics of Socialist Party Ideology'. Paper presented at the Japan Politics Colloquium, Oxford, 11–12 September.

Baerwald, Hans H. 1979. 'Parties, Factions, and the Diet'. In Hyoe Murakami and Johannes Hirschmeier (eds.), *Politics and Economics in Contemporary Japan*. Tokyo: Japan Culture Institute, 21–63.

Baldini, Gianfranco 2009. 'Electoral Reforms in Italy: The (Main) Determinants of the (Many) Electoral Reforms'. Paper presented in the workshop 'Why Electoral Reform? The Determinants, Policy, and Politics of Changing Electoral Systems' at the ECPR Joint Sessions of Workshops, Lisbon, 14–19 April.

Balinski, Michel 2008. 'Redistricting in France under Changing Electoral Rules'. In Lisa Handley and Bernie Grofman (eds.), *Redistricting in Comparative Perspective*. Oxford: Oxford University Press, 173–90.

Banting, Keith G., and Richard Simeon 1985. 'Introduction: The Politics of Constitutional Change'. In Keith G. Banting and Richard Simeon (eds.), *The Politics of Constitutional Change in Industrial Nations: Redesigning the State*. London: Macmillan, 1–29.

Barber, Tony 2005a. 'Berlusconi Buoyed by Reforms'. *Financial Times*, 21 October.

　　2005b. 'Berlusconi under Fire as He Pushes More Election Reforms'. *Financial Times*, 12 December.

　　2006. 'Small Margin of Victory Set to Restrict Prodi Agenda'. *Financial Times*, 12 April.

Bartolini, Stefano 1982. 'The Politics of Institutional Reform in Italy'. *West European Politics* 5: 203–21.

Bartolini, Stefano, and Peter Mair 1990. *Identity, Competition, and Electoral Availability: The Stabilisation of European Electorates 1885–1985.* Cambridge: Cambridge University Press.

Bartolini, Stefano, Alessandro Chiaramonte, and Roberto D'Alimonte 2004. 'The Italian Party System between Parties and Coalitions'. *West European Politics* 27: 1–19.

Baumgartner, Frank R. 1989. 'Strategies of Political Leadership in Diverse Settings'. In Bryan D. Jones (ed.), *Leadership and Politics: New Perspectives in Political Science.* Lawrence, KS: University Press of Kansas, 114–34.

Baumgartner, Frank R., and Bryan D. Jones 1993. *Agendas and Instability in American Politics.* Chicago: University of Chicago Press.

Bawn, Kathleen 1993. 'The Logic of Institutional Preferences: German Electoral Law as a Social Choice Outcome'. *American Journal of Political Science* 37: 965–89.

Bayrou, François 2007. 'Élection Présidentielle 2007: La France de toutes nos forces: Programme d'action de François Bayrou'. Accessed at www. bayrou.fr, 18 December 2008.

Beatty, David 2005. 'Making Democracy Constitutional'. In Paul Howe, Richard Johnston, and André Blais (eds.), *Strengthening Canadian Democracy.* Montreal: Institute for Research on Public Policy, 129–36.

Bell, D. S., and Byron Criddle 1994. *The Communist Party in the Fifth Republic.* Oxford: Oxford University Press.

Bellucci, Paolo, and Martin Bull 2002. 'Introduction: The Return of Berlusconi'. In Paolo Bellucci and Martin Bull (eds.), *Italian Politics: The Return of Berlusconi* (Italian Politics: A Review, Volume 17). New York: Berghahn Books, 29–47.

Bennis, Warren, and Burt Nanus 1985. *Leaders: The Strategies for Taking Charge.* New York: Harper & Row.

Benoit, Kenneth 2004. 'Models of Electoral System Change'. *Electoral Studies* 23: 363–89.

2005. 'Hungary: Holding Back the Tiers'. In Gallagher and Mitchell 2005: 231–52.

2007. 'Electoral Laws as Political Consequences: Explaining the Origins and Change of Electoral Institutions'. *Annual Review of Political Science* 10: 363–90.

Bernhard, Michael 2000. 'Institutional Choice after Communism: A Critique of Theory-Building in an Empirical Wasteland'. *East European Politics and Societies* 14: 316–47.

Birch, Bill 1993 [1992]. 'PR – Taking It Away from the People'. In McRobie 1993: 131–3. Excerpt from address to the National Executive Meeting of the Young Nationals, Wellington, 26 April 1992.

2006. Interview. Auckland, 11 August.

Birch, Sarah, Frances Millard, Marina Popescu, and Kieran Williams 2002. *Embodying Democracy: Electoral System Design in Post-Communist Europe.* Basingstoke: Palgrave Macmillan.

Bisson, T. A. 1949. *Prospects for Democracy in Japan.* New York: Macmillan.

Blais, André (ed.) 2008. *To Keep or to Change First Past the Post? The Politics of Electoral Reform.* Oxford: Oxford University Press.

Blais, André, and Louis Massicotte 1997. 'Electoral Formulas: A Macroscopic Perspective'. *European Journal of Political Research* 32: 107–29.

Blais, André, Agnieszka Dobrzynska, and Indridi H. Indridason 2005. 'To Adopt or Not to Adopt Proportional Representation: The Politics of Institutional Choice'. *British Journal of Political Science* 35: 182–90.

Blau, Adrian 2004. 'Fairness and Electoral Reform'. *British Journal of Politics and International Relations* 6: 165–81.

2008. 'Electoral Reform in the UK: A Veto-Player Analysis'. In Blais 2008: 61–89.

Blitz, James 1998. 'Berlusconi Stirs Reform Pot'. *Financial Times,* 3 February.

Bogdanor, Vernon 1997. *Power and the People: A Guide to Constitutional Reform.* London: Victor Gollancz.

1999. *Devolution in the United Kingdom.* Oxford: Oxford University Press.

Bogdanor, Vernon, and David Butler (eds.) 1983. *Democracy and Elections: Electoral Systems and Their Political Consequences.* Cambridge: Cambridge University Press.

Boissieu, Laurent de 2007. 'Presque tous les candidats sont favorables à un changement du mode de scrutin, ce qui permettrait aux petits partis d'avoir une représentation parlementaire'. *La Croix,* 18 April.

Bolger, Jim 1998. *A View from the Top: My Seven Years as Prime Minister.* Auckland: Viking.

2006. Interview. Wellington, 15 August.

Boix, Carles 1999. 'Setting the Rules of the Game: The Choice of Electoral Systems in Advanced Democracies'. *American Political Science Review* 93: 609–24.

Bonney, Norman 2003. 'The Scottish Parliament and Participatory Democracy: Vision and Reality'. *Political Quarterly* 74: 459–67.

Boscawen, John 2009. Telephone interview, 14 January.

Boston, Jonathan 1987. 'Electoral Reform in New Zealand: The Report of the Royal Commission'. *Electoral Studies* 6: 105–14.

Boston, Jonathan, Stephen Church, and Tim Bale 2003. 'The Impact of Proportional Representation on Government Effectiveness: The New Zealand Experience'. *Australian Journal of Public Administration* 62: 7–22.

Boudon, Raymond 1986. *Theories of Social Change: A Critical Appraisal,* trans. J. C. Whitehouse. Cambridge: Polity.

Bowler, Shaun, and Todd Donovan 2008. 'Election Reform and (the Lack of) Electoral System Change in the USA'. In Blais 2008: 90–111.

Bowler, Shaun, Todd Donovan, and Jeffrey A. Karp 2006. 'Why Politicians Like Electoral Institutions: Self-Interest, Values, or Ideology?' *Journal of Politics* 68: 434–46.

Brady, David, and Jongryn Mo 1992. 'Electoral Systems and Institutional Choice: A Case Study of the 1988 Korean Elections'. *Comparative Political Studies* 24: 405–29.

British Columbia Citizens' Assembly on Electoral Reform 2004. *Making Every Vote Count: The Case for Electoral Reform in British Columbia: Final Report.* Vancouver.

Brown, Alice 2000. 'Designing the Scottish Parliament'. *Parliamentary Affairs* 53: 542–56.

Brown, Bernard E. 1982. *Socialism of a Different Kind: Reshaping the Left in France.* Westport, CT: Greenwood Press.

Browne, Eric C., and Keith E. Hamm 1996. 'Legislative Politics and the Paradox of Voting: Electoral Reform in Fourth Republic France'. *British Journal of Political Science* 26: 165–98.

Bueno De Mesquita, Ethan 2000. 'Strategic and Nonpolicy Voting: A Coalitional Analysis of Israeli Electoral Reform'. *Comparative Politics* 33: 63–80.

Bull, Martin, and James L. Newell 1993. 'Italian Politics and the 1992 Elections: From "Stable Instability" to Instability and Change'. *Parliamentary Affairs* 46: 203–27.

2005. *Italian Politics: Adjustment under Duress.* Cambridge: Polity.

Bull, Martin, and Gianfranco Pasquino 2007. 'A Long Quest in Vain: Institutional Reforms in Italy'. *West European Politics* 30: 670–91.

Bull, Martin, and Martin Rhodes (eds.) 1997. *Crisis and Transition in Italian Politics.* London: Frank Cass.

Burns, James MacGregor 1978. *Leadership.* New York: Harper & Row.

Cain, Bruce E. 2007. 'Reform Studies: Political Science on the Firing Line'. *PS: Political Science and Politics* 40: 635–8.

Cairns, Alan C. 1968. 'The Electoral System and the Party System in Canada, 1921–1965'. *Canadian Journal of Political Science* 1: 55–80.

Calise, Mauro 1993. 'Remaking the Italian Party System: How Lijphart Got It Wrong by Saying It Right'. *West European Politics* 16: 545–60.

Camera dei deputati 2002/3. Legislative proposals C. 2712, C.3304, and C. 2620. Accessed at http://legxiv.camera.it, 8 January 2009.

2005. 'Resoconto della I Commissione Permanente', 23 June. Accessed at http://legxiv.camera.it, 8 January 2009.

Campbell, John Creighton, and Ethan Scheiner 2008. 'Fragmentation and Power: Reconceptualizing Policy Making under Japan's 1955 System'. *Japanese Journal of Political Science* 9: 89–113.

Carlile, Lonny E. 1994. 'Party Politics and the Japanese Labor Movement: Rengo's "New Political Force"'. *Asian Survey* 34: 606–20.

Carlson, Matthew 2007. *Money Politics in Japan: New Rules, Old Practices.* Boulder, CO: Lynne Rienner.

Carstairs, Andrew McLaren 1980. *A Short History of Electoral Systems in Western Europe.* London: George Allen & Unwin.

Carty, R. Kenneth 2004. 'Canadians and Electoral Reform: An Impulse to Doing Democracy Differently'. *Representation* 40: 173–84.

Carty, R. Kenneth, André Blais, and Patrick Fournier 2008. 'When Citizens Choose to Reform SMP: The British Columbia Citizens' Assembly on Electoral Reform'. In Blais 2008: 140–62.

Chang, Eric C. C., Mark Andreas Kayser, and Ronald Rogowski 2008. 'Electoral Systems and Real Prices: Panel Evidence for the OECD Countries, 1970–2000'. *British Journal of Political Science* 38: 739–51.

Chapman, Robert 1999 [1979]. 'On Democracy as Having and Exercising a Clear Choice of Government'. In Elizabeth McLeay (ed.), *New Zealand Politics and Social Patterns: Selected Works by Robert Chapman.* Wellington: Victoria University Press, 278–87. First published in J. Stephen Hoadley (ed.), *Improving New Zealand's Democracy* (Auckland, 1979).

Checkel, Jeffrey T. 2003. '"Going Native" in Europe? Theorizing Social Interaction in European Institutions'. *Comparative Political Studies* 36: 209–31.

Chiaramonte, Alessandro, and Aldo Di Virgilio 2000. 'Le elezioni regionali del 2000: la frammentazione si consolida, le alleanze si assestano'. *Rivista Italiana di Scienza Politica* 30: 513–52.

Christensen, Raymond V. 1994. 'Electoral Reform in Japan: How It Was Enacted and Changes It May Bring'. *Asian Survey* 34: 589–605.

— 2006. 'An Analysis of the 2005 Japanese General Election: Will Koizumi's Political Reforms Endure?' *Asian Survey* 46: 497–516.

Christofferson, Thomas R. 1991. *The French Socialists in Power, 1981–1986: From Autogestion to Cohabitation.* Newark, DE: University of Delaware Press.

Clark, Helen 1993 [1992]. 'Politics a Sobering Experience for Us All'. In McRobie 1993: 112–15. First published in *New Zealand Herald,* 4 January 1992.

Clark, William Roberts, and Matt Golder 2006. 'Rehabilitating Duverger's Theory: Testing the Mechanical and Strategic Modifying Effects of Electoral Laws'. *Comparative Political Studies* 39: 679–708.

Clements, Kevin P. 1976. 'The Citizens for Rowling Campaign: An Insider's View'. *Political Science* 28: 81–96.

Clogg, Richard 1987. *Parties and Elections in Greece: The Search for Legitimacy.* Durham, NC: Duke University Press.

Cole, Alistair, and Peter Campbell 1989. *French Electoral Systems and Elections since 1789.* Gower: Aldershot.

Coleman, James S. 1986. 'Social Theory, Social Research, and a Theory of Action'. *American Journal of Sociology* 91: 1309-35.

Collins, Simon 1989. 'Referendum Proposal Revived'. *New Zealand Herald*, 7 December.

Colomer, Josep M. 2004a. 'The Strategy and History of Electoral System Choice'. In Colomer 2004b: 3-78.

(ed.) 2004b. *Handbook of Electoral System Choice*. Basingstoke: Palgrave Macmillan.

2005. 'It's Parties that Choose Electoral Systems (or, Duverger's Laws Upside Down'. *Political Studies* 53: 1-21.

Comité de Réflexion et de Proposition sur la Modernisation et le Rééquilibrage des Institutions de la Ve République 2007. 'Une Ve République plus démocratique'. Accessed at www.comite-constitutionnel.fr, 18 December 2008.

Connors, Michael Kelly 2002. 'Framing the "People's Constitution"'. In Duncan McCargo (ed.), *Reforming Thai Politics*. Copenhagen: Nordic Institute of Asian Studies, 37-55.

Conradt, David P. 1996. *The German Polity*, 6th edn. New York: Longman.

Conseil Constitutionnel 2003. 'Observations du Conseil Constitutionnel relatives aux élections législatives des 9 et 16 juin 2002', 15 May. Accessed at www.conseil-constitutionnel.fr, 16 December 2008.

2005. 'Observations du Conseil Constitutionnel sur les échéances électorales de 2007', 7 June. Accessed at www.conseil-constitutionnel.fr, 16 December 2008.

2008. 'Observations du Conseil Constitutionnel relatives aux élections législatives des 10 et 17 juin 2007', 29 May. Accessed at www.conseil-constitutionnel.fr, 16 December 2008.

Cousins, John Andrew 2004. 'Prince Edward Island's Cautious Path toward Electoral Reform'. In Milner 2004: 281-9.

Cox, Gary W. 1997. *Making Votes Count: Strategic Coordination in the World's Electoral Systems*. Cambridge: Cambridge University Press.

Cox, Gary W., and Jonathan N. Katz 2002. *Elbridge Gerry's Salamander: The Electoral Consequences of the Reapportionment Revolution*. Cambridge: Cambridge University Press.

Cox, Gary W., Frances McCall Rosenbluth, and Michael F. Thies 1999. 'Electoral Reform and the Fate of Factions: The Case of Japan's Liberal Democratic Party'. *British Journal of Political Science* 29: 33-56.

Crawford, Keith 2001. 'A System of Disproportional Representation: The Proposed Electoral Law for the Czech Republic'. *Representation* 38: 46-58.

Criddle, Byron 1992. 'Electoral Systems in France'. *Parliamentary Affairs* 45: 108-16.

Cronin, Thomas E., and Michael A. Genovese 2004. *The Paradoxes of the American Presidency*, 2nd edn. New York: Oxford University Press.

Cross, William 2005. 'The Rush to Electoral Reform in the Canadian Provinces: Why Now?' *Representation* 41: 75–84.

Curtice, John 1996. 'Why the Additional Member System Has Won Out in Scotland'. *Representation* 33: 119–24.

2009. 'Neither Representative Nor Accountable: First-Past-the-Post in Britain'. In Bernard Grofman, André Blais, and Shaun Bowler (eds.), *Duverger's Law of Plurality Voting: The Logic of Party Competition in Canada, India, the United Kingdom and the United States.* New York: Springer, 27–46.

Curtis, Gerald L. 1988. *The Japanese Way of Politics.* New York: Columbia University Press.

1999. *The Logic of Japanese Politics: Leaders, Institutions, and the Limits of Change.* New York: Columbia University Press.

Cusack, Thomas, Torben Iversen, and David Soskice 2007. 'Economic Interests and the Origins of Electoral Systems'. *American Political Science Review* 101: 373–91.

Daimon, Sayuri 1993. 'Tokyo Success Fuels JNP's Quest in Diet'. *Japan Times*, 12 July.

D'Alimonte, Roberto 2001. 'Mixed Electoral Rules, Partisan Realignment, and Party System Change in Italy'. In Shugart and Wattenberg 2001d: 323–50.

2004. 'Sotto il "Nespolo" 73 seggi in più per la Cdl'. *Il Sole 24 Ore*, 11 December.

2005. 'Italy: A Case of Fragmented Bipolarism'. In Gallagher and Mitchell 2005: 253–76.

Dalton, Russell J. 2004. *Democratic Challenges, Democratic Choices: The Erosion of Political Support in Advanced Industrial Democracies.* Oxford: Oxford University Press.

Daniell, Stella 1983. 'Reform of the New Zealand Political System: How Likely Is It? A Survey of the Attitudes of the Members of the New Zealand Parliament to Reform Proposals'. *Political Science* 35: 151–89.

David, Paul A. 1985. 'Clio and the Economics of QWERTY'. *American Economic Review* 75: 332–7.

Davidson, Ian 1992a. 'French Far Right's Advance Masks Rise on Another Front'. *Financial Times*, 21 February.

1992b. 'A Shock to the Political System'. *Financial Times*, 20 March.

1992c. 'France Delivers Stern Message to Mitterrand: The President and His Party Will Struggle to Recover from the Regional Poll Results'. *Financial Times*, 24 March.

Dawisha, Adeed, and Larry Diamond 2006. 'Electoral Systems Today: Iraq's Year of Voting Dangerously'. *Journal of Democracy* 17: 89–103.

De Gaulle, Charles 1959a. *War Memoirs, Volume 3: Salvation, 1944–1946*, trans. Richard Howard. London: Weidenfeld & Nicolson.

1959b [1946]. 'Speech Delivered by General de Gaulle at Bayeux, June 16 1946'. In Charles De Gaulle, *War Memoirs, Volume 3: Salvation, 1944–1946: Documents,* trans. Joyce Murchie and Hamish Erskine. London: Weidenfeld & Nicolson, 384–90.

1960 [1932]. *The Edge of the Sword*, trans. Gerard Hopkins. London: Faber & Faber. First published as *Le Fil de l'épée*, 1932.

1970 [1950]. 'Conférence de presse tenue au Palais d'Orsay, 16 mars 1950'. In Charles De Gaulle, *Discours et Messages*. Paris: Plon, II, 344–58.

De Grand, Alexander 1989. *The Italian Left in the Twentieth Century: A History of the Socialist and Communist Parties*. Bloomington, IN: Indiana University Press.

De Winter, Lieven 2005. 'Belgium: Empowering Voters and Party Elites?' In Gallagher and Mitchell 2005: 417–32.

Debré, Jean-Louis 1974. *Les Idées constitutionnelles du Général de Gaulle*. Paris: Librairie Générale de Droit et de Jurisprudence.

Debré, Michel 1947. *La Mort de l'état républicain*. Paris: Gallimard.

1981. 'The Constitution of 1958, Its Raison d'Être and How It Evolved'. In William G. Andrews and Stanley Hoffmann (eds.), *The Impact of the Fifth Republic on France*. Albany, NY: State University of New York Press, 1–14.

Department of Justice 1993. 'Electoral Reform Bill: Report of the Department of Justice'. Mimeo. McCully Papers, Archives New Zealand, Agency ABWM, Series 7361, Accession W5295, Box 3, File: 'Electoral Reform Bill [Briefing reports prepared for Electoral Law Select Committee by Department of Justice]'.

Desmond, Edward W. 1995. 'Ichiro Ozawa: Reformer at Bay'. *Foreign Affairs* 74: 117–31.

Diermeier, Daniel, Hülya Eraslan, and Antonio Merlo 2007. 'Bicameralism and Government Formation'. Penn Institute for Economic Research Working Paper 07-010. Accessed at http://ssrn.com/abstract=962395, 12 February 2008.

Diskin, Hanna, and Abraham Diskin 1995. 'The Politics of Electoral Reform in Israel'. *International Political Science Review* 16: 31–45.

Donovan, Mark 1995. 'The Politics of Electoral Reform in Italy'. *International Political Science Review* 16: 47–64.

1996. 'Electoral Reform in Italy'. *Representation* 33: 141–7.

2000. 'The End of Italy's Referendum Anomaly?' In Mark Gilbert and Gianfranco Pasquino (eds.), *Italian Politics: The Faltering Transition* (Italian Politics: A Review, Volume 15). New York: Berghahn, 51–66.

Dunleavy, Patrick 2001. 'Analysing an Institutional Transition Game in an Established Liberal Democracy: The Introduction of Proportional Representation in the UK'. Paper presented at the Public Choice Conference. San Antonio, Texas, 10 March.

Dunleavy, Patrick, and Helen Margetts 1995. 'Understanding the Dynamics of Electoral Reform'. *International Political Science Review* 16: 9–29.

Dunne, Peter 2008. 'Referendum Needed on Maori Seats'. Press release issued 30 May. Accessed at www.unitedfuture.org.nz, 24 December 2008.

Duverger, Maurice 1954. *Political Parties: Their Organization and Activity in the Modern State*. London: Methuen.

1974. *La Cinqième République*. Paris: Presses Universitaires de France.

Dykes, Ray 1979. 'Fresh Stirrings over Voting Reform'. *New Zealand Herald*, 26 May.

East, Paul 2006. Telephone interview. 2 November.

Ebrahim, Hassen 1998. *The Soul of a Nation: Constitution-Making in South Africa*. Cape Town: Oxford University Press.

ECHR 1980. 'Decision of the European Commission of Human Rights as to the Admissibility of Application No. 8765/79 by the Liberal Party, Joyce Dora Hester Rose and Roger James Pincham against the United Kingdom'. Accessed at www.echr.coe.int, 12 March 2008.

Economist Intelligence Unit 1994. *Country Profile: New Zealand, 1994/95*. London: Economist Intelligence Unit.

Eda, Satsuki 1993. 'Sirius: A New Beacon of Political Change'. *Japan Echo* 20(1): 34–9.

Edinger, Lewis J. 1975. 'The Comparative Analysis of Political Leadership'. *Comparative Politics* 7: 253–69.

1990. 'Approaches to the Comparative Analysis of Political Leadership'. *Review of Politics* 52: 509–23.

Edwards, George C., III 2004. *Why the Electoral College Is Bad for America*. New Haven: Yale University Press.

EECR 1992. 'Constitution Watch'. *East European Constitutional Review* 1(2): 2–8.

Ehrhardt, George 2006. 'Factional Influence on the 2001 LDP Primaries: A Quantitative Analysis'. *Japanese Journal of Political Science* 7: 59–69.

Einaudi, Mario 1946. 'Political Change in France and Italy'. *American Political Science Review* 40: 898–923.

EISA 2009. EISA Country Profiles. Accessed at www.eisa.org.za, 27 February 2009.

EJPR 1992–2007. *Political Data Yearbook*. Published annually in the *European Journal of Political Research*, nos. 7–8.

EKA 1999. 'Az Ellenzéki Kerekasztal ülése 1989. július 10. (Videofelvétel szövege)'. In András Bozóki, Márta Elbert, Melinda Kalmár, Béla Révész, Erzsébet Ripp, and Zoltán Ripp (eds.), *A rendszerváltás forgatókönyve: Kerekasztal-tárgyalások 1989-ben*, Volume 2. Budapest: Magvető, 336–89.

Elections BC 2005. 'Statement of Votes: Referendum on Electoral Reform, May 17, 2005'. Accessed at www.elections.bc.ca, 30 July 2007.

2009. '2009 Official Referendum Results'. Accessed at www.elections.bc.ca, 9 July 2009.

Elections Ontario 2007. 'Referendum Statistical Results'. Accessed at www.elections. on.ca, 7 November 2007.

Elections PEI 2005. 'Plebiscite on Mixed Member Proportional Representation System – Official Results'. Accessed at www.electionspei.ca, 14 November 2007.

Electoral Law Select Committee 1988. *Report of the Electoral Law Select Committee: Inquiry into the Report of the Royal Commission on the Electoral System.* Wellington: House of Representatives.

1991. *Report of the Electoral Law Select Committee on the Electoral Poll Bill, December 1991.* Wellington: House of Representatives.

Electoral Reform Coalition 1993. 'Bill Comes Back with Mismatched Options'. *Electoral Reform Coalition Newsletter* 27: 1–2.

Electoral Studies 2000–2009. 'Notes on Recent Elections'.

Electoral System Civic Forum 2007. 'The Electoral System Civic Forum's Recommendations'. Accessed at www.burgerforumkiesstelsel.nl, 9 August 2007.

Elgie, Robert 2005. 'France: Stacking the Deck'. In Gallagher and Mitchell 2005: 119–36.

Elklit, Jørgen, and Palle Svensson 1997. 'What Makes Elections Free and Fair?' *Journal of Democracy* 8(3): 32–46.

Elster, Jon 1993. *Political Psychology.* Cambridge: Cambridge University Press.

Elster, Jon, and Rune Slagstad 1988. 'Introduction'. In Jon Elster and Rune Slagstad (eds.), *Constitutionalism and Democracy.* Cambridge: Cambridge University Press, 1–17.

Elster, Jon, Claus Offe, and Ulrich K. Preuss 1998. *Institutional Design in Post-Communist Societies: Rebuilding the Ship at Sea.* Cambridge: Cambridge University Press.

Engstrom, Richard L. 2004. 'The United States: The Future – Reconsidering Single-Member Districts and the Electoral College'. In Colomer 2004b: 164–76.

Erdos, David 2009. 'Ideology, Power Orientation, and Policy Drag: Explaining the Elite Politics of Britain's Bill of Rights Debate'. *Government and Opposition* 44: 20–41.

Etō, Jun 1993. 'Why I Back Ozawa Ichirō'. *Japan Echo* 20(1): 18–23.

Everson, David H. 1981. 'The Bullet Bites the Dust: Will the Cutback Amendment Bring Competition and Accountability?' *Illinois Issues* 7(3): 10–15.

Fabbrini, Sergio 2001. 'Has Italy Rejected the Referendum Path to Change? The Failed Referenda of May 2000'. *Journal of Modern Italian Studies* 6: 38–56.

Farnsworth, Lee W. 1966. 'Challenges to Factionalism in Japan's Liberal Democratic Party'. *Asian Survey* 6: 501–9.

Farrell, David M. 2001. 'The United Kingdom Comes of Age: The British Electoral Reform "Revolution" of the 1990s'. In Shugart and Wattenberg 2001d: 521–41.

Farrell, David M., and Michael Gallagher 1999. 'British Voters and Their Criteria for Evaluating Electoral Systems'. *British Journal of Politics and International Relations* 1: 293–316.

Farrell, David M., and Ian McAllister 2006. *The Australian Electoral System: Origins, Variations and Consequences.* Sydney: University of New South Wales Press.

Favier, Pierre, and Michel Martin-Roland 1991. *La Décennie Mitterrand, Volume 2: Les Épreuves (1984–1988).* Paris: Éditions du Seuil.

Fiji Constitution Review Commission 1996. *The Fiji Islands: Towards a United Future: Report of the Fiji Constitution Review Commission.* Suva: Parliament of Fiji.

Finer, S. E. 1984. 'The Decline of Party?' In Vernon Bogdanor (ed.), *Parties and Democracy in Britain and America.* New York: Praeger, 1–6.

Fisher, Stephen D. 2006. 'United Kingdom'. *European Journal of Political Research* 45: 1282–91.

Flinders, Matthew, and Dion Curry 2008. 'Deliberative Democracy, Elite Politics and Electoral Reform'. *Policy Studies* 29: 371–92.

Floridia, Antonio 2007. 'The Paradoxes of Popular Electoral Reforms and the Italian Party System: A Trade-Off between Bipolarism and Fragmentation'. Paper presented at the Political Studies Association Annual Conference. Bath, 11–13 April. Accessed at www.psa.ac.uk, 17 April 2007.

Fouchet, Antoine 2007. 'Les Candidats veulent tous changer la Constitution'. *La Croix,* 20 March.

Foulkes, Angela 2006. Interview. Wellington, 14 August.

Fraenkel, Jon 2001. 'The Alternative Vote System in Fiji: Electoral Engineering or Ballot-Rigging?' *Commonwealth and Comparative Politics* 39: 1–31.

2004. 'Electoral Engineering in Papua New Guinea: Lessons from Fiji and Elsewhere'. *Pacific Economic Bulletin* 19: 122–33.

Fraenkel, Jon, and Bernard Grofman 2006. 'Does the Alternative Vote Foster Moderation in Ethnically Divided Societies? The Case of Fiji'. *Comparative Political Studies* 39: 623–51.

Frears, John 1977. *Political Parties and Elections in the Fifth Republic.* London: C. Hurst.

1986. 'The French Electoral System in 1986: PR by Lists and Highest Average'. *Parliamentary Affairs* 39: 489–95.

1988. 'The 1986 Parliamentary Elections'. In Howard R. Penniman (ed.), *France at the Polls, 1981 and 1986: Three National Elections.* Durham, NC: Duke University Press, 209–27.

Friedrich, Carl J. 1949. 'Rebuilding the German Constitution I'. *American Political Science Review* 43: 461–82.

Fukai, Shigeko N., and Haruhiro Fukui 1992. 'Elite Recruitment and Political Leadership'. *PS: Political Science and Politics* 25: 25–36.

Fukui, Haruhiro 1988. 'Electoral Laws and the Japanese Party System'. In Gail
    Lee Bernstein and Haruhiro Fukui (eds.), *Japan and the World: Essays on
    Japanese History and Politics in Honour of Ishida Takeshi*. Basingstoke:
    Macmillan, 119–43.

Fukuoka, Masayuki 1991. 'Political Reform Still Not in Sight'. *Japan Times*,
    28 January.

Furlong, Paul 1991. 'Government Stability and Electoral Systems: The Italian
    Example'. *Parliamentary Affairs* 44: 50–9.

    2002. 'The Italian Political System in 2001: Radical Change and Work in
    Progress'. In James Newell (ed.), *The Italian General Election of 2001:
    Berlusconi's Victory*. Manchester: Manchester University Press, 11–28.

Fusaro, Carlo 1998. 'The Politics of Constitutional Reform in Italy: A Framework
    for Analysis'. *South European Society and Politics* 3(2): 45–74.

Gallagher, Michael 1998. 'The Political Impact of Electoral System Change in
    Japan and New Zealand, 1996'. *Party Politics* 4: 203–28.

    2005. 'Conclusions'. In Gallagher and Mitchell 2005: 535–78.

    2007. 'Election Indices'. Accessed at www.tcd.ie, 31 January 2008.

Gallagher, Michael, and Paul Mitchell (eds.) 2005. *The Politics of Electoral Systems*.
    Oxford: Oxford University Press.

Gambetta, Diego, and Steven Warner 1996. 'The Rhetoric of Reform Revealed (or: If
    You Bite the Ballot May Bite Back)'. *Journal of Modern Italian Studies* 1: 357–76.

    2004. 'Italy: Lofty Ambitions and Unintended Consequences'. In Colomer
    2004b: 237–52.

Gaunder, Alisa 2007. *Political Reform in Japan: Leadership Looming Large*.
    Abingdon: Routledge.

Gaxie, Daniel 1990. 'Les Partis politiques et les modes de scrutin en France
    (1985–1986), croyances et intérêts'. In Serge Noiret (ed.), *Political
    Strategies and Electoral Reforms: Origins of Voting Systems in Europe in
    the 19th and 20th Centuries*. Baden-Baden: Nomos, 423–50.

Gilbert, Mark 1993. 'The Great Reform?' *Conference Group on Italian Politics and
    Society (CONGRIPS) Newsletter* 39: 17–20.

    1994. 'Italy Turns Rightwards'. *Contemporary Review* 265(1542): 4–10.

    1995. *The Italian Revolution: The End of Politics, Italian Style?* Boulder, CO:
    Westview Press.

Ginsborg, Paul 1990. *A History of Contemporary Italy: Society and Politics
    1943–1988*. London: Penguin.

Goffman, Erving 1975. *Frame Analysis: An Essay on the Organization of
    Experience*. Harmondsworth: Penguin.

Goguel, François 1952. *France under the Fourth Republic*. Ithaca, NY: Cornell
    University Press.

Goldey, David 1993. 'The French General Election of 21–28 March 1993'. *Electoral
    Studies* 12: 291–314.

2007. 'De Gaulle and the Paradox of Post-War French Politics'. In Knapp 2007b: 57–74.

Goldey, David, and Philip Williams 1983. 'France'. In Bogdanor and Butler 1983: 62–83.

Goodin, Robert E. 1996. 'Institutions and Their Design'. In Robert E. Goodin (ed.), *The Theory of Institutional Design*. Cambridge: Cambridge University Press, 1–53.

Gouws, Amanda, and Paul Mitchell 2005. 'South Africa: One-Party Dominance Despite Perfect Proportionality'. In Gallagher and Mitchell 2005: 353–73.

Graham, Doug 1988. 'Memorandum to National Caucus from Douglas Graham Re: "Paper on Electoral Law Reform"', 21 April. Mimeo. McCully Papers, Archives New Zealand, Agency ABWM, Series 7361, Accession W5295, Box 2, File: 'Electoral Law [Committee – various papers, including meeting minutes'.

2006. Interview. Drury, Auckland, 11 August.

Graham, Robert 1995. 'Italian MPs Keep Electoral Reform Powers'. *Financial Times*, 13 January.

Grindrod, Muriel 1955. *The Rebuilding of Italy: Politics and Economics, 1945–1955*. London: Royal Institute of International Affairs.

Grofman, Bernard 1982. 'Alternatives to Single-Member Plurality Districts: Legal and Empirical Issues'. In Bernard Grofman, Arend Lijphart, Robert B. McKay, and Howard A. Scarrow (eds.), *Representation and Redistricting Issues*. Lexington, MA: Lexington Books, 107–28.

Grumm, John G. 1958. 'Theories of Electoral Systems'. *Midwest Journal of Political Science* 2: 357–76.

Gumbel, Andrew 1996. 'An Olive Branch to Democracy'. *Independent*, 23 April.

Gundle, Stephen, and Simon Parker 1996a. 'Introduction: The New Italian Republic'. In Gundle and Parker 1996b: 1–15.

(eds.) 1996b. *The New Italian Republic: From the Fall of the Berlin Wall to Berlusconi*. London: Routledge.

Gustafson, Barry 2000. *His Way: A Biography of Robert Muldoon*. Auckland: Auckland University Press.

Guyomarch, Alain 1993. 'The 1993 Parliamentary Election in France'. *Parliamentary Affairs* 46: 605–26.

Hanley, David 1999. 'Compromise, Party Management and Fair Shares: The Case of the French UDF'. *Party Politics* 5: 171–89.

Hargrove, Erwin C. 1966. *Presidential Leadership: Personality and Political Style*. New York: Macmillan.

1998. *The President as Leader: Appealing to the Better Angels of Our Nature*. Lawrence, KS: University Press of Kansas.

Harris, Mary 2002. 'How Is Parliament Performing under MMP?' *New Zealand Law Journal*: 233–6.

Hartlyn, Jonathan 1988. *The Politics of Coalition Rule in Colombia*. Cambridge: Cambridge University Press.

Hayao, Kenji 1993. *The Japanese Prime Minister and Public Policy*. Pittsburgh: University of Pittsburgh Press.

Hazareesingh, Sudhir 1994. *Political Traditions in Modern France*. Oxford: Oxford University Press.

Hellman, Donald C. 1979. 'Case Study: Foreign Policy à la LDP – The 1956 Soviet– Japanese Peace Agreement'. In Hyoe Murakami and Johannes Hirschmeier (eds.), *Politics and Economics in Contemporary Japan*. Tokyo: Japan Culture Institute, 93–108.

Helms, Ludger 2006. 'The Grand Coalition: Precedents and Prospects'. *German Politics and Society* 24: 47–66.

Hermann, Tamar 1995. 'The Rise of Instrumental Voting: The Campaign for Political Reform'. In Asher Arian and Michal Shamir (eds.), *The Elections in Israel 1992*. Albany, NY: State University of New York Press, 275–97.

Hill, Russell 1987. 'First-Past-the-Post Electoral System Difficult to Shake'. *New Zealand Herald*, 27 June.

Hine, David 1981. 'Thirty Years of the Italian Republic: Governability and Constitutional Reform'. *Parliamentary Affairs* 34: 63–80.

1988. 'Italy (1948): Condemned by Its Constitution?' In Vernon Bogdanor (ed.), *Constitutions in Democratic Politics*. Aldershot: Ashgate, 206–28.

1993a. *Governing Italy: The Politics of Bargained Pluralism*. Oxford: Oxford University Press.

1993b. 'The New Italian Electoral System'. *Newsletter of the Association for the Study of Modern Italy* 24: 27–33.

1996. 'Italian Political Reform in Comparative Perspective'. In Gundle and Parker 1996b: 311–25.

Hine, David, and Vincent Della Sala 1992. 'The Italian General Election of 1992'. *Electoral Studies* 11: 362–67.

Hirczy de Miño, Wolfgang, and John C. Lane 2000. 'Malta: STV in a Two-Party System'. In Shaun Bowler and Bernard Grofman (eds.), *Elections in Australia, Ireland, and Malta under the Single Transferable Vote: Reflections on an Embedded Institution*. Ann Arbor: University of Michigan Press, 178–204.

Hooghe, Marc, Jo Noppe, and Bart Maddens 2003. 'The Effect of Electoral Reform on the Belgian Election Results of 18 May 2003'. *Representation* 39: 270–6.

Hooper, John 2005. 'Prodi's Poisoned Chalice'. *Guardian*, 25 October.

Horowitz, Donald L. 1985. *Ethnic Groups in Conflict*. Berkeley: University of California Press.

1991. *A Democratic South Africa? Constitutional Engineering in a Divided Society*. Berkeley: University of California Press.

1997. 'Encouraging Electoral Accommodation in Divided Societies'. In Brij V. Lal and Peter Larmour (eds.), *Electoral Systems in Divided Societies:*

The Fiji Constitution Review. Canberra: National Centre for Development Studies, Research School of Pacific and Asian Studies, Australian National University, 21–37.

2000. 'Constitutional Design: An Oxymoron?' *NOMOS* 42: 253–84.

2002. 'Constitutional Design: Proposals versus Processes'. In Andrew Reynolds (ed.), *The Architecture of Democracy: Constitutional Design, Conflict Management, and Democracy.* Oxford: Oxford University Press, 15–36.

Hosokawa, Morihiro 1993. 'Inaugural Press Conference: Prime Minister Hosokawa Morihiro'. *Japan Echo* 20(4): 30–2.

Housego, David 1985. 'France to Switch to PR Voting'. *Financial Times,* 4 April.

Hrebenar, Ronald J. 1977. 'The Politics of Electoral Reform in Japan'. *Asian Survey* 17: 978–96.

1986. 'Rules of the Game: The Impact of the Electoral System on Political Parties'. In Ronald J. Hrebenar with contributions by Peter Berton, Akira Nakamura, J. A. A. Stockwin, and Nobuo Tomita, *The Japanese Party System: From One-Party Rule to Coalition Government.* Boulder, CO: Westview Press, 32–54.

1992. 'Rules of the Game: The Impact of the Electoral System on Political Parties'. In Ronald J. Hrebenar with contributions by Peter Berton, Akira Nakamura, J. A. A. Stockwin, and Nobuo Tomita, *The Japanese Party System,* 2nd edn. Boulder, CO: Westview Press, 32–53.

Hunt, Graeme 1998. *Why MMP Must Go: The Case for Ditching the Electoral Disaster of the Century.* Auckland: Waddington Press.

Hunt, Jonathan 2006. Interview. London, 10 October.

Huntington, Samuel P. 1991. *The Third Wave: Democratization in the Late Twentieth Century.* Norman, OK: University of Oklahoma Press.

IFES 2009. 'International Foundation for Electoral Systems Election Guide'. Accessed at www.electionguide.org, 27 February 2009.

Independent Commission on the Voting System 1998. *Report of the Independent Commission on the Voting System* (CM 4090-I). London: Stationery Office.

Ingle, Stephen 1995. 'Electoral Reform in New Zealand: The Implications for Westminster Systems'. *Journal of Legislative Studies* 1(4): 76–92.

Inglehart, Ronald 1997. *Modernization and Postmodernization: Cultural, Economic, and Political Change in 43 Societies.* Princeton, NJ: Princeton University Press.

Inglehart, Ronald, and Christian Welzel 2005. *Modernization, Cultural Change, and Democracy: The Human Development Sequence.* Cambridge: Cambridge University Press.

Initiative and Referendum Institute 2008. 'Statewide Initiatives since 1904–2000'. Accessed at http://www.iandrinstitute.org, 25 January 2008.

Inoguchi, Takashi 1990. 'The Political Economy of Conservative Resurgence under Recession: Public Policies and Political Support in Japan, 1977–1983'. In

T. J. Pempel (ed.), *Uncommon Democracies: The One-Party Dominant Regimes*. Ithaca, NY: Cornell University Press, 189–225.

IPU 2009. 'Inter-Parliamentary Union Parline Database on National Parliaments'. Accessed at www.ipu.org/parline-e/parlinesearch.asp, 27 February 2009.

Ishiyama, John T. 1997. 'Transitional Electoral Systems in Post-Communist Eastern Europe'. *Political Science Quarterly* 112: 95–115.

Iversen, Torben, and David Soskice 2006. 'Electoral Institutions and the Politics of Coalitions: Why Some Democracies Redistribute More than Others'. *American Political Science Review* 100: 165–81.

Jackson, Keith, and Alan McRobie 1998. *New Zealand Adopts Proportional Representation: Accident? Design? Evolution?* Aldershot: Ashgate.

Jackson, W. K. 1972. *The New Zealand Legislative Council: A Study of the Establishment, Failure and Abolition of an Upper House*. Dunedin: University of Otago Press.

Jain, Purnendra C. 1993. 'Is the "Mountain" Back in Its Place? Interpreting Japan's House of Councillors Election of 1992'. *Pacific Review* 6: 77–84.

——— 1995. 'Electoral Reform in Japan: Its Process and Implications for Party Politics'. *Journal of East Asian Affairs* 9: 402–27.

James, Colin 1990. 'After the Divide'. In Colin James and Alan McRobie (eds.), *Changes? The 1990 Election*. Wellington: Allen & Unwin, 61–93.

Jesse, Eckhard 1987. 'The West German Electoral System: The Case for Reform, 1949–1987'. *West European Politics* 10: 434–48.

Johnson, Chalmers 1995. *Japan: Who Governs? The Rise of the Developmental State*. New York: W. W. Norton.

Johnson, Stephen 2000. *Opposition Politics in Japan: Strategies under a One-Party Dominant Regime*. London: Routledge.

Kabashima, Ikuo, and Gill Steel 2007. 'How Junichiro Koizumi Seized the Leadership of Japan's Liberal Democratic Party'. *Japanese Journal of Political Science* 8: 95–114.

Kamiński, Marek M. 1999. 'How Communism Could Have Been Saved: Formal Analysis of Electoral Bargaining in Poland in 1989'. *Public Choice* 98: 83–109.

Kaminski, Marek M. 2002. 'Do Parties Benefit from Electoral Manipulation? Electoral Laws and Heresthetics in Poland, 1989–93'. *Journal of Theoretical Politics* 14: 325–58.

Karl, Terry Lynn 1986. 'Petroleum and Political Pacts: The Transition to Democracy in Venezuela'. In Guillermo A. O'Donnell, Philippe C. Schmitter, and Laurence Whitehead (eds.), *Transitions from Authoritarian Rule: Latin America*. Baltimore, MD: Johns Hopkins University Press, 196–219.

Katz, Richard S. 1980. *A Theory of Parties and Electoral Systems*. Baltimore, MD: Johns Hopkins University Press.

1996. 'Electoral Reform and the Transformation of Party Politics in Italy'. *Party Politics* 2: 31–53.

1997. *Democracy and Elections*. New York: Oxford University Press.

1999. 'Electoral Reform and Its Discontents'. In Justin Fisher, Philip Cowley, and David Denver (eds.), *British Elections and Parties Review, Volume 9*. London: Frank Cass, 1–19.

2001. 'Reforming the Italian Electoral Law, 1993'. In Shugart and Wattenberg 2001d: 96–122.

2004. 'Problems in Electoral Reform: Why the Decision to Change Electoral Systems Is Not Simple'. In Milner 2004: 85–101.

2005. 'Why Are There So Many (or So Few) Electoral Reforms?' In Gallagher and Mitchell 2005: 57–76.

2006. 'Electoral Reform in Italy: Expectations and Results'. *Acta Politica* 41: 285–99.

Kaufmann, Bruno, and M. Dane Waters (eds.) 2004. *Direct Democracy in Europe: A Comprehensive Reference Guide to the Initiative and Referendum Process in Europe*. Durham, NC: Carolina Academic Press.

Kawato, Sadafumi 2000. 'Strategic Contexts of the Vote on Political Reform Bills'. *Japanese Journal of Political Science* 1: 23–51.

2002. 'The Study of Japan's Medium-Sized District System'. In Gerhard Loewenberg, Peverill Squire, and D. Roderick Kiewiet (eds.), *Legislatures: Comparative Perspectives on Representative Assemblies*. Ann Arbor: University of Michigan Press, 178–98.

Keith, Kenneth 2006. Interview. Wellington, 21 August.

Kellerman, Barbara 1984a. 'Introductory Remarks'. In Barbara Kellerman (ed.), *Leadership: Multidisciplinary Perspectives*. Englewood Cliffs, NJ: Prentice Hall, ix–xiii.

1984b. *The Political Presidency: Practice of Leadership*. New York: Oxford University Press.

Kellner, Peter 1995. 'Electoral Reform: Principle or Self-Interest'. *Representation* 33(2) 23–7.

Kernell, Samuel 1986. *Going Public: New Strategies of Presidential Leadership*. Washington, DC: CQ Press.

Kingdon, John W. 1995. *Agendas, Alternatives, and Public Policies*, 2nd edn. New York: Longman.

Kishimoto, Koichi 1993. 'Politicians Face Tough Issues as End of Session Nears'. *Japan Times*, 31 May.

Kitazume, Takashi 1993a. 'New Faction Aims for Realignment'. *Japan Times*, 4 January.

1993b. 'New Faction May Lead to Realignment of Party'. *Japan Times*, 4 January.

1993c. 'LDP, Opposition May Strike Reform Plan Compromise'. *Japan Times*, 3 May.

Kitschelt, Herbert, and Steven I. Wilkinson 2007. 'Citizen–Politician Linkages: An Introduction'. In Herbert Kitschelt and Steven I. Wilkinson (eds.), *Patrons, Clients, and Policies: Patterns of Democratic Accountability and Political Competition*. Cambridge: Cambridge University Press, 1–49.

Knapp, Andrew 1987. 'Proportional but Bipolar: France's Electoral System in 1986'. *West European Politics* 10: 89–114.

—— 2007a. 'Introduction: France's "Long" Liberation, 1944–47'. In Knapp 2007b: 1–22.

—— (ed.) 2007b. *The Uncertain Foundation: France at the Liberation, 1944–47*. Basingstoke: Palgrave Macmillan.

Kohno, Masaru 1997. *Japan's Postwar Party Politics*. Princeton, NJ: Princeton University Press.

Kogan, Norman 1966. *A Political History of Postwar Italy*. London: Pall Mall Press.

Köllner, Patrick 2004. 'Factionalism in Japanese Political Parties Revisited or How Do Factions in the LDP and the DPJ Differ?' *Japan Forum* 16(1): 87–109.

—— 2006. 'The Liberal Democratic Party at 50: Sources of Dominance and Changes in the Koizumi Era'. *Social Science Japan Journal* 9: 243–57.

Kopecký, Petr 2004. 'The Czech Republic: Entrenching Proportional Representation'. In Colomer 2004b: 347–58.

Köppl, Stefan 2004. 'Italy: A Transition without Reform? Failed Attempts at Constitutional Reform in Italy in the 1980s and 1990s'. Paper presented at the ASMI Annual Conference. London, 27 November.

Kōsaka, Masataka 1988. 'The Paradox of Japanese Politics'. *Japan Echo* 15(4): 57–62.

—— 1993. 'The Forces at Work in the Political Shakeup'. *Japan Echo* 20(4): 45–53.

Krauss, Ellis 1982. 'Japanese Parties and Parliament: Changing Leadership Rules and Role Conflicts'. In Terry Edward MacDougall (ed.), *Political Leadership in Contemporary Japan*. Ann Arbor: Center for Japanese Studies, University of Michigan, 93–114.

Laakso, Markku, and Rein Taagepera 1979. '"Effective" Number of Parties: A Measure with Application to Western Europe'. *Comparative Political Studies* 12: 3–27.

Laffin, Martin 2000. 'Constitutional Design: A Framework for Analysis'. *Parliamentary Affairs* 53: 532–41.

Lakeman, Enid 1974. *How Democracies Vote. A Study of Electoral Systems*, 4th edn. London: Faber & Faber.

Lal, Brij V. 1998. *Another Way: The Politics of Constitutional Reform in Post-Coup Fiji*. Canberra: Asia Pacific Press, National Centre for Development Studies, Australian National University.

—— 2000. 'Rabuka of Fiji: Coups, Constitution and Confusion: Review and Reflections'. *Journal of Pacific History* 35: 319–26.

Lamare, James W., and Jack Vowles 1996. 'Party Interests, Public Opinion and Institutional Preferences: Electoral System Change in New Zealand'. *Australian Journal of Political Science* 31: 321–45.

Landers, Peter 1991. 'Small Parties Fight to Block Reform'. *Japan Times*, 2 September.

Lange, David 1993 [1992]. 'A Level Playing Field of Contempt'. In McRobie 1993: 141–4. First published in *Dominion*, 9 September 1992.

——— 2005. *My Life*. Auckland: Viking.

LaPalombara, Joseph G. 1953. 'The Italian Elections and the Problem of Representation'. *American Political Science Review* 47: 676–703.

LaPalombara, Joseph 1987. *Democracy, Italian Style*. New Haven: Yale University Press.

Laponce, J. A. 1980. 'The System of Election to the French National Assembly'. *Contemporary French Civilization* 4: 369–83.

Laugesen, Ruth 1992. 'How MPs Vote on Electoral Reform'. *Dominion*, 5 August.

Lavau, Georges, and Janine Mossuz-Lavau 1980. 'The Union of the Left's Defeat: Suicide or Congenital Weakness?' In Howard R. Penniman (ed.), *The French National Assembly Elections of 1978*. Washington, DC: American Enterprise Institute for Public Policy Research, 110–43.

LDP Political Reform Committee 1989. 'A Proposal for Political Reform'. *Japan Echo* 16(3): 22–4. Unofficial translation of the report as summarized in *Nihon Keizai Shimbun*.

LeDuc, Lawrence 2003. *The Politics of Direct Democracy: Referendums in Global Perspective*. Peterborough, Ontario: Broadview Press.

Légifrance 2000. 'Loi constitutionnelle no. 2000-964 du 2 octobre 2000 relative à la durée du mandat du Président de la République'. Accessed at www.legifrance.gouv.fr, 20 December 2008.

——— 2001. 'Loi organique no. 2001-419 du 15 mai 2001 modifiant la date d'expiration des pouvoirs de l'Assemblée Nationale'. Accessed at www.legifrance.gouv.fr, 20 December 2008.

Lehoucq, Fabrice Edouard 1995. 'Institutional Change and Political Conflict: Evaluating Alternative Explanations of Electoral Reform in Costa Rica'. *Electoral Studies* 14: 23–45.

——— 2000. 'Institutionalizing Democracy: Constraint and Ambition in the Politics of Electoral Reform'. *Comparative Politics* 32: 459–77.

Leites, Nathan 1959. *On the Game of Politics in France*. Stanford, CA: Stanford University Press.

Levine, Daniel 1985. 'The Transition to Democracy: Are There Lessons from Venezuela?' *Bulletin of Latin American Research* 4: 47–61.

Levine, Stephen, and Nigel S. Roberts 1993. 'The New Zealand Electoral Referendum of 1992'. *Electoral Studies* 12: 158–67.

1994. 'The New Zealand Electoral Referendum and General Election of 1993'. *Electoral Studies* 13: 240–53.

1997. 'MMP: The Decision'. In Raymond Miller (ed.), *New Zealand Politics in Transition*. Auckland: Oxford University Press, 25–36.

Levy, Jonah D., and Cindy Skach 2008. 'The Return to a Strong Presidency'. In Alistair Cole, Patrick Le Galès, and Jonah D. Levy (eds.), *Developments in French Politics 4*. Basingstoke: Palgrave Macmillan, 111–26.

Lewis, W. Arthur 1965. *Politics in West Africa*. London: George Allen & Unwin.

Lijphart, Arend 1978. 'The Dutch Electoral System in Comparative Perspective: Extreme Proportional Representation, Multipartism, and the Failure of Electoral Reform'. *Netherlands Journal of Sociology* 14: 115–33.

1984. *Democracies: Patterns of Majoritarian and Consensus Government in Twenty-One Countries*. New Haven: Yale University Press.

1985. *Power-Sharing in South Africa*. Berkeley: Institute of International Studies, University of California.

1987. 'The Demise of the Last Westminster System? Comments on the Report of New Zealand's Royal Commission on the Electoral System'. *Electoral Studies* 6: 97–103.

1994. *Electoral Systems and Party Systems: A Study of Twenty-Seven Democracies, 1945–1990*. Oxford: Oxford University Press.

1999. *Patterns of Democracy: Government Forms and Performance in Thirty-Six Countries*. New Haven: Yale University Press.

2002. 'The Wave of Power-Sharing Democracy'. In Andrew Reynolds (ed.), *The Architecture of Democracy: Constitutional Design, Conflict Mangagement, and Democracy*. Oxford: Oxford University Press, 37–54.

Lin, Jih-Wen 2006. 'The Politics of Reform in Japan and Taiwan'. *Journal of Democracy* 17(2): 118–31.

Lindblom, Charles E. 1968. *The Policy-Making Process*. Englewood Cliffs, NJ: Prentice Hall.

Lipset, Seymour Martin, and Stein Rokkan 1967. 'Cleavage Structures, Party Systems, and Voter Alignments: An Introduction'. In Seymour Martin Lipset and Stein Rokkan (eds.), *Party Systems and Voter Alignments: Cross-National Perspectives*. New York: Free Press, 1–64.

Lipson, Leslie 1959. 'Party Systems in the United Kingdom and the Older Commonwealth: Causes, Resemblances and Variations'. *Political Studies* 7: 12–31.

Loeber, Dietrich André 1998. 'Regaining Independence – Constitutional Aspects: Estonia, Latvia, Lithuania'. *Review of Central and East European Law* 24: 1–7.

Long, Richard 1990. 'Teasing the Voters with Dreams of Electoral Reform'. *Dominion*, 17 April.

Longley, Lawrence D., and Alan G. Braun 1975. *The Politics of Electoral College Reform*, 2nd edn. New Haven: Yale University Press.

Longley, Lawrence D., and Neal R. Peirce 1999. *The Electoral College Primer 2000.* New Haven: Yale University Press.

Lord, Carnes 2003. *The Modern Prince: What Leaders Need to Know Now.* New Haven: Yale University Press.

Lundberg, Thomas Carl 2007. *Proportional Representation and the Constituency Role in Britain.* Basingstoke: Palgrave Macmillan.

Lundell, Krister 2005. *Contextual Determinants of Electoral System Choice: A Macro-Comparative Study 1945-2003.* Åbo, Finland: Åbo Akademi University Press.

Lupia, Arthur, and John G. Matsusaka 2004. 'Direct Democracy: New Approaches to Old Questions'. *Annual Review of Political Science* 7: 463-82.

Lutz, Georg 2004. 'Switzerland: Introducing Proportional Representation from Below'. In Colomer 2004b: 279-93.

MacArthur, General Douglas 1949 [1945]. 'Statement to the Japanese Government Concerning Required Reforms', 11 October 1945. In Government Section, Supreme Commander for the Allied Powers, *Political Reorientation of Japan, September 1945 to September 1948.* Washington, DC: US Government Printing Office, 741.

McCarthy, Patrick 1992. 'The Referendum of 9 June'. In Stephen Hellman and Gianfranco Pasquino (eds.), *Italian Politics: A Review, Volume 7.* London: Pinter, 11-28.

McCully, Murray 1988. 'Memo to: D. A. M. Graham MP, John Luxton MP, From: Murray McCully MP, Subject: Proposed Private Member's Bill – Second Chamber of Parliament, Date: 22 March 1988'. Mimeo. McCully Papers, Archives New Zealand, Agency ABWM, Series 7361, Accession W5295, Box 1, File: '1988 Inquiry, Electoral Law Committee (2)'.

———. 1989a. Letter from McCully to Phil Saxby, dated 1 February 1989. Mimeo. McCully Papers, Archives New Zealand, Agency ABWM, Series 7361, Accession W5295, Box 1, File: '1989 Correspondence (Electoral Reform)'.

———. 1989b. 'Speech to the Banks Peninsula Meeting, Selwyn Electorate', 3 November. Mimeo. McCully Papers, Archives New Zealand, Agency ABWM, Series 7361, Accession W5295, Box 6, File: 'Media – Speeches and Press Releases, Part 2: 1988-1990'.

———. 1990. 'Address to the Annual General Meeting of the Auckland Division of the Young Nationals by Murray McCully MP'. Mimeo. McCully Papers, Archives New Zealand, Agency ABWM, Series 7361, Accession W5295, Box 6, File: 'Media – Speeches and Press Releases, Part 1, 1987-1988'.

———. 2006. Interview. Wellington, 21 August.

McCully, Murray, and Wayne Eagleson 1991. 'Electoral Reform: The 1992 Referendum – An Issues Paper for [the National Party's] National Executive', 25 June. Mimeo. McCully Papers, Archives New Zealand,

Agency ABWM, Series 7361, Accession W5295, Box 1, File: '1991 Electoral Law Committee'.

McElwain, Kenneth Mori 2008. 'Manipulating Electoral Rules to Manufacture Single-Party Dominance'. *American Journal of Political Science* 52: 32–47.

McGann, Anthony J., and Teresa Moran 2005. 'The Myth of the Disproportionate Influence of Small Parties in Israel'. Center for the Study of Democracy, Paper 05-08. Accessed at http://repositories.cdlib.org/csd/05–08, 6 February 2008.

Machiavelli, Niccolò 1979 [1513]. *The Prince.* In *The Portable Machiavelli*, ed. and trans. Peter Bondanella and Mark Musa. New York: Penguin, 77–166.

Machin, Howard 1993a. 'How the Socialists Lost the 1993 Elections to the French Parliament'. *West European Politics* 16: 595–606.

1993b. 'Representation and Distortion in the 1993 French Election'. *Parliamentary Affairs* 46: 627–36.

Mackerras, Malcolm 1994. 'Reform of New Zealand's Voting System, 1985–1996'. *Representation* 32(118): 36–40.

Mackie, Thomas T., and Richard Rose 1991. *The International Almanac of Electoral History*, 3rd edn. Basingstoke: Macmillan.

McKinnon, Don 2006. Interview. London, 10 October.

McLean, Iain 1987. *Public Choice.* Oxford: Blackwell.

2001. *Rational Choice and British Politics: An Analysis of Rhetoric and Manipulation from Peel to Blair.* Oxford: Oxford University Press.

2002. 'Review Article: William H. Riker and the Invention of Heresthetic(s)'. *British Journal of Political Science* 32: 535–58.

McLeay, Elizabeth 1996. 'Restructuring the State and the Electoral System in New Zealand: Public Choice Theory and Elite Behaviour'. Paper presented to the Shaping Political Behaviour Workshop, European Consortium of Political Research, Oslo, 29 March–3 April.

McLeay, Elizabeth, Jonathan Boston, Stephen Levine, and Nigel S. Roberts 1996. 'Contradictions and Compatibility: Electoral System Change and the New Zealand Political Culture'. *New Zealand Studies* 6 (November): 23–8.

McRobie, Alan 1980. 'The Electoral System and the 1978 Election'. In Howard R. Penniman (ed.), *New Zealand at the Polls: The General Election of 1978.* Washington, DC: American Enterprise Institute for Public Policy Research, 64–98.

1989. 'Challenging the Elective Dictatorship: Proposals for Reforming New Zealand's Electoral System'. In Hyam Gold (ed.), *New Zealand Politics in Perspective*, 2nd edn. Auckland: Longman Paul, 388–408.

1991. 'The New Zealand General Election of 1990'. *Electoral Studies* 10: 158–71.

(ed.) 1993. *Taking It to the People? The New Zealand Electoral Referendum Debate.* Christchurch: Hazard Press.

1994. 'Final and Binding: The 1993 Electoral Referendum'. In Jack Vowles and Peter Aimer (eds.), *Double Decision: The 1993 Election and Referendum in New Zealand*. Wellington: Department of Politics, Victoria University of Wellington, 101–24.

Maeno, J. Rey 1974. 'Japan 1973: The End of an Era?' *Asian Survey* 14: 52–64.

Magri, Ugo 2004. 'Discorso di 25 minuti al Senato e alla Camera per ricomporre il crisis: Federalismo e legge elettorale, il premier apre'. *La Stampa*, 15 July.

Mahoney, James 2000. 'Path Dependence in Historical Sociology'. *Theory and Society* 29: 507–48.

Mahoney, James, and Dietrich Rueschemeyer 2003. 'Comparative Historical Analysis: Achievements and Agendas'. In James Mahoney and Dietrich Rueschemeyer, *Comparative Historical Analysis in the Social Sciences*. Cambridge: Cambridge University Press, 3–38.

Mainwaring, Scott 1991. 'Politicians, Parties, and Electoral Systems: Brazil in Comparative Perspective'. *Comparative Political Studies* 24: 21–43.

Maisrikrod, Surin 2002. 'Political Reform and the New Thai Electoral System: Old Habits Die Hard?' In John Fuh-sheng Hsieh and David Newman (eds.), *How Asia Votes*. New York: Chatham House Publishers of Seven Bridges Press, 187–209.

Majone, Giandomenico 1989. *Evidence, Argument, and Persuasion in the Policy Process*. New Haven: Yale University Press.

Malone, Ryan 2008. *Rebalancing the Constitution: The Challenge of Government Law-Making under MMP*. Wellington: Institute of Policy Studies, Victoria University of Wellington.

Mandonnet, Eric, and Ludovic Vigogne 2008. 'Institutions: le oui, mais de Morin'. Interview with Hervé Morin. *L'Express*, 17 April.

Mannheimer, Renato 2005. 'Il centro-sinistra vince, ma di meno'. *Corriere della Sera*, 4 October.

Māori Party 2008. 'Election Policy'. Accessed at www.maoriparty.org, 12 December 2008.

Marchais, Georges 1973. *Le Défi démocratique*. Paris: Bernard Grasset.

Marshall, John 1989. *Memoirs, Volume 2: 1960 to 1988*. Auckland: William Collins.

Masaki, Hisane 1991. 'Takeshita Faction Backs Miyazawa for Premiership: Patrons Cast Shadow on Candidacy'. *Japan Times*, 21 October.

1992. 'Abe Arrest Another Blow to Miyazawa'. *Japan Times*, 27 January.

Massetti, Emanuele 2006. 'Electoral Reform in Italy: From PR to Mixed System and (Almost) Back Again'. *Representation* 42: 261–9.

Massicotte, Louis 2008. 'Electoral Reform in Canada'. In Blais 2008: 112–39.

Massicotte, Louis, and André Blais 1999. 'Mixed Electoral Systems: A Conceptual and Empirical Survey'. *Electoral Studies* 18: 341–66.

Massicotte, Louis, André Blais, and Antoine Yoshinaka 2004. *Establishing the Rules of the Game: Election Laws in Democracies*. Toronto: University of Toronto Press.

Masumi, Junnosuke 1985. *Postwar Politics in Japan, 1945–1955*, trans. Lonny E. Carlile. Berkeley, CA: Center for Japanese Studies, Institute of East Asian Studies, University of California, Berkeley.

1995. *Contemporary Politics in Japan*, trans. Lonny E. Carlile. Berkeley, CA: University of California Press.

Masuzoe, Yōichi 1991. 'Tremors in the Political System'. *Japan Echo* 18 (special issue): 2–5.

Matsuzaki, Tetsuhisa 1989. 'Electoral Reform: A Flawed LDP Initiative'. *Japan Echo* 16(3): 7–13.

May, John D. 1973. 'Opinion Structure of Political Parties: The Special Law of Curvilinear Disparity'. *Political Studies* 21: 135–51.

Merkl, Peter 1963. *The Origin of the West German Republic*. New York: Oxford University Press.

Mershon, Carol, and Gianfranco Pasquino (eds.) 1995. *Italian Politics: Ending the First Republic* (Italian Politics: A Review, Volume 9). Boulder, CO: Westview Press.

Merton, Robert K. 1967. 'On Sociological Theories of the Middle Range'. In Robert K. Merton, *On Theoretical Sociology: Five Essays, Old and New*. New York: Free Press, 39–72.

Michels, Robert 1962 [1911]. *Political Parties: A Sociological Survey of the Oligarchical Tendencies of Modern Democracy*, trans. Eden and Cedar Paul. New York: Free Press.

Milner, Henry (ed.) 2004. *Steps toward Making Every Vote Count: Electoral System Reform in Canada and Its Provinces*. Peterborough, Ontario: Broadview Press.

Ministero dell'Interno 1992. 'Elezioni della Camera dei Deputati del 5 Aprile 1992'. Accessed at http://elezionistorico.interno.it, 12 March 2008.

2009. 'Ballotaggi amministrative e referendum del 21 e 22 giugno'. Accessed at www.interno.it, 9 July 2009.

Minogue, Michael J. 1976. 'Parliamentary Democracy Today'. *New Zealand Law Journal* 21: 485–9.

Mishima, Ko 2007. 'Grading Japanese Prime Minister Koizumi's Revolution: How Far Has the LDP's Policymaking Changed?' *Asian Survey* 47: 727–48.

Mitterrand, François 1981. 'Les 110 propositions'. Accessed at http://www.psinfo.net, 19 December 2008.

Moore, Mike 1987. *Hard Labour*. Auckland: Penguin.

Morin, Hervé 2007. Speech at the National Council of the Nouveau Centre, 16 December. Accessed at www.le-nouveaucentre.org, 18 December 2008.

Morita, Minoru 1991. 'The Hidden Obstacles to Electoral Reform'. *Japan Echo* 18 (special issue): 80–4.

Morlino, Leonardo 1996. 'Crisis of Parties and Change of Party System in Italy'. *Party Politics* 2: 5–30.

Morton, F. L., and Rainer Knopf 2000. *The Charter Revolution and the Court Party*. Peterborough, Ontario: Broadview Press.

Mozaffar, Shaheen 1998. 'Electoral Systems and Conflict Management in Africa: A Twenty-Eight-State Comparison'. In Timothy D. Sisk and Andrew Reynolds (eds.), *Elections and Conflict Management in Africa*. Washington, DC: United States Institute of Peace Press, 81–98.

Mulgan, Aurelia George 2002. *Japan's Failed Revolution: Koizumi and the Politics of Economic Reform*. Canberra: Asia Pacific Press at the Australian National University.

Mulgan, Richard 1980. 'Palmer, Parliament and the Constitution'. *Political Science* 32: 171–7.

——— 1984. *Democracy and Power in New Zealand: A Study of New Zealand Politics*. Auckland: Oxford University Press.

——— 1989. 'Recent Writing on New Zealand Politics'. *Politics* 24: 118–22.

——— 1990. 'Moderates Converted to Radical Electoral Reform'. *New Zealand Herald*, 22 April.

——— 1995. 'The Democratic Failure of Single-Party Government: The New Zealand Experience'. *Australian Journal of Political Science* 30 (special issue): 82–96.

——— 2006. Interview. Canberra, 31 July.

Müller, Wolfgang 2005. 'Austria: A Complex Electoral System with Subtle Effects'. In Gallagher and Mitchell 2005: 397–415.

Muramatsu, Michio, and Ellis S. Krauss 1990. 'The Dominant Party and Social Coalitions in Japan'. In T. J. Pempel (ed.), *Uncommon Democracies: The One-Party Dominant Regimes*. Ithaca, NY: Cornell University Press, 282–305.

Nagel, Jack H. 1994. 'What Political Scientists Can Learn from the 1993 Electoral Reform in New Zealand'. *PS: Political Science and Politics* 27: 525–9.

——— 2004. 'New Zealand: Reform by (Nearly) Immaculate Design'. In Colomer 2004b: 530–43.

Naoumova, Natalia 2007. 'Moscow, the Parti Communiste Français and France's Political Recovery'. In Knapp 2007b: 160–82.

National Popular Vote 2009. '22 Legislative Chambers Have Now Passed Bill'. Accessed at www.nationalpopularvote.com, 9 July 2009.

Neary, Ian 2002. *The State and Politics in Japan*. Cambridge: Polity.

Neumann, Robert G. 1951. 'The Struggle for Electoral Reform in France'. *American Political Science Review* 45: 741–55.

Neustadt, Richard E. 1960. *Presidential Power: The Politics of Leadership*. New York: John Wiley & Sons.

Newell, James L. 2006. 'The Italian Election of May 2006: Myths and Realities'. *West European Politics* 29: 802–13.

Newell, James L., and Martin J. Bull 1993. 'The Italian Referenda of April 1993: Real Change at Last?' *West European Politics* 16: 607–15.

New Zealand Democratic Party 1985. Written submission to the Royal Commission on the Electoral System, no. 742 (untitled). Mimeo. Papers of the Royal Commission on the Electoral System, Archives New Zealand, Agency AAYI (RCES), Accession W3047, Item 1, 4 – Submissions.

New Zealand Election Study 1993. '1993 New Zealand Election Survey'. Accessed at www.nzes.org/exec/show/1993, 10 February 2008.

New Zealand Federation of Labour 1979. *Minutes and Report of the Proceedings of the Forty-Second Annual Conference held in the Town Hall, Wellington, on May 1, 2, 3 and 4, 1979.* Wellington: New Zealand Federation of Labour.

   1982. *Minutes and Report of the Proceedings of the Forty-Fifth Annual Conference held in the Town Hall, Wellington, on May 4, 5, 6 and 7, 1982.* Wellington: New Zealand Federation of Labour.

New Zealand Government 2008. 'Speech from the Throne', 9 December. Accessed at www.beehive.govt.nz, 11 December 2008.

New Zealand Labour Party 1978. *New Zealand Labour Party 1978 Manifesto: To Rebuild the Nation.* Wellington: New Zealand Labour Party.

   1981. 'Open Government Policy – 1981'. In *Manifesto 1981: Labour ... Positive, Practical Solutions.* Wellington: New Zealand Labour Party.

   1984. 'Open Government Policy 1984'. In New Zealand Labour Party 1984 Policy Compendium (untitled). Wellington: New Zealand Labour Party.

   1985. Submission to the Royal Commission on the Electoral System, 25 July. Mimeo. Papers of the Royal Commission on the Electoral System, Archives New Zealand, Agency AAYI (RCES), Accession W3047, Item 1, 4 – Submissions.

   1987. New Zealand Labour Party 1987 Policy Document (untitled). Wellington: New Zealand Labour Party.

New Zealand National Party 1960. *New Zealand National Party 1960 General Election Policy.* Wellington: New Zealand National Party.

   1990a. 'National's Policy on Electoral Reform: Improving New Zealand's Democracy', 11 September. Mimeo.

   1990b. *National Party Policies for the 1990s: Creating a Decent Society.* Wellington: New Zealand National Party.

   2008. 'Electoral Law Policy'. Accessed at www.national.org.nz, 19 November 2008.

New Zealand National Party Electoral Law Reform Caucus Committee 1990. 'Report of the Electoral Law Reform Committee to Caucus', September. Mimeo. *New Zealand Parliamentary Debates (Hansard).* Wellington.

Nicholle, Brian 2009. Telephone interview, 17 January.

Nishibe, Susumu 1991. 'Challenging the Politics of Expediency'. *Japan Echo* 18(3): 24–7.

Nohlen, Dieter 1984. 'Changes and Choices in Electoral Systems'. In Arend Lijphart and Bernard Grofman (eds.), *Choosing an Electoral System: Issues and Alternatives*. Westport, CT: Praeger, 217–24.

Nordic Research Group 2005. 'Post Election STV Poll Results', 13 June. Accessed at www.nrgresearchgroup.com, 19 January 2009.

Norris, Pippa 1995a. 'Introduction: The Politics of Electoral Reform'. *International Political Science Review* 16: 3–8.

1995b. 'May's Law of Curvilinear Disparity Revisited: Leaders, Officers, Members and Voters in British Political Parties'. *Party Politics* 1: 29–47.

2004. *Electoral Engineering: Voting Rules and Political Behavior*. Cambridge: Cambridge University Press.

North, Douglass C. 1990. *Institutions, Institutional Change and Economic Performance*. Cambridge: Cambridge University Press.

Northey, Richard 2006. Telephone interview. 19 August.

O'Leary, Cornelius 1979. *Irish Elections 1918–77: Parties, Voters and Proportional Representation*. Dublin: Gill and Macmillan.

Ontario Citizens' Assembly on Electoral Reform 2007. *One Ballot, Two Votes: A New Way to Vote in Ontario: Recommendation of the Ontario Citizens' Assembly on Electoral Reform*. Toronto.

Ordeshook, Peter C., and Olga V. Shvetsova 1994. 'Ethnic Heterogeneity, District Magnitude, and the Number of Parties'. *American Journal of Political Science* 38: 100–23.

Otake, Hideo 1996. 'Forces for Political Reform: The Liberal Democratic Party's Young Reformers and Ozawa Ichirō'. *Journal of Japanese Studies* 22: 269–94.

Ottolenghi, Emanuele 2001. 'Why Direct Election Failed in Israel'. *Journal of Democracy* 12(4): 109–22.

Ozawa, Ichirō 1993 [1992]. 'My Commitment to Political Reform'. *Japan Echo* 20(1): 8–12. Translated and abridged from 'Wareware wa naze Kaikaku o mezasu ka', *Bunjei Shunjū*, December 1992: 136–49.

1994 [1993]. *Blueprint for a New Japan: The Rethinking of a Nation*. Tokyo: Kodansha International. First published as *Nihon Kaizō Keikaku* (Tokyo: Kodansha, 1993).

Palmer, Geoffrey 1979. *Unbridled Power? An Interpretation of New Zealand's Constitution and Government*. Wellington: Oxford University Press.

1992. *New Zealand's Constitution in Crisis: Reforming Our Political System*. Dunedin: John McIndoe.

2004. 'Muldoon and the Constitution'. In Margaret Clark (ed.), *Muldoon Revisited*. Palmerston North: Dunmore Press, 167–214.

2006. Interview. Wellington, 9 August.

Park, Cheol Hee 2001. 'Factional Dynamics in Japan's LDP since Political Reform'. *Asian Survey* 41: 428–61.

Parker, Simon 1996. 'Electoral Reform and Political Change in Italy, 1991–1994'. In Gundle and Parker 1996b: 40–56.

Pasquino, Gianfranco 1986. 'The Debate on Institutional Reform'. In Robert Leonardi and Raffaella Y. Nanetti (eds.), *Italian Politics: A Review, Volume 1*. London: Frances Pinter, 117–33.

1987. 'La proposta Pasquino'. In Roberto Ruffilli (ed.), *Materiali per la riforma elettorale*. Bologna: Il Mulino, 61–76.

1989. 'That Obscure Object of Desire: A New Electoral Law for Italy'. *West European Politics* 12: 280–94.

1991. 'The De Mita Government Crisis and the Powers of the President of the Republic: Which Form of Government?' In Filippo Sabetti and Raimondo Catanzaro (eds.), *Italian Politics: A Review, Volume 5*. London: Pinter, 40–54.

1992. 'The Electoral Reform Referendums'. In Robert Leonardi and Fausto Anderlini (eds.), *Italian Politics: A Review, Volume 6*. London: Pinter, 9–24.

1994. 'The Birth of the "Second Republic"'. *Journal of Democracy* 5(3): 107–13.

1998. 'Reforming the Italian Constitution'. *Journal of Modern Italian Studies* 3: 42–54

2000. 'A Postmortem of the Bicamerale'. In David Hine and Salvatore Vassallo (eds.), *Italian Politics: The Return of Politics* (Italian Politics: A Review, Volume 14). New York: Berghahn, 101–20.

2001. 'Premiership and Leadership from D'Alema to Amato and Beyond'. In Mario Caciagli and Alan S. Zuckerman (eds.), *Italian Politics: Emerging Themes and Institutional Responses* (Italian Politics: A Review, Volume 16). New York: Berghahn, 37–51.

2007. 'Tricks and Treats: The 2005 Italian Electoral Law and Its Consequences'. *South European Society and Politics* 12: 79–93.

Pasquino, Gianfranco, and Stephen Hellman 1992. 'Introduction'. In Stephen Hellman and Gianfranco Pasquino (eds.), *Italian Politics: A Review, Volume 7*. London: Pinter, 1–10.

PCF 1971. *Changer de cap: programme pour un gouvernement démocratique d'union populaire*. Paris: Éditions Sociales.

Pearse, Hilary 2005. 'Geographic Representation and Electoral Reform'. *Canadian Parliamentary Review* 28(3): 26–32.

Peirce, Neal R. 2004. 'Foreword'. In Edwards 2004: ix–xiii.

Perry, Paul, and Alan Webster 1999. *New Zealand Politics at the Turn of the Millennium: Attitudes and Values about Politics and Government*. Auckland: Alpha Publications.

Persson, Torsten, and Guido Tabellini 2005. *The Economic Effects of Constitutions*. Cambridge, MA: MIT Press.

Pickles, Dorothy 1958. *France: The Fourth Republic*, 2nd edn. Westport, CT: Greenwood Press.

Pierson, Paul 2000. 'Increasing Returns, Path Dependence, and the Study of Politics'. *American Political Science Review* 94: 251–67.

2004. *Politics in Time: History, Institutions, and Social Analysis*. Princeton, NJ: Princeton University Press.

Pilet, Jean-Benoit 2006. 'Confronting the Influence of Ideas and Interests in Electoral Reforms: Analysis of Two Electoral Reforms in Belgium'. Paper presented at the Annual Congress of the International Political Science Association. Fukuoka, Japan, 9–13 July.

2007. 'Strategies under the Surface: The Determinants of Redistricting in Belgium'. *Comparative European Politics* 5: 205–25.

Pilon, Dennis 2004. 'The Uncertain Path of Democratic Renewal in Ontario'. In Milner 2004: 249–65.

Piretti, Maria Serena 2003. *La legge truffa: il fallimento dell'ingegneria politica*. Bologna: Il Mulino.

Plant, Raymond 1995. 'The Plant Report: A Retrospective'. *Representation* 33(2): 5–16.

Powell, G. Bingham, Jr. 2000. *Elections as Instruments of Democracy: Majoritarian and Proportional Visions*. New Haven: Yale University Press.

Preddey, Elspeth 2003. *The WEL Herstory: The Women's Electoral Lobby in New Zealand 1975–2002*. Wellington: WEL New Zealand.

Programme Commun de Gouvernement 1972. *Programme Commun de Gouvernement du Parti Communiste et du Parti Socialiste (27 juin 1972)*. Paris: Éditions Sociales.

Pryce, Roy 1952. 'The New Italian Electoral Law'. *Parliamentary Affairs* 6: 269–76.

1957. 'The Italian General Election, 1958'. *Parliamentary Affairs* 11: 318–27.

Przeworski, Adam 1991. *Democracy and the Market: Political and Economic Reforms in Eastern Europe and Latin America*. Cambridge: Cambridge University Press.

PS 1972. *Changer la vie: programme de gouvernement du Parti Socialiste*. Paris: Flammarion.

Pulzer, Peter 1983. 'Germany'. In Bogdanor and Butler 1983: 84–109.

Putnam, Robert D. 1988. 'Diplomacy and Domestic Politics: The Logics of Two-Level Games'. *International Organization* 42: 427–60.

Quagliariello, Gaetano 2003. *La legge elettorale del 1953: dibattiti storici in Parlamento*. Bologna: Il Mulino.

Quigley, Harold S. 1926. 'The New Japanese Electoral Law'. *American Political Science Review* 20: 392–5.

Quintal, David P. 1970. 'The Theory of Electoral Systems'. *Western Political Quarterly* 23: 752–61.

Rae, Douglas W. 1971 [1967]. *The Political Consequences of Electoral Laws*. New Haven: Yale University Press.

Rahat, Gideon 2001. 'The Politics of Reform in Israel: How the Israeli Mixed System Came to Be'. In Shugart and Wattenberg 2001d: 123–51.

—— 2008. *The Politics of Regime Structure Reform in Democracies: Israel in Comparative and Theoretical Perspective*. Albany, NY: State University of New York Press.

Rahat, Gideon, and Reuven Y. Hazan 2005. 'Israel: The Politics of an Extreme Electoral System'. In Gallagher and Mitchell 2005: 333–51.

Rahat, Gideon, and Mario Sznajder 1998. 'Electoral Engineering in Chile: The Electoral System and Limited Democracy'. *Electoral Studies* 17: 429–42.

Ramseyer, J. Mark, and Frances M. Rosenbluth 1995. *The Politics of Oligarchy: Institutional Choice in Imperial Japan*. Cambridge: Cambridge University Press.

Rawls, John 1971. *A Theory of Justice*. Cambridge, MA: Belknap Press of Harvard University Press.

Reed, Steven R. 1990. 'Structure and Behaviour: Extending Duverger's Law to the Japanese Case'. *British Journal of Political Science* 20: 335–56.

—— 1997. 'Providing Clear Cues: Voter Response to the Reform Issue in the 1993 Japanese General Election'. *Party Politics* 3: 265–77.

—— 1999. 'Political Reform in Japan: Combining Scientific and Historical Analysis'. *Social Science Japan Journal* 2: 177–93.

—— 2003a. 'The 1993 Election and the End of LDP One-Party Dominance'. In Steven R. Reed (ed.), *Japanese Electoral Politics: Creating a New Party System*. London: RoutledgeCurzon, 7–23.

—— 2003b. 'Realignment between the 1993 and 1996 Elections'. In Steven R. Reed (ed.), *Japanese Electoral Politics: Creating a New Party System*. London: RoutledgeCurzon, 24–39.

—— 2005. 'Japan: Haltingly Towards a Two-Party System'. In Gallagher and Mitchell 2005: 277–93.

Reed, Steven R., and John M. Bolland 1999. 'The Fragmentation Effect of SNTV in Japan'. In Bernard Grofman, Sung-Chull Lee, Edwin A. Winckler, and Brian Woodall (eds.), *Elections in Japan, Korea, and Taiwan under the Single Non-Transferable Vote: The Comparative Study of an Embedded Institution*. Ann Arbor: University of Michigan Press, 211–26.

Reed, Steven R., and Michael F. Thies 2001. 'The Causes of Electoral Reform in Japan'. In Shugart and Wattenberg 2001d: 152–72.

Reid, Nicola 2003. 'ACT'. In Raymond Miller (ed.), *New Zealand Government and Politics*, 3rd edn. Melbourne: Oxford University Press, 274–82.

Reilly, Ben 1996. 'The Effects of the Electoral System in Papua New Guinea'. In Yaw Saffu (ed.), *The 1992 PNG Election: Change and Continuity in Electoral Politics*. Canberra: Department of Political and Social Change,

Research School of Pacific and Asian Studies, Australian National University, 43–76.

1997a. 'Constitutional Engineering and the Alternative Vote in Fiji: An Assessment'. In Brij V. Lal and Peter Larmour (eds.), *Electoral Systems in Divided Societies: The Fiji Constitution Review*. Canberra: National Centre for Development Studies, Research School of Pacific and Asian Studies, Australian National University, 73–96.

1997b. 'Preferential Voting and Political Engineering: A Comparative Study'. *Journal of Commonwealth and Comparative Politics* 35: 1–19.

2002. 'Back to the Future? The Political Consequences of Electoral Reform in Papua New Guinea'. *Journal of Pacific History* 37: 239–53.

2004. 'The Global Spread of Preferential Voting: Australian Institutional Imperialism?' *Australian Journal of Political Science* 39: 253–66.

2006. *Democracy and Diversity: Political Engineering in the Asia-Pacific*. Oxford: Oxford University Press.

2007. 'Political Engineering in the Asia Pacific'. *Journal of Democracy* 18(1): 58–72.

Rejai, Mostafa, and Kay Phillips 1997. *Leaders and Leadership: An Appraisal of Theory and Research*. Westport, CT: Praeger.

Remington, Thomas F., and Steven S. Smith 1998. 'Theories of Legislative Institutions and the Organization of the Russian Duma'. *American Journal of Political Science* 42: 545–72.

Renwick, Alan 2005. 'Modelling Multiple Goals: Electoral System Preferences in Hungary in 1989'. *Europe-Asia Studies* 57: 995–1019.

2007. 'Why Did National Promise a Referendum on Electoral Reform in 1990?' *Political Science* 59: 7–22.

2009a. 'How Likely Is Proportional Representation in the House of Commons? Lessons from International Experience'. *Government and Opposition* 44: 366–84.

2009b. 'Do "Wrong Winner" Elections Trigger Electrol Reform? Lessons from New Zealand'. *Representation* 45: 357–67.

Renwick, Alan, Chris Hanretty, and David Hine 2009. 'Partisan Self-Interest and Electoral Reform: The New Italian Electoral Law of 2005'. *Electoral Studies* 28: 437–47.

Reynolds, Andrew 1995. 'Constitutional Engineering in Southern Africa'. *Journal of Democracy* 6(1): 86–99.

2006. 'Electoral Systems Today: The Curious Case of Afghanistan'. *Journal of Democracy* 17(2): 104–17.

Reynolds, Andrew, and Ben Reilly 1997. *The International IDEA Handbook of Electoral System Design*. Stockholm: International Institute for Democracy and Electoral Assistance.

Reynolds, Andrew, Ben Reilly, and Andrew Ellis 2005. *Electoral System Design: The New International IDEA Handbook*. Stockholm: International Institute for Democracy and Electoral Assistance.

Rich, Clifford A. L. 1953. 'Political Trends in Italy'. *Western Political Quarterly* 6: 469–88.

Richie, Robert, and Steven Hill 2004. 'The Fair Elections Movement in the United States: What It Has Done and Why It Is Needed'. In Milner 2004: 215–32.

Ridet, Philippe 2007. 'M. Sarkozy transforme son meeting parisien en démonstration de force et de popularité'. Le Monde, 2 May.

Riding, Alan 1992. 'Socialist Party Is Dealt a Loss in French Vote'. New York Times, 23 March.

Riker, William H. 1982. 'The Two-Party System and Duverger's Law: An Essay on the History of Political Science'. American Political Science Review 76: 753–66.

——— 1984. 'Electoral Systems and Constitutional Restraints'. In Arend Lijphart and Bernard Grofman (eds.), Choosing an Electoral System: Issues and Alternatives. Westport, CT: Praeger, 103–10.

——— 1986. The Art of Political Manipulation. New Haven: Yale University Press.

Rioux, Jean-Pierre 1987. The Fourth Republic, 1944–1958, trans. Godfrey Rogers. Cambridge: Cambridge University Press.

Rizzo, Alessandra 2005. 'Italian Legislators Approve Berlusconi-Backed Electoral Reform'. Associated Press, 13 October.

Rogowski, Ronald 1987. 'Trade and the Variety of Democratic Institutions'. International Organization 41: 203–23.

Rokkan, Stein 1970. 'Electoral Systems'. In Stein Rokkan with Angus Campbell, Per Torsvik, and Henry Valen, Citizens, Elections, Parties: Approaches to the Comparative Study of the Processes of Development. Oslo: Universitetsforlaget, 147–68.

Rose, Richard 1983. 'Elections and Electoral Systems: Choices and Alternatives'. In Bogdanor and Butler 1983: 20–45.

Royal Commission on the Electoral System 1986. Report of the Royal Commission on the Electoral System: Towards a Better Democracy. Wellington: Government Printer.

Royal, Ségolène 2007. 'Le Pacte présidentiel'. Accessed at www.desirsdavenir.org, April 2007.

Ruff, Norman J. 2004. 'Electoral Reform and Deliberative Democracy: The British Columbia Citizens' Assembly'. In Milner 2004: 235–48.

Ruffilli, Roberto 1987. 'La quota riservata alle coalizioni'. In Roberto Ruffilli (ed.), Materiali per la riforma elettorale. Bologna: Il Mulino, 43–60.

Ryan, Louise 2006. Telephone interview, 22 August.

Rydon, Joan 1987. 'Issues in Electoral Reform with Special Reference to Australia and New Zealand'. Political Science 39: 58–69.

Sakamoto, Takayuki 1999a. Building Policy Legitimacy in Japan: Political Behaviour beyond Rational Choice. Basingstoke: Macmillan.

——— 1999b. 'Explaining Electoral Reform: Japan versus Italy and New Zealand'. Party Politics 5: 419–38.

Samuels, David, and Timothy Hellwig 2008. 'Electoral Accountability: A Conceptual and Empirical Reassessment'. Paper presented at the Annual Meeting of the American Political Science Association. Boston, MA, 28–31 August.

Samuels, Richard J. 2003. *Machiavelli's Children: Leaders and Their Legacies in Italy and Japan.* Ithaca, NY: Cornell University Press.

Sarkozy, Nicolas 2007a. *Mon projet: ensemble tout devient possible.* Accessed at www.sarkozy.fr, 15 December 2008.

—— 2007b. Speech delivered at Épinal, 12 July, on the theme of 'la démocratie irréprochable'. Accessed at www.elysee.fr, 15 December 2008.

Särlvik, Bo 1983. 'Scandinavia'. In Bogdanor and Butler 1983: 122–48.

Sartori, Giovanni 2000. 'The Party Effects of Electoral Systems'. In Reuven Y. Hazan and Moshe Maor (eds.), *Parties, Elections and Cleavages: Israel in Comparative and Theoretical Perspective.* London: Frank Cass, 13–28.

—— 2005. 'La riforma con il veleno: il sistema elettorale proposto dal Polo'. *Corriere della Sera*, 15 September 2005.

Satō, Seizaburō 1991. 'Political Reform Imperatives'. *Japan Echo* 18(2): 27–8.

Saxby, P. J. 1985. Written submission to the Royal Commission on the Electoral System, no. 687 (untitled). Mimeo. Papers of the Royal Commission on the Electoral System, Archives New Zealand, Agency AAYI (RCES), Accession W3047, Item 1, 4 – Submissions.

Saxby, Phil 2006. Interview. Wellington, 8 August.

Scarrow, Susan 2001. 'Germany: The Mixed-Member System as a Political Compromise'. In Shugart and Wattenberg 2001d: 57–69.

—— 2003. 'Making Elections More Direct? Reducing the Role of Parties in Elections'. In Bruce E. Cain, Russell J. Dalton, and Susan E. Scarrow (eds.), *Democracy Transformed? Expanding Political Opportunities in Advanced Industrial Democracies.* Oxford: Oxford University Press, 44–58.

Scharpf, Fritz W. 1997. *Games Real Actors Play: Actor-Centered Institutionalism in Policy Research.* Boulder, CO: Westview Press.

Schattschneider, E. E. 1942. *Party Government.* New York: Holt, Rinehart & Winston.

—— 1975 [1960]. *The Semisovereign People: A Realist's View of Democracy in America.* Hinsdale, IL: Dryden Press.

Scheiner, Ethan 2007. 'Clientelism in Japan: The Importance and Limits of Institutional Explanations'. In Herbert Kitschelt and Steven I. Wilkinson (eds.), *Patrons, Clients, and Policies: Patterns of Democratic Accountability and Political Competition.* Cambridge: Cambridge University Press, 276–97.

—— 2008. 'Does Electoral System Reform Work? Electoral System Lessons from Reforms of the 1990s'. *Annual Review of Political Science* 11: 161–81.

Schelling, Thomas C. 1963. *The Strategy of Conflict.* New York: Oxford University Press.

Schiemann, John W. 2001. 'Hedging against Uncertainty: Regime Change and the Origins of Hungary's Mixed-Member System'. In Shugart and Wattenberg 2001d: 231–54.

Schlesinger, Jacob M. 1997. *Shadow Shoguns: The Rise and Fall of Japan's Postwar Political Machine*. New York: Simon & Schuster.

Schonberger, Howard B. 1989. *Aftermath of War: Americans and the Remaking of Japan 1945–1952*. Kent, OH: Kent State University Press.

Schuller, Philipp A. 1998. 'Money Politics and the Transformation of the Japanese Political System'. DPhil thesis, University of Oxford.

Scottish Elections Review 2007. *Scottish Elections 2007: The Independent Review of the Scottish Parliamentary and Local Government Elections*. London: Electoral Commission. Accessed at www.electoralcommission.org.uk, 27 October 2007.

Seton-Watson, Christopher 1967. *Italy from Liberalism to Fascism, 1870–1925*. London: Methuen.

— 1983. 'Italy'. In Bogdanor and Butler 1983: 110–21.

Shennan, Andrew 1989. *Rethinking France: Plans for Renewal 1940–1946*. Oxford: Clarendon Press.

Shepsle, Kenneth A. 2001. 'A Comment on Institutional Change'. *Journal of Theoretical Politics* 13: 321–5.

Shiratori, Rei 1995. 'The Politics of Electoral Reform in Japan'. *International Political Science Review* 16: 79–94.

Shugart, Matthew Soberg 2001. '"Extreme" Electoral Systems and the Appeal of the Mixed-Member Alternative'. In Shugart and Wattenberg 2001d: 25–51.

— 2008. 'Inherent and Contingent Factors in Reform Initiation in Plurality Systems'. In Blais 2008: 7–60.

Shugart, Matthew Soberg, and Martin P. Wattenberg 2001a. 'Introduction: The Electoral Reform of the Twenty-First Century'. In Shugart and Wattenberg 2001d: 1–6.

— 2001b. 'Mixed-Member Electoral Systems: A Definition and Typology'. In Shugart and Wattenberg 2001d: 9–24.

— 2001c. 'Conclusion: Are Mixed-Member Electoral Systems the Best of Both Worlds?' In Shugart and Wattenberg 2001d: 571–96.

— (eds.) 2001d. *Mixed-Member Electoral Systems: The Best of Both Worlds?* Oxford: Oxford University Press.

Siaroff, Alan 2003. 'Spurious Majorities, Electoral Systems and Electoral System Change'. *Commonwealth and Comparative Politics* 41: 143–60.

Siavelis, Peter M. 2005. 'Chile: The Unexpected (and Expected) Consequences of Electoral Engineering'. In Gallagher and Mitchell 2005: 433–52.

Sidoti, Franceso 1993. 'Italy: A Clean-Up after the Cold War'. *Government and Opposition* 28: 105–14.

Simon, Herbert, A. 1959. 'Theories of Decision-Making in Economics and Behavioral Science'. *American Economic Review* 49: 253–83.

— 1985. 'Human Nature in Politics: The Dialogue of Psychology with Political Science'. *American Political Science Review* 79: 293–304.

Sisk, Timothy D. 1995. 'Electoral System Choice in South Africa: Implications for Intergroup Moderation'. *Nationalism and Ethnic Politics* 1: 178–204.

Skocpol, Theda, and Margaret Somers 1980. 'The Uses of Comparative History in Macrosocial Inquiry'. *Comparative Studies in Society and History* 22: 174–97.

Smith, Kaapua 2006. 'Māori Party'. In Raymond Miller (ed.), *New Zealand Government and Politics*, 4th edn. Melbourne: Oxford University Press, 405–16.

Smyth, Howard McGaw 1948. 'Italy: From Fascism to the Republic'. *Western Political Quarterly* 1: 205–22.

Snow, David A., E. Burke Rochford, Jr, Steven K. Worden, and Robert D. Benford 1986. 'Frame Alignment Processes, Micromobilization, and Movement Participation'. *American Sociological Review* 51: 464–81.

Southall, Roger 2003. 'An Unlikely Success: South Africa and Lesotho's Election of 2002'. *Journal of Modern African Studies* 41: 269–96.

Spotts, Frederic, and Theodor Wieser 1986. *Italy: A Difficult Democracy: A Survey of Italian Politics*. Cambridge: Cambridge University Press.

Standish, Bill 1996. 'Elections in Simbu: Towards Gunpoint Democracy?' In Yaw Saffu (ed.), *The 1992 PNG Election: Change and Continuity in Electoral Politics*. Canberra: Department of Political and Social Change, Research School of Pacific and Asian Studies, Australian National University, 277–322.

Stanley, Alessandra 1998. 'In a First for Italy, Former Communist Is Named Premier'. *New York Times*, 22 October.

Statistics New Zealand 2003. 'Labour Market Statistics 2003'. Accessed at www.stats.govt.nz, 5 March 2008.

Steel, David 1989. *Against Goliath: David Steel's Story*. London: Weidenfeld & Nicolson.

Stepanek, Marcia 1980. 'Pat Quinn – A Man Politicians Love To Hate'. *Illinois Issues* 6(1): 4–8.

Stickley, Tony 1990. 'Peters Suggests Voting Reform'. *New Zealand Herald*, 30 March.

Stockley, Andrew P. 2004. 'What Difference Does Proportional Representation Make?' *Public Law Review* 15: 121–36.

Stockwin, J. A. A. 1983. 'Japan'. In Bogdanor and Butler 1983: 209–27.

—— 1988a. 'Dynamic and Immobilist Aspects of Japanese Politics'. In J. A. A. Stockwin, Alan Rix, Aurelia George, James Home, Daiichi Itō, and Martin Collick, *Dynamic and Immobilist Politics in Japan*. Basingstoke: Macmillan, 1–21.

—— 1988b. 'Parties, Politicians and the Political System'. In J. A. A. Stockwin, Alan Rix, Aurelia George, James Home, Daiichi Itō, and Martin Collick, *Dynamic and Immobilist Politics in Japan*. Basingstoke: Macmillan, 22–53.

1991a. 'Japan's Opposition Parties and the Prospects for Political Change'. *Japan Foundation Newsletter* 19(2): 1–6 and 17.

1991b. 'From JSP to SDPJ: The New Wave Society and the "New" *Nihon Shakaitō*'. *Japan Forum* 3(2): 287–300.

1992. 'The Japan Socialist Party: Resurgence after Long Decline'. In Ronald J. Hrebenar with contributions by Peter Berton, Akira Nakamura, J. A. A. Stockwin and Nobuo Tomita, *The Japanese Party System*, 2nd edn. Boulder, CO: Westview Press, 81–115.

1996. 'New Directions in Japanese Politics'. In Ian Neary (ed.), *Leaders and Leadership in Japan*. Richmond: Japan Library, 265–75.

2008. *Governing Japan: Divided Politics in a Resurgent Economy*, 4th edn. Oxford: Blackwell.

Strand, Per 2000. 'Decisions on Democracy: The Politics of Constitution-Making in South Africa, 1990–1996'. PhD Thesis, Uppsala University.

Strøm, Kaare, and Wolfgang C. Müller 1999. 'Political Parties and Hard Choices'. In Wolfgang C. Müller and Kaare Strøm (eds.), *Policy, Office, or Votes? How Political Parties in Western Europe Make Hard Decisions*. Cambridge: Cambridge University Press, 1–35.

Taagepera, Rein 1994. 'Estonia's Constitutional Assembly, 1991–1992'. *Journal of Baltic Studies* 25: 211–32.

1998. 'Effective Magnitude and Effective Threshold'. *Electoral Studies* 17: 393–404.

Taagepera, Rein, and Matthew Soberg Shugart 1989. *Seats and Votes: The Effects and Determinants of Electoral Systems*. New Haven: Yale University Press.

Takenaka, Harukata 2007. 'Fukuda's Rise and the Return of the Old LDP'. *Japan Echo* 34(6): 11–14.

Taylor, Brian 2002. *The Road to the Scottish Parliament*, revised edn. Edinburgh: Edinburgh University Press.

Temple, Philip 1995. 'Changing the Rules in New Zealand: The Electoral Reform Referenda of 1992 and 1993'. *Political Quarterly* 66: 234–8.

Test Case Centre 2006. 'The "Green Party Case": *Joan Russow v The Attorney General of Canada, The Chief Electoral Officer of Canada and Her Majesty the Queen in Right of Canada*'. Accessed at www.law-lib.utoronto.ca/testcase/, 20 January 2007.

Thacher, George A. 1907. 'The Initiative and Referendum in Oregon'. *Proceedings of the American Political Science Association* 4: 198–221.

Thelen, Kathleen 1999. 'Historical Institutionalism in Comparative Politics'. *Annual Review of Political Science* 2: 369–404.

Thies, Michael F. 2002. 'Changing How the Japanese Vote: The Promise and Pitfalls of the 1994 Electoral Reform'. In John Fuh-sheng Hsieh and David Newman (eds.), *How Asia Votes*. New York: Chatham House Publishers of Seven Bridges Press, 92–117.

Tiersky, Ronald 2000. *François Mitterrand: The Last French President*. New York: St Martin's Press.

Tokumoto, Teruhito 1990. 'A Labor Leader Endorses Single-Member Districts'. *Japan Echo* 17(3): 52–4.

Travett, Claire 2008. 'Referendum "No" Wouldn't Need to Spell End for Proportionality'. *New Zealand Herald*, 9 August.

Tsebelis, George 1990. *Nested Games: Rational Choice in Comparative Politics*. Berkeley: University of California Press.

2002. *Veto Players: How Political Institutions Work*. Princeton, NJ: Princeton University Press.

Tucker, Robert C. 1995. *Politics as Leadership*, revised edn. Columbia, MS: University of Missouri Press.

Uchida, Kenzō 1987. 'Japan's Postwar Conservative Parties'. In Robert E. Ward and Sakamoto Yoshikazu (eds.), *Democratizing Japan: The Allied Occupation*. Honolulu, HI: Hawaii University Press, 306–38.

Uchida, Kenzo 1988. 'Politics' High Cost'. *Japan Times*, 18 June.

Uleri, Pier Vincenzo 2002. 'On Referendum Voting in Italy: YES, NO, or Non-Vote? How Italian Parties Learned to Control Referendums'. *European Journal of Political Research* 41: 863–83.

United Future 2008. 'Purposeful Democracy'. Constitution policy statement. Wellington. Accessed at www.unitedfuture.org.nz, 12 December 2008.

Upton, Simon 1993 [1992]. 'Electoral Reform No Answer'. In McRobie 1993: 115–17. First published in *New Zealand Herald*, 8 January 1992.

US Government 1949 [1945]. 'United States Initial Post-Surrender Policy for Japan', 29 August 1945. In Government Section, Supreme Commander for the Allied Powers, *Political Reorientation of Japan, September 1945 to September 1948*. Washington, DC: US Government Printing Office, 423–6.

Van der Kolk, Henk, and Jacques Thomassen 2006. 'The Dutch Electoral System on Trial'. *Acta Politica* 41: 117–32.

Van Wolferen, Karel 1986/1987. 'The Japan Problem'. *Foreign Affairs* 65: 288–303.

Vassallo, Salvatore 2005. 'The Constitutional Reforms of the Center-Right'. In Carlo Guarnieri and James L. Newell (eds.), *Italian Politics: Quo Vadis?* (Italian Politics: A Review, Volume 20). New York: Berghahn, 117–35.

Verderami, Francesco 2004. 'Dobbiamo rivedere le nostre promesse: parla il vicepremier Gianfranco Fini'. *Corrierre della Sera*, 28 October.

Vowles, Jack 1995. 'The Politics of Electoral Reform in New Zealand'. *International Political Science Review* 16: 95–115.

1997. 'The New Zealand General Election of 1996'. *Electoral Studies* 16: 258–62.

2000. 'Introducing Proportional Representation: The New Zealand Experience'. *Parliamentary Affairs* 53: 680–96.

2008a. 'Systemic Failure, Coordination, and Contingencies: Understanding Electoral System Change in New Zealand'. In Blais 2008: 163–83.

2008b. 'Making a Difference? Public Perceptions of Coalition, Single-Party, and Minority Governments'. Paper presented at the Elections, Public Opinion, and Parties Conference. Manchester, 12–14 September.

Vowles, Jack, and Peter Aimer 1993. *Voters' Vengeance: The 1990 Election in New Zealand and the Fate of the Fourth Labour Government*. Auckland: Auckland Unversity Press.

Vowles, Jack, Peter Aimer, Helena Catt, Jim Lamare, and Raymond Miller 1995. *Towards Consensus? The 1993 Election in New Zealand and the Transition to Proportional Representation*. Auckland: Auckland University Press.

Wahl, Nicholas 1959a. 'The French Constitution of 1958: II. The Initial Draft and Its Origins'. *American Political Science Review* 53: 358–82.

1959b. *The Fifth Republic: France's New Political System*. New York: Random House.

Wallace, John 2002. 'Reflections on Constitutional and Other Issues Concerning Our Electoral System: The Past and the Future'. *Political Science* 54: 47–66.

2006. Interview. Auckland, 12 August.

Ward, Robert E. 1966. 'Recent Electoral Developments in Japan'. *Asian Survey* 6: 547–67.

Ware, Alan 1996. *Political Parties and Party Systems*. Oxford: Oxford University Press.

Washio, Akira 1993. 'Hata Tsutomu: Portrait of a Tenacious Politician'. *Japan Echo* 20(1): 24–8.

Wasi, Prawase 2002. 'An Overview of Political Reform'. In Duncan McCargo (ed.), *Reforming Thai Politics*. Copenhagen: Nordic Institute of Asian Studies, 21–7.

Weaver, R. Kent 2001. 'Electoral Rules and Electoral Reform in Canada'. In Shugart and Wattenberg 2001d: 542–69.

Welsh, David, and Jack Spence 2000. 'F. W. de Klerk: Enlightened Conservative'. In Martin Westlake (ed.), *Leaders of Transition*. Basingstoke: Macmillan, 29–52.

Westlake, Martin 2000. 'Conclusions: Vision and Will'. In Martin Westlake (ed.), *Leaders of Transition*. Basingstoke: Macmillan, 157–71.

Whitney, Courtney 1955. *MacArthur: His Rendezvous with History*. Westport, CT: Greenwood Press.

Williams, Daniel 1996. 'New Italian Prime Minister Named, Will Oversee Electoral Reform'. *Washington Post*, 2 February.

Williams, David 1996. 'Ozawa Ichirō: The Making of a Japanese Kingmaker'. In
　　Ian Neary (ed.), *Leaders and Leadership in Japan*. Richmond: Japan Library,
　　276–97.
Williams, Justin, Sr. 1979. *Japan's Political Revolution under MacArthur:
　　A Participant's Account*. Athens, GA: University of Georgia Press.
Williams, Kieran 2005. 'Judicial Review of Electoral Thresholds in Germany,
　　Russia, and the Czech Republic'. *Election Law Journal* 4: 191–206.
　　2007. 'The Growing Litigiousness of Czech Elections'. *Europe-Asia Studies*
　　59: 937–69.
Williams, Philip 1954. *Politics in Post-War France: Parties and the Constitution in
　　the Fourth Republic*. London: Longmans, Green.
　　1964. *Crisis and Compromise: Politics in the Fourth Republic*. London:
　　Longman.
Williams, Philip M., and Martin Harrison 1959. 'France 1958'. In D. E. Butler,
　　Philip M. Williams, Martin Harrison, Zbigniew Pelczynski, Basil Chubb,
　　and R. R. Farquharson, *Elections Abroad*. London: Macmillan, 11–90.
　　1961. *De Gaulle's Republic*, 2nd edn. London: Longmans.
Wilson, Margaret 1989. *Labour in Government 1984–1987*. Wellington: Allen &
　　Unwin.
　　2006. Interview. Wellington, 23 August.
Wolfe, Eugene, L., III 1992. 'Japan's LDP Considers Electoral Reform: A Neglected
　　Political Debt'. *Asian Survey* 32: 773–86.
　　1995. 'Japanese Electoral and Political Reform: Role of the Young Turks'. *Asian
　　Survey* 35: 1059–74.
Woodall, Brian 1999. 'The Politics of Reform in Japan's Lower House Electoral
　　System'. In Bernard Grofman, Sung-Chull Lee, Edwin A. Winckler, and
　　Brian Woodall (eds.), *Elections in Japan, Korea, and Taiwan under the
　　Single Non-Transferable Vote: The Comparative Study of an Embedded
　　Institution*. Ann Arbor: University of Michigan Press, 23–50.
　　2007. 'Campaign Finance on Steroids: The Roots of Change, Inertia, and
　　Corruption in Japanese Political Funding'. Paper presented at the annual
　　meeting of the American Political Science Association. Chicago, 30 August–
　　2 September.
Woollaston, Philip 2006. Interview. Wellington, 25 August.
Wriggins, W. Howard 1969. *The Ruler's Imperative: Strategies for Political Survival
　　in Asia and Africa*. New York: Columbia University Press.
Wright, Gordon 1950. *The Reshaping of French Democracy*. London: Methuen.
Wyles, John 1987. 'Italians Launch Reform Manifesto'. *Financial Times*, 22 December.
Yayama, Tarō 1991. 'Following Through on Electoral Reform'. *Japan Echo*
　　18(2): 29–34.
Yomiuri Electoral System Study Group 1990. 'Estimating the Impact of Reform
　　Scenarios'. *Japan Echo* 17(3): 36–42.

Zahariadis, Nikolaos 2003. *Ambiguity and Choice in Public Policy: Political Decision Making in Modern Democracies*. Washington, DC: Georgetown University Press.

———— 2007. 'The Multiple Streams Framework: Structure, Limitations, Prospects'. In Paul A. Sabatier, *Theories of the Policy Process*, 2nd edn. Boulder, CO: Westview Press, 65–92.

INDEX

accountability 40, 54
  in Italy 170, 171, 176, 222
  in Japan 212
  in New Zealand 222
Acerbo Law 111, 114, 155–6
ACT (New Zealand) 208, 209
act contingencies 28–9
  and leadership 75–6
  and legitimacy constraints 60–1
  in elite majority imposition 144, 146, 159
  in elite–mass interaction 217, 225
  mechanisms 30, 31–2, 33–5, 36, 37, 41–2
Afghanistan 15
Africa 42
  see also individual countries
agenda setting 65, 162–3, 216–17, 232–4
Alleanza Nazionale (AN) see National Alliance, Italian
alternation in power see accountability
alternative vote 14, 32, 45–6, 54, 59, 206
Amato, Giuliano 121, 175
Andreotti, Giulio 172, 174, 178
Asia-Pacific 43
  see also individual countries
Australia 14, 32
Austria 40

Balladur, Édouard 108
Baltic States 45
bargained reform 109–10
bargaining
  as leadership strategy 73–4, 162, 233–5
  between electoral reform and other issues 34, 109–10, 126, 162

Bayrou, François 107–8
Belgium 31, 37
Benoit, Kenneth 7, 9, 246
Bérégovoy, Pierre 105, 106
Berlusconi, Silvio 120
  changing stance 1994–2000 120, 121, 123, 144
  and 2005 reform 124, 126, 146, 158
Bicameral Commission, 1997–1998 (Italy) 121
  see also Bozzi Commission
bipolar v. centripetal competition 33
  in France 102–3
  in Italy 116, 122–3, 125–7, 173, 177
Bolger, Jim
  1990 referendum promise 201–3, 205, 237
  implementation of referendum 205, 207
bonus-adjusted systems
  in Italy 111, 114, 121, 124, 155–6, 171
  in New Zealand 231–2
Bossi, Umberto 123, 174
bounded rationality 74, 81, 83, 236
  see also cognitive constraints; uncertainty
Bozzi Commission 170–1, 216–17
Brazil 62
British Columbia
  citizens' assembly, 2004 40
  2005 referendum 77, 219, 253–4
  2009 referendum 219, 254
bureaucrats 15
  and Japan 1945 131

302